ORIGINAL NARRATIVES
OF EARLY AMERICAN HISTORY

REPRODUCED UNDER THE AUSPICES OF THE
AMERICAN HISTORICAL ASSOCIATION

GENERAL EDITOR, J. FRANKLIN JAMESON, PH.D., LL.D.
DIRECTOR OF THE DEPARTMENT OF HISTORICAL RESEARCH IN THE
CARNEGIE INSTITUTION OF WASHINGTON

THE NORTHMEN, COLUMBUS, AND CABOT
985 — 1503

ORIGINAL NARRATIVES
OF EARLY AMERICAN HISTORY

THE NORTHMEN
COLUMBUS AND CABOT

985—1503

THE VOYAGES OF THE NORTHMEN

EDITED BY

JULIUS E. OLSON

PROFESSOR OF THE SCANDINAVIAN LANGUAGES AND LITERATURES
IN THE UNIVERSITY OF WISCONSIN

THE VOYAGES OF COLUMBUS
AND OF JOHN CABOT

EDITED BY

EDWARD GAYLORD BOURNE, Ph.D.

PROFESSOR OF HISTORY IN YALE UNIVERSITY

*WITH MAPS AND A FACSIMILE
REPRODUCTION*

CHARLES SCRIBNER'S SONS
NEW YORK

GENERAL PREFACE TO THE ORIGINAL NAR-RATIVES OF EARLY AMERICAN HISTORY

AT its annual meeting in December, 1902, the American Historical Association approved and adopted the plan of the present series, and the undersigned was chosen as its general editor. The purpose of the series was to provide individual readers of history, and the libraries of schools and colleges, with a comprehensive and well-rounded collection of those classical narratives on which the early history of the United States is founded, or of those narratives which, if not precisely classical, hold the most important place as sources of American history anterior to 1700. The reasons for undertaking such a project are for the most part obvious. No modern history, however excellent, can give the reader all that he can get from the *ipsissima verba* of the first narrators, Argonauts or eye-witnesses, vivacious explorers or captains courageous. There are many cases in which secondary narrators have quite hidden from view these first authorities, whom it is therefore a duty to restore to their rightful position. In a still greater number of instances, the primitive narrations have become so scarce and expensive that no ordinary library can hope to possess anything like a complete set of the classics of early American history.

The series is to consist of such volumes as will illustrate the early history of all the chief parts of the country, with an additional volume of general index. The plan contemplates, not a body of extracts, but in general the publication or republication of whole works or distinct parts of works. In the case of narratives originally issued in some other language than English, the best available translations will be used, or fresh versions made. In a few instances, important narratives hitherto unprinted will be inserted. The English texts will be taken from the earliest editions, or those having the highest historical value, and will be reproduced with literal exactness. The maps will be such as will give real help toward understanding the events narrated in the volume. The special editors of the individual works will supply introductions, setting forth briefly the author's career and opportunities, when known, the status of the work in the literature of American history, and its value as a source, and indicating previous editions; and they will furnish such annotations, scholarly but simple, as will enable the intelligent reader to understand and to estimate rightly the statements of the text. The effort has been made to secure for each text the most competent editor.

The results of all these endeavors will be laid before the public in the confident hope that they will be widely useful in making more real and more vivid the apprehension of early American history. The general editor would not have undertaken the serious labors of preparation and supervision if he had not felt sure that it was a genuine benefit to American historical knowledge and American patriotism to make accessible, in one collection, so large a body of pioneer narrative. No subsequent sources can have quite the intellectual interest, none quite the sentimental value, which attaches to these early narrations, springing direct from the brains and hearts of the nation's founders.

Sacra recognosces annalibus eruta priscis.

J. FRANKLIN JAMESON.

CARNEGIE INSTITUTION, WASHINGTON, D.C.

NOTE

SPECIAL acknowledgments and thanks are due to the representatives of the late Arthur Middleton Reeves, who have kindly permitted the use of his translations of the Vinland sagas, originally printed in his *Finding of Wineland the Good*, published in London by the Clarendon Press in 1890; to the President and Council of the Hakluyt Society, for permission to use Sir Clements Markham's translation of the Journal of Columbus's first voyage, printed in Vol. LXXXVI. of the publications of that Society (London, 1893), and that of Dr. Chanca's letter and of the letter of Columbus respecting his fourth voyage, by the late Mr. R. H. Major, in their second and forty-third volumes, *Select Letters of Columbus* (London, 1847, 1870); to the Honorable John Boyd Thacher, of Albany, for permission to use his version of Las Casas's narrative of the third voyage, as printed by him in his *Christopher Columbus* (New York, 1904), published by Messrs. G. P. Putnam's Sons; to Messrs. Houghton, Mifflin and Company for permission to use, out of the third volume of Winsor's *Narrative and Critical History of America*, the late Dr. Charles Deane's translation, revised by Professor Bennet H. Nash, of the second letter of Raimondo de Soncino respecting John Cabot's expedition; and to George Philip and Son, Limited, of London, for permission to use the map in Markham's *Life of Christopher Columbus* as the basis for the map in the present volume, showing the routes of Columbus's four voyages.

CONTENTS

ORIGINAL NARRATIVES OF THE VOYAGES OF THE NORTHMEN

EDITED BY PROFESSOR JULIUS E. OLSON

ORIGINAL NARRATIVES OF THE VOYAGES OF COLUMBUS

EDITED BY PROFESSOR EDWARD G. BOURNE

ORIGINAL NARRATIVES OF THE VOYAGES OF JOHN CABOT

EDITED BY PROFESSOR EDWARD G. BOURNE

MAPS AND FACSIMILE REPRODUCTION

ORIGINAL NARRATIVES OF THE VOYAGES OF THE NORTHMEN

INTRODUCTION

THE important documents from Norse sources that may be classed as "Original Narratives of Early American History" are the Icelandic sagas (prose narratives) that tell of the voyages of Northmen to Vinland. There are two sagas that deal mainly with these voyages, while in other Icelandic sagas and annals there are a number of references to Vinland and adjacent regions. These two sagas are the "Saga of Eric the Red" and another, which, for the lack of a better name, we may call the "Vinland History of the Flat Island Book," but which might well bear the same name as the other. This last history is composed of two disjointed accounts found in a fine vellum manuscript known as the Flat Island Book (Flateyjarbok), so-called because it was long owned by a family that lived on Flat Island in Broad Firth, on the northwestern coast of Iceland. Bishop Brynjolf, an enthusiastic collector, got possession of this vellum, "the most extensive and most perfect of Icelandic manuscripts," and sent it, in 1662, with other vellums, as a gift to King Frederick III. of Denmark, where it still is one of the great treasures of the Royal Library.

On account of the beauty of the Flat Island vellum, and the number of sagas that it contained (when printed it made 1700 octavo pages), it early attracted the attention of Old Norse collectors and scholars, and hence the narrative relating to Vinland that it contained came to be better known than the vellum called Hauk's Book, containing the "Saga of Eric the Red," and was the only account of Vinland that received any particular attention from the scholars of the seventeenth and eighteenth centuries. The Flat Island Book narrative

3

was also given first place in Rafn's *Antiquitates Americanæ*
(Copenhagen, 1837). This ponderous volume contained all
the original sources, but it has given rise to much needless
controversy on the Norse voyages, for many of the author's
conclusions were soon found to be untenable. He failed to win-
now the sound historical material from that which was unsub-
stantiated or improbable. And so far as the original sources
are concerned, it was particularly unfortunate that he followed in the footsteps of seventeenth and eighteenth century
scholars and gave precedence to the Flat Island Book narrative. In various important respects this saga does not agree
with the account given in the "Saga of Eric the Red," which
modern scholarship has pronounced the better and more reliable version, for reasons that we shall consider later.

The Flat Island Book consists of transcripts of various
sagas made by the Icelandic priests Jon Thordsson and Magnus Thorhallsson. Very little of their lives is known, but
there is evidence to show that the most important portion of
the copying was completed about 1380. There is, however,
no information concerning the original from which the transcripts were made. From internal evidence, however, Dr.
Storm of the University of Christiania thinks that this original
account was a late production, possibly of the fourteenth
century.[1] It is, moreover, evident that this original account
was quite different from the one from which the existing "Saga
of Eric the Red" was made, so that we have two distinct accounts of the same set of events, both separately derived from
oral tradition, a fact which, on account of the lack of harmony
in details, has been the source of much confusion, but which
nevertheless gives strong testimony concerning the verity of
the Vinland tradition in its general outlines.

The saga which has best stood the test of modern criticism,
namely the "Saga of Eric the Red," has beyond this fact the

---

[1] *Eiriks Saga Raudha* (Copenhagen, 1891), p. xv.

additional advantage of having come down to us in two different vellums. The one is found in Hauk's Book, No. 544 of the Arne-Magnæan Collection in Copenhagen, and the other is in No. 557 of the same collection. These two narratives (in vellums 544 and 557) tell the same story. They are so closely allied that the translation which appears in this volume has been made from a collation of both texts, that of Hauk's Book (544) having been more closely followed.[1] The Hauk's Book text is clearly legible; No. 557 is not in such good condition.

Many facts in the life of Hauk Erlendsson, who with the assistance of two secretaries made Hauk's Book, are known. He was in 1294 made a "lawman" in Iceland, and died in Norway in 1334. There are reasons for believing that the vellum bearing his name was written a number of years before his death, probably during the period 1310–1320. Hauk was particularly interested in the "Saga of Eric the Red," as he was descended from Thorfinn Karlsefni, the principal character of the saga, a fact that perhaps lends a certain authority to this version as against that of the Flat Island Book. Hauk brings the genealogical data of the saga down to his own time, which is not done in No. 557, one fact among others which shows that 557 is not a copy of 544.

The early history of AM. 557 is not known. The orthography and hand indicate that it was made later than Hauk's Book, probably in the early part of the fifteenth century. Vigfusson considered it a better text than the Hauk's Book version, though rougher and less carefully written.[2] Other critics (Jonsson and Gering) consider 544 the safer text.

In regard to the date of composition of the archetype, it may be remarked that both 544 and 557 speak of Bishop Brand "the Elder," which presupposes a knowledge of the second

---

[1] A translation, with the title "The Story of Thorfinn Carlsemne," based on AM. 557, may be found in *Origines Islandicae*, II. 610.

[2] *Origines Islandicae*, II. 590.

Bishop Brand, whose accession occurred in 1263.   Before this date, therefore, the originals used in making 544 and 557 could not have been written.   But this mention of Bishop Brand "the Elder" does not, we think, give an adequate basis for fixing the date of the *composition* of the saga, as Dr. Storm believes, who places it somewhere between 1263 and 1300, with an inclination toward the earlier date.   Dr. Finnur Jonsson,[1] who accepts Dr. Storm's opinion in other respects, says on this point: "The classic form of the saga and its vivid and excellent tradition surely carry it back to about 1200. . . . To assume that the saga was first written down about 1270 or after, I consider to be almost an impossibility."   Nor does this conservative opinion by Dr. Jonsson preclude the possibility, or even probability, that written accounts of the Vinland voyages existed before this date.   John Fiske's[2] well-considered opinion of this same saga (544 and 557) has weight: "Its general accuracy in the statement and grouping of so many remote details is proof that its statements were controlled by an exceedingly strong and steady tradition, — altogether too strong and steady, in my opinion, to have been maintained simply by word of mouth."   And Vigfusson,[3] in speaking of the sagas in general, says: "We believe that when once the first saga was written down, the others were in quick succession committed to parchment, some still keeping their original form through a succession of copies, others changed.   The saga time was short and transitory, as has been the case with the highest literary periods of every nation, whether we look at the age of Pericles in Athens, or of our own Elizabeth in England, and that which was not written down quickly, in due time, was lost and forgotten forever."

The absence of contemporary record has caused some

---

[1] *Den oldnorske og oldislandske Litteraturs Historie* (Copenhagen, 1901), II. 648.

[2] *The Discovery of America*, p. 212.

[3] Prolegomena, *Sturlunga Saga*, p. lxix.

American historians to view the narratives of the Vinland
voyages as ordinary hearsay. But it is important to remember that before the age of writing in Iceland there was a saga-
telling age, a most remarkable period of intellectual activity,
by means of which the deeds and events of the seething life
of the heroic age were carried over into the age of writing.[1]
The general trustworthiness of this saga-telling period has been
attested in numerous ways from foreign records. Thus Snorri
Sturlason's "The Sagas of the Kings of Norway," one of the
great history books of the world, written in Iceland in the
thirteenth century, was based primarily on early tradition,
brought over the sea to Iceland. Yet the exactness of its
descriptions and the reliability of its statements have been
verified in countless cases by modern Norwegian historians.[2]

With reference to the Vinland voyages, there is proof of
an unusually strong tradition in the fact that it has come
down from two sources, the only case of such a phenomenon
among the Icelandic sagas proper. It does not invalidate the
general truth of the tradition that these two sources clash in
various matters. These disagreements are not so serious but
that fair-minded American scholars have found it "easy to
believe that the narratives contained in the sagas are true in

[1] Snorri, the Icelandic historian, says that "it was more than 240 years
from the settlement of Iceland (about 870) before sagas began to be written"
and that "Ari (1067–1148) was the first man who wrote in the vernacular
stories of things old and new."

[2] "Among the mediaeval literatures of Europe, that of Iceland is un-
rivalled in the profusion of detail with which the facts of ordinary life are
recorded, and the clearness with which the individual character of numberless real persons stands out from the historic background. . . . The Ice-
landers of the Saga-age were not a secluded self-centred race; they were
untiring in their desire to learn all that could be known of the lands round
about them, and it is to their zeal for this knowledge, their sound historical
sense, and their trained memories, that we owe much information regarding
the British Isles themselves from the ninth to the thirteenth century. The
contact of the Scandinavian peoples with the English race on the one hand,
and the Gaelic on the other, has been an important factor in the subsequent
history of Britain; and this is naturally a subject on which the Icelandic
evidence is of the highest value." Prefatory Note to *Origines Islandicae*.

their general outlines and important features." It lies within the province of Old Norse scholarship to determine which of the two Vinland sagas has the better literary and historical antecedents. After this point has been established, the truthfulness and credibility of the selected narrative in its details must be maintained on the internal evidence in conjunction with the geographical and other data of early America. And here American scholarship may legitimately speak.

These sagas have in recent years been subjected, especially by Dr. Gustav Storm of Christiania,[1] to most searching textual and historical criticism, and the result has been that the simpler narrative of Hauk's Book and AM. 557 is pronounced the more reliable account.[2] In respect to literary quality, it has the characteristics of the Icelandic sagas proper, as distinguished from the later sagas by well-known literary men like Snorri. Where it grazes facts of Northern history it is equally strong. Thus, there is serious question as to the first sighting of land by Biarni Herjulfson, who is mentioned only in the Flat Island narrative, and nowhere else in the rich genealogical literature of Iceland, although his alleged father was an important man, of whom there are reliable accounts. On the other hand, the record of the "Saga of Eric the Red," giving the priority of discovery to Leif Ericson, can be collaterally confirmed.[3] The whole account of Biarni seems sus-

---

[1] *Studies on the Vinland Voyages* (Copenhagen, 1889) and *Eiriks Saga Raudha* (Copenhagen, 1891).

[2] Of the same opinion are Professor Hugo Gering of Kiel, *Zeitschrift für deutsche Philologie*, XXIV. (1892), and Professor Finnur Jonsson of Copenhagen, *Den oldnorske og oldislandske Litteraturs Historie*, II. 646.

[3] The Kristni-Saga, which tells of the conversion of Iceland, says: "That summer [1000] King Olaf [of Norway] went out of the country to Wendland in the south, and he sent Leif Eric's son to Greenland to preach the faith there. It was then that Leif discovered Vinland the Good. He also discovered a crew on the wreck of a ship out in the deep sea, and so he got the name of Leif the Lucky." For passages from other sagas that corroborate Leif's discovery on his voyage from Norway to Greenland (*i.e.*, in the year that Olaf Tryggvason fell, namely, 1000), see Reeves, *The Finding of Wineland the Good* (London, 1895), pp. 7–18.

picious, and the main facts, viewed with reference to Leif's discovery, run counter to Northern chronology and history. There are, however, two incidental touches in the Flat Island Book narrative, which are absent from the other saga, namely, the observation concerning the length of the day in Vinland, and the reference to finding "three skin-canoes, with three men under each." The improbabilities of the Flat Island Book saga are easily detected, if one uses as a guide the simpler narrative of the "Saga of Eric the Red," the only doubtful part of which is the "uniped" episode, a touch of mediaeval superstition so palpable as not to be deceptive.

Aside from such things as picking grapes in the spring, sipping sweet dew from the grass, and the presence of an apparition, the Flat Island Book account, when read by itself, with no attempt to make it harmonize with the statements of the "Saga of Eric the Red" or other facts of Scandinavian history, is a sufficiently straightforward narrative. The difficulty begins when it is placed in juxtaposition to these facts and statements. It should not be and need not be discarded, but in giving an account of the Vinland voyages it must be used with circumspection. From an historical standpoint it must occupy a subordinate place. If Rafn in his *Antiquitates Americanæ* had given emphatic precedence to the saga as found in Hauk's Book and AM. 557, had left to American scholars the Dighton Rock and the Newport Tower, and had not been so confident in the matter of identifying the exact localities that the explorers visited, he might have carried conviction, instead of bringing confusion, to American scholars.

The general results of the work of the Norwegian scholar Dr. Storm, together with a unique presentation of the original narratives, are accessible in *The Finding of Wineland* (London, 1890 and 1895), by an American scholar, the late Arthur Middleton Reeves. This work contains a lucid account of the important investigations on the subject, photographs of all the vellum pages that give the various narratives, a printed text accompanying these, page by page and line by line, and also translations into English.   There is one phase of the subject that this work does not discuss: the identifications of the regions visited by the Northmen.   Dr. Storm, however, has gone into this subject, and is convinced that Helluland, Markland, and Vinland of the sagas, are Labrador, Newfoundland, and Nova Scotia.[1] The sailing directions in the "Saga of Eric the Red" are given with surprising detail.   These, with other observations, seem to fit Nova Scotia remarkably well. Only one thing appears to speak against Storm's view, and that is the *abundance* of grapes to which the Flat Island Book account testifies.   But coupled with this testimony are statements (to say nothing of the unreliability of this saga in other respects) that indicate that the Icelandic narrators had come to believe that grapes were gathered in the spring, thus invalidating the testimony as to abundance.

Whether the savages that the sagas describe were Indians or Eskimos is a question of some interest.   John Fiske [2] believes that the explorers came in contact with American Indians; Vigfusson, on the other hand, believes that the sagas describe Eskimos.   Here, however, the American has the better right to an opinion.

On this point, it is of importance to call attention to the fact that the Norse colonists in Greenland found no natives there, only vestiges of them.   They were at that time farther north in Greenland; the colonists came in contact with them much later, — too late to admit of descriptions of them in any of the classical Icelandic sagas, in which the Greenland colonists play no inconspicuous part.   Ari, the great authority on early Norse history, speaking of the Greenland colonists,

---

[1] See, in support of Storm, Juul Dieserud's paper, "Norse Discoveries in America," *Bulletin of the American Geographical Society*, Feb., 1901.

[2] *Discovery of America*, p. 182.

says, in his *Libellus Islandorum*:[1] "They found there men's habitations both east and west in the land [*i.e.*, in both the Eastern and Western settlements] both broken cayaks and stone-smithery, whereby it may be seen that the same kind of folk had been there as they which inhabited Vinland, and whom the men of Greenland [*i.e.*, the explorers] called Skrellings."

A sort of negative corroboration of this is offered by a work of high rank, the famous *Speculum Regale*, written in Old Norse in Norway in the middle of the thirteenth century. It contains much trustworthy information on Greenland; it tells, "with bald common sense," of such characteristic things as glaciers and northern lights, discusses the question as to whether Greenland is an island or a peninsula, tells of exports and imports, the climate, the means of subsistence, and especially the fauna, *but not one word concerning any natives*. Moreover Ivar Bardsen's account[2] of Greenland, which is entirely trustworthy, gives a distinct impression that the colonists did not come into conflict with the Eskimos until the fourteenth century.

There is consequently no valid reason for doubting that the savages described in the sagas were natives of Vinland and Markland. But whether it can ever be satisfactorily demonstrated that the Norse explorers came in contact with Algonquin, Micmac, or Beothuk Indians, and just where they landed, are not matters of essential importance. The incontrovertible facts of the various Norse expeditions are that Leif Ericson and Thorfinn Karlsefni are as surely historical characters as Christopher Columbus, that they visited, in the early part of the eleventh century, some part of North America where the grape grew, and that in that region the colonists found savages, whose hostility upset their plans of permanent settlement.

[1] See *Origines Islandicae*, I. 294.
[2] See notes 6 and 8 to Papal Letters, p. 71 of this volume.

According to the usually accepted chronology, Leif's voyage from Norway to Greenland (during which voyage he found Vinland) was made in the year 1000, and Karlsefni's attempt at colonization within the decade following. On the basis of genealogical records (so often treacherous) some doubt has recently been cast on this chronology by Vigfusson, in *Origines Islandicae* [1] (1905). Vigfusson died in 1889, sixteen years before the publication of this work. He had no opportunity to consider the investigations of Dr. Storm, who accepts without question the first decade of the eleventh century for the Vinland voyages. Nor do Storm's evidences and arguments on this point appear in the work as published. Therefore we are obliged to say of Vigfusson's observations on the chronology of the Vinland voyages, that they stand as question-marks which call for confirmation.

We are surprised, moreover, to find that *Origines Islandicae* prints the Flat Island Book story first, apparently on account of the belief that this story contains the "truer account of the first sighting of the American continent" by Biarni Herjulfson.[2] It is impossible to believe that this would have been done, if the editors (Vigfusson and Powell) had known the results of Dr. Storm's work, which is not mentioned. There is, furthermore, no attempt in the *Origines Islandicae* to refute or explain away an opinion on AM. 557 expressed by the same authorities, in 1879,[3] to the effect that "it is free from grave errors of fact which disfigure the latter [the Flat Island Book saga]."

[1] See note 1, p. 43.

[2] In other respects the editors speak highly of the saga as found in Hauk's Book and AM. 557: "This saga has never been so well known as the other, though it is probably of even higher value. Unlike the other, it has the form and style of one of the 'Islendinga Sogor' [the Icelandic sagas proper]; its phrasing is broken, its dialogue is excellent, it contains situations of great pathos, such as the beautiful incident at the end of Bearne's self-sacrifice, and scenes of high interest, such as that of the Sibyl's prophesying in Greenland. . . ." II. 591.

[3] *Icelandic Prose Reader* (where AM. 557 is printed), notes, p. 377.

We are almost forced to the conclusion that a hand less cunning than Vigfusson's has had to do with the unfinished section of the work.

In regard to the extract from Adam of Bremen, which we print, it should be observed that its only importance lies in the fact that it corroborates the Icelandic tradition of a land called Vinland, where there were grapes and "unsown grain," and thus serves to strengthen faith in the trustworthiness of the saga narrative. The annals and papal letters that follow need no further discussion, we think, than that contained in the annotations.

Besides the texts in Icelandic, already described, by Rafn, Reeves, Vigfusson and Powell, and Storm, it may be mentioned that the Flat Island text is given in Vol. I. of *Flateyjar-bok*, ed. Vigfusson and Unger, Christiania, 1860. There are translations of both texts in Beamish, *Discovery of North America by the Northmen* (London, 1841), in Slafter, *Voyages of the Northmen* (Boston, 1877), and in De Costa, *Pre-Columbian Discovery of America by the Northmen* (Albany, 1901). But most of these are confused in arrangement, and the best is that by the late Mr. Reeves, which by the kind consent of his representatives we are permitted to use in this volume.

JULIUS E. OLSON.

THE SAGA OF ERIC THE RED

Also called the Saga of Thorfinn Karlsefni[1]

The Saga of Eric the Red, also called the Saga of Thorfinn Karlsefni and Snorri Thorbrandsson.[2] — Olaf was the name of a warrior-king, who was called Olaf the White. He was the son of King Ingiald, Helgi's son, the son of Olaf, Gudraud's son, son of Halfdan Whiteleg, king of the Uplands-men.[3] Olaf engaged in a Western freebooting expedition and captured Dublin in Ireland and the Shire of Dublin, over which he became king.[4] He married Aud the Wealthy, daughter of Ketil Flatnose, son of Biorn Buna, a famous man of Norway. Their son was called Thorstein the Red. Olaf was killed in battle in Ireland, and Aud and Thorstein went then to the Hebrides; there Thorstein married Thurid, daughter of Eyvind Easterling, sister of Helgi the Lean; they had many children. Thorstein became a warrior-king, and entered into fellowship with Earl Sigurd the Mighty, son of Eystein the Rattler. They conquered Caithness and Sutherland, Ross and Moray, and more than the half of Scotland. Over these Thorstein became king, ere he was betrayed by the Scots, and was slain there in battle. Aud was at Caithness when she heard of Thorstein's death; she thereupon caused a ship to be secretly built in the forest, and when she was ready, she sailed out to the Orkneys. There she bestowed Groa, Thorstein the Red's daughter, in marriage; she was the mother of Grelad, whom

---

[1] The translation that follows, by Arthur Middleton Reeves, is based on the text of Hauk's Book, No. 544 of the Arna-Magnæan Collection, collated with No. 557 of the same collection. In *Origines Islandicae*, II. 610, this saga is called "The Story of Thorfinn Carlsemne."

[2] The rubrics here given in italics are found in the original manuscript.

[3] In eastern Norway.

[4] From 853 to 871.

14

Earl Thorfinn, Skull-cleaver, married. After this Aud set out to seek Iceland, and had on board her ship twenty freemen. Aud arrived in Iceland, and passed the first winter at Biarnarhöfn with her brother, Biorn. Aud afterwards took possession of all the Dale country between Dögurdar river and Skraumuhlaups river. She lived at Hvamm, and held her orisons at Krossholar, where she caused crosses to be erected, for she had been baptized and was a devout believer. With her there came out [to Iceland] many distinguished men, who had been captured in the Western freebooting expedition, and were called slaves. Vifil was the name of one of these: he was a highborn man, who had been taken captive in the Western sea, and was called a slave, before Aud freed him; now when Aud gave homesteads to the members of her crew, Vifil asked wherefore she gave him no homestead as to the other men. Aud replied, that this should make no difference to him, saying, that he would be regarded as a distinguished man wherever he was. She gave him Vifilsdal, and there he dwelt. He married a woman whose name was . . . ;[1] their sons were Thorbiorn and Thorgeir. They were men of promise, and grew up with their father.[2]

Eric the Red finds Greenland. — There was a man named Thorvald; he was a son of Asvald, Ulf's son, Eyxna-Thori's son. His son's name was Eric. He and his father went from Jaederen [3] to Iceland, on account of manslaughter, and settled on Hornstrandir, and dwelt at Drangar. There Thorvald died, and Eric then married Thorhild, a daughter of Jorund, Atli's son, and Thorbiorg the Ship-chested, who had been married before to Thorbiorn of the Haukadal family. Eric then removed from the North, and cleared land in Haukadal, and dwelt at Ericsstadir by Vatnshorn. Then Eric's thralls caused a land-slide on Valthiof's farm, Valthiofsstadir. Eyiolf

---

[1] A blank in the original manuscript.

[2] This introductory paragraph, giving at the end the ancestry of Gudrid, the daughter of Thorbiorn Vifilson and a prominent figure in the Vinland voyages, seems to come first on account of the earlier historical allusions that it contains. The account of Gudrid is continued in the third paragraph.

[3] In southwestern Norway.

the Foul, Valthiof's kinsman, slew the thralls near Skeids-brekkur above Vatnshorn.   For this Eric killed Eyiolf the Foul, and he also killed Duelling-Hrafn, at Leikskalar.   Geir-stein and Odd of Jorva, Eyiolf's kinsmen, conducted the prose-cution for the slaying of their kinsmen, and Eric was, in conse-quence, banished from Haukadal.   He then took possession of Brokey and Eyxney, and dwelt at Tradir on Sudrey, the first winter.   It was at this time that he loaned Thorgest his outer daïs-boards;[1] Eric afterwards went to Eyxney, and dwelt at Ericsstad.   He then demanded his outer daïs-boards, but did not obtain them.   Eric then carried the outer daïs-boards away from Breidabolstad, and Thorgest gave chase. They came to blows a short distance from the farm of Drangar. There two of Thorgest's sons were killed and certain other men besides.   After this each of them retained a considerable body of men with him at his home.   Styr gave Eric his support, as did also Eyiolf of Sviney, Thorbiorn, Vifil's son, and the sons of Thorbrand of Alptafirth; while Thorgest was backed by the sons of Thord the Yeller, and Thorgeir of Hitardal, Aslak of Langadal and his son, Illugi.   Eric and his people were con-demned to outlawry at Thorsness-thing.   He equipped his ship for a voyage, in Ericsvag; while Eyiolf concealed him in Dimunarvag, when Thorgest and his people were searching for him among the islands.   He said to them, that it was his in-tention to go in search of that land which Gunnbiorn, son of Ulf the Crow, saw when he was driven out of his course, west-ward across the main, and discovered Gunnbiorns-skerries.[2] He told them that he would return again to his friends, if he should succeed in finding that country.   Thorbiorn, and Eyiolf, and Styr accompanied Eric out beyond the islands, and they parted with the greatest friendliness; Eric said to them that he would render them similar aid, so far as it might lie within his power, if they should ever stand in need of his help.   Eric

---

[1] Movable planks used in constructing the lock-beds of the sleeping apart-ment.   They were often beautifully carved, and hence valuable.

[2] An island midway between Iceland and Greenland, discovered in the latter part of the ninth century.   Gunnbiorn was a Norwegian.   This island is no longer above the surface.   See Fiske, *The Discovery of America*, p. 242.

sailed out to sea from Snaefells-iokul, and arrived at that ice-mountain which is called Blacksark. Thence he sailed to the southward, that he might ascertain whether there was habitable country in that direction. He passed the first winter at Ericsey, near the middle of the Western Settlement.[1] In the following spring he proceeded to Ericsfirth, and selected a site there for his homestead. That summer he explored the western uninhabited region, remaining there for a long time, and assigning many local names there. The second winter he spent at Ericsholms beyond Hvarfsgnipa. But the third summer he sailed northward to Snaefell,[2] and into Hrafnsfirth. He believed then that he had reached the head of Ericsfirth; he turned back then, and remained the third winter at Ericsey at the mouth of Ericsfirth. The following summer he sailed to Iceland, and landed in Breidafirth. He remained that winter with Ingolf at Holmlatr. In the spring he and Thorgest fought together, and Eric was defeated; after this a reconciliation was effected between them. That summer Eric set out to colonize the land which he had discovered, and which he called Greenland, because, he said, men would be the more readily persuaded thither if the land had a good name.[3]

[1] This should read *Eastern* Settlement, evidently a clerical error in an original manuscript, as both Hauk's Book and AM. 557 reproduce it. There were two settlements in Greenland, the Eastern and Western, both, however, to the westward of Cape Farewell, and between that cape on the south and Disco Island on the north. Ericsey (*i.e.*, Eric's Island) was at the mouth of Ericsfirth, near the present Julianshaab. For further details on the geography of these settlements, see Reeves, *The Finding of Wineland the Good*, p. 166, (25), and Fiske, *The Discovery of America*, I. 158, note.

[2] On the western coast of Greenland, about 70° N. Lat.

[3] The saga up to this point is taken from Landnama-bok, the great Icelandic authority on early genealogy and history. It might well have included one more paragraph (the succeeding one), which gives an approximate date to the colonization of Greenland: "Ari, Thorgil's son, says that that summer twenty-five ships sailed to Greenland out of Borgfirth and Broadfirth; but fourteen only reached their destination; some were driven back, and some were lost. This was sixteen [S: fifteen] winters before Christianity was legally adopted in Iceland." That is, in about 985, as Christianity was accepted in 1000 (or 1001). There is a possible variation of a year in the usually accepted date. See *Origines Islandicae*, I. 369.

C

Concerning Thorbiorn. — Thorgeir, Vifil's son, married, and took to wife Arnora, daughter of Einar of Laugarbrekka, Sigmund's son, son of Ketil Thistil, who settled Thistilsfirth. Einar had another daughter named Hallveig; she was married to Thorbiorn, Vifil's son, who got with her Laugarbrekka-land on Hellisvellir. Thorbiorn moved thither, and became a very distinguished man. He was an excellent husbandman, and had a great estate. Gudrid was the name of Thorbiorn's daughter. She was the most beautiful of her sex, and in every respect a very superior woman. There dwelt at Arnarstapi a man named Orm, whose wife's name was Halldis. Orm was a good husbandman, and a great friend of Thorbiorn, and Gudrid lived with him for a long time as a foster-daughter. There was a man named Thorgeir, who lived at Thorgeirsfell; he was very wealthy and had been manumitted; he had a son named Einar, who was a handsome, well-bred man, and very showy in his dress. Einar was engaged in trading-voyages from one country to the other, and had prospered in this. He always spent his winters alternately either in Iceland or in Norway.

Now it is to be told, that one autumn, when Einar was in Iceland, he went with his wares out along Snaefellsness, with the intention of selling them. He came to Arnarstapi, and Orm invited him to remain with him, and Einar accepted this invitation, for there was a strong friendship [between Orm and himself]. Einar's wares were carried into a store-house, where he unpacked them, and displayed them to Orm and the men of his household, and asked Orm to take such of them as he liked. Orm accepted this offer, and said that Einar was a good merchant, and was greatly favored by fortune. Now, while they were busied about the wares, a woman passed before the door of the store-house. Einar inquired of Orm: "Who was that handsome woman who passed before the door? I have never seen her here before." Orm replies: "That is Gudrid, my foster-child, the daughter of Thorbiorn of Laugar-brekka." "She must be a good match," said Einar; "has she had any suitors?" Orm replies: "In good sooth she has been

courted, friend, nor is she easily to be won, for it is believed
that both she and her father will be very particular in their
choice of a husband." "Be that as it may," quoth Einar,
"she is a woman to whom I mean to pay my addresses, and I
would have thee present this matter to her father in my behalf,
and use every exertion to bring it to a favorable issue, and I
shall reward thee to the full of my friendship, if I am successful.   It may be that Thorbiorn will regard the connection as
being to our mutual advantage, for [while] he is a most honorable man and has a goodly home, his personal effects, I am
told, are somewhat on the wane; but neither I nor my father
are lacking in lands or chattels, and Thorbiorn would be greatly
aided thereby, if this match should be brought about."
"Surely I believe myself to be thy friend," replies Orm, "and
yet I am by no means disposed to act in this matter, for Thorbiorn hath a very haughty spirit, and is moreover a most
ambitious man." Einar replied that he wished for nought
else than that his suit should be broached; Orm replied, that
he should have his will.   Einar fared again to the South until
he reached his home.   Sometime after this, Thorbiorn had
an autumn feast, as was his custom, for he was a man of high
position.   Hither came Orm of Arnarstapi, and many other
of Thorbiorn's friends.   Orm came to speech with Thorbiorn,
and said, that Einar of Thorgeirsfell had visited him not long
before, and that he was become a very promising man.   Orm
now makes known the proposal of marriage in Einar's behalf,
and added that for some persons and for some reasons it might
be regarded as a very appropriate match: "thou mayest
greatly strengthen thyself thereby, master, by reason of the
property."   Thorbiorn answers: "Little did I expect to hear
such words from thee, that I should marry my daughter to
the son of a thrall; and that, because it seems to thee that my
means are diminishing, wherefore she shall not remain longer
with thee since thou deemest so mean a match as this suitable
for her."   Orm afterward returned to his home, and all of the
invited guests to their respective households, while Gudrid
remained behind with her father, and tarried at home that

winter.　But in the spring Thorbiorn gave an entertainment
to his friends, to which many came, and it was a noble feast,
and at the banquet Thorbiorn called for silence, and spoke:
"Here have I passed a goodly lifetime, and have experienced
the good-will of men toward me, and their affection; and, methinks, our relations together have been pleasant; but now I
begin to find myself in straitened circumstances, although my
estate has hitherto been accounted a respectable one.　Now
will I rather abandon my farming, than lose my honor, and
rather leave the country, than bring disgrace upon my family;
wherefore I have now concluded to put that promise to the
test, which my friend Eric the Red made, when we parted
company in Breidafirth.　It is my present design to go to
Greenland this summer, if matters fare as I wish."　The folk
were greatly astonished at this plan of Thorbiorn's, for he was
blessed with many friends, but they were convinced that he
was so firmly fixed in his purpose, that it would not avail to
endeavor to dissuade him from it.　Thorbiorn bestowed gifts
upon his guests, after which the feast came to an end, and the
folk returned to their homes.　Thorbiorn sells his lands and
buys a ship, which was laid up at the mouth of Hraunhöfn.
Thirty persons joined him in the voyage; among these were
Orm of Arnarstapi, and his wife, and other of Thorbiorn's
friends, who would not part from him.　Then they put to sea.
When they sailed the weather was favorable, but after they
came out upon the high-seas the fair wind failed, and there
came great gales, and they lost their way, and had a very
tedious voyage that summer.　Then illness appeared among
their people, and Orm and his wife Halldis died, and the half
of their company.　The sea began to run high, and they had a
very wearisome and wretched voyage in many ways, but arrived, nevertheless, at Heriolfsness in Greenland, on the very
eve of winter.[1]　At Heriolfsness lived a man named Thorkel.
He was a man of ability and an excellent husbandman.　He
received Thorbiorn and all of his ship's company, and entertained them well during the winter.　At that time there was a

---

[1] "Winter-night-tide" was about the middle of October.

season of great dearth in Greenland; those who had been at the fisheries had had poor hauls, and some had not returned. There was a certain woman there in the settlement, whose name was Thorbiorg. She was a prophetess, and was called Little Sibyl. She had had nine sisters, all of whom were prophetesses, but she was the only one left alive. It was Thorbiorg's custom in the winters, to go to entertainments, and she was especially sought after at the homes of those who were curious to know their fate, or what manner of season might be in store for them; and inasmuch as Thorkel was the chief yeoman in the neighborhood, it was thought to devolve upon him to find out when the evil time, which was upon them, would cease. Thorkel invited the prophetess to his home, and careful preparations were made for her reception, according to the custom which prevailed, when women of her kind were to be entertained. A high seat was prepared for her, in which a cushion filled with poultry feathers was placed. When she came in the evening, with the man who had been sent to meet her, she was clad in a dark-blue cloak, fastened with a strap, and set with stones quite down to the hem. She wore glass beads around her neck, and upon her head a black lamb-skin hood, lined with white cat-skin. In her hands she carried a staff, upon which there was a knob, which was ornamented with brass, and set with stones up about the knob. Circling her waist she wore a girdle of touch-wood, and attached to it a great skin pouch, in which she kept the charms which she used when she was practising her sorcery. She wore upon her feet shaggy calf-skin shoes, with long, tough latchets, upon the ends of which there were large brass buttons. She had cat-skin gloves upon her hands, which were white inside and lined with fur. When she entered, all of the folk felt it to be their duty to offer her becoming greetings. She received the salutations of each individual according as he pleased her. Yeoman Thorkel took the sibyl by the hand, and led her to the seat which had been made ready for her. Thorkel bade her run her eyes over man and beast and home. She had little to say concerning all these. The tables were brought forth in the evening, and it remains to be told what manner of food was prepared for the prophetess. A porridge of goat's beestings was made for her, and for meat there were dressed the hearts of every kind of beast, which could be obtained there. She had a brass spoon, and a knife with a handle of walrus tusk, with a double hasp of brass around the haft, and from this the point was broken. And when the tables were removed, Yeoman Thorkel approaches Thorbiorg, and asks how she is pleased with the home, and the character of the folk, and how speedily she would be likely to become aware of that concerning which he had questioned her, and which the people were anxious to know. She replied that she could not give an opinion in this matter before the morrow, after that she had slept there through the night. And on the morrow, when the day was far spent, such preparations were made as were necessary to enable her to accomplish her soothsaying. She bade them bring her those women, who knew the incantation, which she required to work her spells, and which she called Warlocks; but such women were not to be found. Thereupon a search was made throughout the house, to see whether any one knew this [incantation]. Then says Gudrid: "Although I am neither skilled in the black art nor a sibyl, yet my foster-mother, Halldis, taught me in Iceland that spell-song, which she called Warlocks." Thorbiorg answered: "Then art thou wise in season!" Gudrid replies: "This is an incantation and ceremony of such a kind, that I do not mean to lend it any aid, for that I am a Christian woman." Thorbiorg answers: "It might so be that thou couldst give thy help to the company here, and still be no worse woman than before; however I leave it with Thorkel to provide for my needs." Thorkel now so urged Gudrid, that she said she must needs comply with his wishes. The women then made a ring round about, while Thorbiorg sat up on the spell-daïs. Gudrid then sang the song, so sweet and well, that no one remembered ever before to have heard the melody sung with so fair a voice as this. The sorceress thanked her for the song, and said: "She has indeed lured many spirits hither, who think it pleasant to hear this song, those who were wont

to forsake us hitherto and refuse to submit themselves to us.
Many things are now revealed to me, which hitherto have been
hidden, both from me and from others.   And I am able to
announce that this period of famine will not endure longer,
but the season will mend as spring approaches.   The visitation of disease, which has been so long upon you, will disappear
sooner than expected.   And thee, Gudrid, I shall reward out of
hand, for the assistance, which thou hast vouchsafed us, since
the fate in store for thee is now all made manifest to me.   Thou
shalt make a most worthy match here in Greenland, but it
shall not be of long duration for thee, for thy future path leads
out to Iceland, and a lineage both great and goodly shall
spring from thee, and above thy line brighter rays of light
shall shine, than I have power clearly to unfold.   And now
fare well and health to thee, my daughter !"   After this the
folk advanced to the sibyl, and each besought information concerning that about which he was most curious.   She was very
ready in her responses, and little of that which she foretold
failed of fulfilment.   After this they came for her from a
neighboring farmstead, and she thereupon set out thither.
Thorbiorn was then sent for, since he had not been willing to
remain at home while such heathen rites were practising.
The weather improved speedily, when the spring opened,
even as Thorbiorg had prophesied.   Thorbiorn equipped his
ship and sailed away, until he arrived at Brattahlid.[1]   Eric
received him with open arms, and said that it was well that he
had come thither.   Thorbiorn and his household remained
with him during the winter, while quarters were provided
for the crew among the farmers.   And the following spring
Eric gave Thorbiorn land on Stokkaness, where a goodly
farmstead was founded, and there he lived thenceforward.

*Concerning Leif the Lucky and the Introduction of Chris-
tianity into Greenland.* — Eric was married to a woman named
Thorhild, and had two sons; one of these was named Thorstein, and the other Leif.   They were both promising men.
Thorstein lived at home with his father, and there was not at

---

[1] The home of Eric the Red, in the Eastern Settlement.

that time a man in Greenland who was accounted of so great promise as he. Leif had sailed to Norway,[1] where he was at the court of King Olaf Tryggvason. When Leif sailed from Greenland, in the summer, they were driven out of their course to the Hebrides. It was late before they got fair winds thence, and they remained there far into the summer. Leif became enamored of a certain woman, whose name was Thorgunna. She was a woman of fine family, and Leif observed that she was possessed of rare intelligence. When Leif was preparing for his departure Thorgunna asked to be permitted to accompany him. Leif inquired whether she had in this the approval of her kinsmen. She replied that she did not care for it. Leif responded that he did not deem it the part of wisdom to abduct so high-born a woman in a strange country, "and we so few in number." "It is by no means certain that thou shalt find this to be the better decision," said Thorgunna. "I shall put it to the proof, notwithstanding," said Leif. "Then I tell thee," said Thorgunna, "that I am no longer a lone woman, for I am pregnant, and upon thee I charge it. I foresee that I shall give birth to a male child. And though thou give this no heed, yet will I rear the boy, and send him to thee in Greenland, when he shall be fit to take his place with other men. And I foresee that thou wilt get as much profit of this son as is thy due from this our parting; moreover, I mean to come to Greenland myself before the end comes." Leif gave her a gold finger-ring, a Greenland wadmal mantle, and a belt of walrus-tusk. This boy came to Greenland, and was called Thorgils. Leif acknowledged his paternity, and some men will have it that this Thorgils came to Iceland in the summer before the Froda-wonder.[2] However, this Thorgils was afterwards in Greenland, and there seemed to be something not altogether natural about him before the end came. Leif and his com-

---

[1] This was evidently the first time that the voyage from Greenland to Norway was accomplished without going by way of Iceland, and was a remarkable achievement. The aim was evidently to avoid the dangerous passage between Greenland and Iceland.

[2] A reference to some strange happenings in the winter of 1000–1001 at the Icelandic farmstead Froda, as related in the Eyrbyggja Saga.

panions sailed away from the Hebrides, and arrived in Norway in the autumn.[1] Leif went to the court of King Olaf Tryggvason.[2] He was well received by the king, who felt that he could see that Leif was a man of great accomplishments. Upon one occasion the king came to speech with Leif, and asks him, "Is it thy purpose to sail to Greenland in the summer?" "It is my purpose," said Leif, "if it be your will." "I believe it will be well," answers the king, "and thither thou shalt go upon my errand, to proclaim Christianity there." Leif replied that the king should decide, but gave it as his belief that it would be difficult to carry this mission to a successful issue in Greenland. The king replied that he knew of no man who would be better fitted for this undertaking, "and in thy hands the cause will surely prosper." "This can only be," said Leif, "if I enjoy the grace of your protection." Leif put to sea when his ship was ready for the voyage. For a long time he was tossed about upon the ocean, and came upon lands of which he had previously had no knowledge. There were self-sown wheat[3] fields and vines growing there. There were also those trees there which are called "mausur,"[4] and of all these they took specimens. Some of the timbers were so large that they were used in building. Leif found men upon a wreck, and took them home with him, and procured quarters for them all during the winter. In this wise he showed

---

[1] Of the year 999. See next note.

[2] King Olaf ruled from 995 to 1000. He fell at the battle of Svolder (in the Baltic) in September, 1000. It was in the same year that Leif started out as the King's missionary to Greenland. See p. 43, note 1.

[3] A wild cereal of some sort. Fiske is convinced that it was Indian corn, while Storm thinks it was wild rice, contending with much force that Indian corn was a product entirely unknown to the explorers, and that they could not by any possibility have confused it with wheat, even if they had found it. There is, moreover, no indication in this saga that they found cultivated fields. Storm cites Sir William Alexander, *Encouragement to Colonies* (1624), who, in speaking of the products of Nova Scotia, refers, among other things, to "some eares of wheate, barly and rie growing there wild." He also cites Jacques Cartier, who, in 1534, found in New Brunswick "wild grain like rye, which looked as though it had been sowed and cultivated." See Reeves, p. 174, (50).

[4] Supposed to be maple.

his nobleness and goodness, since he introduced Christianity
into the country, and saved the men from the wreck; and he
was called Leif the Lucky ever after.   Leif landed in Ericsfirth, and then went home to Brattahlid; he was well received
by every one.   He soon proclaimed Christianity throughout
the land, and the Catholic faith, and announced King Olaf
Tryggvason's messages to the people, telling them how much
excellence and how great glory accompanied this faith.   Eric
was slow in forming the determination to forsake his old belief,
but Thiodhild [1] embraced the faith promptly, and caused a
church to be built at some distance from the house.   This
building was called Thiodhild's Church, and there she and those
persons who had accepted Christianity, and they were many,
were wont to offer their prayers.   Thiodhild would not have
intercourse with Eric after that she had received the faith,
whereat he was sorely vexed.

At this time there began to be much talk about a voyage
of exploration to that country which Leif had discovered.
The leader of this expedition was Thorstein Ericsson, who was
a good man and an intelligent, and blessed with many friends.
Eric was likewise invited to join them, for the men believed
that his luck and foresight would be of great furtherance.
He was slow in deciding, but did not say nay, when his friends
besought him to go.   They thereupon equipped that ship in
which Thorbiorn had come out, and twenty men were selected
for the expedition.   They took little cargo with them, nought
else save their weapons and provisions.   On that morning
when Eric set out from his home he took with him a little
chest containing gold and silver; he hid this treasure, and then
went his way.   He had proceeded but a short distance, however, when he fell from his horse and broke his ribs and dis-
located his shoulder, whereat he cried "Ai, ai!"   By reason
of this accident he sent his wife word that she should procure
the treasure which he had concealed, for to the hiding of the
treasure he attributed his misfortune.   Thereafter they sailed
cheerily out of Ericsfirth in high spirits over their plan.   They

[1] Also called Thorhild.

were long tossed about upon the ocean, and could not lay the
course they wished. They came in sight of Iceland, and likewise saw birds from the Irish coast.[1] Their ship was, in sooth,
driven hither and thither over the sea. In the autumn they
turned back, worn out by toil, and exposure to the elements,
and exhausted by their labors, and arrived at Ericsfirth at
the very beginning of winter. Then said Eric, "More cheerful
were we in the summer, when we put out of the firth, but we
still live, and it might have been much worse." Thorstein
answers, "It will be a princely deed to endeavor to look well
after the wants of all these men who are now in need, and to
make provision for them during the winter." Eric answers,
"It is ever true, as it is said, that 'it is never clear ere the
answer comes,' and so it must be here. We will act now upon
thy counsel in this matter." All of the men, who were not
otherwise provided for, accompanied the father and son.
They landed thereupon, and went home to Brattahlid, where
they remained throughout the winter.

Thorstein Ericsson weds Gudrid; Apparitions. — Now it
is to be told that Thorstein Ericsson sought Gudrid, Thorbiorn's daughter, in wedlock. His suit was favorably received
both by herself and by her father, and it was decided that
Thorstein should marry Gudrid, and the wedding was held at
Brattahlid in the autumn. The entertainment sped well,
and was very numerously attended. Thorstein had a home
in the Western Settlement at a certain farmstead, which is
called Lysufirth. A half interest in this property belonged
to a man named Thorstein, whose wife's name was Sigrid.
Thorstein went to Lysufirth, in the autumn, to his namesake,
and Gudrid bore him company. They were well received,
and remained there during the winter. It came to pass that
sickness appeared in their home early in the winter. Gard
was the name of the overseer there; he had few friends; he fell
sick first, and died. It was not long before one after another
fell sick and died. Then Thorstein, Eric's son, fell sick,
and Sigrid, the wife of Thorstein, his namesake; and one even-

---

[1] That is, were near Ireland.

ing Sigrid wished to go to the house, which stood over against the outer-door, and Gudrid accompanied her; they were facing the outer-door when Sigrid uttered a loud cry. "We have acted thoughtlessly," exclaimed Gudrid, "yet thou needest not cry, though the cold strikes thee; let us go in again as speedily as possible." Sigrid answers, "This may not be in this present plight. All of the dead folk are drawn up here before the door now; among them I see thy husband, Thorstein, and I can see myself there, and it is distressful to look upon." But directly this had passed she exclaimed, "Let us go now, Gudrid; I no longer see the band!" The overseer had vanished from her sight, whereas it had seemed to her before that he stood with a whip in his hand and made as if he would scourge the flock. So they went in, and ere the morning came she was dead, and a coffin was made ready for the corpse; and that same day the men planned to row out to fish, and Thorstein accompanied them to the landing-place, and in the twilight he went down to see their catch. Thorstein, Eric's son, then sent word to his namesake that he should come to him, saying that all was not as it should be there, for the housewife was endeavoring to rise to her feet, and wished to get in under the clothes beside him, and when he entered the room she was come up on the edge of the bed. He thereupon seized her hands and held a pole-axe [1] before her breast. Thorstein, Eric's son, died before night-fall. Thorstein, the master of the house, bade Gudrid lie down and sleep, saying that he would keep watch over the bodies during the night; thus she did, and early in the night, Thorstein, Eric's son, sat up and spoke saying that he desired Gudrid to be called thither, for that it was his wish to speak to her: "It is God's will that this hour be given me for my own and for the betterment of my condition." Thorstein, the master, went in search of Gudrid, and waked her, and bade her cross herself, and pray God to help her; "Thorstein, Eric's son, has said to me that he wishes to see thee; thou must take counsel with thyself now, what thou

---

[1] The display of an axe seems to have been thought efficacious in laying fetches. See Reeves, p. 171, (39), citing a passage from another saga.

wilt do, for I have no advice to give thee." She replies, "It
may be that this is intended to be one of those incidents which
shall afterward be held in remembrance, this strange event,
and it is my trust that God will keep watch over me; wherefore, under God's mercy, I shall venture to him and learn
what it is that he would say, for I may not escape this if it
be designed to bring me harm. I will do this, lest he go further, for it is my belief that the matter is a grave one." So
Gudrid went and drew near to Thorstein, and he seemed to her
to be weeping. He spoke a few words in her ear, in a low tone,
so that she alone could hear them; but this he said so that all
could hear, that those persons would be blessed who kept well
the faith, and that it carried with it all help and consolation,
and yet many there were, said he, who kept it but ill. "This
is no proper usage which has obtained here in Greenland since
Christianity was introduced here, to inter men in unconsecrated
earth, with nought but a brief funeral service. It is my wish
that I be conveyed to the church, together with the others
who have died here; Gard, however, I would have you burn
upon a pyre, as speedily as possible, since he has been the cause
of all of the apparitions which have been seen here during the
winter." He spoke to her also of her own destiny, and said that
she had a notable future in store for her, but he bade her be-
ware of marrying any Greenlander; he directed her also to give
their property to the church and to the poor, and then sank
down again a second time. It had been the custom in Greenland, after Christianity was introduced there, to bury persons
on the farmsteads where they died, in unconsecrated earth; a
pole was erected in the ground, touching the breast of the dead,
and subsequently, when the priests came thither, the pole was
withdrawn and holy water poured in [the orifice], and the funeral service held there, although it might be long thereafter.
The bodies of the dead were conveyed to the church at Ericsfirth, and the funeral services held there by the clergy. Thorbiorn died soon after this, and all of his property then passed
into Gudrid's possession. Eric took her to his home and carefully looked after her affairs.

Concerning Thord of Höfdi. — There was a man named Thord, who lived at Höfdi on Höfdi-strands. He married Fridgerd, daughter of Thori the Loiterer and Fridgerd, daughter of Kiarval the King of the Irish. Thord was a son of Biorn Chestbutter, son of Thorvald Spine, Asleik's son, the son of Biorn Iron-side, the son of Ragnar Shaggy-breeks. They had a son named Snorri. He married Thorhild Ptarmigan, daughter of Thord the Yeller. Their son was Thord Horse-head. Thorfinn Karlsefni [1] was the name of Thord's son. Thorfinn's mother's name was Thorunn. Thorfinn was engaged in trading voyages, and was reputed to be a successful merchant. One summer Karlsefni equipped his ship, with the intention of sailing to Greenland. Snorri, Thorbrand's son, of Alptafirth accompanied him, and there were forty men on board the ship with them. There was a man named Biarni, Grimolf's son, a man from Breidafirth, and another named Thorhall, Gamli's son, an East-firth man. They equipped their ship, the same summer as Karlsefni, with the intention of making a voyage to Greenland; they had also forty men in their ship. When they were ready to sail, the two ships put to sea together. It has not been recorded how long a voyage they had; but it is to be told, that both of the ships arrived at Ericsfirth in the autumn. Eric and other of the inhabitants of the country rode to the ships, and a goodly trade was soon established between them. Gudrid was requested by the skippers to take such of their wares as she wished, while Eric, on his part, showed great munificence in return, in that he extended an invitation to both crews to accompany him home for winter quarters at Brattahlid. The merchants accepted this invitation, and went with Eric. Their wares were then conveyed to Brattahlid; nor was there lack there of good and commodious store-houses, in which to keep them; nor was there wanting much of that, which they needed, and the merchants were well pleased with their entertainment at Eric's

---

[1] Thorfinn Karlsefni, the explorer of the Vinland expeditions, was of excellent family. His lineage is given at greater length in the *Landnamabok* (Book of Settlements).

home during that winter.   Now as it drew toward Yule, Eric became very taciturn, and less cheerful than had been his wont. On one occasion Karlsefni entered into conversation with Eric, and said: "Hast thou aught weighing upon thee, Eric?   The folk have remarked, that thou art somewhat more silent than thou hast been hitherto.   Thou hast entertained us with great liberality, and it behooves us to make such return as may lie within our power.   Do thou now but make known the cause of thy melancholy."   Eric answers: "Ye accept hospitality gracefully, and in manly wise, and I am not pleased that ye should be the sufferers by reason of our intercourse; rather am I troubled at the thought, that it should be given out elsewhere, that ye have never passed a worse Yule than this, now drawing nigh, when Eric the Red was your host at Brattahlid in Greenland."   "There shall be no cause for that," replies Karlsefni, "we have malt, and meal, and corn in our ships, and you are welcome to take of these whatsoever you wish, and to provide as liberal an entertainment as seems fitting to you."   Eric accepts this offer, and preparations were made for the Yule feast, and it was so sumptuous, that it seemed to the people they had scarcely ever seen so grand an entertainment before.   And after Yule, Karlsefni broached the subject of a marriage with Gudrid to Eric, for he assumed that with him rested the right to bestow her hand in marriage.   Eric answers favorably, and says, that she would accomplish the fate in store for her, adding that he had heard only good reports of him.   And, not to prolong this, the result was, that Thorfinn was betrothed to Thurid,[1] and the banquet was augmented, and their wedding was celebrated; and this befell at Brattahlid during the winter.

Beginning of the Wineland Voyages. — About this time there began to be much talk at Brattahlid, to the effect that Wineland the Good should be explored, for, it was said, that country must be possessed of many goodly qualities.   And so it came to pass, that Karlsefni and Snorri fitted out their ship, for the purpose of going in search of that country in the spring.   Biarni

---

[1] Usually called Gudrid.

and Thorhall joined the expedition with their ship, and the men who had borne them company. There was a man named Thorvard; he was wedded to Freydis, a natural daughter of Eric the Red. He also accompanied them, together with Thorvald, Eric's son, and Thorhall, who was called the Huntsman. He had been for a long time with Eric as his hunter and fisherman during the summer, and as his steward during the winter. Thorhall was stout and swarthy, and of giant stature; he was a man of few words, though given to abusive language, when he did speak, and he ever incited Eric to evil. He was a poor Christian; he had a wide knowledge of the unsettled regions. He was on the same ship with Thorvard and Thorvald. They had that ship which Thorbiorn had brought out. They had in all one hundred and sixty men, when they sailed to the Western Settlement,[1] and thence to Bear Island. Thence they bore away to the southward two "dœgr." [2] Then they saw land, and launched a boat, and explored the land, and found there large flat stones [hellur], and many of these were twelve ells wide; there were many Arctic foxes there. They gave a name to the country, and called it Helluland [the land of flat stones]. Then they sailed with northerly winds two "dœgr," and land then lay before them, and upon it was a great wood and many wild beasts; an island lay off the land to the south-east, and there they found a bear, and they called this Biarney [Bear Island], while the land where the wood was they called Markland [Forest-land]. Thence they sailed southward along the land for a long time, and came to a cape; the land lay upon the starboard; there were long strands and sandy banks there. They rowed to the land and found upon the cape there the

---

[1] There is doubt as to why the expedition sailed northwest to the Western Settlement. Possibly Thorfinn desired to make a different start than Thorstein, whose expedition was a failure. See Reeves, p. 172, (45).

[2] Dœgr was a period of twelve hours. Reeves quotes the following from an old Icelandic work: "In the day there are two dœgr; in the dœgr twelve hours." A dœgr's sailing is estimated to have been about one hundred miles. There is evidently a clerical error in this passage after the number of days' sailing. The words for "two" and "seven" are very similar in old Norse.

keel of a ship, and they called it there Kialarnes [Keelness]; they also called the strands Furdustrandir [Wonder-strands], because they were so long to sail by.[1] Then the country became indented with bays, and they steered their ships into a bay. It was when Leif was with King Olaf Tryggvason, and he bade him proclaim Christianity to Greenland, that the king gave him two Gaels; the man's name was Haki, and the woman's Haekia. The king advised Leif to have recourse to these people, if he should stand in need of fleetness, for they were swifter than deer. Eric and Leif had tendered Karlsefni the services of this couple. Now when they had sailed past Wonder-strands, they put the Gaels ashore, and directed them to run to the southward, and investigate the nature of the country, and return again before the end of the third half-day. They were each clad in a garment, which they called "kiafal," [2] which was so fashioned, that it had a hood at the top, was open at the sides, was sleeveless, and was fastened between the legs with buttons and loops, while elsewhere they were naked. Karlsefni and his companions cast anchor, and lay there during their absence; and when they came again, one of them carried a bunch of grapes, and the other an ear of new-sown wheat. They went on board the ship, whereupon Karlsefni and his followers held on their way, until they came to where the coast was indented with bays. They stood into a bay with their ships. There was an island out at the mouth of the bay, about which there were strong currents, wherefore they called it Straumey [Stream Isle]. There were so many birds [3] there, that it was scarcely possible to step between

[1] The language of the vellum AM. 557 is somewhat different in this and the previous sentence. It does not say that "they sailed southward along the land for a long time, and came to a cape," but, "when two *dœgr* had elapsed, they descried land, and they sailed off this land; there was a cape to which they came. They beat into the wind along this coast, having the land upon the starboard side. This was a bleak coast, with long and sandy shores. They went ashore in boats, and found the keel of a ship, so they called it Keelness there; they likewise gave a name to the strands and called them Wonderstrands, because they were long to sail by."

[2] AM. 557 says *biafal*. Neither word has been identified.

[3] Hauk's Book says "eider-ducks."

D

the eggs. They sailed through the firth, and called it Straum-fiord [Streamfirth], and carried their cargoes ashore from the ships, and established themselves there. They had brought with them all kinds of live-stock. It was a fine country there. There were mountains thereabouts. They occupied themselves exclusively with the exploration of the country. They remained there during the winter, and they had taken no thought for this during the summer. The fishing began to fail, and they began to fall short of food. Then Thorhall the Huntsman disappeared. They had already prayed to God for food, but it did not come as promptly as their necessities seemed to demand. They searched for Thorhall for three half-days, and found him on a projecting crag. He was lying there, and looking up at the sky, with mouth and nostrils agape, and mumbling something. They asked him why he had gone thither; he replied, that this did not concern any one. They asked him then to go home with them, and he did so. Soon after this a whale appeared there, and they captured it, and flensed it, and no one could tell what manner of whale it was; and when the cooks had prepared it, they ate of it, and were all made ill by it. Then Thorhall, approaching them, says: "Did not the Red-beard [1] prove more helpful than your Christ? This is my reward for the verses which I composed to Thor, the Trustworthy; seldom has he failed me." When the people heard this, they cast the whale down into the sea, and made their appeals to God. The weather then improved, and they could now row out to fish, and thenceforward they had no lack of provisions, for they could hunt game on the land, gather eggs on the island, and catch fish from the sea.

Concerning Karlsefni and Thorhall. — It is said, that Thorhall wished to sail to the northward beyond Wonder-strands, in search of Wineland, while Karlsefni desired to proceed to the southward, off the coast. Thorhall prepared for his voyage out below the island, having only nine men in his party, for all of the remainder of the company went with Karlsefni.

---

[1] The god Thor.

And one day when Thorhall was carrying water aboard his ship, and was drinking, he recited this ditty:[1]

> When I came, these brave men told me,
> Here the best of drink I'd get,
> Now with water-pail behold me, —
> Wine and I are strangers yet.
> Stooping at the spring, I've tested
> All the wine this land affords;
> Of its vaunted charms divested,
> Poor indeed are its rewards.

And when they were ready, they hoisted sail; whereupon Thorhall recited this ditty:[2]

> Comrades, let us now be faring
> Homeward to our own again!
> Let us try the sea-steed's daring,
> Give the chafing courser rein.
> Those who will may bide in quiet,
> Let them praise their chosen land,
> Feasting on a whale-steak diet,
> In their home by Wonder-strand.

Then they sailed away to the northward past Wonder-strands and Keelness, intending to cruise to the westward around the cape. They encountered westerly gales, and were driven ashore in Ireland,[3] where they were grievously maltreated and thrown into slavery. There Thorhall lost his life, according to that which traders have related.

It is now to be told of Karlsefni, that he cruised southward off the coast, with Snorri and Biarni, and their people. They

---

[1] The prose sense is: "Men promised me, when I came hither, that I should have the best of drink; it behooves me before all to blame the land. See, oh, man! how I must raise the pail; instead of drinking wine, I have to stoop to the spring" (Reeves).

[2] The prose sense is: "Let us return to our countrymen, leaving those who like the country here, to cook their whale on Wonder-strand." From an archaic form in these lines it is apparent that they are older than either of the vellums, and must have been composed at least a century before Hauk's Book was written; they may well be much older than the beginning of the thirteenth century (Reeves). The antiquity of the verses of the saga is also attested by a certain metrical irregularity, as in poetry of the tenth and beginning of the eleventh centuries (Storm).

[3] In the next sentence the authority for this doubtful statement seems to be placed upon "traders."

sailed for a long time, and until they came at last to a river, which flowed down from the land into a lake, and so into the sea. There were great bars at the mouth of the river, so that it could only be entered at the height of the flood-tide. Karlsefni and his men sailed into the mouth of the river, and called it there Hop [a small land-locked bay]. They found self-sown wheat-fields on the land there, wherever there were hollows, and wherever there was hilly ground, there were vines.[1] Every brook there was full of fish. They dug pits, on the shore where the tide rose highest, and when the tide fell, there were halibut in the pits. There were great numbers of wild animals of all kinds in the woods. They remained there half a month, and enjoyed themselves, and kept no watch. They had their live-stock with them. Now one morning early, when they looked about them, they saw a great number of skin-canoes,[2] and staves were brandished from the boats, with a noise like flails, and they were revolved in the same direction in which the sun moves. Then said Karlsefni: "What may this betoken?" Snorri, Thorbrand's son, answers him: "It may be, that this is a signal of peace, wherefore let us take a white shield and display it." And thus they did. Thereupon the strangers rowed toward them, and went upon the land, marvelling at those whom they saw before them. They were swarthy men,[3] and ill-looking, and the hair of their heads was ugly. They had great eyes,[4] and were broad of cheek.

[1] Note the word "hollows" with reference to the contention that "wild wheat" is "wild rice." See p. 25, note 3.

[2] "Skin-canoes," or kayaks, lead one to think of Eskimos. Both Storm and Fiske think that the authorities of the saga-writer may have failed to distinguish between bark-canoes and skin-canoes.

[3] The vellum AM. 557 says "small men" instead of "swarthy men." The explorers called them *Skrælingar*, a disparaging epithet, meaning inferior people, *i.e.*, savages. The name is applied, in saga literature, to the natives of Greenland as well as to the natives of Vinland. Storm thinks the latter were the Micmac Indians of Nova Scotia.

[4] "Lescarbot, in his minute and elaborate description of the Micmacs of Acadia, speaks with some emphasis of their large eyes. Dr. Storm quite reasonably suggests that the Norse expression may refer to the size not of the eyeball but of the eye-socket, which in the Indian face is apt to be large." Fiske, *The Discovery of America*, p. 190.

They tarried there for a time looking curiously at the people they saw before them, and then rowed away, and to the southward around the point.

Karlsefni and his followers had built their huts above the lake, some of their dwellings being near the lake, and others farther away. Now they remained there that winter. No snow came there, and all of their live-stock lived by grazing.[1] And when spring opened, they discovered, early one morning, a great number of skin-canoes, rowing from the south past the cape, so numerous, that it looked as if coals had been scattered broadcast out before the bay; and on every boat staves were waved. Thereupon Karlsefni and his people displayed their shields, and when they came together, they began to barter with each other. Especially did the strangers wish to buy red cloth, for which they offered in exchange peltries and quite gray skins. They also desired to buy swords and spears, but Karlsefni and Snorri forbade this. In exchange for perfect unsullied skins, the Skrellings would take red stuff a span in length, which they would bind around their heads. So their trade went on for a time, until Karlsefni and his people began to grow short of cloth, when they divided it into such narrow pieces, that it was not more than a finger's breadth wide, but the Skrellings still continued to give just as much for this as before, or more.

It so happened, that a bull,[2] which belonged to Karlsefni and his people, ran out from the woods, bellowing loudly. This so terrified the Skrellings, that they sped out to their canoes, and then rowed away to the southward along the coast. For three entire weeks nothing more was seen of them. At

---

[1] This would seem to place Vinland farther south than Nova Scotia, but not necessarily. Storm cites the Frenchman Denys, who as colonist and governor of Nova Scotia passed a number of years there, and in a work published in 1672 says of the inner tracts of the land east of Port Royal that "there is very little snow in the country, and very little winter." He adds: "It is certain that the country produces the vine naturally, — that it bears a grape that ripens perfectly, the berry as large as the muscat."

[2] An animal unknown to the natives. As Fiske suggests, "It is the unknown that frightens."

the end of this time, however, a great multitude of Skrelling
boats was discovered approaching from the south, as if a
stream were pouring down, and all of their staves were waved
in a direction contrary to the course of the sun, and the Skrellings were all uttering loud cries.   Thereupon Karlsefni and
his men took red shields and displayed them.   The Skrellings
sprang from their boats, and they met then, and fought together.   There was a fierce shower of missiles, for the Skrellings had war-slings.   Karlsefni and Snorri observed, that the
Skrellings raised up on a pole a great ball-shaped body, almost the size of a sheep's belly, and nearly black in color,
and this they hurled from the pole up on the land above Karlsefni's followers, and it made a frightful noise, where it fell.
Whereat a great fear seized upon Karlsefni, and all his men,
so that they could think of nought but flight, and of making
their escape up along the river bank, for it seemed to them,
that the troop of the Skrellings was rushing towards them from
every side, and they did not pause, until they came to certain
jutting crags, where they offered a stout resistance.   Freydis
came out, and seeing that Karlsefni and his men were fleeing,
she cried: "Why do ye flee from these wretches, such worthy
men as ye, when, meseems, ye might slaughter them like cattle.
Had I but a weapon, methinks, I would fight better than any
one of you!"   They gave no heed to her words.   Freydis
sought to join them, but lagged behind, for she was not hale; [1]
she followed them, however, into the forest, while the Skrellings pursued her; she found a dead man in front of her;
this was Thorbrand, Snorri's son, his skull cleft by a flat stone;
his naked sword lay beside him; she took it up, and prepared
to defend herself with it.   The Skrellings then approached her,
whereupon she stripped down her shift, and slapped her breast
with the naked sword.   At this the Skrellings were terrified
and ran down to their boats, and rowed away.   Karlsefni
and his companions, however, joined her and praised her valor.
Two of Karlsefni's men had fallen, and a great number of the
Skrellings.   Karlsefni's party had been overpowered by dint

---

[1] A euphemism for pregnant; the original is *eigi heil*.

of superior numbers.   They now returned to their dwellings, and bound up their wounds, and weighed carefully what throng of men that could have been, which had seemed to descend upon them from the land; it now seemed to them, that there could have been but the one party, that which came from the boats, and that the other troop must have been an ocular delusion.   The Skrellings, moreover, found a dead man, and an axe lay beside him.   One of their number picked up the axe, and struck at a tree with it, and one after another [they tested it], and it seemed to them to be a treasure, and to cut well; then one of their number seized it, and hewed at a stone with it, so that the axe broke, whereat they concluded that it could be of no use, since it would not withstand stone, and they cast it away.

It now seemed clear to Karlsefni and his people, that although the country thereabouts was attractive, their life would be one of constant dread and turmoil by reason of the [hostility of the] inhabitants of the country, so they forthwith prepared to leave, and determined to return to their own country.   They sailed to the northward off the coast, and found five Skrellings, clad in skin-doublets, lying asleep near the sea. There were vessels beside them, containing animal marrow, mixed with blood.   Karlsefni and his company concluded that they must have been banished from their own land.   They put them to death.   They afterwards found a cape, upon which there was a great number of animals, and this cape looked as if it were one cake of dung, by reason of the animals which lay there at night.   They now arrived again at Streamfirth, where they found great abundance of all those things of which they stood in need.   Some men say, that Biarni and Freydis remained behind here with a hundred men, and went no further; while Karlsefni and Snorri proceeded to the southward with forty men, tarrying at Hop barely two months, and returning again the same summer.   Karlsefni then set out with one ship, in search of Thorhall the Huntsman, but the greater part of the company remained behind.   They sailed to the northward around Keelness, and then bore to the westward,

having land to the larboard.[1] The country there was a wooded
wilderness, as far as they could see, with scarcely an open space;
and when they had journeyed a considerable distance, a river
flowed down from the east toward the west. They sailed into
the mouth of the river, and lay to by the southern bank.

The Slaying of Thorvald, Eric's son. — It happened one
morning, that Karlsefni and his companions discovered in an
open space in the woods above them, a speck, which seemed
to shine toward them, and they shouted at it: it stirred, and
it was a Uniped,[2] who skipped down to the bank of the river
by which they were lying. Thorvald, a son of Eric the Red,
was sitting at the helm, and the Uniped shot an arrow into
his inwards. Thorvald drew out the arrow, and exclaimed:
"There is fat around my paunch; we have hit upon a fruitful
country, and yet we are not like to get much profit of it."
Thorvald died soon after from this wound. Then the Uniped
ran away back toward the north. Karlsefni and his men
pursued him, and saw him from time to time. The last they
saw of him, he ran down into a creek. Then they turned back;
whereupon one of the men recited this ditty:[3]

> Eager, our men, up hill down dell,
>   Hunted a Uniped;
> Hearken, Karlsefni, while they tell
>   How swift the quarry fled!

Then they sailed away back toward the north, and believed
they had got sight of the land of the Unipeds; nor were they
disposed to risk the lives of their men any longer. They concluded that the mountains of Hop, and those which they had

---

[1] Thus reaching the western coast of Cape Breton Island and Nova Scotia,
according to Storm.

[2] The Norse word is *Ein-fœtingr*, one-footer. The mediaeval belief in a
country in which there lived a race of unipeds was not unknown in Iceland.
It has been suggested by Vigfusson that Thorvald being an important per-
sonage, his death must be adorned in some way. It is a singular fact that
Jacques Cartier brought back from his Canadian explorations reports of a
land peopled by a race of one-legged folk. See Reeves, *The Finding of
Wineland*, p. 177, (56).

[3] The literal translation is: "The men drove, it is quite true, a one-footer
down to the shore. The strange man ran hard over the banks. Hearken,
Karlsefni!"

now found, formed one chain, and this appeared to be so because they were about an equal distance removed from Streamfirth, in either direction.[1] They sailed back, and passed the third winter at Streamfirth. Then the men began to divide into factions, of which the women were the cause; and those who were without wives, endeavored to seize upon the wives of those who were married, whence the greatest trouble arose. Snorri, Karlsefni's son, was born the first autumn, and he was three winters old when they took their departure. When they sailed away from Wineland, they had a southerly wind, and so came upon Markland, where they found five Skrellings,[2] of whom one was bearded, two were women, and two were children. Karlsefni and his people took the boys, but the others escaped, and these Skrellings sank down into the earth. They bore the lads away with them, and taught them to speak, and they were baptized. They said, that their mother's name was Vætilldi, and their father's Uvægi. They said, that kings governed the Skrellings, one of whom was called Avalldamon, and the other Valldidida.[3] They stated, that there were no houses there, and that the people lived in caves or holes. They said, that there was a land on the other side over against their country, which was inhabited by people who wore white garments, and yelled loudly, and carried poles before them, to

[1] As skilled mariners the explorers were undoubtedly competent to make such a deduction as this. If Storm and Dieserud are correct, the explorers saw from the north coast of Nova Scotia the same mountains that they had seen from the south coast.

[2] The Beothuk Indians of Newfoundland, according to Storm.

[3] Nothing can with certainty be extracted from these names. The chances that they were incorrectly recorded are of course great. Storm contends that they cannot be Eskimo. Captain Holm of the Danish navy, an authority on the Eskimos, says, "It is not *impossible* that the names may have been derived from Eskimo originals." Fiske says, p. 189, note: "There is not the slightest reason for supposing that there were any Eskimos south of Labrador so late as nine hundred years ago." In this connection Captain Holm says: "It appears to me not sufficiently proven that the now extinct race on America's east coast, the Beothuk, were Indians. I wish to direct attention to the possibility that in the Beothuk we may perhaps have one of the transition links between the Indians and the Eskimo." See Reeves, p. 177, (57).

which rags were attached;[1] and people believe that this must
have been Hvitramanna-land [White-men's-land], or Ireland
the Great.[2]   Now they arrived in Greenland, and remained
during the winter with Eric the Red.

Biarni, Grimolf's son, and his companions were driven out
into the Atlantic,[3] and came into a sea, which was filled with
worms, and their ship began to sink beneath them.   They had
a boat, which had been coated with seal-tar; this the sea-worm
does not penetrate.   They took their places in this boat,
and then discovered that it would not hold them all.   Then
said Biarni: "Since the boat will not hold more than half
of our men, it is my advice, that the men who are to go in the
boat, be chosen by lot, for this selection must not be made
according to rank."   This seemed to them all such a manly
offer, that no one opposed it.   So they adopted this plan, the
men casting lots; and it fell to Biarni to go in the boat, and half
of the men with him, for it would not hold more.   But when
the men were come into the boat, an Icelander, who was in
the ship, and who had accompanied Biarni from Iceland, said:
"Dost thou intend, Biarni, to forsake me here?"   "It must
be even so," answers Biarni.   "Not such was the promise thou
gavest my father," he answers, "when I left Iceland with thee,
that thou wouldst thus part with me, when thou saidst, that
we should both share the same fate."   "So be it, it shall not
rest thus," answers Biarni; "do thou come hither, and I will
go to the ship, for I see that thou art eager for life."   Biarni
thereupon boarded the ship, and this man entered the boat,
and they went their way, until they came to Dublin in Ireland,
and there they told this tale; now it is the belief of most peo-

---

[1] The description is clearly suggestive of processions of Christian priests,
in white vestments, with banners, and singing (Storm).

[2] Vellum AM. 557 has not the words "Ireland the Great."   As to "White-
men's-land" (mentioned also once in the *Landnama-bok*), Storm traces its
quasi-historical origin to the Irish visitation of Iceland prior to the Norse
settlement.   See *Studies on the Vineland Voyages*, p. 61.   The explanation
is, however, hardly convincing.   See *Origines Islandicae*, Vol. II., p. 625.

[3] AM. 557 says "Iceland's sea" (*i.e.*, between Iceland and Markland),
and Hauk's Book, "Greenland's sea" (*i.e.*, between Iceland and Greenland).

ple, that Biarni and his companions perished in the maggot-sea, for they were never heard of afterward.

Karlsefni and his Wife Thurid's Issue. — The following summer Karlsefni sailed to Iceland and Gudrid with him, and he went home to Reyniness. His mother believed that he had made a poor match, and she was not at home the first winter. However, when she became convinced that Gudrid was a very superior woman, she returned to her home, and they lived happily together. Hallfrid was a daughter of Snorri, Karlsefni's son, she was the mother of Bishop Thorlak,[1] Runolf's son. They had a son named Thorbiorn, whose daughter's name was Thorunn, [she was] Bishop Biorn's [2] mother. Thorgeir was the name of a son of Snorri, Karlsefni's son, [he was] the father of Ingveld, mother of Bishop Brand the Elder. Steinunn was a daughter of Snorri, Karlsefni's son, who married Einar, a son of Grundar-Ketil, a son of Thorvald Crook, a son of Thori of Espihol. Their son was Thorstein the Unjust, he was the father of Gudrun, who married Jorund of Keldur. Their daughter was Halla, the mother of Flosi, the father of

[1] Thorlak was born in 1085, consecrated bishop in 1118, and died Feb. 1, 1133. These dates are definitely known, and are important. "The bishop's birth-year being certainly known, one can reckon back, and according to the regular allowances, we shall have Hallfrid born about 1060, and her father about 1030, in Vinland, and Karlsefni as far back as 1000." Vigfusson in *Origines Islandicae*, Vol. II., p. 592. Vigfusson seeks to corroborate the above by other allied lineages. If his deductions are correct, they are revolutionary with reference to the generally accepted chronology of the Vinland voyages. He is convinced that Leif belongs to an older generation than Karlsefni and his wife, and that Leif's declining years coincide with Karlsefni's appearance on the scene. The expeditions would then stand in the year 1025–1035, or 1030–1040, while Leif may have headed the first expedition, say in 1025. And he thinks that various things outside of the genealogies point to this. See Introduction, p. 12, of this volume.

[2] Biorn was consecrated bishop in 1147, and died in 1162. His successor was Bishop Brand "the Elder," who died in 1201. Both Hauk's Book and AM. 557 refer to him as "the Elder"; hence the originals could not have been written before the accession of the second bishop Brand, which was in 1263. He died the following year. AM. 557 concludes with the words "Bishop Brand the Elder." But in Hauk's Book the genealogical information is carried down to Hauk's own time. He was a descendant of Karlsefni and Gudrid, through Snorri, born in Vinland.

Valgerd, the mother of Herra Erlend the Stout, the father of Herra Hauk the Lawman. Another daughter of Flosi was Thordis, the mother of Fru Ingigerd the Mighty. Her daughter was Fru Hallbera, Abbess of Reyniness at Stad. Many other great people in Iceland are descended from Karlsefni and Thurid, who are not mentioned here. God be with us, Amen!

THE VINLAND HISTORY OF THE FLAT ISLAND BOOK[1]

A Brief History of Eric the Red.[2] — There was a man named Thorvald, a son of Osvald, Ulf's son, Eyxna-Thori's son. Thorvald and Eric the Red, his son, left Jaederen [in Norway], on account of manslaughter, and went to Iceland. At that time Iceland was extensively colonized. They first lived at Drangar on Horn-strands, and there Thorvald died. Eric then married Thorhild, the daughter of Jorund and Thorbiorg the Ship-chested, who was then married to Thorbiorn of the Haukadal family. Eric then removed from the north, and made his home at Ericsstadir by Vatnshorn. Eric and Thorhild's son was called Leif.

After the killing of Eyiulf the Foul, and Duelling-Hrafn, Eric was banished from Haukadal, and betook himself westward to Breidafirth, settling in Eyxney at Ericsstadir. He loaned his outer daïs-boards to Thorgest, and could not get these again when he demanded them. This gave rise to broils and battles between himself and Thorgest, as Eric's Saga relates. Eric was backed in the dispute by Styr Thorgrimsson, Eyiulf of Sviney, the sons of Brand of Alptafirth and Thorbiorn Vifilsson, while the Thorgesters were upheld by the sons of Thord the Yeller and Thorgeir of Hitardal. Eric was declared an outlaw at Thorsnessthing. He thereupon equipped his ship for a voyage, in Ericsvag, and when he was ready to sail, Styr and the others accompanied him out beyond the islands. Eric told them, that it was his purpose to go in search

---

[1] Reeves's translation. In *Origines Islandicae*, Vol. II., p. 598, this saga is called "The Story of the Wineland Voyages, commonly called The Story of Eric the Red."

[2] The original word for "Brief History" also means "section," "episode," "little story," *i.e.*, extract or abbreviated account.

of that country which Gunnbiorn, son of Ulf the Crow, had
seen, when he was driven westward across the main, at the
time when he discovered Gunnbiorns-skerries; he added,
that he would return to his friends, if he should succeed in
finding this country. Eric sailed out from Snæfellsiokul,
and found the land. He gave the name of Midiokul to his
landfall; this is now called Blacksark. From thence he proceeded southward along the coast, in search of habitable land.
He passed the first winter at Ericsey, near the middle of the
Eastern Settlement, and the following spring he went to Ericsfirth, where he selected a dwelling-place. In the summer he
visited the western uninhabited country, and assigned names
to many of the localities. The second winter he remained at
Holmar by Hrafnsgnipa, and the third summer he sailed
northward to Snæfell, and all the way into Hrafnsfirth; then
he said he had reached the head of Ericsfirth. He then returned and passed the third winter in Ericsey at the mouth of
Ericsfirth. The next summer he sailed to Iceland, landing in
Breidafirth. He called the country, which he had discovered,
Greenland, because, he said, people would be attracted thither,
if the country had a good name. Eric spent the winter in
Iceland, and the following summer set out to colonize the country. He settled at Brattahlid in Ericsfirth, and learned men
say, that in this same summer, in which Eric set out to settle
Greenland, thirty-five ships sailed out of Breidafirth and Bor-
garfirth; fourteen of these arrived there safely, some were
driven back and some were lost. This was fifteen years before
Christianity was legally adopted in Iceland.[1] During the same
summer Bishop Frederick[2] and Thorvald Kodransson went
abroad [from Iceland]. Of those men, who accompanied Eric
to Greenland, the following took possession of land there:
Heriulf, Heriulfsfirth, he dwelt at Heriulfsness; Ketil, Ketils-

---

[1] About 985 (983–986). One vellum of the *Landnama-bok* (Book of
Settlements) says sixteen, the other fifteen years.

[2] Bishop Frederick was from "Saxland" (Saxony). According to the
Kristni-Saga he came to Iceland "in the summer when the land had been
settled one-hundred-and-seven winters," *i.e.*, in 981. He made but little
headway in preaching Christianity.

firth; Hrafn, Hrafnsfirth; Solvi, Solvadal; Helgi Thorbrandsson, Alptafirth; Thorbiorn Gleamer, Siglufirth; Einar, Einars-
firth; Hafgrim, Hafgrimsfirth and Vatnahverfi; Arnlaug,
Arnlaugsfirth; while some went to the Western Settlement.

Leif the Lucky Baptized. — After that sixteen winters had
lapsed, from the time when Eric the Red went to colonize
Greenland, Leif, Eric's son, sailed out from Greenland to Norway. He arrived in Drontheim in the autumn, when King
Olaf Tryggvason was come down from the north, out of Hala-
goland. Leif put in to Nidaros with his ship, and set out at
once to visit the king. King Olaf expounded the faith to him,
as he did to other heathen men who came to visit him. It
proved easy for the king to persuade Leif, and he was accordingly baptized, together with all of his shipmates. Leif remained throughout the winter with the king, by whom he was
well entertained.

Biarni goes in Quest of Greenland. — Heriulf was a son of
Bard Heriulfsson. He was a kinsman of Ingolf, the first colonist. Ingolf allotted land to Heriulf between Vag and Rey-
kianess, and he dwelt at first at Drepstokk. Heriulf's wife's
name was Thorgerd, and their son, whose name was Biarni,
was a most promising man. He formed an inclination for
voyaging while he was still young, and he prospered both in
property and public esteem. It was his custom to pass his
winters alternately abroad and with his father. Biarni soon
became the owner of a trading-ship, and during the last winter
that he spent in Norway, [his father] Heriulf determined to
accompany Eric on his voyage to Greenland, and made his
preparations to give up his farm. Upon the ship with Heriulf
was a Christian man from the Hebrides, he it was who composed the Sea-Rollers' Song, which contains this stave:[1]

> Mine adventure to the Meek One,
> Monk-heart-searcher, I commit now;
> He, who heaven's halls doth govern,
> Hold the hawk's-seat ever o'er me!

[1] *Hafgerdingar* (sea-rollers) are supposed to have been earthquake waves,
and the lines evidently refer to such tidal-waves caused by an unusually

Heriulf settled at Heriulfsness, and was a most distinguished man.   Eric the Red dwelt at Brattahlid, where he was held in the highest esteem, and all men paid him homage.   These were Eric's children: Leif, Thorvald, and Thorstein, and a daughter whose name was Freydis; she was wedded to a man named Thorvard, and they dwelt at Gardar, where the episcopal seat now is.   She was a very haughty woman, while Thorvard was a man of little force of character, and Freydis had been wedded to him chiefly because of his wealth.   At that time the people of Greenland were heathen.

Biarni arrived with his ship at Eyrar [in Iceland] in the summer of the same year, in the spring of which his father had sailed away.   Biarni was much surprised when he heard this news, and would not discharge his cargo.   His shipmates inquired of him what he intended to do, and he replied that it was his purpose to keep to his custom, and make his home for the winter with his father; "and I will take the ship to Greenland, if you will bear me company."   They all replied that they would abide by his decision.   Then said Biarni, "Our voyage must be regarded as foolhardy, seeing that no one of us has ever been in the Greenland Sea."   Nevertheless they put out to sea when they were equipped for the voyage, and sailed for three days, until the land was hidden by the water, and then the fair wind died out, and north winds arose, and fogs, and they knew not whither they were drifting, and thus it lasted for many "dœgr."   Then they saw the sun again, and were able to determine the quarters of the heavens; they hoisted sail, and sailed that "dœgr" through before they saw land.   They discussed among themselves what land it could be, and Biarni said that he did not believe that it could be Greenland.   They asked whether he wished to sail to this land or not.   "It is my counsel" [said he], "to sail close to the land."   They did so, and soon saw that the land was level, and covered with woods, and that there were small hillocks

severe earthquake in the year 986. See Reeves, p. 180, (63). The prose sense of the stave is: "I beg the blessed friend of the monks to further our voyage. May the Lord of the heavens hold his hand over me."

upon it.   They left the land on their larboard, and let the sheet turn toward the land.   They sailed for two "dœgr" before they saw another land.   They asked whether Biarni thought this was Greenland yet.   He replied that he did not think this any more like Greenland than the former, "because in Greenland there are said to be many great ice-mountains." They soon approached this land, and saw that it was a flat and wooded country.   The fair wind failed them then, and the crew took counsel together, and concluded that it would be wise to land there, but Biarni would not consent to this.   They alleged that they were in need of both wood and water.   "Ye have no lack of either of these," says Biarni — a course, forsooth, which won him blame among his shipmates.   He bade them hoist sail, which they did, and turning the prow from the land they sailed out upon the high seas, with southwesterly gales, for three "dœgr," when they saw the third land; this land was high and mountainous, with ice-mountains upon it.   They asked Biarni then whether he would land there, and he replied that he was not disposed to do so, "because this land does not appear to me to offer any attractions." Nor did they lower their sail, but held their course off the land, and saw that it was an island.   They left this land astern, and held out to sea with the same fair wind.   The wind waxed amain, and Biarni directed them to reef, and not to sail at a speed unbefitting their ship and rigging.   They sailed now for four "dœgr," when they saw the fourth land.   Again they asked Biarni whether he thought this could be Greenland or not. Biarni answers, "This is likest Greenland, according to that which has been reported to me concerning it, and here we will steer to the land."   They directed their course thither, and landed in the evening, below a cape upon which there was a boat, and there, upon this cape, dwelt Heriulf,[1] Biarni's father, whence the cape took its name, and was afterwards called Her-

---

[1] "Certainly a marvellous coincidence, but it is quite in character with the no less surprising accuracy with which the explorers of this history [*i.e.*, the Flat Island Book narrative] succeeded in finding ' Leif's-booths ' in a country which was as strange to them as Greenland to Biarni."   (Reeves.)

E

iulfsness. Biarni now went to his father, gave up his voyaging, and remained with his father while Heriulf lived, and continued to live there after his father.

Here begins the Brief History of the Greenlanders. — Next to this is now to be told how Biarni Heriulfsson came out from Greenland on a visit to Earl Eric,[1] by whom he was well received. Biarni gave an account of his travels [upon the occasion] when he saw the lands, and the people thought that he had been lacking in enterprise, since he had no report to give concerning these countries, and the fact brought him reproach. Biarni was appointed one of the Earl's men, and went out to Greenland the following summer. There was now much talk about voyages of discovery. Leif, the son of Eric the Red, of Brattahlid, visited Biarni Heriulfsson and bought a ship of him, and collected a crew, until they formed altogether a company of thirty-five men. Leif invited his father, Eric, to become the leader of the expedition, but Eric declined, saying that he was then stricken in years, and adding that he was less able to endure the exposure of sea-life than he had been. Leif replied that he would nevertheless be the one who would be most apt to bring good luck, and Eric yielded to Leif's solicitation, and rode from home when they were ready to sail. When he was but a short distance from the ship, the horse which Eric was riding stumbled, and he was thrown from his back and wounded his foot, whereupon he exclaimed, "It is not designed for me to discover more lands than the one in which we are now living, nor can we now continue longer together." Eric returned home to Brattahlid, and Leif pursued his way to the ship with his companions, thirty-five men; one of the company was a German named Tyrker. They put the ship in order, and when they were ready, they sailed out to sea, and found first that land which Biarni and his ship-mates found last. They sailed up to the land and cast anchor, and launched a boat and went ashore, and saw no grass there; great ice mountains lay inland back from the sea, and it was as a [table-land of] flat rock all the way from the sea to the ice moun-

---

[1] Earl Eric ruled in Norway from 1000 to 1015.

tains, and the country seemed to them to be entirely devoid of good qualities. Then said Leif, "It has not come to pass with us in regard to this land as with Biarni, that we have not gone upon it. To this country I will now give a name, and call it Helluland." They returned to the ship, put out to sea, and found a second land. They sailed again to the land, and came to anchor, and launched the boat, and went ashore. This was a level wooded land, and there were broad stretches of white sand, where they went, and the land was level by the sea. Then said Leif, "This land shall have a name after its nature, and we will call it Markland." They returned to the ship forthwith, and sailed away upon the main with north-east winds, and were out two "dœgr" before they sighted land. They sailed toward this land, and came to an island which lay to the northward off the land. There they went ashore and looked about them, the weather being fine, and they observed that there was dew upon the grass, and it so happened that they touched the dew with their hands, and touched their hands to their mouths, and it seemed to them that they had never before tasted anything so sweet as this. They went aboard their ship again and sailed into a certain sound, which lay between the island and a cape, which jutted out from the land on the north, and they stood in westering past the cape. At ebb-tide there were broad reaches of shallow water there, and they ran their ship aground there, and it was a long distance from the ship to the ocean; yet were they so anxious to go ashore that they could not wait until the tide should rise under their ship, but hastened to the land, where a certain river flows out from a lake. As soon as the tide rose beneath their ship, however, they took the boat and rowed to the ship, which they conveyed up the river, and so into the lake, where they cast anchor and carried their hammocks ashore from the ship, and built themselves booths there. They afterwards determined to establish themselves there for the winter, and they accordingly built a large house. There was no lack of salmon there either in the river or in the lake, and larger salmon than they had ever seen before. The country thereabouts seemed to be possessed of such good qualities that cattle would need no fodder there during the winters. There was no frost there in the winters, and the grass withered but little. The days and nights there were of more nearly equal length than in Greenland or Iceland. On the shortest day of winter the sun was up between "eyktarstad" and "dagmala-stad." [1] When they had completed their house Leif said to his companions, "I propose now to divide our company into two groups, and to set about an exploration of the country; one half of our party shall remain at home at the house, while the other half shall investigate the land, and they must not go beyond a point from which they can return home the same evening, and are not to separate [from each other.]" Thus they did for a time; Leif himself, by turns, joined the exploring party or remained behind at the house. Leif was a large and powerful man, and of a most imposing bearing, a man of sagacity, and a very just man in all things.

Leif the Lucky finds Men upon a Skerry at Sea. — It was discovered one evening that one of their company was missing, and this proved to be Tyrker, the German. Leif was sorely troubled by this, for Tyrker had lived with Leif and his father for a long time, and had been very devoted to Leif, when he was a child. Leif severely reprimanded his companions, and prepared to go in search of him, taking twelve men with him. They had proceeded but a short distance from the house, when they were met by Tyrker, whom they received most cordially. Leif observed at once that his foster-father was in lively spirits. Tyrker had a prominent forehead, restless eyes, small features,

---

[1] These two words designate positions of the sun at two points of time. Early commentators got much more definite results from this observation than later ones, with scientific assistance, have succeeded in getting. Largely on the basis of it, Rafn (in *Antiquitates Americanæ*), concluded that Vinland was in Rhode Island. Both Storm and Reeves, after detailed investigation, declare that it cannot be shown from this passage how far to the south Vinland was located. Captain Phythian, U.S.N., who has given the question careful consideration, says: "The data furnished are not sufficiently definite to warrant a more positive assertion than that the explorers could not have been, when the record was made, farther north than Lat. [say] 49°." See Reeves, p. 181, (66).

was diminutive in stature, and rather a sorry-looking individual withal, but was, nevertheless, a most capable handicraftsman. Leif addressed him, and asked: "Wherefore art thou so belated, foster-father mine, and astray from the others?" In the beginning Tyrker spoke for some time in German, rolling his eyes, and grinning, and they could not understand him; but after a time he addressed them in the Northern tongue: "I did not go much further [*than you*], and yet I have something of novelty to relate. I have found vines and grapes." "Is this indeed true, foster-father?" said Leif. "Of a certainty it is true," quoth he, "for I was born where there is no lack of either grapes or vines." They slept the night through, and on the morrow Leif said to his shipmates: "We will now divide our labors, and each day will either gather grapes or cut vines and fell trees, so as to obtain a cargo of these for my ship." They acted upon this advice, and it is said, that their after-boat was filled with grapes. A cargo sufficient for the ship was cut, and when the spring came, they made their ship ready, and sailed away; and from its products Leif gave the land a name, and called it Wineland. They sailed out to sea, and had fair winds until they sighted Greenland, and the fells below the glaciers; then one of the men spoke up, and said, "Why do you steer the ship so much into the wind?" Leif answers: "I have my mind upon my steering, but on other matters as well. Do ye not see anything out of the common?" They replied, that they saw nothing strange. "I do not know," says Leif, "whether it is a ship or a skerry that I see." Now they saw it, and said, that it must be a skerry; but he was so much keener of sight than they, that he was able to discern men upon the skerry. "I think it best to tack," says Leif, "so that we may draw near to them, that we may be able to render them assistance, if they should stand in need of it; and if they should not be peaceably disposed, we shall still have better command of the situation than they." They approached the skerry, and lowering their sail, cast anchor, and launched a second small boat, which they had brought with them. Tyrker inquired who was the leader of the party.

He replied that his name was Thori, and that he was a Norseman; "but what is thy name?" Leif gave his name. "Art thou a son of Eric the Red of Brattahlid?" says he. Leif responded that he was. "It is now my wish," says Leif, "to take you all into my ship, and likewise so much of your possessions as the ship will hold." This offer was accepted, and [with their ship] thus laden, they held away to Ericsfirth, and sailed until they arrived at Brattahlid. Having discharged the cargo, Leif invited Thori, with his wife, Gudrid, and three others, to make their home with him, and procured quarters for the other members of the crew, both for his own and Thori's men. Leif rescued fifteen persons from the skerry. He was afterward called Leif the Lucky. Leif had now goodly store both of property and honor. There was serious illness that winter in Thori's party, and Thori and a great number of his people died. Eric the Red also died that winter. There was now much talk about Leif's Wineland journey, and his brother, Thorvald, held that the country had not been sufficiently explored. Thereupon Leif said to Thorvald: "If it be thy will, brother, thou mayest go to Wineland with my ship, but I wish the ship first to fetch the wood, which Thori had upon the skerry." And so it was done.

Thorvald goes to Wineland. — Now Thorvald, with the advice of his brother, Leif, prepared to make this voyage with thirty men. They put their ship in order, and sailed out to sea; and there is no account of their voyage before their arrival at Leif's-booths in Wineland. They laid up their ship there, and remained there quietly during the winter, supplying themselves with food by fishing. In the spring, however, Thorvald said that they should put their ship in order, and that a few men should take the after-boat, and proceed along the western coast, and explore [the region] thereabouts during the summer. They found it a fair, well-wooded country; it was but a short distance from the woods to the sea, and [there were] white sands, as well as great numbers of islands and shallows. They found neither dwelling of man nor lair of beast; but in one of the westerly islands, they found a wooden building for

the shelter of grain. They found no other trace of human
handiwork, and they turned back, and arrived at Leif's-booths
in the autumn. The following summer Thorvald set out toward the east with the ship, and along the northern coast. They
were met by a high wind off a certain promontory, and were
driven ashore there, and damaged the keel of their ship, and
were compelled to remain there for a long time and repair the
injury to their vessel. Then said Thorvald to his companions:
"I propose that we raise the keel upon this cape, and call it
Keelness," and so they did. Then they sailed away, to the
eastward off the land, and into the mouth of the adjoining
firth, and to a headland, which projected into the sea there,
and which was entirely covered with woods. They found an
anchorage for their ship, and put out the gangway to the land,
and Thorvald and all of his companions went ashore. "It
is a fair region here," said he, "and here I should like to make
my home." They then returned to the ship, and discovered on
the sands, in beyond the headland, three mounds; they went
up to these, and saw that they were three skin-canoes, with
three men under each. They thereupon divided their party,
and succeeded in seizing all of the men but one, who escaped
with his canoe. They killed the eight men, and then ascended
the headland again, and looked about them, and discovered
within the firth certain hillocks, which they concluded must be
habitations. They were then so overpowered with sleep
that they could not keep awake, and all fell into a [heavy]
slumber, from which they were awakened by the sound of a
cry uttered above them; and the words of the cry were these:
"Awake, Thorvald, thou and all thy company, if thou wouldst
save thy life; and board thy ship with all thy men, and sail
with all speed from the land!" A countless number of skin-
canoes then advanced toward them from the inner part of the
firth, whereupon Thorvald exclaimed: "We must put out the
war-boards, on both sides of the ship, and defend ourselves to
the best of our ability, but offer little attack." This they did,
and the Skrellings, after they had shot at them for a time,
fled precipitately, each as best he could. Thorvald then in-

quired of his men, whether any of them had been wounded, and they informed him that no one of them had received a wound. "I have been wounded in my arm-pit," says he; "an arrow flew in between the gunwale and the shield, below my arm. Here is the shaft, and it will bring me to my end! I counsel you now to retrace your way with the utmost speed. But me ye shall convey to that headland which seemed to me to offer so pleasant a dwelling-place; thus it may be fulfilled, that the truth sprang to my lips, when I expressed the wish to abide there for a time. Ye shall bury me there, and place a cross at my head, and another at my feet, and call it Crossness for ever after." At that time Christianity had obtained in Greenland; Eric the Red died, however, before [the introduction of] Christianity.

Thorvald died, and when they had carried out his injunctions, they took their departure, and rejoined their companions, and they told each other of the experiences which had befallen them. They remained there during the winter, and gathered grapes and wood with which to freight the ship. In the following spring they returned to Greenland, and arrived with their ship in Ericsfirth, where they were able to recount great tidings to Leif.

Thorstein Ericsson dies in the Western Settlement. — In the meantime it had come to pass in Greenland, that Thorstein of Ericsfirth had married, and taken to wife Gudrid, Thorbiorn's daughter, [she] who had been the spouse of Thori Eastman,[1] as has been already related. Now Thorstein Ericsson, being minded to make the voyage to Wineland after the body of his brother, Thorvald, equipped the same ship, and selected a crew of twenty-five men of good size and strength, and taking with him his wife, Gudrid, when all was in readiness, they sailed out into the open ocean, and out of sight of land. They were driven hither and thither over the sea all that sum-

---

[1] Evidently an incorrect statement. *Landnama-bok*, the authority on genealogical matters, says: "His son was Thorbiorn, father of Gudrid who married Thorstein, son of Eric the Red, and afterwards Thorfinn Karlsefni." Thori Eastman (the Norwegian) is not mentioned in the *Landnama-bok*.

mer, and lost all reckoning, and at the end of the first week of winter they made the land at Lysufirth in Greenland, in the Western Settlement. Thorstein set out in search of quarters for his crew, and succeeded in procuring homes for all of his shipmates; but he and his wife were unprovided for, and remained together upon the ship for two or more days. At this time Christianity was still in its infancy in Greenland. It befell, early one morning, that men came to their tent, and the leader inquired who the people were within the tent. Thorstein replies: "We are twain," says he; "but who is it who asks?" "My name is Thorstein, and I am known as Thorstein the Swarthy, and my errand hither is to offer you two, husband and wife, a home with me." Thorstein replied, that he would consult with his wife, and she bidding him decide, he accepted the invitation. "I will come after you on the morrow with a sumpter-horse, for I am not lacking in means wherewith to provide for you both, although it will be lonely living with me, since there are but two of us, my wife and myself, for I, forsooth, am a very hard man to get on with; moreover, my faith is not the same as yours, albeit methinks that is the better to which you hold." He returned for them on the morrow, with the beast, and they took up their home with Thorstein the Swarthy, and were well treated by him. Gudrid was a woman of fine presence, and a clever woman, and very happy in adapting herself to strangers.

Early in the winter Thorstein Ericsson's party was visited by sickness, and many of his companions died. He caused coffins to be made for the bodies of the dead, and had them conveyed to the ship, and bestowed there; "for it is my purpose to have all the bodies taken to Ericsfirth in the summer." It was not long before illness appeared in Thorstein's home, and his wife, whose name was Grimhild, was first taken sick. She was a very vigorous woman, and as strong as a man, but the sickness mastered her; and soon thereafter Thorstein Ericsson was seized with the illness, and they both lay ill at the same time, and Grimhild, Thorstein the Swarthy's wife, died, and when she was dead Thorstein went out of the room to procure a deal, upon which to lay the corpse. Thereupon Gudrid spoke. "Do not be absent long, Thorstein mine!" says she. He replied, that so it should be. Thorstein Ericsson then exclaimed: "Our house-wife is acting now in a marvellous fashion, for she is raising herself up on her elbow, and stretching out her feet from the side of the bed, and groping after her shoes." At that moment Thorstein, the master of the house, entered, and Grimhild laid herself down, wherewithal every timber in the room creaked. Thorstein now fashioned a coffin for Grimhild's body, and bore it away, and cared for it. He was a big man, and strong, but it called for all [his strength], to enable him to remove the corpse from the house. The illness grew upon Thorstein Ericsson, and he died, whereat his wife, Gudrid, was sorely grieved. They were all in the room at the time, and Gudrid was seated upon a chair before the bench, upon which her husband, Thorstein, was lying. Thorstein, the master of the house, then taking Gudrid in his arms [carried her] from the chair, and seated himself, with her, upon another bench, over against her husband's body, and exerted himself in divers ways to console her, and endeavored to reassure her, and promised her that he would accompany her to Ericsfirth with the body of her husband, Thorstein, and those of his companions: "I will likewise summon other persons hither," says he, "to attend upon thee, and entertain thee." She thanked him. Then Thorstein Ericsson sat up, and exclaimed: "Where is Gudrid?" Thrice he repeated the question, but Gudrid made no response. She then asked Thorstein, the master, "Shall I give answer to his question, or not?" Thorstein, the master, bade her make no reply, and he then crossed the floor, and seated himself upon the chair, with Gudrid in his lap, and spoke, saying: "What dost thou wish, namesake?" After a little while, Thorstein replies: "I desire to tell Gudrid of the fate which is in store for her, to the end that she may be better reconciled to my death, for I am indeed come to a goodly resting-place. This I have to tell thee, Gudrid, that thou art to marry an Icelander, and that ye are to have a long wedded life together, and a numerous and noble progeny, illustrious, and famous, of good odor and sweet virtues. Ye shall go from Greenland to Norway, and thence to Iceland, where ye shall build your home. There ye shall dwell together for a long time, but thou shalt outlive him, and shalt then go abroad and to the South, and shalt return to Iceland again, to thy home, and there a church shall then be raised, and thou shalt abide there and take the veil, and there thou shalt die." When he had thus spoken, Thorstein sank back again, and his body was laid out for burial, and borne to the ship. Thorstein, the master, faithfully performed all his promises to Gudrid. He sold his lands and livestock in the spring, and accompanied Gudrid to the ship, with all his possessions. He put the ship in order, procured a crew, and then sailed to Ericsfirth. The bodies of the dead were now buried at the church, and Gudrid then went home to Leif at Brattahlid, while Thorstein the Swarthy made a home for himself on Ericsfirth, and remained there as long as he lived, and was looked upon as a very superior man.

Of the Wineland Voyages of Thorfinn and his Companions. — That same summer a ship came from Norway to Greenland. The skipper's name was Thorfinn Karlsefni; he was a son of Thord Horsehead, and a grandson of Snorri, the son of Thord of Höfdi. Thorfinn Karlsefni, who was a very wealthy man, passed the winter at Brattahlid with Leif Ericsson. He very soon set his heart upon Gudrid, and sought her hand in marriage; she referred him to Leif for her answer, and was subsequently betrothed to him, and their marriage was celebrated that same winter. A renewed discussion arose concerning a Wineland voyage, and the folk urged Karlsefni to make the venture, Gudrid joining with the others. He determined to undertake the voyage, and assembled a company of sixty men and five women, and entered into an agreement with his shipmates that they should each share equally in all the spoils of the enterprise. They took with them all kinds of cattle, as it was their intention to settle the country, if they could. Karlsefni asked Leif for the house in Wineland, and he replied, that he would lend it but not give it. They sailed out to sea with the ship, and arrived safe and sound at Leif's-booths, and carried their hammocks ashore there. They were soon provided with an abundant and goodly supply of food, for a whale of good size and quality was driven ashore there, and they secured it, and flensed it, and had then no lack of provisions. The cattle were turned out upon the land, and the males soon became very restless and vicious; they had brought a bull with them. Karlsefni caused trees to be felled, and to be hewed into timbers, wherewith to load his ship, and the wood was placed upon a cliff to dry. They gathered somewhat of all of the valuable products of the land, grapes, and all kinds of game and fish, and other good things. In the summer succeeding the first winter, Skrellings were discovered. A great troop of men came forth from out the woods. The cattle were hard by, and the bull began to bellow and roar with a great noise, whereat the Skrellings were frightened, and ran away, with their packs wherein were gray furs, sables, and all kinds of peltries. They fled towards Karlsefni's dwelling, and sought to effect an entrance into the house, but Karlsefni caused the doors to be defended [against them]. Neither [people] could understand the other's language. The Skrellings put down their bundles then, and loosed them, and offered their wares [for barter], and were especially anxious to exchange these for weapons, but Karlsefni forbade his men to sell their weapons, and taking counsel with himself, he bade the women carry out milk to the Skrellings, which they no sooner saw, than they wanted to buy it, and nothing else. Now the outcome of the Skrellings' trading was, that they carried their wares away in their stomachs, while they left their packs and peltries behind with Karlsefni and his companions, and having accomplished this [exchange] they went away. Now it is to be told, that Karlsefni caused a strong wooden palisade to be constructed and set up around the house. It was at this time that Gudrid, Karlsefni's wife, gave birth to a male child, and the boy was called Snorri. In the early part of the second winter the Skrellings came to them again, and these were now much more numerous than before, and brought with them the same wares as at first. Then said Karlsefni to the women: "Do ye carry out now the same food, which proved so profitable before, and nought else." When they saw this they cast their packs in over the palisade. Gudrid was sitting within, in the doorway, beside the cradle of her infant son, Snorri, when a shadow fell upon the door, and a woman in a black namkirtle entered. She was short in stature, and wore a fillet about her head; her hair was of a light chestnut color, and she was pale of hue, and so big-eyed, that never before had eyes so large been seen in a human skull. She went up to where Gudrid was seated, and said: "What is thy name?" "My name is Gudrid; but what is thy name?" "My name is Gudrid," says she. The housewife, Gudrid, motioned her with her hand to a seat beside her; but it so happened, that at that very instant Gudrid heard a great crash, whereupon the woman vanished, and at that same moment one of the Skrellings, who had tried to seize their weapons, was killed by one of Karlsefni's followers. At this the Skrellings fled precipitately, leaving their garments and wares behind them; and not a soul, save Gudrid alone, beheld this woman. "Now we must needs take counsel together," says Karlsefni, "for that I believe they will visit us a third time, in great numbers, and attack us. Let us now adopt this plan: ten of our number shall go out upon the cape, and show themselves there, while the remainder of our company shall go into the woods and hew a clearing for our cattle, when the troop approaches from the forest. We will also take our bull, and let him go in advance of us." The lie of the land was such that the proposed meeting-place had the lake upon the one side, and the forest upon the other. Karlsefni's advice was now carried into execution. The Skrellings advanced to the spot which Karlsefni had selected for the encounter, and a battle was fought there, in which great numbers of the band of the Skrellings were slain. There was one man among the Skrellings, of large size and fine bearing, whom Karlsefni concluded must be their chief. One of the Skrellings picked up an axe, and having looked at it for a time, he brandished it about one of his companions, and hewed at him, and on the instant the man fell dead. Thereupon the big man seized the axe, and after examining it for a moment, he hurled it as far as he could, out into the sea; then they fled helter-skelter into the woods, and thus their intercourse came to an end. Karlsefni and his party remained there throughout the winter, but in the spring Karlsefni announces, that he is not minded to remain there longer, but will return to Greenland. They now made ready for the voyage, and carried away with them much booty in vines and grapes, and peltries. They sailed out upon the high seas, and brought their ship safely to Ericsfirth, where they remained during the winter.

Freydis causes the Brothers to be put to Death. — There was now much talk anew, about a Wineland-voyage, for this was reckoned both a profitable and an honorable enterprise. The same summer that Karlsefni arrived from Wineland, a ship from Norway arrived in Greenland. This ship was commanded by two brothers, Helgi and Finnbogi, who passed the winter in Greenland. They were descended from an Icelandic family of the East-firths. It is now to be added, that Freydis,[1] Eric's daughter, set out from her home at Gardar, and waited upon the brothers, Helgi and Finnbogi, and invited them to sail with their vessel to Wineland, and to share with her equally all of the good things which they might succeed in obtaining there. To this they agreed, and she departed thence to visit her brother, Leif, and ask him to give her the house which he had caused to be erected in Wineland, but he made her the same answer [as that which he had given Karlsefni], saying, that he would lend the house, but not give it. It was stipulated between Karlsefni and Freydis, that each should have on shipboard thirty able-bodied men, besides the women; but Freydis immediately violated this compact, by concealing five men more [than this number], and this the brothers did not discover before they arrived in Wineland. They now put out to sea, having agreed beforehand, that they would sail in company,

[1] This cruel virago plays a much less conspicuous part in the version of Hauk's Book and AM. 557.

if possible, and although they were not far apart from each other, the brothers arrived somewhat in advance, and carried their belongings up to Leif's house. Now when Freydis arrived, her ship was discharged, and the baggage carried up to the house, whereupon Freydis exclaimed: "Why did you carry your baggage in here?" "Since we believed," said they, "that all promises made to us would be kept." "It was to me that Leif loaned the house," says she, "and not to you." Whereupon Helgi exclaimed: "We brothers cannot hope to rival thee in wrong-dealing." They thereupon carried their baggage forth, and built a hut, above the sea, on the bank of the lake, and put all in order about it; while Freydis caused wood to be felled, with which to load her ship. The winter now set in, and the brothers suggested, that they should amuse themselves by playing games. This they did for a time, until the folk began to disagree, when dissensions arose between them, and the games came to an end, and the visits between the houses ceased; and thus it continued far into the winter. One morning early, Freydis arose from her bed, and dressed herself, but did not put on her shoes and stockings. A heavy dew had fallen, and she took her husband's cloak, and wrapped it about her, and then walked to the brothers' house, and up to the door, which had been only partly closed by one of the men, who had gone out a short time before. She pushed the door open, and stood, silently, in the doorway for a time. Finnbogi, who was lying on the innermost side of the room, was awake, and said: "What dost thou wish here, Freydis?" She answers: "I wish thee to rise, and go out with me, for I would speak with thee." He did so, and they walked to a tree, which lay close by the wall of the house, and seated themselves upon it. "How art thou pleased here?" says she. He answers: "I am well pleased with the fruitfulness of the land, but I am ill-content with the breach which has come between us, for, methinks, there has been no cause for it." "It is even as thou sayest," says she, "and so it seems to me; but my errand to thee is, that I wish to exchange ships with you brothers, for that ye have a larger ship than I, and I wish to depart from here." "To this I must accede," says he, "if it is thy pleasure." Therewith they parted, and she returned home, and Finnbogi to his bed. She climbed up into bed, and awakened Thorvard with her cold feet, and he asked her why she was so cold and wet. She answered, with great passion: "I have been to the brothers," says she, "to try to buy their ship, for I wished to have a larger vessel, but they received my overtures so ill, that they struck me, and handled me very roughly; what time thou, poor wretch, wilt neither avenge my shame nor thy own, and I find, perforce, that I am no longer in Greenland, moreover I shall part from thee unless thou wreakest vengeance for this." And now he could stand her taunts no longer, and ordered the men to rise at once, and take their weapons, and this they did, and they then proceeded directly to the house of the brothers, and entered it, while the folk were asleep, and seized and bound them, and led each one out, when he was bound; and as they came out, Freydis caused each one to be slain. In this wise all of the men were put to death, and only the women were left, and these no one would kill. At this Freydis exclaimed: "Hand me an axe!" This was done, and she fell upon the five women, and left them dead. They returned home, after this dreadful deed, and it was very evident that Freydis was well content with her work. She addressed her companions, saying: "If it be ordained for us, to come again to Greenland, I shall contrive the death of any man who shall speak of these events. We must give it out, that we left them living here, when we came away." Early in the spring, they equipped the ship, which had belonged to the brothers, and freighted it with all of the products of the land, which they could obtain, and which the ship would carry. Then they put out to sea, and, after a prosperous voyage, arrived with their ship in Ericsfirth early in the summer. Karlsefni was there, with his ship all ready to sail, and was awaiting a fair wind; and people say, that a ship richer laden, than that which he commanded, never left Greenland.

Concerning Freydis. — Freydis now went to her home,

since it had remained unharmed during her absence. She bestowed liberal gifts upon all of her companions, for she was anxious to screen her guilt. She now established herself at her home; but her companions were not all so close-mouthed, concerning their misdeeds and wickedness, that rumors did not get abroad at last. These finally reached her brother, Leif, and he thought it a most shameful story. He thereupon took three of the men, who had been of Freydis's party, and forced them all at the same time to a confession of the affair, and their stories entirely agreed. "I have no heart," says Leif, "to punish my sister, Freydis, as she deserves, but this I predict of them, that there is little prosperity in store for their offspring." Hence it came to pass, that no one from that time forward thought them worthy of aught but evil. It now remains to take up the story from the time when Karlsefni made his ship ready, and sailed out to sea. He had a successful voyage, and arrived in Norway safe and sound. He remained there during the winter, and sold his wares, and both he and his wife were received with great favor by the most distinguished men of Norway. The following spring he put his ship in order for the voyage to Iceland; and when all his preparations had been made, and his ship lying at the wharf, awaiting favorable winds, there came to him a Southerner, a native of Bremen in the Saxonland, who wished to buy his "house-neat." [1] "I do not wish to sell it," said he. "I will give thee half a 'mörk' in gold for it," says the Southerner. This Karlsefni thought a good offer, and accordingly closed the bargain. The Southerner went his way, with the "house-neat," and Karlsefni knew not what wood it was, but it was "mösur," come from Wineland.

Karlsefni sailed away, and arrived with his ship in the north of Iceland, in Skagafirth. His vessel was beached there during the winter, and in the spring he bought Glaumbœiar-land, and made his home there, and dwelt there as long as he lived, and was a man of the greatest prominence. From him and

---

[1] "A weather-vane, or other ornament at the point of the gable of a house or upon a ship." (Fritzner.)

his wife, Gudrid, a numerous and goodly lineage is descended. After Karlsefni's death, Gudrid, together with her son, Snorri, who was born in Wineland, took charge of the farmstead; and when Snorri was married, Gudrid went abroad, and made a pilgrimage to the South, after which she returned again to the home of her son, Snorri, who had caused a church to be built at Glaumbœr. Gudrid then took the veil and became an anchorite, and lived there the rest of her days. Snorri had a son, named Thorgeir, who was the father of Ingveld, the mother of Bishop Brand. Hallfrid was the name of the daughter of Snorri, Karlsefni's son; she was the mother of Runolf, Bishop Thorlak's father. Biorn was the name of [another] son of Karlsefni and Gudrid; he was the father of Thorunn, the mother of Bishop Biorn. Many men are descended from Karlsefni, and he has been blessed with a numerous and famous posterity; and of all men Karlsefni has given the most exact accounts of all these voyages, of which something has now been recounted.

FROM ADAM OF BREMEN'S[1] DESCRIPTIO
INSULARUM AQUILONIS

MOREOVER he [2] spoke of an island in that ocean [3] discovered by many, which is called Vinland, for the reason that vines grow wild there, which yield the best of wine. Moreover that grain unsown [4] grows there abundantly, is not a fabulous fancy, but, from the accounts of the Danes, we know to be a fact. Beyond this island, it is said, that there is no habitable land in that ocean, but all those regions which are beyond are filled with insupportable ice and boundless gloom, to which Martian thus refers: "One day's sail beyond Thile the sea is frozen." This was essayed not long since by that very enter-

---

[1] Adam of Bremen was a prebendary and writer on ecclesiastical history. The *Descriptio Insularum Aquilonis* is an appendix to his *Gesta Hammaburgensis Ecclesiae Pontificum.* For the preparation of his work on the "Northern Islands," Adam spent some time at the Danish court, where he obtained much information from the king, Svend Estridson (1047–1076), an unusually well informed monarch. Adam's work was undoubtedly completed before the king's death, which occurred in 1076. The *Descriptio* was first printed in Lindenbrog's edition of Adam's work, published in 1595, which thus contains the first printed allusions to Vinland. Rafn gives a facsimile of one of the manuscripts, for part of the passage.

[2] Svend Estridson, king of Denmark.

[3] Immediately before this extract, the author describes the islands in the northern seas — among them Iceland — and then proceeds to speak of newer lands "deeper in the ocean," first of all Greenland, "far up towards the Swedish or Riphaean mountains," distant five or seven days' sailing from Norway, then Halagland, somewhat nearer, where the sun is above the horizon fourteen days in summer, and lastly Vinland. That is, according to Adam, Vinland was in a northern region.

[4] The reference to the "unsown grain," and vines in the preceding sentence, are sufficiently characteristic to have enabled any one familiar with the "Saga of Eric the Red" to identify the new land as Vinland, even though it had not been named. It is interesting to note that the reference to "unsown grain" does not appear in the Flat Island Book saga.

prising Northmen's prince, Harold,[1] who explored the extent of the northern ocean with his ship, but was scarcely able by retreating to escape in safety from the gulf's enormous abyss, where before his eyes the vanishing bounds of earth were hidden in gloom.

[1] Evidently a reference to Harold the Stern-ruler (Haardraade). He was a contemporary of Svend Estridson, and ruler in Norway from 1047 to 1066. The saga of Harold Haardraade in Snorri Sturlason's "Saga of the Kings of Norway" contains no reference to any such expedition. Yet it would be quite in keeping with the other adventures of this much-travelled king to have undertaken such an expedition. It is to be noted that he did not, according to Adam, go in search of Vinland.

FROM THE ICELANDIC ANNALS[1]

ANNALES REGII

A.D. 1121. Bishop Eric[2] of Greenland went in search of Vinland.

FROM THE ELDER SKALHOLT[3] ANNALS

A.D. 1347. There came also a ship from Greenland, less in size than small Icelandic trading vessels. It came into the outer Stream-firth.[4] It was without an anchor. There were seventeen men on board, and they had sailed to Markland,[5] but had afterwards been driven hither by storms at sea.

---

[1] Besides the Annales Regii, which are the most important, there are several other Icelandic annals. All have, under the year 1121, the entry given here, (facsimile in Rafn). It is the only information that they give concerning Vinland, and is the last surviving mention of Vinland in the older Icelandic records. It must be remarked, however, that there were no contemporary annals as early as 1121; the earliest entries on Scandinavian events are gleaned from various sources, especially the early historians.

[2] According to the *Landnama-bok* he was an Icelander, his full name being Eric Gnupson. He is also known as Eric Uppsi. He was, according to some accounts, the first bishop of Greenland. The exact date of his consecration is not known; but the Lawman's Annals have, under date of 1112, these words: "Bishop Eric's expedition," referring no doubt to his departure from Iceland. There is no record of his consecration at Lund (Sweden), the seat of the primate at that time, as in the case of his successor, Bishop Arnold. In regard to Bishop Eric's seeking Vinland, there is no indication anywhere why he went, or whether he ever returned. At any rate, the Greenlanders applied for a new bishop, and, according to the annals, one was consecrated in 1124; this was Bishop Arnold, and he reached Greenland the following year. See "The Tale of the Greenlanders," in *Origines Islandicae*, II. 748.

[3] So called because the manuscript was found at Skalholt, in southern Iceland. This entry (facsimile in Rafn) is corroborated, in abbreviated form, by the Annals of Gottskalk, in these words: "A ship came then from Greenland, which had sailed to Markland, and there were eighteen men on board."

[4] Stream-firth is on the western coast of Iceland.

[5] One of the new lands mentioned in the sagas of the Vinland voyages.

PAPAL LETTERS CONCERNING THE BISH-OPRIC OF GARDAR IN GREENLAND DURING THE FIFTEENTH CENTURY[1]

LETTER OF NICHOLAS V., *September* 20, 1448

CALLED by a command from on high to preside over all the churches in the exercise of our apostolic duty, with the Lord's help we employ all our solicitude in laboring for the salvation of souls redeemed by the precious blood of Christ, and we strive earnestly to restore to a state of peace and tranquillity, not only those who are frequently tossed about by the storms of impiety and error, but also those who are involved in the hardships and whirlwinds of persecution. Profoundly im-

---

[1] In 1893 an American in Rome, Mr. J. C. Heywood, one of the papal chamberlains, brought out, in a very small edition (twenty-five copies), a book of photographic facsimiles of documents in the Vatican relating to Greenland and the discovery of America, *Documenta Selecta e Tabulario Secreto Vaticano*. The Latin text of those here presented may be found in Fischer, *Discoveries of the Northmen*, pp. 49-51. A translation of all was made for the Tennessee Historical Society by Rev. John B. Morris and printed in Vol. IX. of the society's organ, the *American Historical Magazine*. Using this translation, we have printed Letters IX. and X. as the only ones that contain anything of particular interest concerning the Gardar bishopric in Greenland, excepting, possibly, the following sentence from Letter II. (December 4, 1276), to the Archbishop of Drontheim: "Your Fraternity having been explicitly directed by letters apostolic to visit personally all parts of the kingdom of Norway, for the purpose of collecting the tithes due the Holy Land, has informed us that this seems almost impossible, when it is taken into consideration that the diocese of Gardar in Greenland is so remote from your metropolitan see and kingdom, that five years or more would be consumed in going thither and returning." It has been inferred, on account of the length of this time, that the Vinland colony was included. There is no documentary evidence of this. The papal letters contain no reference to Vinland.

pressed therefore with the responsibility of our position, it is
not difficult to understand how our mind was filled with bit-
terness by the tearful lamentations [1] which have reached our
ears from our beloved children, the native and other inhabitants of the island of Greenland, a region situated at the utter-
most end of the earth.   The island, belonging [2] to the kingdom of Norway, and under the ecclesiastical jurisdiction of the
Archbishop of Drontheim,[3] received the faith of Christ almost
six [4] centuries ago, through the piety of blessed King Olaf, and
preserved it steadfastly and inviolably in accordance with the
tradition of the Roman Church, and the Apostolic See.   After
their conversion, the people of this island, with untiring and
characteristic devotion, erected many temples [5] to the worship
of God and his saints, as well as a magnificent cathedral,[6] in
which divine worship was diligently celebrated, until about
thirty [7] years ago, when God permitting it, a barbarous and
pagan fleet from neighboring shores [8] invaded the island, lay-

[1] No record of these reports from Greenland has been found.

[2] Both Iceland and Greenland came under Norwegian rule in 1261, during the reign of Haakon Haakonson (1217–1263).

[3] In Norway.

[4] Only four and a half centuries before this time.   Olaf Tryggvason, who
reigned from 995 to 1000, sent Leif Ericson as a missionary to Greenland in
the year 1000.

[5] According to Northern chorography, the Eastern Settlement had one
hundred and ninety farmsteads, twelve churches, and two monasteries; the
Western Settlement had ninety farmsteads and three churches.

[6] The cathedral (hardly magnificent) was in the Eastern Settlement (i.e.,
in southern Greenland), no doubt the present Kakortok.   The village of
Gardar, which gave its name to the bishopric, was at the present Kaksiarsuk.
The authority which makes this identification possible, is Ivar Bardsen's
description of Greenland written in that country in the fourteenth century.
He was for many years steward to the Gardar bishopric.   An English
version of Bardsen's description is printed in Major's The Voyages of the
Venetian Brothers Zeno (London, 1873).   See also Fiske, The Discovery of
America, pp. 239 and 242.

[7] That is, about 1418.   The last notice of Greenland based on Northern
tradition is from the year 1409, telling of a marriage ceremony performed by
Endride Andreson, the last bishop.   See Laing's The Sagas of the Norse
Kings (London, 1889), p. 177.

[8] From Ivar Bardsen's description of Greenland it is known that the
Greenlanders first came in conflict with the Eskimos during the fourteenth

ing waste the land with fire and sword, and destroying the sacred temples. Just nine parish churches were left standing. To these are attached, it is said, parishes of very great extent. These churches are left intact, because being situated in the mountain fastnesses, they were inaccessible to the barbarian hordes, who, after completing their work of destruction, led captive to their shores the unfortunate inhabitants of both sexes, and more particularly those who seemed best able to bear the hardships of servitude and tyranny. But as the same complaint sets forth, many of these captives, after a time, returned to their native land. They set to work to re-build their ruined homes, and were particularly desirous of restoring divine worship to its former splendor. Because, however, of their past calamities, as well as the added trials of famine and want, they had not wherewith to support priests or bishop. They have been consequently during these thirty years past without the comfort and ministry of bishop or priest, unless some one of a very zealous disposition, and at long intervals, and in spite of danger from the raging sea, ventured to visit the island and minister to them in those churches which the barbarians had left standing. Having acquainted us with this deplorable state of affairs, and knowing our paternal solicitude, they have supplicated us to come to their rescue in this their hour of spiritual need. Our hearts have been moved by the prayers of the people of Greenland, but not being sufficiently acquainted with the circumstances,

century. He was appointed to lead an expedition from the Eastern Settlement against the Skrellings (Eskimos), who had taken possession of the Western Settlement. When he arrived there the Skrellings had departed, and they found nothing but ruins and some cattle running wild. See *Antiquitates Americanæ*, p. 316.

The letter of Nicholas V. refers to an attack on the Western Settlement, of which there is no other recorded evidence. It is not likely that it will ever be possible to determine whether the settlement owed its final destruction to the irruptions of the Eskimos, "to the ravages of pestilence, to the enforced neglect of the mother country — itself during the fifteenth century too often in sore straits — to the iniquitous restrictions in commerce imposed by the home government, or to a combination of several of these evils." There was a regular succession of bishops from 1124 to the end of the fourteenth, or perhaps the beginning of the fifteenth century.

we direct and command you, or either of you,[1] beloved brothers, who as we understand are the bishops living nearest to
that island, to institute a diligent inquiry as to whether things
are as they have been reported to us, and if you should find
them so, and the number of people warrant it, and if they
are in a condition to provide sufficiently, we command you or
either of you, to send worthy priests who will minister to them,
erect churches, govern parishes, and administer the sacraments.

Moreover, if you or either of you should deem it expedient,
and in this you will consult, of course, the metropolitan,[2] if his
residence be not too far away from you, we empower you to
select and consecrate a bishop, having first required him to
take the usual oath to us and the Roman See. Be mindful,
however, that we burden your conscience with this work, and
we grant you, or either of you, full authority to carry it out,
even if there should exist any constitution of the Apostolic
See, general councils, canonical or other statutes to the contrary.

Given at Rome as dated above in the second year of our
pontificate.

LETTER OF ALEXANDER VI.; WRITTEN IN THE FIRST YEARS OF HIS PONTIFICATE[3]

It has been reported to us that in the diocese of Gardar in
Greenland, situated at the confines of the known world, the
inhabitants, because of the scarcity of bread, wine and oil,
live for the most part on dried fish and milk products. Wherefore because of the difficulty of passing through such immense
quantities of ice, and likewise because of the poverty of the
land, and the scant means of living, ships rarely visit its
shores. We have learned in fact that no vessel has touched
there during the past eighty years, and if a voyage be made
at all, it must be in the month of August, when the ice has

---

[1] Addressed to the two bishops of Skalholt and Holar, in Iceland.
[2] The Archbishop of Drontheim in Norway.
[3] Alexander VI. was pope from 1492 to 1503.

broken up. On this account, during eighty years no bishop or priest has resided personally among those people, and by reason of this, we are informed that many who were formerly Catholics have forgotten the faith of their baptism, and that no memory of the Christian religion is found, except a corporal, which is shown to the people once a year, and on which it is said the last priest who officiated there consecrated the body of Christ a hundred years ago.[1] In consideration of these things, Innocent the VIII., our predecessor of happy memory, wishing to provide a proper pastor for those forlorn people, conferred with his brethren, of whom we were one, and elected Matthias, our venerable brother, a member of the Order of St. Benedict, as well as professed monk, at our suggestion, and while we were still in minor orders, to be Bishop of Gardar. This good man, fired with great zeal to recall those people from the way of error to the practice of their faith, is about to undertake this perilous voyage and laborious duty.[2] We, on our part, accordingly, recognizing the pious and praiseworthy purpose of the same elect, and wishing to succor in some manner his poverty, which is very great indeed, command the officials of our chancery, as well as those of our palace, under pain of excommunication *ipso facto* to be incurred, that all apostolic letters destined for the church of Gardar, be written gratis for the glory of God alone, without exacting or charging any stipend; and we command the clergy and notaries of our palace to forward all letters to the above mentioned bishop, without demanding any payment whatsoever for services rendered.

To him everything must be free, other things to the contrary notwithstanding.

[1] Evidently this is only an approximate statement.

[2] There are no records that this man ever reached either Greenland or Iceland. The Greenland colony was not entirely forgotten by the home government (Denmark-Norway). In the beginning of the sixteenth century, Archbishop Valkendorf of Drontheim had agitated the question of searching for the Greenland colony. During the reign of Frederick II. of Denmark-Norway, Mogens Heinesen was in 1579 sent out, but he did not reach the island. The Englishman John Davis, in 1585, visited the western coast of Greenland, but found no Europeans.

ORIGINAL NARRATIVES OF THE
VOYAGES OF COLUMBUS

ARTICLES OF AGREEMENT BETWEEN THE LORDS THE CATHOLIC SOVEREIGNS AND CRISTÓBAL COLON[1]

THE things prayed for, and which Your Highnesses give and grant to Don Cristóbal Colon [2] as some recompense for what he is to discover in the Oceans, and for the voyage which now, with the help of God, he has engaged to make therein in the service of Your Highnesses, are the following:

Firstly, that Your Highnesses, as actual Lords of the said Oceans, appoint from this date the said Don Cristóbal Colon to be your Admiral in all those islands and mainlands which

[1] The Spanish text is that printed by Navarrete in his *Coleccion de los Viages y Descubrimientos*, etc. (Madrid, 1825), II. 7–8, and taken from the Archives of the Duke of Veragua. The translation is that of George F. Barwick printed by Benjamin Franklin Stevens in his *Christopher Columbus His Own Book of Privileges*, 1502, etc. (London, 1893), pp. 42–45, with such slight changes (chiefly of tenses) as were necessary to bring it into conformity with the text of Navarrete. This document is also given in English translation in *Memorials of Columbus* (London, 1823), pp. 40–43. That volume is a translation of G. B. Spotorno, *Codice Diplomatico Colombo-Americano* (Genoa, 1823).

[2] In this edition of the Narratives of the Voyages of Columbus his name in the translation of the original documents will be given in the form used in the originals. During his earlier years in Spain Columbus was known as Colomo, the natural Spanish form corresponding to the Italian Colombo. At some time prior to 1492 he adopted the form Colon, apparently to make more probable his claim to be descended from a Roman general, Colonius, and to be related to the French admiral, Coullon, called in contemporary Italian sources Colombo, and Columbus in Latin. In modern texts of Tacitus the Roman general's name is Cilonius, and modern research has shown that the French admiral's real name was Caseneuve and that Coullon was a sobriquet added for some unknown reason. On the two French naval commanders known as Colombo or Coullon and the baselessness of Columbus's alleged relationship see Vignaud, *Études Critiques sur la Vie de Colomb*, pp. 131 ff.

by his activity and industry shall be discovered or acquired
in the said oceans, during his lifetime, and likewise, after his
death, his heirs and successors one after another in perpetuity,
with all the pre-eminences and prerogatives appertaining to
the said office, and in the same manner as Don Alfonso Enriques, your High Admiral of Castile,[1] and his predecessors in
the said office held it in their districts. — It so pleases their
Highnesses. Juan de Coloma.

Likewise, that Your Highnesses appoint the said Don Cristóbal Colon to be your Viceroy and Governor General in all
the said islands and mainlands and in the islands which, as
aforesaid, he may discover and acquire [2] in the said seas; and
that for the government of each and any of them he may
make choice of three persons for each office, and that Your
Highnesses may select and choose the one who shall be most
serviceable to you; and thus the lands which our Lord shall
permit him to discover and acquire for the service of Your
Highnesses, will be the better governed. — It so pleases their
Highnesses. Juan de Coloma.

[1] In 1497 Columbus at his own request was supplied with a copy of the
ordinances establishing the admiralty of Castile so that he might have a documentary enumeration of his prerogatives in the Indies. This official copy
he preserved in the collection of his papers known as the *Book of Privileges*,
and the translation of the documents relating to the Admiralty of Castile is
given in Stevens's edition of the *Book of Privileges*, pp. 14 ff. This dignity
of Admiral comprised supreme or vice-regal authority on the sea and the
general range of legal jurisdiction in determining suits of law that is enjoyed
by modern courts of admiralty. A translation of Columbus's exposition of
his rights derived from his admiralty of the islands in the Ocean may be
found in P. L. Ford, *Writings of Columbus* (New York, 1892), pp. 177–198,
taken from *Memorials of Columbus* (London, 1823), pp. 205–223. For a
summary of these powers *cf.* the *Titulo* that follows.

[2] It is a remarkable fact that nothing is said in this patent of discovering
a route to the Indies. It is often said that the sole purpose of Columbus
was to discover such a route, yet it is clear that he expected to make some
new discoveries, and that if he did not, the sovereigns were under no specified
obligations to him. Patents are usually drawn on the lines indicated by the
petitioner. Can we conclude that the complete silence of the articles as
to the Indies means that Ferdinand and Isabella refused to make any promises
if Columbus only succeeded in reaching the known East Indies and could gain
for them no new possessions?

Item, that of all and every kind of merchandise, whether pearls, precious stones, gold, silver, spices, and other objects and merchandise whatsoever, of whatever kind, name and sort, which may be bought, bartered, discovered, acquired and obtained within the limits of the said Admiralty, Your Highnesses grant from now henceforth to the said Don Cristóbal, and will that he may have and take for himself, the tenth part of the whole, after deducting all the expenses which may be incurred therein, so that of what shall remain clear and free he may have and take the tenth part for himself, and may do therewith as he pleases, the other nine parts being reserved for Your Highnesses. — It so pleases their Highnesses. Juan de Coloma.

Likewise, that if on account of the merchandise which he might bring from the said islands and lands which thus, as aforesaid, may be acquired or discovered, or of that which may be taken in exchange for the same from other merchants here, any suit should arise in the place where the said commerce and traffic shall be held and conducted; and if by the pre-eminence of his office of Admiral it appertains to him to take cognizance of such suit; it may please Your Highnesses that he or his deputy, and not another judge, shall take cognizance thereof and give judgment in the same from henceforth. — It so pleases their Highnesses, if it appertains to the said office of Admiral, according as it was held by Admiral Don Alfonso Enriques, and others his successors in their districts, and if it be just. Juan de Coloma.

Item, that in all the vessels which may be equipped for the said traffic and business, each time and whenever and as often as they may be equipped, the said Don Cristóbal Colon may, if he chooses, contribute and pay the eighth part of all that may be spent in the equipment, and that likewise he may have and take the eighth part of the profits that may result from such equipment. — It so pleases their Highnesses. Juan de Coloma.

These are granted and despatched, with the replies of Your Highnesses at the end of each article, in the town of Santa Fe

de la Vega of Granada, on the seventeenth day of April in the
year of the nativity of our Saviour Jesus Christ, one thousand
four hundred and ninety-two.   I the King.   I the Queen.
By command of the King and of the Queen.   Juan de Coloma.
Registered, Calcena.

TITLE GRANTED BY THE CATHOLIC SOVEREIGNS TO CRISTÓBAL COLON OF ADMIRAL, VICEROY AND GOVERNOR OF THE ISLANDS AND MAINLAND THAT MAY BE DISCOVERED [1]

DON FERDINAND and Donna Isabella, by the grace of God King and Queen of Castile, Leon, Aragon, Sicily, Granada, Toledo, Valencia, Galicia, Majorca, Seville, Sardinia, Cordova, Corsica, Murcia, Jaen, Algarbe, Algeciras, Gibraltar, and the Canary Islands; Count and Countess of Barcelona; Lords of Biscay and Molina; Dukes of Athens and Neopatria; Counts of Roussillon and Cerdagne, Marquises of Oristano and Goziano; Forasmuch as you, Cristóbal Colon, are going by our command, with some of our ships and with our subjects, to discover and acquire certain islands and mainland in the ocean, and it is hoped that, by the help of God, some of the said islands and mainland in the said ocean will be discovered and acquired by your pains and industry; and as it is a just and reasonable thing that since you incur the said danger for our service you should be rewarded for it, and since we desire to honor and favor you on account of what is aforesaid, it is our will and pleasure that you, the said Cristóbal Colon, after you have discovered and acquired the said islands and mainland in the said ocean, or any of them whatsoever, shall be our Admiral of the said islands and mainland which you may thus discover and acquire, and shall be our Admiral and Viceroy

[1] Spanish text in Navarrete, II. 9–11. We omit the long preamble. Spanish text and facsimile of Paris Codex in Stevens, *Christopher Columbus His Own Book of Privileges*, pp. 49 ff. The translation is that of George F. Barwick. This document is also to be found in English in *Memorials of Columbus* (London, 1823), pp. 52–57.

and Governor therein, and shall be empowered from that time
forward to call and entitle yourself Don Cristóbal Colon, and
that your sons and successors in the said office and charge may
likewise entitle and call themselves Don, and Admiral and
Viceroy and Governor thereof; and that you may have power
to use and exercise the said office of Admiral, together with
the said office of Viceroy and Governor of the said islands and
mainland which you may thus discover and acquire, by yourself or by your lieutenants, and to hear and determine all the
suits and causes civil and criminal appertaining to the said
office of Admiralty, Viceroy, and Governor according as you
shall find by law, and as the Admirals of our kingdoms are
accustomed to use and exercise it; and may have power to
punish and chastise delinquents, and exercise the said offices
of Admiralty, Viceroy, and Governor, you and your said
lieutenants, in all that concerns and appertains to the said
offices and to each of them; and that you shall have and
levy the fees and salaries annexed, belonging and appertaining to the said offices and to each of them, according as our
High Admiral in the Admiralty of our kingdoms levies and is
accustomed to levy them. And by this our patent, or by the
transcript thereof signed by a public scrivener, we command
Prince Don Juan, our very dear and well beloved son, and
the Infantes, dukes, prelates, marquises, counts, masters of
orders, priors, commanders, and members of our council, and
auditors of our audiencia, alcaldes, and other justices whom-
soever of our household, court, and chancery, and sub-com-
manders, alcaldes of castles and fortified and unfortified
houses, and all councillors, assistants, regidores, alcaldes, bail-
iffs, judges, veinticuatros, jurats, knights, esquires, officers,
and liege men [1] of all the cities, towns, and places of our kingdoms and dominions, and of those which you may conquer

---

[1] Audiencia means the king's court of justice; regidores are roughly equivalent to members of a town council. The Navarrete text has *corregidores*,
town governors appointed by the king. Veinticuatros were town councillors,
so called because commonly 24 in number. Jurats were municipal executive
officers in Aragon. The original which is translated "liege men" is *Homes-
Buenos*. Further explanations of these offices may be found in Hume,

and acquire, and the captains, masters, mates, officers, mariners, and seamen, our natural subjects who now are or hereafter shall be, and each and any of them, that upon the said
islands and mainland in the said ocean being discovered and
acquired by you, and the oath and formality requisite in such
case having been made and done by you or by him who may
have your procuration,[1] they shall have and hold you from
thenceforth for the whole of your life, and your son and successor after you, and successor after successor for ever and
ever, as our Admiral of the said ocean, and as Viceroy and
Governor of the said islands and mainland, which you, the
said Don Cristóbal Colon, may discover and acquire; and they
shall treat with you, and with your said lieutenants whom
you may place in the said offices of Admiral, Viceroy, and
Governor, about everything appertaining thereto, and shall
pay and cause to be paid to you the salary, dues and other
things annexed and appertaining to the said offices, and shall
observe and cause to be observed toward you all the honors,
graces, favors, liberties, pre-eminences, prerogatives, exemptions, immunities, and all other things, and each of them,
which in virtue of the said offices of Admiral, Viceroy, and
Governor you shall be entitled to have and enjoy, and which
ought to be observed towards you in every respect fully and
completely so that nothing may be diminished therefrom; and
that neither therein nor in any part thereof shall they place
or consent to place hindrance or obstacle against you; for we
by this our patent from now henceforth grant to you the said
offices of Admiralty, Viceroy, and Governor, by right of inheritance for ever and ever, and we give you actual and pro-
spective possession thereof, and of each of them, and power
and authority to use and exercise it, and to collect the dues
and salaries annexed and appertaining to them and to each
of them, according to what is aforesaid. Concerning all that
is aforesaid, if it should be necessary and you should require

Spain, Its Greatness and Decay, pp. 18 ff., and in *The Cambridge Modern
History*, I. 348 ff.

[1] Procuration = power of attorney.

it of them, we command our chancellor and notaries and the other officers who are at the board of our seals to give, deliver, pass, and seal for you our patent of privilege with the circle of signatures, in the strongest, firmest, and most sufficient manner that you may request and may find needful, and neither one nor the other of you or them shall do contrary hereto in any manner, under penalty of our displeasure and of ten thousand maravedis [1] to our chamber, upon every one who shall do to the contrary. And further we command the man who shall show them this our patent, to cite them to appear before us in our court, wheresoever we may be, within fifteen days from the day of citation, under the said penalty, under which we command every public scrivener who may be summoned for this purpose, to give to the person who shall show it to him a certificate thereof signed with his signature, whereby we may know in what manner our command is executed. Given in our city of Granada, on the thirtieth day of the month of April, in the year of the nativity of our Lord Jesus Christ one thousand four hundred and ninety-two. I the King. I the Queen. I, Juan de Coloma, Secretary of the King and of the Queen, our Lords, caused this to be written by their command. Granted in form, Roderick, Doctor. Registered, Sebastian de Olano. Francisco de Madrid, Chancellor.

[1] The maravedi at this time was equal in coin value to about two-thirds of a cent.

JOURNAL OF THE FIRST VOYAGE OF COLUMBUS

INTRODUCTION

The contents of Columbus's Journal of his first voyage were first made known to the public in the epitome incorporated in Ferdinand Columbus's life of the Admiral, which has come down to us only in the Italian translation of Alfonso Ulloa, the *Historie del S. D. Fernando Colombo nelle quali s'ha particolare e vera relazione della vita e de' fatti dell' Ammiraglio D. Christoforo Colombo suo padre*, etc. (Venice, 1571). This account is accessible in English in Churchill's *Voyages*, Vol. II., and in Pinkerton's *Voyages*, Vol. XII.

Another epitome was prepared by Bartolomé de Las Casas and inserted in his *Historia de las Indias*. This account was embodied in the main by Antonio de Herrera in his *Historia General de las Indias Occidentales* (Madrid, 1601). It is accessible in English in John Stevens's translation of Herrera (London, 1725–1726).

These independent epitomes of the original were supplemented in 1825 by the publication by the Spanish archivist Martin Fernandez de Navarrete in his *Coleccion de los Viages y Descubrimientos que hicieron por mar los Españoles desde fines del siglo XV*. of a considerably more detailed narrative (likewise independently abridged from the original) which existed in two copies in the archives of the Duke del Infantado. Navarrete says that the handwriting of the older copy is that of Las Casas and that Las Casas had written some explanatory notes in the margin. This longer narrative, here reprinted, was first translated by Samuel Kettell of Boston and published in 1827 under the title *Personal Narrative of the First*

Voyage of Columbus. The next translation was that of Clements R. Markham for the Hakluyt Society in 1893. A third and very exact rendering appeared in 1903 in John Boyd Thacher's *Christopher Columbus,* Vol. I.

The translation given here is that of Sir Clements R. Markham with some slight revisions. When we recall the very scanty and fragmentary knowledge which we have of the Cabot voyages, and how few in fact of the great discoverers of this era left personal narratives of their achievements, we realize our singular good fortune in possessing so full a daily record from the hand of Columbus himself which admits us as it were "into the very presence of the Admiral to share his thoughts and impressions as the strange panorama of his experiences unfolded before him."[1] Sir Clements R. Markham declares the Journal "the most important document in the whole range of the history of geographical discovery, because it is a record of the enterprise which changed the whole face, not only of that history, but of the history of mankind."[2]

EDWARD G. BOURNE.

[1] Bourne, *Spain in America,* p. 22.
[2] *Journal of Christopher Columbus,* p. viii.

JOURNAL OF THE FIRST VOYAGE OF COLUMBUS

This is the first voyage and the routes and direction taken by the Admiral Don Cristóbal Colon when he discovered the Indies, summarized; except the prologue made for the Sovereigns, which is given word for word and commences in this manner

In the name of our Lord Jesus Christ

BECAUSE, O most Christian, and very high, very excellent, and puissant Princes, King and Queen of the Spains and of the islands of the Sea, our Lords, in this present year of 1492, after your Highnesses had given an end to the war with the Moors who reigned in Europe, and had finished it in the very great city of Granada, where in this present year, on the second day of the month of January, by force of arms, I saw the royal banners of your Highnesses placed on the towers of Alfambra,[1] which is the fortress of that city, and I saw the Moorish King come forth from the gates of the city and kiss the royal hands of your Highnesses, and of the Prince my Lord, and presently in that same month, acting on the information that I had given to your Highnesses touching the lands of India, and respecting a Prince who is called Gran Can, which means in our language King of Kings, how he and his ancestors had sent to Rome many times to ask for learned men [2] of our holy faith to teach him, and how the Holy Father

---

[1] The Alhambra.

[2] This information Columbus is ordinarily supposed to have derived from Toscanelli's letter which may be found in Fiske, *Discovery of America*, I. 356 ff. and II. App. The original source of the information, however, is Marco Polo, and Columbus summarized the passage on the margin in his copy of Marco Polo, Lib. I., ch. IV., as follows: "Magnus Kam misit legatos ad pontificem:" *Raccolta Colombiana*, Part I, Tomo 2, p. 446. That he read

had never complied, insomuch that many people believing in idolatries were lost by receiving doctrine of perdition: YOUR HIGHNESSES, as Catholic Christians and Princes who love the holy Christian faith, and the propagation of it, and who are enemies to the sect of Mahoma and to all idolatries and heresies, resolved to send me, Cristóbal Colon, to the said parts of India to see the said princes, and the cities and lands, and their disposition, with a view that they might be converted to our holy faith; [1] and ordered that I should not go by land to the eastward, as had been customary, but that I should go by way of the west, whither up to this day, we do not know for certain that any one has gone.

Thus, after having turned out all the Jews from all your kingdoms and lordships, in the same month of January, [2] your Highnesses gave orders to me that with a sufficient fleet I should go to the said parts of India, and for this they made great concessions to me, and ennobled me, so that henceforward I should be called Don, and should be Chief Admiral of the Ocean Sea, perpetual Viceroy and Governor of all the islands and continents that I should discover and gain, and that I might hereafter discover and gain in the Ocean Sea, and that my eldest son should succeed, and so on from generation to generation for ever.

I left the city of Granada on the 12th day of May, in the same year of 1492, being Saturday, and came to the town of Palos, which is a seaport; where I equipped three vessels well suited for such service; and departed from that port, well supplied with provisions and with many sailors, on the 3d day of August of the same year, being Friday, half an hour before sunrise,

and annotated these passages before 1492 seems most probable. See Bourne, *Spain in America*, pp. 10–15, and Vignaud, *Toscanelli and Columbus*, p. 284.

[1] It is interesting to notice the emphasis of the missionary motive in this preamble. Nothing is said in regard to the search for a new route to the Indies for commercial reasons. Nor is reference made to the expectation of new discoveries which is prominent in the royal patent granted to Columbus, see above p. 78.

[2] The edict of expulsion bears the date of March 30.

taking the route to the islands of Canaria, belonging to your Highnesses, which are in the said Ocean Sea, that I might thence take my departure for navigating until I should arrive at the Indies, and give the letters of your Highnesses to those princes, so as to comply with my orders. As part of my duty I thought it well to write an account of all the voyage very punctually, noting from day to day all that I should do and see, and that should happen, as will be seen further on. Also, Lords Princes, I resolved to describe each night what passed in the day, and to note each day how I navigated at night. I propose to construct a new chart for navigating, on which I shall delineate all the sea and lands of the Ocean in their proper positions under their bearings; and further, I propose to prepare a book, and to put down all as it were in a picture, by latitude from the equator, and western longitude. Above all, I shall have accomplished much, for I shall forget sleep, and shall work at the business of navigation, that so the service may be performed; all which will entail great labor.

Friday, 3d of August

We departed on Friday, the 3d of August, in the year 1492, from the bar of Saltes, at 8 o'clock, and proceeded with a strong sea breeze until sunset, towards the south, for 60 miles, equal to 15 leagues;[1] afterwards S.W. and W.S.W., which was the course for the Canaries.

Saturday, 4th of August

They steered S.W. ¼ S.

Sunday, 5th of August

They continued their course day and night more than 40 leagues.

[1] Columbus reckoned in Italian miles, four of which make a league. (Navarrete.)

Monday, 6th of August

The rudder of the caravel *Pinta* became unshipped, and Martin Alonso Pinzon, who was in command, believed or suspected that it was by contrivance of Gomes Rascon and Cristóbal Quintero, to whom the caravel belonged, for they dreaded to go on that voyage. The Admiral says that, before they sailed, these men had been displaying a certain backwardness, so to speak. The Admiral was much disturbed at not being able to help the said caravel without danger, and he says that he was eased of some anxiety when he reflected that Martin Alonso Pinzon was a man of energy and ingenuity. They made, during the day and night, 29 leagues.

Tuesday, 7th of August

The rudder of the *Pinta* was shipped and secured, and they proceeded on a course for the island of Lanzarote, one of the Canaries. They made, during the day and night, 25 leagues.

Wednesday, 8th of August

Opinions respecting their position varied among the pilots of the three caravels; but that of the Admiral proved to be nearer the truth. He wished to go to Gran Canaria, to leave the caravel *Pinta*, because she was disabled by the faulty hanging of her rudder, and was making water. He intended to obtain another there if one could be found. They could not reach the place that day.

Thursday, 9th of August

The Admiral was not able to reach Gomera until the night of Sunday, while Martin Alonso remained on that coast of Gran Canaria by order of the Admiral, because his vessel could not be navigated. Afterwards the Admiral took her to Canaria, and they repaired the *Pinta* very thoroughly through the pains and labor of the Admiral, of Martin Alonso, and of the rest. Finally they came to Gomera. They saw a great fire issue from the mountain of the island of Tenerife, which is of great height. They rigged the *Pinta* with square sails, for she was lateen rigged; and the Admiral reached Gomera on Sunday, the 2nd of September, with the *Pinta* repaired.

The Admiral says that many honorable Spanish gentlemen who were at Gomera with Doña Ines Peraza, mother of Guillen Peraza (who was afterwards the first Count of Gomera), and who were natives of the island of Hierro, declared that every year they saw land to the west of the Canaries; and others, natives of Gomera, affirmed the same on oath. The Admiral here says that he remembers, when in Portugal in the year 1484, a man came to the King from the island of Madeira, to beg for a caravel to go to this land that was seen, who swore that it could be seen every year, and always in the same way.[1] He also says that he recollects the same thing being affirmed in the islands of the Azores; and all these lands were described as in the same direction, and as being like each other, and of the same size. Having taken in water, wood, and meat, and all else that the men had who were left at Gomera by the Admiral when he went to the island of Canaria to repair the caravel *Pinta*, he finally made sail from the said island of Gomera, with his three caravels, on Thursday, the 6th day of September.

Thursday, 6th of September

He departed on that day from the port of Gomera in the morning, and shaped a course to go on his voyage; having received tidings from a caravel that came from the island of Hierro that three Portuguese caravels were off that island with the object of taking him. (This must have been the result

---

[1] On June 30, 1484, King John II. of Portugal granted to Fernam Domimguez do Arco, "resident in the island of Madeyra, if he finds it, an island which he is now going in search of." *Alguns Documentos do Archivo Nacional da Torre do Tombo*, p. 56.

of the King's annoyance that Colon should have gone to Castile.) There was a calm all that day and night, and in the morning he found himself between Gomera and Tenerife.

Friday, 7th of September

The calm continued all Friday and Saturday, until the third hour of the night.

Saturday, 8th of September

At the third hour of Saturday night [1] it began to blow from the N.E., and the Admiral shaped a course to the west. He took in much sea over the bows, which retarded progress, and 9 leagues were made in that day and night.

Sunday, 9th of September

This day the Admiral made 19 leagues, and he arranged to reckon less than the number run, because if the voyage was of long duration, the people would not be so terrified and disheartened. In the night he made 120 miles, at the rate of 12 miles an hour, which are 30 leagues. The sailors steered badly, letting the ship fall off to N.E., and even more, respecting which the Admiral complained many times. [2]

Monday, 10th of September

In this day and night he made 60 leagues, at the rate of 10 miles an hour, which are 2½ leagues; but he only counted

---

[1] *Tres horas de noche* means three hours after sunset.

[2] "On this day [Sunday, Sept. 9] they lost sight of land; and many, fearful of not being able to return for a long time to see it, sighed and shed tears. But the admiral, after he had comforted all with big offers of much land and wealth to keep them in hope and to lessen their fear which they had of the long way, when that day the sailors reckoned the distance 18 leagues, said he had counted only 15, having decided to lessen the record so that the crew would not think they were as far from Spain as in fact they were." *Historie del Signor Don Fernando Colombo* (London ed., 1867), pp. 61–62.

48 leagues, that the people might not be alarmed if the voyage should be long.

Tuesday, 11th of September

That day they sailed on their course, which was west, and made 20 leagues and more.   They saw a large piece of the mast of a ship of 120 tons, but were unable to get it.   In the night they made nearly 20 leagues, but only counted 16, for the reason already given.

Wednesday, 12th of September

That day, steering their course, they made 33 leagues during the day and night, counting less.

Thursday, 13th of September

That day and night, steering their course, which was west, they made 33 leagues, counting 3 or 4 less.   The currents were against them.   On this day, at the commencement of the night, the needles turned a half point to north-west, and in the morning they turned somewhat more north-west.[1]

[1] Las Casas in his *Historia*, I. 267, says "on that day at nightfall the needles northwested that is to say the fleur de lis which marks the north was not pointing directly at it but verged somewhat to the left of north and in the morning northeasted that is to say the fleur de lis pointed to right of the north until sunset."

The *Historie* agrees with the text of the Journal that the needle declined more to the west, instead of shifting to an eastern declination.

The author of the *Historie* remarks: "This variation no one had ever observed up to this time," p. 62.   "Columbus had crossed the point of no variation, which was then near the meridian of Flores, in the Azores, and found the variation no longer easterly, but more than a point westerly. His explanation that the pole-star, by means of which the change was detected, was not itself stationary, is very plausible.   For the pole-star really does describe a circle round the pole of the earth, equal in diameter to about six times that of the sun; but this is not equal to the change observed in the direction of the needle."   (Markham.)

Friday, 14th of September

That day they navigated, on their westerly course, day and night, 20 leagues, counting a little less. Here those of the caravel *Niña* reported that they had seen a tern [1] and a boatswain bird,[2] and these birds never go more than 25 leagues from the land.[3]

Saturday, 15th of September

That day and night they made 27 leagues and rather more on their west course; and in the early part of the night there fell from heaven into the sea a marvellous flame of fire, at a distance of about 4 or 5 leagues from them.

Sunday, 16th of September

That day and night they steered their course west, making 39 leagues, but the Admiral only counted 36. There were some clouds and small rain. The Admiral says that on that day, and ever afterwards, they met with very temperate breezes, so that there was great pleasure in enjoying the mornings, nothing being wanted but the song of nightingales. He says that the weather was like April in Andalusia. Here they began to see many tufts of grass which were very green, and appeared to have been quite recently torn from the land. From this they judged that they were near some island, but

---

[1] *Garjao.* This word is not in the Spanish dictionaries that I have consulted. The translator has followed the French translators MM. Chalumeau de Verneuil and de la Roquette who accepted the opinion of the naturalist Cuvier that the *Garjao* was the *hirondelle de mer*, the *Sterna maxima* or royal tern.

[2] *Rabo de junco*, literally, reedtail, is the tropic bird or Phaethon. The name "boatswain-bird" is applied to some other kinds of birds, besides the tropic bird. *Cf.* Alfred Newton, *Dictionary of Birds* (London, 1896). Ferdinand Columbus says: *rabo di giunco*, "a bird so called because it has a long feather in its tail," p. 63.

[3] This remark is, of course, not true of the tropic bird or *rabo de junco*, as was abundantly proved on this voyage.

not the main land, according to the Admiral, "because," as he says, "I make the main land to be more distant."

Monday, 17th of September

They proceeded on their west course, and made over 50 leagues in the day and night, but the Admiral only counted 47. They were aided by the current. They saw much very fine grass and herbs from rocks, which came from the west. They, therefore, considered that they were near land. The pilots observed the north point, and found that the needles turned a full point to the west of north. So the mariners were alarmed and dejected, and did not give their reason. But the Admiral knew, and ordered that the north should be again observed at dawn. They then found that the needles were true. The cause was that the star makes the movement, and not the needles. At dawn, on that Monday, they saw much more weed appearing, like herbs from rivers, in which they found a live crab, which the Admiral kept. He says that these crabs are certain signs of land. The sea-water was found to be less salt than it had been since leaving the Canaries. The breezes were always soft. Every one was pleased, and the best sailers went ahead to sight the first land. They saw many tunny-fish, and the crew of the *Niña* killed one. The Admiral here says that these signs of land came from the west, "in which direction I trust in that high God in whose hands are all victories that very soon we shall sight land." In that morning he says that a white bird was seen which has not the habit of sleeping on the sea, called *rabo de junco* (boatswain-bird).[1]

Tuesday, 18th of September

This day and night they made over 55 leagues, the Admiral only counting 48. In all these days the sea was very smooth, like the river at Seville. This day Martin Alonso, with the *Pinta*, which was a fast sailer, did not wait, for he said to the

---

[1] See p. 96, note 2.

H

Admiral, from his caravel, that he had seen a great multitude
of birds flying westward, that he hoped to see land that night,
and that he therefore pressed onward. A great cloud appeared
in the north, which is a sign of the proximity of land.

Wednesday, 19th of September

The Admiral continued on his course, and during the day
and night he made but 25 leagues because it was calm. He
counted 22. This day, at 10 o'clock, a booby [1] came to the
ship, and in the afternoon another arrived, these birds not
generally going more than 20 leagues from the land. There
was also some drizzling rain without wind, which is a sure
sign of land. The Admiral did not wish to cause delay by
beating to windward to ascertain whether land was near, but
he considered it certain that there were islands both to the
north and south of his position, (as indeed there were, and he
was passing through the middle of them). For his desire was
to press onwards to the Indies, the weather being fine. For
on his return, God willing, he could see all. These are his
own words. Here the pilots found their positions. He of the
Niña made the Canaries 440 leagues distant, the *Pinta* 420.
The pilot of the Admiral's ship made the distance exactly 400
leagues.

Thursday, 20th of September

This day the course was W.b.N., and as her head was all
round the compass owing to the calm that prevailed,[2] the
ship made only 7 or 8 leagues. Two boobies came to the ship,

---

[1] *Alcatraz.* The rendering "booby" follows Cuvier's note to the
French translation. The "booby" is the "booby gannet." The Spanish
dictionaries give pelican as the meaning of *Alcatraz.* The gannets and the
pelicans were formerly classed together. The word *Alcatraz* was taken over
into English and corrupted to *Albatros.* Alfred Newton, *Dictionary of Birds*
(London, 1896), art. "Albatros."

[2] More exactly, "He sailed this day toward the West a quarter northwest
and half the division [*i.e.*, west by north and west by one eighth northwest]
because of the veering winds and calm that prevailed."

and afterwards another, a sign of the proximity of land. They saw much weed, although none was seen on the previous day. They caught a bird with the hand, which was like a tern. But it was a river-bird, not a sea-bird, the feet being like those of a gull. At dawn two or three land-birds came singing to the ship, and they disappeared before sunset. Afterwards a booby came from W.N.W., and flew to the S.W., which was a sign that it left land in the W.N.W.; for these birds sleep on shore, and go to sea in the mornings in search of food, not extending their flight more than 20 leagues from the land.

Friday, 21st of September

Most of the day it was calm, and later there was a little wind. During the day and night they did not make good more than 13 leagues. At dawn they saw so much weed that the sea appeared to be covered with it, and it came from the west. A booby was seen. The sea was very smooth, like a river, and the air the best in the world. They saw a whale, which is a sign that they were near land, because they always keep near the shore.

Saturday, 22nd of September

They shaped a course W.N.W. more or less, her head turning from one to the other point, and made 30 leagues. Scarcely any weed was seen. They saw some sandpipers and another bird. Here the Admiral says: "This contrary wind was very necessary for me, because my people were much excited at the thought that in these seas no wind ever blew in the direction of Spain." Part of the day there was no weed, and later it was very thick.

Sunday, 23rd of September

They shaped a course N.W., and at times more northerly; occasionally they were on their course, which was west, and they made about 22 leagues. They saw a dove and a booby, another river-bird, and some white birds.   There was a great deal of weed, and they found crabs in it.   The sea being smooth and calm, the crew began to murmur, saying that here there was no great sea, and that the wind would never blow so that they could return to Spain.   Afterwards the sea rose very much, without wind, which astonished them. The Admiral here says: " Thus the high sea was very necessary to me, such as had not appeared but in the time of the Jews when they went out of Egypt and murmured against Moses, who delivered them out of captivity." [1]

Monday, 24th of September

The Admiral went on his west course all day and night, making 14 leagues.   He counted 12.   A booby came to the ship, and many sandpipers. [2]

Tuesday, 25th of September

This day began with a calm, and afterwards there was wind.   They were on their west course until night.   The Admiral conversed with Martin Alonso Pinzon, captain of the other caravel *Pinta*, respecting a chart which he had sent to the caravel three days before, on which, as it would appear,

---

[1] The abridger of the original journal missed the point here and his epitome is unintelligible.   Las Casas says in his *Historia*, I. 275: "The Admiral says in this place that the adverseness of the winds and the high sea were very necessary to him since they freed the crew of their erroneous idea that there would be no favorable sea and winds for their return and thereby they received some relief of mind or were not in so great despair, yet even then some objected, saying that that wind would not last, up to the Sunday following, when they had nothing to answer when they saw the sea so high. By which means, Cristóbal Colon says here, God dealt with him and with them as he dealt with Moses and the Jews when he drew them from Egypt showing signs to favor and aid him and to their confusion."

[2] Las Casas, *Historia*, I. 275-276, here describes with detail the discontent of the sailors and their plots to put Columbus out of the way.   The passage is translated in Thacher, *Christopher Columbus*, I. 524.   The word rendered "sandpipers" is *pardelas*, petrels.   The French translation has *petrels tachetes*, *i.e.*, "pintado petrels," or cape pigeons.

the Admiral had certainis lands depicted in that sea.[1] Martin
Alonso said that the ships were in the position on which the
islands were placed, and the Admiral replied that so it appeared
to him: but it might be that they had not fallen in with them,
owing to the currents which had always set the ships to the
N.E., and that they had not made so much as the pilots reported. The Admiral then asked for the chart to be returned,
and it was sent back on a line.[2] The Admiral then began to

[1] More exactly, "On which it seems the Admiral had painted certain islands." The Spanish reads: "*donde segun parece tenia pintadas el
Almirante ciertas islas*," etc. The question is whether Columbus made the
map or had it made. The rendering of the note is supported by the
French translators and by Harrisse.

[2] Las Casas, I. 279, says: "This map is the one which Paul, the physician, the Florentine, sent, which I have in my possession with other articles
which belonged to the Admiral himself who discovered these Indies, and writings in his own hand which came into my possession. In it he depicted many
islands and the main land which were the beginning of India and in that
region the realms of the Grand Khan," etc. Las Casas does not tell us how
he knew that the Toscanelli map which he found in Columbus's papers was
the map that the Admiral used on the first voyage. That is the general
assumption of scholars, but there is no positive evidence of the fact. The
Toscanelli map is no longer extant, and all reconstructions of it are based on
the globe of Martin Behaim constructed in 1492. The reconstruction by
H. Wagner which may be seen in S. Ruge, *Columbus*, 2te aufl. (Berlin, 1902)
is now accepted as the most successful.

According to the reckoning of the distances in the Journal, Columbus
was now about 550 leagues or 2200 Italian miles west of the Canaries. The
Toscanelli map was divided off into spaces each containing 250 miles. Columbus was therefore nine spaces west of the Canaries. No reconstruction of
Toscanelli's map puts any islands at nine spaces from the Canaries except
so far as the reconstructors insert the island of Antilia on the basis of Behaim's
globe. The Antilia of Behaim according to Wagner was eight spaces west
of the Canaries. Again Ferdinand Columbus, in his *Historie* under date of
October 7 (p. 72), says the sailors "had been frequently told by him that he
did not look for land until they had gone 750 leagues west from the Canaries,
at which distance he had told them he would have found Española then
called Cipango." 750 leagues or 3000 Italian miles would be 12 spaces
on the Toscanelli map. But according to the Toscanelli letter Cipango
was 10 spaces west of Antilia, and therefore 18 spaces or 4500 miles west
of the Canaries. Columbus then seems to have expected to find Cipango
some 1500 miles to the east of where it was placed on the Toscanelli map.
These considerations justify a very strong doubt whether Columbus was
shaping his course and basing his expectations on the data of the Toscanelli letter and map, or whether the fact that Las Casas found what he

plot the position on it, with the pilot and mariners. At sunset Martin Alonso went up on the poop of his ship, and with much joy called to the Admiral, claiming the reward as he had sighted land. When the Admiral heard this positively declared, he says that he gave thanks to the Lord on his knees, while Martin Alonso said the *Gloria in excelsis* with his people. The Admiral's crew did the same. Those of the *Niña* all went up on the mast and into the rigging, and declared that it was land. It so seemed to the Admiral, and that it was distant 25 leagues. They all continued to declare it was land until night. The Admiral ordered the course to be altered from W. to S.W., in which direction the land had appeared. That day they made 4 leagues on a west course, and 17 S.W. during the night, in all 21; but the people were told that 13 was the distance made good: for it was always feigned to them that the distances were less, so that the voyage might not appear so long. Thus two reckonings were kept on this voyage, the shorter being feigned, and the longer being the true one. The sea was very smooth, so that many sailors bathed alongside. They saw many *dorados*[1] and other fish.

Wednesday, 26th of September

The Admiral continued on the west course until afternoon. Then he altered course to S.W., until he made out that what had been said to be land was only clouds. Day and night they made 31 leagues, counting 24 for the people. The sea was like a river, the air pleasant and very mild.

Thursday, 27th of September

The course west, and distance made good during day and night 24 leagues, 20 being counted for the people. Many *dorados* came. One was killed. A boatswain-bird came.

took to be the Toscanelli map in the Admiral's papers proves that it was that map which he had on his first voyage.

[1] *Dorado* is defined by Stevens as the dory or gilt head.

Friday, 28th of September

The course was west, and the distance, owing to calms, only 14 leagues in day and night, 13 leagues being counted. They met with little weed; but caught two *dorados*, and more in the other ships.

Saturday, 29th of September

The course was west, and they made 24 leagues, counting 21 for the people. Owing to calms, the distance made good during day and night was not much. They saw a bird called *rabiforcado* [1] (man-o'-war bird), which makes the boobies vomit what they have swallowed, and eats it, maintaining itself on nothing else. It is a sea-bird, but does not sleep on the sea, and does not go more than 20 leagues from the land. There are many of them at the Cape Verde Islands. Afterwards they saw two boobies. The air was very mild and agreeable, and the Admiral says that nothing was wanting but to hear the nightingale. The sea smooth as a river. Later, three boobies and a man-o'-war bird were seen three times. There was much weed.

Sunday, 30th of September

The western course was steered, and during the day and night, owing to calms, only 14 leagues were made, 11 being counted. Four boatswain-birds came to the ship, which is a great sign of land, for so many birds of this kind together is a sign that they are not straying or lost. They also twice saw four boobies. There was much weed. *Note* that the stars which are called *Las Guardias* (the Pointers [2]), when night

---

[1] *Rabiforcado*, Portuguese. The Spanish form is *rabihorcado*. It means "forked tail." The modern English equivalent is "frigate bird." It is "the Fregata aquila of most ornithologists, the Frégate of French and the Rabihorcado of Spanish mariners." Newton, *Dictionary of Birds*, art. "Frigate-Bird." Newton says that the name "man-of-war bird" has generally passed out of use in books.

[2] Rather, the Guards, the name given to the two brightest stars in the constellation of the Little Bear. The literal translation is: "the Guards,

comes on, are near the western point, and when dawn breaks they are near the N.E. point; so that, during the whole night, they do not appear to move more than three lines or 9 hours, and this on each night. The Admiral says this, and also that at nightfall the needles vary a point westerly, while at dawn they agree exactly with the star. From this it would appear that the north star has a movement like the other stars, while the needles always point correctly.

Monday, 1st of October

Course west, and 25 leagues made good, counted for the crew as 20 leagues. There was a heavy shower of rain. At dawn the Admiral's pilot made the distance from Hierro 578 leagues to the west. The reduced reckoning which the Admiral showed to the crew made it 584 leagues; but the truth which the Admiral observed and kept secret was 707.

Tuesday, 2nd of October

Course west, and during the day and night 39 leagues were made good, counted for the crew as 30. The sea always smooth. Many thanks be given to God, says the Admiral, that the weed is coming from east to west, contrary to its usual course. Many fish were seen, and one was killed. A white bird was also seen that appeared to be a gull.

Wednesday, 3rd of October

They navigated on the usual course, and made good 47 leagues, counted as 40. Sandpipers appeared, and much weed, some of it very old and some quite fresh and having fruit. They saw no birds. The Admiral, therefore, thought that they had left the islands behind them which were depicted

when night comes on, are near the arm on the side to the west, and when dawn breaks they are on the line under the arm to the northeast," etc. What Columbus meant I cannot explain. Neither Navarrete nor the French translators offer any suggestions.

on the charts.   The Admiral here says that he did not wish to keep the ships beating about during the last week, and in the last few days when there were so many signs of land, although he had information of certain islands in this region.   For he wished to avoid delay, his object being to reach the Indies. He says that to delay would not be wise.[1]

Thursday, 4th of October

Course west, and 63 leagues made good during the day and night, counted as 46.   More than forty sandpipers came to the ship in a flock, and two boobies, and a ship's boy hit one with a stone.   There also came a man-o'-war bird and a white bird like a gull.

Friday, 5th of October

The Admiral steered his course, going 11 miles an hour, and during the day and night they made good 57 leagues, as the wind increased somewhat during the night: 45 were counted. The sea was smooth and quiet.   "To God," he says, "be many thanks given, the air being pleasant and temperate, with no weed, many sandpipers, and flying-fish coming on the deck in numbers."

---

[1] Las Casas, I. 282, adds to the foregoing under date of October 3: "He says here that it would not have been good sense to beat about and in that way to be delayed in search of them [*i.e.*, the islands] since he had favorable weather and his chief intention was to go in search of the Indies by way of the west, and this was what he proposed to the King and Queen, and they had sent him for that purpose.   Because he would not turn back to beat up and down to find the islands which the pilots believed to be there, particularly Martin Alonzo by the chart which, as was said, Cristóbal Colon had sent to his caravel for him to see, and it was their opinion that he ought to turn, they began to stir up a mutiny, and the disagreement would have gone farther if God had not stretched out his arm as he was wont, showing immediately new signs of their being near land since now neither soft words nor entreaties nor prudent reasoning of Cristóbal Colon availed to quiet them and to persuade them to persevere."   Ferdinand Columbus says simply, "For this reason the crew began to be mutinous, persevering in their complaints and plots," p. 71.   See page 108, note 1.

Saturday, 6th of October

The Admiral continued his west course, and during day and night they made good 40 leagues, 33 being counted. This night Martin Alonso said that it would be well to steer south of west,[1] and it appeared to the Admiral that Martin Alonso did not say this with respect to the island of Cipango.[2] He saw that if an error was made the land would not be reached so quickly, and that consequently it would be better to go at once to the continent and afterwards to the islands.

Sunday, 7th of October

The west course was continued; for two hours they went at the rate of 12 miles an hour, and afterwards 8 miles an hour. They made good 23 leagues, counting 18 for the people. This day, at sunrise, the caravel *Niña*, which went ahead, being the best sailer, and pushed forward as much as possible to sight the land first, so as to enjoy the reward which the Sovereigns had promised to whoever should see it first, hoisted a flag at the mast-head and fired a gun, as a signal that she had sighted land, for such was the Admiral's order. He had also ordered that, at sunrise and sunset, all the ships should join him; because those two times are most proper for seeing the greatest distance, the haze clearing away. No land was seen during the afternoon, as reported by the caravel *Niña*, and they passed a great number of birds flying from N. to S.W. This gave rise to the belief that the birds were either going to sleep on land, or were flying from the winter which might be supposed to be near in the land whence they were coming. The Admiral was aware that most of the islands held by the Portuguese were discovered by the flight of birds. For this reason he

[1] *Á la cuarta del Oueste, á la parte del Sudueste,* at the quarter from the west toward the southwest, *i.e.,* west by south.

[2] Las Casas, in the *Historia de las Indias,* I. 283, writes, "That night Martin Alonso said that it would be well to sail west by south for the island of Cipango which the map that Cristóbal Colon showed him represented.' *Cf.* page 101, note 2.

resolved to give up the west course, and to shape a course
W.S.W. for the two following days.[1]   He began the new course
one hour before sunset.   They made good, during the night,
about 5 leagues, and 23 in the day, altogether 28 leagues.

Monday, 8th of October

The course was W.S.W., and 11½ or 12 leagues were made
good in the day and night; and at times it appears that they
went at the rate of 15 miles an hour during the night (if the
handwriting is not deceptive).[2]   The sea was like the river at
Seville.   "Thanks be to God," says the Admiral, "the air
is very soft like the April at Seville; and it is a pleasure to be
here, so balmy are the breezes."   The weed seemed to be very
fresh.   There were many land-birds, and they took one that
was flying to the S.W.   Terns,[3] ducks, and a booby were also
seen.

Tuesday, 9th of October

The course was S.W., and they made 5 leagues.   The
wind then changed, and the Admiral steered W. by N. 4 leagues.
Altogether, in day and night, they made 11 leagues by day
and 20½ leagues by night; counted as 17 leagues altogether.
Throughout the night birds were heard passing.

Wednesday, 10th of October

The course was W.S.W., and they went at the rate of 10
miles an hour, occasionally 12 miles, and sometimes 7.   During

[1] Las Casas remarks, I. 285, "If he had kept up the direct westerly course
and the impatience of the Castilians had not hindered him, there is no doubt
that he would have struck the main land of Florida and from there to New
Spain, although the difficulties would have been unparalleled and the losses
unbearable that they would have met with, and it would have been a divine
miracle if he had ever returned to Castile."

[2] A remark by the abridger who noted the inconsistency between a total
of 48 miles for a day and night and even an occasional 15 miles per hour.

[3] Grajaos.   The translator assumed this to be the same as garjao; the
French translators, on the other hand, took it to be the same as grajos,
crows.   In Portuguese dictionaries the word grajão is found as the name of
"an Indian bird."

the day and night they made 59 leagues, counted as no more than 44. Here the people could endure no longer. They complained of the length of the voyage. But the Admiral cheered them up in the best way he could, giving them good hopes of the advantages they might gain from it. He added that, however much they might complain, he had to go to the Indies, and that he would go on until he found them, with the help of our Lord.[1]

Thursday, 11th of October

The course was W.S.W., and there was more sea than there had been during the whole of the voyage. They saw sandpipers, and a green reed near the ship. Those of the caravel *Pinta* saw a cane and a pole, and they took up another small pole which appeared to have been worked with iron; also another bit of cane, a land-plant, and a small board. The crew of the caravel *Niña* also saw signs of land, and a small branch covered with berries.[2] Every one breathed afresh and rejoiced at these signs. The run until sunset was 27 leagues.

After sunset the Admiral returned to his original west course, and they went along at the rate of 12 miles an hour. Up to two hours after midnight they had gone 90 miles, equal to 22½ leagues. As the caravel *Pinta* was a better sailer, and went ahead of the Admiral, she found the land, and made the

---

[1] The trouble with the captains and the sailors is told in greatest detail by Oviedo, *Historia de las Indias*, lib. ii., cap. v. He is the source of the story that the captains finally declared they would go on three days longer and not another hour. Oviedo does not say that Columbus acquiesced in this arrangement. Modern critics have been disposed to reject Oviedo's account, but strictly interpreted, it is not inconsistent with our other sources. Columbus recalls in his Journal, February 14, 1493, the terror of the situation which was evidently more serious than the entry of October 10 would imply. Peter Martyr too says that the sailors plotted to throw Columbus overboard and adds: "After the thirtieth day roused by madness they declared they were going back," but that Columbus pacified them. *De Rebus Oceanicis*, Dec. lib. i., fol. 2, ed. of 1574. Oviedo says that he derived information from Vicente Yañez Pinzon, "since with him I had a friendship up to the year 1514 when he died." *Historia de las Indias*, ii., cap. xiii.

[2] *Escaramojos*. Wild roses.

signals ordered by the Admiral.   The land was first seen by a
sailor named Rodrigo de Triana.[1]   But the Admiral, at ten
o'clock, being on the castle of the poop,[2] saw a light, though
it was so uncertain that he could not affirm it was land.   He
called Pero Gutierrez, a gentleman of the King's bed-chamber,
and said that there seemed to be a light, and that he should
look at it.   He did so, and saw it.[3]   The Admiral said the same
to Rodrigo Sanchez of Segovia, whom the King and Queen
had sent with the fleet as inspector, but he could see nothing,
because he was not in a place whence anything could be seen.
After the Admiral had spoken he saw the light once or twice,
and it was like a wax candle rising and falling.   It seemed to
few to be an indication of land; but the Admiral made certain
that land was close.   When they said the *Salve*, which all the
sailors were accustomed to sing in their way, the Admiral
asked and admonished the men to keep a good look-out on the
forecastle, and to watch well for land; and to him who should
first cry out that he saw land, he would give a silk doublet,
besides the other rewards promised by the Sovereigns, which
were 10,000 maravedis to him who should first see it.[4]   At
two hours after midnight the land was sighted at a distance of

---

[1] It was full moon on October 5.   On the night of the 11th the moon rose
at 11 P.M. and at 2 A.M. on the morning of the 12th it was 39° above the
horizon.   It would be shining brightly on the sandy shores of an island some
miles ahead, being in its third quarter, and a little behind Rodrigo de Triana,
when he sighted land at 2 A.M.   (Markham.)

[2] The high decks fore and aft were called castles.   The name survives in
the English forecastle.   Stevens gives poop alone as the English for *Castilla
de popa*.

[3] Oviedo, lib. II., cap. V., says that, as they were sailing along, a sailor, a
native of Lepe, cried out, "Light," "Land," but was immediately told that
the admiral had already seen it and remarked upon it.

[4] Columbus received this award.   His claiming or accepting it under the
circumstances has been considered discreditable and a breach of faith by
many modern writers.   Oviedo says the native of Lepe was so indignant at
not getting the reward that " he went over into Africa and denied the faith,"
i.e., became a Mohammedan.   Las Casas seems to have seen no impropriety
in Columbus' accepting the award.   He tells us, I. 289, that this annuity
was paid to Columbus throughout his life and was levied from the butcher
shops of Seville.   A maravedi was equal to two-thirds of a cent.

two leagues.   They shortened sail, and lay by under the mainsail without the bonnets.

[*Friday, 12th of October*]

The vessels were hove to, waiting for daylight; and on
Friday they arrived at a small island of the Lucayos, called,
in the language of the Indians, Guanahani.[1]   Presently they
saw naked people.   The Admiral went on shore in the armed
boat, and Martin Alonso Pinzon, and Vicente Yañez, his
brother, who was captain of the *Niña*.   The Admiral took the
royal standard, and the captains went with two banners of the
green cross, which the Admiral took in all the ships as a sign,
with an F and a Y [2] and a crown over each letter, one on one
side of the cross and the other on the other.   Having landed,
they saw trees very green, and much water, and fruits of diverse
kinds.   The Admiral called to the two captains, and to the
others who leaped on shore, and to Rodrigo Escovedo, secretary of the whole fleet, and to Rodrigo Sanchez of Segovia,[3] and
said that they should bear faithful testimony that he, in
presence of all, had taken, as he now took, possession of the
said island [4] for the King and for the Queen his Lords, making
the declarations that are required, as is now largely set forth
in the testimonies which were then made in writing.

Presently many inhabitants of the island assembled.
What follows is in the actual words of the Admiral in his book
of the first navigation and discovery of the Indies.[5]   "I," he
says, "that we might form great friendship, for I knew that
they were a people who could be more easily freed and converted to our holy faith by love than by force, gave to some

---

[1] Pronounced originally, according to Las Casas, I. 291, with the accent
on the last syllable.   Guanahani is now generally accepted to have been
Watling Island.   See Markham, *Christopher Columbus*, pp. 89–107, for a
lucid discussion of the landfall.

[2] Fernando and Ysabel.

[3] The royal inspector.

[4] Las Casas adds, I. 293, "To which he gave the name Sant Salvador."

[5] We have here perhaps the original title of what in its abridged form
we now call the Journal.

of them red caps, and glass beads to put round their necks, and many other things of little value, which gave them great pleasure, and made them so much our friends that it was a marvel to see. They afterwards came to the ship's boats where we were, swimming and bringing us parrots, cotton threads in skeins, darts, and many other things; and we exchanged them for other things that we gave them, such as glass beads and small bells. In fine, they took all, and gave what they had with good will. It appeared to me to be a race of people very poor in everything. They go as naked as when their mothers bore them, and so do the women, although I did not see more than one young girl. All I saw were youths, none more than thirty years of age. They are very well made, with very handsome bodies, and very good countenances. Their hair is short and coarse, almost like the hairs of a horse's tail. They wear the hairs brought down to the eyebrows, except a few locks behind, which they wear long and never cut. They paint themselves black, and they are the color of the Canarians, neither black nor white. Some paint themselves white, others red, and others of what color they find. Some paint their faces, others the whole body, some only round the eyes, others only on the nose. They neither carry nor know anything of arms, for I showed them swords, and they took them by the blade and cut themselves through ignorance. They have no iron, their darts being wands without iron, some of them having a fish's tooth at the end, and others being pointed in various ways. They are all of fair stature and size, with good faces, and well made. I saw some with marks of wounds on their bodies, and I made signs to ask what it was, and they gave me to understand that people from other adjacent islands came with the intention of seizing them, and that they defended themselves. I believed, and still believe, that they come here from the mainland to take them prisoners. They should be good servants and intelligent, for I observed that they quickly took in what was said to them, and I believe that they would easily be made Christians, as it appeared to me that they had no religion.

I, our Lord being pleased, will take hence, at the time of my departure, six natives for your Highnesses, that they may learn to speak. I saw no beast of any kind except parrots, on this island." The above is in the words of the Admiral.

Saturday, 13th of October

"As soon as dawn broke many of these people came to the beach, all youths, as I have said, and all of good stature, a very handsome people. Their hair is not curly, but loose and coarse, like horse hair. In all the forehead is broad, more so than in any other people I have hitherto seen. Their eyes are very beautiful and not small, and themselves far from black, but the color of the Canarians. Nor should anything else be expected, as this island is in a line east and west from the island of Hierro in the Canaries. Their legs are very straight, all in one line, and no belly, but very well formed. They came to the ship in small canoes, made out of the trunk of a tree like a long boat, and all of one piece, and wonderfully worked, considering the country. They are large, some of them holding 40 to 45 men, others smaller, and some only large enough to hold one man. They are propelled with a paddle like a baker's shovel, and go at a marvellous rate. If the canoe capsizes, they all promptly begin to swim, and to bale it out with calabashes that they take with them. They brought skeins of cotton thread, parrots, darts, and other small things which it would be tedious to recount, and they give all in exchange for anything that may be given to them. I was attentive, and took trouble to ascertain if there was gold. I saw that some of them had a small piece fastened in a hole they have in the nose, and by signs I was able to make out that to the south, or going from the island to the south, there was a king who had great cups full, and who possessed a great quantity. I tried to get them to go there, but afterwards I saw that they had no inclination. I resolved to wait until to-morrow in the afternoon and then to depart, shaping a course to the S.W., for, according to what many of them told me, there was land to the S., to the S.W., and N.W., and that the natives from the N.W. often came to attack them, and went on to the S.W. in search of gold and precious stones.

"This island is rather large and very flat, with bright green trees, much water, and a very large lake in the centre, without any mountain, and the whole land so green that it is a pleasure to look on it. The people are very docile, and for the longing to possess our things, and not having anything to give in return, they take what they can get, and presently swim away. Still, they give away all they have got, for whatever may be given to them, down to broken bits of crockery and glass. I saw one give 16 skeins of cotton for three *ceotis* [1] of Portugal, equal to one *blanca* of Spain, the skeins being as much as an *arroba* of cotton thread. I shall keep it, and shall allow no one to take it, preserving it all for your Highnesses, for it may be obtained in abundance. It is grown in this island, though the short time did not admit of my ascertaining this for a certainty. Here also is found the gold they wear fastened in their noses. But, in order not to lose time, I intend to go and see if I can find the island of Cipango. [2] Now, as it is night, all the natives have gone on shore with their canoes."

Sunday, 14th of October

"At dawn I ordered the ship's boat and the boats of the caravels to be got ready, and I went along the coast of the island to the N.N.E., to see the other side, which was on the other side to the east, and also to see the villages. Presently I saw two or three, and the people all came to the shore, calling out and giving thanks to God. Some of them brought us water, others came with food, and when they saw that I did not want to land, they got into the sea, and came swimming to us. We understood that they asked us if we had come from heaven. One old man came into the boat, and others cried

[1] The Portuguese *ceitil* (pl. *ceitis*) was a small coin deriving its name from Ceuta, opposite Gibraltar, in Africa, a Portuguese possession. The *blanca* was one-half a maravedi, or about one-third of a cent.

[2] Cipango. Marco Polo's name for Japan.

I

out, in loud voices, to all the men and women, to come and see the men who had come from heaven, and to bring them to eat and drink. Many came, including women, each bringing something, giving thanks to God, throwing themselves on the ground and shouting to us to come on shore. But I was afraid to land, seeing an extensive reef of rocks which sur-- rounded the island, with deep water between it and the shore forming a port large enough for as many ships as there are in Christendom, but with a very narrow entrance. It is true that within this reef there are some sunken rocks, but the sea has no more motion than the water in a well. In order to see all this I went this morning, that I might be able to give a full account to your Highnesses, and also where a fortress might be established. I saw a piece of land which appeared like an island, although it is not one, and on it there were six houses. It might be converted into an island in two days, though I do not see that it would be necessary, for these people are very simple as regards the use of arms, as your Highnesses will see from the seven that I caused to be taken, to bring home and learn our language and return; unless your Highnesses should order them all to be brought to Castile, or to be kept as captives on the same island; for with fifty men they can all be subjugated and made to do what is required of them. Close to the above peninsula there are gardens of the most beautiful trees I ever saw, and with leaves as green as those of Castile in the month of April and May, and much water. I examined all that port, and afterwards I returned to the ship and made sail. I saw so many islands that I hardly knew how to determine to which I should go first. Those natives I had with me said, by signs, that there were so many that they could not be numbered, and they gave the names of more than a hundred. At last I looked out for the largest, and resolved to shape a course for it, and so I did. It will be dis- tant five leagues from this of *San Salvador*, and the others some more, some less. All are very flat, and all are inhabited. The natives make war on each other, although these are very simple-minded and handsomely-formed people."

Monday, 15th of October

"I had laid by during the night, with the fear of reaching the land to anchor before daylight,[1] not knowing whether the coast was clear of rocks, and at dawn I made sail. As the island was more than 5 leagues distant and nearer 7, and the tide checked my way, it was noon when we arrived at the said island. I found that side facing towards the island of San Salvador trended north and south with a length of 5 leagues, and the other which I followed ran east and west for more than 10 leagues.[2] As from this island I saw another larger one to the west, I clued up [3] the sails, after having run all that day until night, otherwise I could not have reached the western cape. I gave the name of Santa Maria de la Concepcion [4] to the island, and almost as the sun set I anchored near the said cape to ascertain if it contained gold. For the people I had taken from the island of San Salvador told me that here they wore very large rings of gold on their arms and legs. I really believed that all they said was nonsense, invented that they might escape. My desire was not to pass any island without taking possession, so that, one having been taken, the same may be said of all. I anchored, and remained until to-day, Tuesday, when I went to the shore with the boats armed, and landed. The people, who were numerous, went naked, and were like those of the other island of San Salvador. They let us go over the island, and gave us what we required. As the wind changed to the S.E., I did not like to stay, and returned to the ship. A large canoe was alongside the *Niña*, and one of the men of the island of San Salvador, who was on board, jumped into the sea and got into the canoe. In the middle of the night before, another swam away behind the canoe,

---

[1] Rather, "I had lain to during the night for fear of reaching the land," etc.

[2] These lengths are exaggerated.

[3] The word is *cargué* and means "raised" or "hoisted." The same word seven lines above was translated "made sail." Las Casas in the corresponding passage in his *Historia* uses *alzar*.

[4] Identified as Rum Cay.

which fled, for there never was boat that could have overtaken her, seeing that in speed they have a great advantage.[1]   So they reached the land and left the canoe.   Some of my people went on shore in chase of them, but they all fled like fowls, and the canoe they had left was brought alongside the caravel *Niña*, whither, from another direction, another small canoe came, with a man who wished to barter with skeins of cotton. Some sailors jumped into the sea, because he would not come on board the caravel, and seized him.   I was on the poop of my ship, and saw everything.   So I sent for the man, gave him a red cap, some small beads of green glass, which I put on his arms, and small bells, which I put in his ears, and ordered his canoe, which was also on board, to be returned to him. I sent him on shore, and presently made sail to go to the other large island which was in sight to the westward.   I also ordered the other large canoe, which the caravel *Niña* was towing astern, to be cast adrift; and I soon saw that it reached the land at the same time as the man to whom I had given the above things.   I had not wished to take the skein of cotton that he offered me.   All the others came round him and seemed astonished, for it appeared clear to them that we were good people.   The other man who had fled might do us some harm, because we had carried him off, and for that reason I ordered this man to be set free and gave him the above things, that he might think well of us, otherwise, when your Highnesses again send an expedition, they might not be friendly.   All the presents I gave were not worth four maravedis.   At 10 we departed with the wind S.W., and made for the south, to reach that other island, which is very large, and respecting which all the men that I bring from San Salvador make signs that there is much gold, and that they wear it as bracelets on the arms, on the legs, in the ears and nose, and round the neck.

---

[1] A line is missing in the original.   The text may be restored as follows, beginning with the end of the preceding sentence, "jumped into the sea and got into the canoe; in the middle of the night before the other threw [himself into the sea and swam off.   The boat was lowered] and put after the canoe which escaped since there never was a boat which could have overtaken him, since we were far behind him."

The distance of this island from that of Santa Maria is 9 leagues on a course east to west. All this part of the island trends N.W. and S.E., and it appeared that this coast must have a length of 28 leagues. It is very flat, without any mountain, like San Salvador and Santa Maria, all being beach without rocks, except that there are some sunken rocks near the land, whence it is necessary to keep a good lookout when it is desired to anchor, and not to come to very near the land; but the water is always very clear, and the bottom is visible. At a distance of two shots of a lombard, there is, off all these islands, such a depth that the bottom cannot be reached. These islands are very green and fertile, the climate very mild. They may contain many things of which I have no knowledge, for I do not wish to stop, in discovering and visiting many islands, to find gold. These people make signs that it is worn on the arms and legs; and it must be gold, for they point to some pieces that I have. I cannot err, with the help of our Lord, in finding out where this gold has its origin. Being in the middle of the channel between these two islands, that is to say, that of Santa Maria and this large one, to which I give the name of Fernandina,[1] I came upon a man alone in a canoe going from Santa Maria to Fernandina. He had a little of their bread, about the size of a fist, a calabash of water, a piece of brown earth powdered and then kneaded, and some dried leaves, which must be a thing highly valued by them,[2] for they bartered with it at San Salvador. He also had with him a native basket with a string of glass beads, and two *blancas*, by which I knew that he had come from the island of San Salvador, and had been to Santa Maria, and thence to Fernandina. He came alongside the ship, and I made him come on board as he desired, also getting the canoe inboard, and taking care of all his property. I ordered him to be given to eat bread and treacle, and also to drink: and so I shall take him on to Fernandina, where I shall return everything to him, in order that he may give a good account of us, that, our

[1] Long Island. (Markham.)
[2] Possibly a reference to tobacco.

Lord pleasing, when your Highnesses shall send here, those who come may receive honor, and that the natives may give them all they require."

Tuesday, 16th of October

"I sailed from the island of Santa Maria de la Concepcion at about noon, to go to Fernandina Island, which appeared very large to the westward, and I navigated all that day with light winds. I could not arrive in time to be able to see the bottom, so as to drop the anchor on a clear place, for it is necessary to be very careful not to lose the anchors. So I stood off and on all that night until day, when I came to an inhabited place where I anchored, and whence that man had come that I found yesterday in the canoe in mid channel. He had given such a good report of us that there was no want of canoes alongside the ship all that night, which brought us water and what they had to offer. I ordered each one to be given something, such as a few beads, ten or twelve of those made of glass on a thread, some timbrels made of brass such as are worth a maravedi in Spain, and some straps, all which they looked upon as most excellent. I also ordered them to be given treacle to eat when they came on board. At three o'clock [1] I sent the ship's boat on shore for water, and the natives with good will showed my people where the water was, and they themselves brought the full casks down to the boat, and did all they could to please us.

"This island is very large, and I have determined to sail round it, because, so far as I can understand, there is a mine in or near it. The island is eight leagues from Santa Maria, nearly east and west; and this point I had reached, as well as all the coast, trends N.N.W. and S.S.E. I saw at least 20 leagues of it, and then it had not ended. Now, as I am writing this, I made sail with the wind at the south, to sail round the island,

---

[1] It should be "about nine o'clock." The original is *á horas de tercia*, which means "at the hour of tierce," *i.e.*, the period between nine and twelve.

and to navigate until I find Samaot, which is the island or city where there is gold, as all the natives say who are on board, and as those of San Salvador and Santa Maria told us. These people resemble those of the said islands, with the same language and customs, except that these appear to me a rather more domestic and tractable people, yet also more subtle. For I observed that those who brought cotton and other trifles to the ship, knew better than the others how to make a bargain. In this island I saw cotton cloths made like mantles. The people were better disposed, and the women wore in front of their bodies a small piece of cotton which scarcely covered them.

"It is a very green island, level and very fertile, and I have no doubt that they sow and gather corn [1] all the year round, as well as other things. I saw many trees very unlike those of our country. Many of them have their branches growing in different ways and all from one trunk, and one twig is one form, and another in a different shape, and so unlike that it is the greatest wonder in the world to see the great diversity; thus one branch has leaves like those of a cane, and others like those of a mastick tree: and on a single tree there are five or six different kinds. Nor are these grafted, for it may be said that grafting is unknown, the trees being wild, and untended by these people. They do not know any religion, and I believe they could easily be converted to Christianity, for they are very intelligent. Here the fish are so unlike ours that it is wonderful. Some are the shape of dories, and of the finest colors in the world, blue, yellow, red, and other tints, all painted in various ways, and the colors are so bright that there is not a man who would not be astonished, and would not take great delight in seeing them. There are also whales. I saw no beasts on the land of any kind, except parrots and lizards. A boy told me that he saw a large serpent. I saw

---

[1] *Panizo*, literally "panic grass." Here Columbus seems to use the word as descriptive of maize or Indian corn, and later the word came to have this meaning. On the different species of panic grass, see Candolle, *Origin of Cultivated Plants* (index under *panicum*).

neither sheep, nor goats, nor any other quadruped. It is true I have been here a short time, since noon,[1] yet I could not have failed to see some if there had been any. I will write respecting the circuit of this island after I have been round it."

Wednesday, 17th of October

"At noon I departed from the village off which I was anchored, and where I took in water, to sail round this island of Fernandina. The wind was S.W. and South. My wish was to follow the coast of this island to the S.E., from where I was, the whole coast trending N.N.W. and S.S.E.; because all the Indians I bring with me, and others, made signs to this southern quarter, as the direction of the island they call Samoet, where the gold is. Martin Alonso Pinzon, captain of the caravel *Pinta*, on board of which I had three of the Indians, came to me and said that one of them had given him to understand very positively that the island might be sailed round much quicker by shaping a N.N.W. course. I saw that the wind would not help me to take the course I desired, and that it was fair for the other, so I made sail to the N.N.W. When I was two leagues from the cape of the island, I discovered a very wonderful harbor.[2] It has one mouth, or, rather, it may be said to have two, for there is an islet in the middle. Both are very narrow, and within it is wide enough for a hundred ships, if there was depth and a clean bottom, and the entrance was deep enough. It seemed desirable to explore it and take soundings, so I anchored outside, and went in with all the ship's boats, when we saw there was insufficient depth. As I thought, when I first saw it, that it was the mouth of some river, I ordered the water-casks to be brought. On shore I found eight or ten men, who presently came to us and showed us the village, whither I sent the people for water, some with arms, and others with the casks; and, as it was some little distance, I waited two hours for them.

---

[1] Rather, "since it is noon."
[2] Port Clarence in Long Island.   (Markham.)

"During that time I walked among the trees, which was the most beautiful thing I had ever seen, beholding as much verdure as in the month of May in Andalusia. The trees are as unlike ours as night from day, as are the fruits, the herbs, the stones, and everything. It is true that some of the trees bore some resemblance to those in Castile, but most of them are very different, and some were so unlike that no one could compare them to anything in Castile. The people were all like those already mentioned: like them naked, and the same size. They give what they possess in exchange for anything that may be given to them. I here saw some of the ship's boys bartering broken bits of glass and crockery for darts. The men who went for water told me that they had been in the houses of the natives, and that they were very plain and clean inside. Their beds and bags for holding things[1] were like nets of cotton.[2] The houses are like booths, and very high, with good chimneys.[3] But, among many villages that I saw, there was none that consisted of more than from twelve to fifteen houses. Here they found that the married women wore clouts of cotton, but not the young girls, except a few who were over eighteen years of age. They had dogs, mastiffs, and hounds;[4] and here they found a man who had a piece of gold in his nose, the size of half a *castellano*,[5] on which they saw letters. I quarrelled with these people because they would not exchange or give what was required; as I wished to see

---

[1] Rather, "beds and hangings." The original is *paramentos de cosas*, but in the corresponding passage in his *Historia*, I. 310, Las Casas has *paramentos de casa*, which is almost certainly the correct reading.

[2] "These are called Hamacas in Española." Las Casas, I. 310, where will be found an elaborate description of them.

[3] For ornament. Las Casas calls them caps or crowns, I. 311.

[4] Rather: "mastiffs and beagles." Las Casas, I. 311, says the Admiral called these dogs mastiffs from the report of the sailors. "If he had seen them, he would not have called them so but that they resembled hounds. These and the small ones never bark but merely a grunt in the throat."

[5] The *castellano* was one-sixth of an ounce. Las Casas, I. 311, remarks: "They were deceived in believing the marks to be letters since those people are wont to work it in their fashion, since never anywhere in all the Indies was there found any trace of money of gold or silver or other metal."

what and whose this money was; and they replied that they were not accustomed to barter.

"After the water was taken I returned to the ship, made sail, and shaped a course N.W., until I had discovered all the part of the coast of the island which trends east to west. Then all the Indians turned round and said that this island was smaller than Samoet, and that it would be well to return back so as to reach it sooner. The wind presently went down, and then sprang up from W.N.W., which was contrary for us to continue on the previous course. So I turned back, and navigated all that night to E.S.E., sometimes to east and to S.E. This course was steered to keep me clear of the land, for there were very heavy clouds and thick weather, which did not admit of my approaching the land to anchor. On that night it rained very heavily from midnight until nearly dawn, and even afterwards the clouds threatened rain. We found ourselves at the S.W. end of the island, where I hoped to anchor until it cleared up, so as to see the other island whither I have to go. On all these days, since I arrived in these Indies, it has rained more or less. Your Highnesses may believe that this land is the best and most fertile, and with a good climate, level, and as good as there is in the world."

Thursday, 18th of October

"After it had cleared up I went before the wind, approaching the island as near as I could, and anchored when it was no longer light enough to keep under sail. But I did not go on shore, and made sail at dawn. . . ."

Friday, 19th of October

"I weighed the anchors at daylight, sending the caravel *Pinta* on an E.S.E. course, the caravel *Niña* S.S.E., while I shaped a S.E. course, giving orders that these courses were to be steered until noon, and that then the two caravels should alter course so as to join company with me. Before we had sailed for three hours we saw an island to the east, for which we steered, and all three vessels arrived at the north point before noon. Here there is an islet, and a reef of rocks to seaward of it, besides one between the islet and the large island. The men of San Salvador, whom I bring with me, called it Saomete, and I gave it the name of Isabella.[1] The wind was north, and the said islet bore from the island of Fernandina, whence I had taken my departure, east and west. Afterwards we ran along the coast of the island, westward from the islet, and found its length to be 12 leagues as far as a cape, which I named Cabo Hermoso, at the western end. The island is beautiful, and the coast very deep, without sunken rocks off it. Outside the shore is rocky, but further in there is a sandy beach, and here I anchored on that Friday night until morning. This coast and the part of the island I saw is almost flat, and the island is very beautiful; for if the other islands are lovely, this is more so. It has many very green trees, which are very large. The land is higher than in the other islands, and in it there are some hills, which cannot be called mountains; and it appears that there is much water inland. From this point to the N.E. the coast makes a great angle, and there are many thick and extensive groves. I wanted to go and anchor there, so as to go on shore and see so much beauty; but the water was shallow, and we could only anchor at a distance from the land. The wind also was fair for going to this cape, where I am now anchored, to which I gave the name of Cabo Hermoso,[2] because it is so. Thus it was that I do not anchor in that angle, but as I saw this cape so green and so beautiful, like all the other lands of these islands, I scarcely knew which to visit first; for I can never tire my eyes in looking at such lovely vegetation, so different from ours. I believe that there are many herbs and many trees that are worth much in Europe for dyes and for medicines; but I do not know them, and this causes me great sorrow. Arriving at this cape, I found the smell of the trees and flowers so delicious that it seemed the pleasantest thing in the world.

[1] Crooked Island. (Markham.)   [2] Cape Beautiful.

To-morrow, before I leave this place, I shall go on shore to see what there is at this cape. There are no people, but there are villages in the interior, where, the Indians I bring with me say, there is a king who has much gold. To-morrow I intend to go so far inland as to find the village, and see and have some speech with this king, who, according to the signs they make, rules over all the neighboring islands, goes about clothed, and wears much gold on his person. I do not give much faith to what they say, as well because I do not understand them well as because they are so poor in gold that even a little that this king may have would appear much to them. This cape, to which I have given the name of Cabo Fermoso, is, I believe, on an island separated from Saometo, and there is another small islet between them. I did not try to examine them in detail, because it could not be done in 50 years. For my desire is to see and discover as much as I can before returning to your Highnesses, our Lord willing, in April. It is true that in the event of finding places where there is gold or spices in quantity I should stop until I had collected as much as I could. I, therefore, proceed in the hope of coming across such places."

Saturday, 20th of October

"To-day, at sunrise, I weighed the anchors from where I was with the ship, and anchored off the S.W. point of the island of Saometo, to which I gave the name of Cabo de la Laguna, and to the island Isabella. My intention was to navigate to the north-east and east from the south-east and south, where, I understood from the Indians I brought with me, was the village of the king. I found the sea so shallow that I could not enter nor navigate in it, and I saw that to follow a route by the south-east would be a great round. So I determined to return by the route that I had taken from the N.N.E. to the western part, and to sail round this island to [reconnoitre it].

"I had so little wind that I never could sail along the coast, except during the night. As it was dangerous to anchor off these islands except in the day, when one can see where to let go the anchor, for the bottom is all in patches, some clear and some rocky, I lay to all this Sunday night. The caravels anchored because they found themselves near the shore, and they thought that, owing to the signals that they were in the habit of making, I would come to anchor, but I did not wish to do so."

Sunday, 21st of October

"At ten o'clock I arrived here, off this islet, and anchored, as well as the caravels. After breakfast I went on shore, and found only one house, in which there was no one, and I supposed they had fled from fear, because all their property was left in the house. I would not allow anything to be touched, but set out with the captains and people to explore the island. If the others already seen are very beautiful, green, and fertile, this is much more so, with large trees and very green. Here there are large lagoons with wonderful vegetation on their banks. Throughout the island all is green, and the herbage like April in Andalusia. The songs of the birds were so pleasant that it seemed as if a man could never wish to leave the place. The flocks of parrots concealed the sun; and the birds were so numerous, and of so many different kinds, that it was wonderful. There are trees of a thousand sorts, and all have their several fruits; and I feel the most unhappy man in the world not to know them, for I am well assured that they are all valuable. I bring home specimens of them, and also of the land. Thus walking along round one of the lakes I saw a serpent, which we killed, and I bring home the skin for your Highnesses. As soon as it saw us it went into the lagoon, and we followed, as the water was not very deep, until we killed it with lances. It is 7 spans long, and I believe that there are many like it in these lagoons.[1] Here

---

[1] "The Indians of this island of Española call it *iguana*." Las Casas, I. 314. He gives a minute description of it.

I came upon some aloes, and I have determined to take ten quintals on board to-morrow, for they tell me that they are worth a good deal. Also, while in search of good water, we came to a village about half a league from our anchorage. The people, as soon as they heard us, all fled and left their houses, hiding their property in the wood. I would not allow a thing to be touched, even the value of a pin. Presently some men among them came to us, and one came quite close. I gave him some bells and glass beads, which made him very content and happy. That our friendship might be further increased, I resolved to ask him for something; I requested him to get some water. After I had gone on board, the natives came to the beach with calabashes full of water, and they delighted much in giving it to us. I ordered another string of glass beads to be presented to them, and they said they would come again to-morrow. I wished to fill up all the ships with water at this place, and, if there should be time, I intended to search the island until I had had speech with the king, and seen whether he had the gold of which I had heard. I shall then shape a course for another much larger island, which I believe to be Cipango, judging from the signs made by the Indians I bring with me. They call it Cuba, and they say that there are ships and many skilful sailors there. Beyond this island there is another called Bosio,[1] which they also say is very large, and others we shall see as we pass, lying between. According as I obtain tidings of gold or spices I shall settle what should be done. I am still resolved to go to the mainland and the city of Guisay,[2] and to deliver the letters of your Highnesses to the Gran Can, requesting a reply and returning with it."

[1] The names in the Spanish text are Colba and Bosio, errors in transcription for Cuba and Bohio. Las Casas, I. 315, says in regard to the latter: "To call it Bohio was to misunderstand the interpreters, since throughout all these islands, where the language is practically the same, they call the huts in which they live *bohio* and this great island Española they called Hayti, and they must have said that in Hayti there were great *bohios*."

[2] The name is spelled Quinsay in the Latin text of Marco Polo which Columbus annotated.

Monday, 22nd of October

"All last night and to-day I was here, waiting to see if the king or other person would bring gold or anything of value. Many of these people came, like those of the other islands, equally naked, and equally painted, some white, some red, some black, and others in many ways. They brought darts and skeins of cotton to barter, which they exchanged with the sailors for bits of glass, broken crockery, and pieces of earthenware. Some of them had pieces of gold fastened in their noses, which they willingly gave for a hawk's bell and glass beads. But there was so little that it counts for nothing. It is true that they looked upon any little thing that I gave them as a wonder, and they held our arrival to be a great marvel, believing that we came from heaven. We got water for the ships from a lagoon which is near the Cabo del Isleo (Cape of the Islet), as we named it. In the said lagoon Martin Alonso Pinzon, captain of the *Pinta*, killed another serpent 7 *spans* long, like the one we got yesterday. I made them gather here as much of the aloe as they could find."

Tuesday, 23rd of October

"I desired to set out to-day for the island of Cuba, which I think must be Cipango, according to the signs these people make, indicative of its size and riches, and I did not delay any more here nor [attempt to sail] . . .[1] round this island to the residence of this king or lord, and have speech with him, as I had intended. This would cause me much delay, and I see that there is no gold mine here. To sail round would need several winds, for it does not blow here as men may wish. It is better to go where there is great entertainment, so I say that it is not reasonable to wait, but rather to continue the voyage and inspect much land, until some very profitable country is reached, my belief being that it will be rich in spices. That I have no personal knowledge of these

---

[1] One or two words are missing in the original.

products causes me the greatest sorrow in the world, for I see a thousand kinds of trees, each one with its own special fruit, all green now as in Spain during the months of May and June, as well as a thousand kinds of herbs with their flowers; yet I know none of them except this aloe, of which I ordered a quantity to be brought on board to bring to your Highnesses. I have not made sail for Cuba because there is no wind, but a dead calm with much rain. It rained a great deal yesterday without causing any cold. On the contrary, the days are hot and the nights cool, like May in Andalusia."

Wednesday, 24th of October

"At midnight I weighed the anchors and left the anchorage at Cabo del Isleo, in the island of Isabella.[1]　From the northern side, where I was, I intended to go to the island of Cuba, where I heard of the people who were very great, and had gold, spices, merchandise, and large ships. They showed me that the course thither would be W.S.W., and so I hold. For I believe that it is so, as all the Indians of these islands, as well as those I brought with me in the ships, told me by signs. I cannot understand their language, but I believe that it is of the island of Cipango that they recount these wonders.[2]　On the spheres I saw, and on the delineations of the map of the world,[3] Cipango is in this region. So I shaped a course W.S.W. until daylight, but at dawn it fell calm and began to rain, and went on nearly all night. I remained thus, with little wind,

---

[1] The translation here should be, "raised the anchors at the island of Isabella at Cabo del Isleo, which is on the northern side where I tarried to go to the island of Cuba, which I heard from this people is very great and has gold," etc.

[2] These two lines should read, "I believe that it is the island of Cipango of which marvellous things are related."

[3] The exact translation is, "On the spheres that I saw and on the paintings of world-maps it is this region." The plural number is used in both cases. Of the globes of this date, i.e., 1492 or earlier, that of Behaim is the only one that has come down to us. Of the world maps Toscanelli's, no longer extant, may have been one, but it is to be noted that Columbus uses the plural.

until the afternoon, when it began to blow fresh.   I set all the sails in the ship, the mainsail with two bonnets, the foresail, spritsail, mizzen, main topsail, and the boat's sail on the poop. So I proceeded until nightfall, when the Cabo Verde of the island of Fernandina, which is at the S.W. end, bore N.W. distant 7 leagues.   As it was now blowing hard, and I did not know how far it was to this island of Cuba, I resolved not to go in search of it during the night; all these islands being very steep-to, with no bottom round them for a distance of two shots of a lombard.   The bottom is all in patches, one bit of sand and another of rock, and for this reason it is not safe to anchor without inspection with the eye.   So I determined to take in all the sails except the foresail, and to go on under that reduced canvas.   Soon the wind increased, while the route was doubtful, and there was very thick weather, with rain.   I ordered the foresail to be furled, and we did not make two leagues during that night."

Thursday, 25th of October

"I steered W.S.W. from after sunset until 9 o'clock, making 5 leagues.   Afterwards I altered course to west, and went 8 miles an hour until one in the afternoon; and from that time until three made good 44 miles.   Then land was sighted, consisting of 7 or 8 islands, the group running north and south, distant from us 5 leagues."

Friday, 26th of October

"The ship was on the south side of the islands, which were all low, distant 5 or 6 leagues.   I anchored there.   The Indians[1] on board said that thence to Cuba was a voyage in their canoes of a day and a half; these being small dug-outs without a sail.   Such are their canoes.   I departed thence for Cuba,

---

[1] Columbus's conviction that he has reached the Indies is registered by his use from now on of the word "Indians" for the people.

K

for by the signs the Indians made of its greatness, and of its gold and pearls, I thought that it must be Cipango."

Saturday, 27th of October

"I weighed from these islands at sunrise, and gave them the name of Las Islas de Arena, owing to the little depth the sea had for a distance of 6 leagues to the southward of them. We went 8 miles an hour on a S.S.W. course until one o'clock, having made 40 miles. Until night we had run 28 miles on the same course, and before dark the land was sighted. At night there was much rain. The vessels, on Saturday until sunset, made 17 leagues on a S.S.W. course."

Sunday, 28th of October

"I went thence in search of the island of Cuba on a S.S.W. course, making for the nearest point of it, and entered a very beautiful river without danger of sunken rocks or other impediments. All the coast was clear of dangers up to the shore. The mouth of the river was 12 *brazas* across, and it is wide enough for a vessel to beat in.[1] I anchored about a lombard-shot inside." The Admiral says that "he never beheld such a beautiful place, with trees bordering the river, handsome, green, and different from ours, having fruits and flowers each one according to its nature. There are many birds, which sing very sweetly. There are a great number of palm trees of a different kind from those in Guinea and from ours, of a middling height, the trunks without that covering, and the leaves very large, with which they thatch their houses. The country is very level." The Admiral jumped into his boat and went on shore. He came to two houses, which he believed to belong to fishermen who had fled from fear. In one of them he found a kind of dog that never barks, and in both there were nets of

---

[1] This should be, "The mouth of the river is 12 fathoms deep and it is wide enough," etc.

palm-fibre and cordage, as well as horn fish-hooks, bone har-
poons, and other apparatus "for fishing, and several hearths.
He believed that many people lived together in one house. He
gave orders that nothing in the houses should be touched, and
so it was done." The herbage was as thick as in Andalusia
during April and May. He found much purslane and wild
amaranth.[1] He returned to the boat and went up the river
for some distance, and he says it was great pleasure to see the
bright verdure, and the birds, which he could not leave to go
back. He says that this island is the most beautiful that eyes
have seen, full of good harbors and deep rivers, and the sea
appeared as if it never rose; for the herbage on the beach nearly
reached the waves, which does not happen where the sea is
rough. (Up to that time they had not experienced a rough
sea among all those islands.) He says that the island is full
of very beautiful mountains, although they are not very extensive as regards length, but high; and all the country is
high like Sicily. It is abundantly supplied with water, as
they gathered from the Indians they had taken with them from
the island of Guanahani. These said by signs that there are
ten great rivers, and that they cannot go round the island in
twenty days. When they came near land with the ships,
two canoes came out; and, when they saw the sailors get into
a boat and row about to find the depth of the river where
they could anchor, the canoes fled. The Indians say that in
this island there are gold mines and pearls, and the Admiral
saw a likely place for them and mussel-shells, which are signs
of them. He understood that large ships of the Gran Can
came here, and that from here to the mainland was a voyage
of ten days.[2] The Admiral called this river and harbor San
Salvador.[3]

[1] *Bledos.* The French translators give *cresson sauvage,* wild cress, as
the equivalent.
[2] Las Casas, I. 320, says Columbus understood "that from these to the
mainland would be a sail of ten days by reason of the notion he had derived
from the chart or picture which the Florentine sent him."
[3] Baracoa (Las Casas); Puerto Naranjo (Markham); Nipe (Navarrete);
Nuevitas (Thacher).

Monday, 29th of October

The Admiral weighed anchor from this port and sailed to the westward, to go to the city, where, as it seemed, the Indians said that there was a king. They doubled a point six leagues to the N.W.,[1] and then another point,[2] then east ten leagues. After another league he saw a river with no very large entrance, to which he gave the name of Rio de la Luna.[3] He went on until the hour of vespers. He saw another river much larger than the others, as the Indians told him by signs, and near he saw goodly villages of houses. He called the river Rio de Mares.[4] He sent two boats on shore to a village to communicate, and one of the Indians he had brought with him, for now they understood a little, and show themselves content with Christians. All the men, women, and children fled, abandoning their houses with all they contained. The Admiral gave orders that nothing should be touched. The houses were better than those he had seen before, and he believed that the houses would improve as he approached the mainland. They were made like booths, very large, and looking like tents in a camp without regular streets, but one here and another there. Within they were clean and well swept, with the furniture well made. All are of palm branches beautifully constructed. They found many images in the shape of women, and many heads like masks,[5] very well carved. It was not known whether these were used as ornaments, or to be worshipped. They had dogs which never bark, and wild birds tamed in their houses. There was a wonderful supply of nets and other fishing implements, but nothing was touched. He believed that all the people on the coast were fishermen, who took the fish inland, for this island is very large, and so beautiful, that he is never tired of praising it. He says that he found trees

[1] Punta de Mulas.   (Navarrete.)
[2] Punta de Cabañas.   (Navarrete.)
[3] Puerto de Banes.   (Navarrete.)
[4] Puerto de las Nuevitas del Principe.   (Navarrete.)
[5] Las Casas, I. 321, has "many heads well carved from wood."   Possibly these were totems.

and fruits of very marvellous taste; and adds that they must
have cows or other cattle, for he saw skulls which were like
those of cows.[1] The songs of the birds and the chirping of
crickets throughout the night lulled everyone to rest, while
the air was soft and healthy, and the nights neither hot nor
cold. On the voyage through the other islands there was great
heat, but here it is tempered like the month of May. He
attributed the heat of the other islands to their flatness, and
to the wind coming from the east, which is hot. The water
of the rivers was salt at the mouth, and they did not know
whence the natives got their drinking-water, though they have
sweet water in their houses. Ships are able to turn in this
river, both entering and coming out, and there are very good
leading-marks. He says that all this sea appears to be constantly smooth, like the river at Seville, and the water suitable
for the growth of pearls. He found large shells unlike those
of Spain. Remarking on the position of the river and port,
to which he gave the name of San Salvador,[2] he describes its
mountains as lofty and beautiful, like the Peña de las Enamo-
radas,[3] and one of them has another little hill on its summit,
like a graceful mosque. The other river and port, in which he
now was,[4] has two round mountains to the S.W., and a fine
low cape running out to the W.S.W.

Tuesday, 30th of October

He left the Rio de Mares and steered N.W., seeing a cape
covered with palm trees, to which he gave the name of Cabo
de Palmas,[5] after having made good 15 leagues. The Indians
on board the caravel *Pinta* said that beyond that cape there was

---

[1] Las Casas, I. 321, comments, "These must have been skulls of the
manati, a very large fish, like large calves, which has a skin with no scales
like a whale and its head is like that of a cow."

[2] "I believe that this port was Baracoa, which name Diego Velasquez,
the first of the Spaniards to settle Cuba, gave to the harbor of Asump-
cion." Las Casas, I. 322.

[3] Near Granada in Spain.

[4] Nuevitas del Principe. (Navarrete.)

[5] "Alto de Juan Dañue." (Navarrete.)

a river,[1] and that from the river to Cuba it was four days' journey. The captain of the *Pinta* reported that he understood from that, that this Cuba was a city, and that the land was a great continent trending far to the north. The king of that country, he gathered, was at war with the Gran Can, whom they called Cami, and his land or city Fava, with many other names. The Admiral resolved to proceed to that river, and to send a present, with the letter of the Sovereigns,[2] to the king of that land. For this service there was a sailor who had been to Guinea, and some of the Indians of Guanahani wished to go with him, and afterwards to return to their homes. The Admiral calculated that he was forty-two degrees to the north of the equinoctial line (but the handwriting is here illegible).[3] He says that he must attempt to reach the Gran Can, who he thought was here or at the city of Cathay,[4] which belongs to him, and is very grand, as he was informed before leaving Spain. All this land, he adds, is low and beautiful, and the sea deep.

Wednesday, 31st of October

All Tuesday night he was beating to windward, and he saw a river, but could not enter it because the entrance was narrow. The Indians fancied that the ships could enter wherever their canoes could go. Navigating onwards, he came to a cape running out very far, and surrounded by sunken rocks,[5]

---

[1] Rio Maximo.   (Navarrete.)

[2] See above, p. 91.

[3] Rather, "The text here is corrupt." Las Casas, I. 324, gives the same figures and adds, "yet I think the text is erroneous." Navarrete says the quadrants of that period measured the altitude double and so we should take half of forty-two as the real altitude. If so, one wonders why there was no explanation to this effect in the original journal which Las Casas saw or why Las Casas was not familiar with this fact and did not make this explanation. Ruge, *Columbus*, pp. 144, 145, says there were no such quadrants, and regards these estimates as proofs of Columbus's ignorance as a scientific navigator.

[4] In Toscanelli's letter Cathay is a province in one place and a city in another.

[5] Boca de Carabelas grandes.   (Navarrete.)

and he saw a bay where small vessels might take shelter. He could not proceed because the wind had come round to the north, and all the coast runs N.W. and S.E. Another cape further on ran out still more.[1] For these reasons, and because the sky showed signs of a gale, he had to return to the Rio de Mares.

Thursday, November the 1st

At sunrise the Admiral sent the boats on shore to the houses that were there, and they found that all the people had fled. After some time a man made his appearance. The Admiral ordered that he should be left to himself, and the sailors returned to the boats. After dinner, one of the Indians on board was sent on shore. He called out from a distance that there was nothing to fear, because the strangers were good people and would do no harm to anyone, nor were they people of the Gran Can, but they had given away their things in many islands where they had been. The Indian then swam on shore, and two of the natives took him by the arms and brought him to a house, where they heard what he had to say. When they were certain that no harm would be done to them they were reassured, and presently more than sixteen canoes came to the ships with cotton-thread and other trifles. The Admiral ordered that nothing should be taken from them, that they might understand that he sought for nothing but gold, which they call *nucay*.[2] Thus they went to and fro between the ships and the shore all day, and they came to the Christians on shore with confidence. The Admiral saw no gold whatever among them, but he says that he saw one of them with a piece of worked silver fastened to his nose. They said, by signs, that within three days many merchants from inland would come to buy the things brought by the Christians, and would give information respecting the king of that land. So far as could

---

[1] Punta del Maternillo. (Navarrete.)

[2] Las Casas says, I. 326, "I think the Christians did not understand, for the language of all these islands is the same, and in this island of Española gold is called *caona*."

be understood from their signs, he resided at a distance of four days' journey. They had sent many messengers in all directions, with news of the arrival of the Admiral. "These people," says the Admiral, "are of the same appearance and have the same customs as those of the other islands, without any religion so far as I know, for up to this day I have never seen the Indians on board say any prayer; though they repeat the *Salve* and *Ave Maria* with their hands raised to heaven, and they make the sign of the cross. The language is also the same, and they are all friends; but I believe that all these islands are at war with the Gran Can, whom they called Cavila, and his province Bafan. They all go naked like the others." This is what the Admiral says. "The river," he adds, "is very deep, and the ships can enter the mouth, going close to the shore. The sweet water does not come within a league of the mouth. It is certain," says the Admiral, "that this is the mainland, and that I am in front of Zayto and Guinsay, a hundred leagues, a little more or less, distant the one from the other.[1] It is very clear that no one before has been so far as this by sea. Yesterday, with wind from the N.W., I found it cold."

Friday, 2nd of November

The Admiral decided upon sending two Spaniards, one named Rodrigo de Jerez, who lived in Ayamonte, and the other Luis de Torres, who had served in the household of the Ade-

---

[1] The last words should be, "distant from the one and from the other." Las Casas, I. 327, says: "Zayton and Quisay are certain cities or provincias of the mainland which were depicted on the map of Paul the physician as mentioned above." These Chinese cities were known from Marco Polo's description of them. This passage in the Journal is very perplexing if it assumes that Columbus was guided by the Toscanelli letter. Again a few days earlier Columbus was sure that Cuba was Cipango, and now he is equally certain that it is the mainland of Asia asserted by Toscanelli to be 26 spaces or 6500 Italian miles west of Lisbon, but the next day his estimate of his distance from Lisbon is 4568 miles. It would seem as if Columbus attached no importance to the estimate of distances on the Toscanelli map which was the only original information in it.

lantado of Murcia, and had been a Jew, knowing Hebrew, Chaldee, and even some Arabic. With these men he sent two Indians, one from among those he had brought from Guanahani, and another a native of the houses by the river-side. He gave them strings of beads with which to buy food if they should be in need, and ordered them to return in six days. He gave them specimens of spices, to see if any were to be found. Their instructions were to ask for the king of that land, and they were told what to say on the part of the Sovereigns of Castile, how they had sent the Admiral with letters and a present, to inquire after his health and establish friendship, favoring him in what he might desire from them. They were to collect information respecting certain provinces, ports, and rivers of which the Admiral had notice, and to ascertain their distances from where he was.

This night the Admiral took an altitude with a quadrant, and found that the distance from the equinoctial line was 42 degrees.[1] He says that, by his reckoning, he finds that he has gone over 1142 leagues from the island of Hierro.[2] He still believes that he has reached the mainland.

Saturday, 3rd of November

In the morning the Admiral got into the boat, and, as the river is like a great lake at the mouth, forming a very excellent port, very deep, and clear of rocks, with a good beach for careening ships, and plenty of fuel, he explored it until he came to fresh water at a distance of two leagues from the mouth. He ascended a small mountain to obtain a view of the surrounding country, but could see nothing, owing to the dense foliage of the trees, which were very fresh and odoriferous, so that he felt no doubt that there were aromatic herbs among them. He said that all he saw was so beautiful that his eyes could never tire of gazing upon such loveliness, nor his ears of listening to the songs of birds. That day many canoes came

---

[1] *Cf.* p. 134, note 3.
[2] The true distance was 1105 leagues.   (Navarrete.)

to the ships, to barter with cotton threads and with the nets in which they sleep, called *hamacas*.

Sunday, 4th of November

At sunrise the Admiral again went away in the boat, and landed to hunt the birds he had seen the day before. After a time, Martin Alonso Pinzon came to him with two pieces of cinnamon, and said that a Portuguese, who was one of his crew, had seen an Indian carrying two very large bundles of it; but he had not bartered for it, because of the penalty imposed by the Admiral on any one who bartered. He further said that this Indian carried some brown things like nutmegs. The master [1] of the *Pinta* said that he had found the cinnamon trees. The Admiral went to the place, and found that they were not cinnamon trees. The Admiral showed the Indians some specimens of cinnamon and pepper he had brought from Castile, and they knew it, and said, by signs, that there was plenty in the vicinity, pointing to the S.E. He also showed them gold and pearls, on which certain old men said that there was an infinite quantity in a place called *Bohio*,[2] and that the people wore it on their necks, ears, arms, and legs, as well as pearls. He further understood them to say that there were great ships and much merchandise, all to the S.E. He also understood that, far away, there were men with one eye, and others with dogs' noses [3] who were cannibals, and that when they captured an enemy, they beheaded him and drank his blood, and cut off his private parts.

[1] *Contramaestre* is boatswain.

[2] "*Bohio* means in their language 'house,' and therefore it is to be supposed that they did not understand the Indians, but that it was Hayti, which is this island of Española where they made signs there was gold." Las Casas, I. 329.

[3] Columbus understood the natives to say these things because of his strong preconceptions as to what he would find in the islands off the coast of Asia based on his reading of the Book of Sir John Maundeville. Cf. ch. XVIII. of that work, *e.g.*, "a great and fair isle called Nacumera. . . . And all the men and women have dogs' heads," and ch. XIX., *e.g.*, "In one of these isles are people of great stature, like giants, hideous to look upon; and they have but one eye in the middle of the forehead."

The Admiral then determined to return to the ship and wait for the return of the two men he had sent, intending to depart and seek for those lands, if his envoys brought some good news touching what he desired. The Admiral further says: "These people are very gentle and timid; they go naked, as I have said, without arms and without law. The country is very fertile. The people have plenty of *mames* which are like carrots and have the flavor of chestnuts; and they have *faxones* and beans of kinds very different from ours.[1] They also have much cotton, which they do not sow, as it is wild in the mountains, and I believe they collect it throughout the year, because I saw pods empty, others full, and flowers all on one tree. There are a thousand other kinds of fruits, which it is impossible for me to write about, and all must be profitable." All this the Admiral says.

Monday, 5th of November

This morning the Admiral ordered the ship to be careened, afterwards the other vessels, but not all at the same time. Two were always to be at the anchorage, as a precaution; although he says that these people were very safe, and that without fear all the vessels might have been careened at the same time. Things being in this state, the master[2] of the *Niña* came to claim a reward from the Admiral because he had found mastic, but he did not bring the specimen, as

---

[1] Las Casas, I. 329, identifies the *mames* as *ajes* and *batatas*. The batatas, whence our word "potato," is the sweet potato. *Mames* is more commonly written *ñames* or *ignames*. This is the Guinea Negro name of the *Dioscorea sativa*, in English "Yam." *Ajes* is the native West Indies name. See Peschel, *Zeitalter der Entdeckungen*, p. 139, and Columbus's Journal, Dec. 13 and Dec. 16. *Faxones* are the common haricot kidney beans or string beans, *Phaseolus vulgaris*. This form of the name seems a confusion of the Spanish *jásoles* and the Portuguese *feijões*. That Columbus, an Italian by birth who had lived and married in Portugal and removed to Spain in middle life, should occasionally make slips in word-forms is not strange. More varieties of this bean are indigenous in America than were known in Europe at the time of the discoveries. Cf. De Candolle, *Origin of Cultivated Plants*, pp. 338 ff.

[2] The word is *contramaestre*, boatswain.

he had dropped it. The Admiral promised him a reward, and sent Rodrigo Sanchez and master Diego to the trees. They collected some, which was kept to present to the Sovereigns, as well as the tree. The Admiral says that he knew it was mastic, though it ought to be gathered at the proper season. There is enough in that district for a yield of 1000 *quintals* every year. The Admiral also found here a great deal of the plant called aloe. He further says that the *Puerto de Mares* is the best in the world, with the finest climate and the most gentle people. As it has a high, rocky cape, a fortress might be built, so that, in the event of the place becoming rich and important, the merchants would be safe from any other nations. He adds: "The Lord, in whose hands are all victories, will ordain all things for his service. An Indian said by signs that the mastic was good for pains in the stomach."

Tuesday, 6th of November

Yesterday, at night, says the Admiral, the two men came back who had been sent to explore the interior. They said that after walking 12 leagues they came to a village of 50 houses, where there were a thousand inhabitants, for many live in one house. These houses are like very large booths. They said that they were received with great solemnity, according to custom, and all, both men and women, came out to see them. They were lodged in the best houses, and the people touched them, kissing their hands and feet, marvelling and believing that they came from heaven, and so they gave them to understand. They gave them to eat of what they had. When they arrived, the chief people conducted them by the arms to the principal house, gave them two chairs on which to sit, and all the natives sat round them on the ground. The Indian who came with them described the manner of living of the Christians, and said that they were good people. Presently the men went out, and the women came sitting round them in the same way, kissing their hands and feet, and looking to see if they were of flesh and bones like themselves. They begged the Spaniards to remain with them at least five days. The Spaniards showed the natives specimens of cinnamon, pepper, and other spices which the Admiral had given them, and they said, by signs, that there was plenty at a short distance from thence to S.E., but that there they did not know whether there was any.[1] Finding that they had no information respecting cities, the Spaniards returned; and if they had desired to take those who wished to accompany them, more than 500 men and women would have come, because they thought the Spaniards were returning to heaven. There came, however, a principal man of the village and his son, with a servant. The Admiral conversed with them, and showed them much honor. They made signs respecting many lands and islands in those parts. The Admiral thought of bringing them to the Sovereigns. He says that he knew not what fancy took them; either from fear, or owing to the dark night, they wanted to land. The ship was at the time high and dry, but, not wishing to make them angry, he let them go on their saying that they would return at dawn, but they never came back. The two Christians met with many people on the road going home, men and women with a half-burnt weed in their hands, being the herbs they are accustomed to smoke.[2] They

---

[1] The last line should read, "but that they did not know whether there was any in the place where they were."

[2] The last line should read, "with a brand in their hand, [and] herbs to smoke as they are accustomed to do." This is the earliest reference to smoking tobacco. Las Casas, I. 332, describes the process as the natives practised it: "These two Christians found on their way many people, men and women, going to and from their villages and always the men with a brand in their hands and certain herbs to take their smoke, which are dry herbs placed in a certain leaf, also dry like the paper muskets which boys make at Easter time. Having lighted one end of it, they suck at the other end or draw in with the breath that smoke with which they make themselves drowsy and as if drunk, and in that way, they say, cease to feel fatigue. These muskets, or whatever we call them, they call *tabacos*. I knew Spaniards in this island of Española who were accustomed to take them, who, when they were rebuked for it as a vice, replied they could not give it up. I do not know what pleasant taste or profit they found in them." Las Casas' last remarks show that smoking was not yet common in his later life in Spain. The paper muskets of Las Casas are blow-pipes. Oviedo, lib. v., cap. II., gives a detailed description of the use of tobacco. He says that the Indians

did not find villages on the road of more than five houses,
all receiving them with the same reverence. They saw many
kinds of trees, herbs, and sweet-smelling flowers; and birds
of many different kinds, unlike those of Spain, except the par-
tridges, geese, of which there are many, and singing nightingales. They saw no quadrupeds except the dogs that do not
bark.[1] The land is very fertile, and is cultivated with yams
and several kinds of beans different from ours, as well as corn.[2]
There were great quantities of cotton gathered, spun, and
worked up. In a single house they saw more than 500 *arrobas*,[3]
and as much as 4000 *quintals* could be yielded every year.
The Admiral said that "it did not appear to be cultivated,
and that it bore all the year round. It is very fine, and has
a large boll. All that was possessed by these people they gave
at a very low price, and a great bundle of cotton was exchanged
for the point of a needle or other trifle. They are a people,"
says the Admiral, "guileless and unwarlike. Men and women
go as naked as when their mothers bore them. It is true that
the women wear a very small piece of cotton-cloth which covers
their private parts and no more, and they are of very good
appearance, not very dark, less so than the Canarians. I hold,
most serene Princes, that if devout religious persons were here,
knowing the language, they would all turn Christians. I
trust in our Lord that your Highnesses will resolve upon this
with much diligence, to bring so many great nations within
the Church, and to convert them; as you have destroyed those
who would not confess the Father, the Son, and the Holy

smoked by inserting these tubes in the nostrils and that after two or three
inhalations they lost consciousness. He knew some Christians who used it
as an anesthetic when in great pain.

[1] On this indigenous species of dumb dogs, *cf.* Oviedo, lib. XII. cap.
v. They have long been extinct in the Antilles. Oviedo says there were
none in Española when he wrote. He left the island in 1546.

[2] This last part of this sentence should read, "and is cultivated with
mames, kidney beans, other beans, this same panic [*i.e.*, Indian corn], etc."
The corresponding passage in the *Historie* of Ferdinand Columbus reads,
"and another grain like panic called by them *mahiz* of very excellent flavor
cooked or roasted or pounded in porridge (polenta)," p. 87.

[3] The *arroba* was 25 pounds and the *quintal* one hundred weight.

Ghost.   And after your days, all of us being mortal, may your kingdoms remain in peace, and free from heresy and evil, and may you be well received before the eternal Creator, to whom I pray that you may have long life and great increase of kingdoms and lordships, with the will and disposition to increase the holy Christian religion as you have done hitherto. Amen !"

"To-day I got the ship afloat, and prepared to depart on Thursday, in the name of God, and to steer S.E. in search of gold and spices, and to discover land."

These are the words of the Admiral, who intended to depart on Thursday, but, the wind being contrary, he could not go until the 12th of November.

Monday, 12th of November

The Admiral left the port and river of Mares before dawn to visit the island called Babeque, so much talked of by the Indians on board, where, according to their signs, the people gather the gold on the beach at night with candles, and afterwards beat it into bars with hammers.[1]   To go thither it was necessary to shape a course E. b. S.   After having made 8 leagues along the coast, a river was sighted, and another 4 leagues brought them to another river, which appeared to be of great volume, and larger than any they had yet seen.   The Admiral did not wish to stop nor to enter any of these rivers, for two reasons: the first and principal one being that wind and weather were favorable for going in search of the said island of Babeque; the other, that, if there was a populous and famous city near the sea, it would be visible, while, to go up the rivers, small vessels are necessary, which those of the expedition were not.   Much time would thus be lost; moreover, the exploration of such rivers is a separate enterprise. All that coast was peopled near the river, to which the name of Rio del Sol was given.

---

[1] In Las Casas, I. 339, Bohio is mentioned with Babeque, and it is in Bohio that the people were reported to gather gold on the beach.

The Admiral says that, on the previous Sunday, the 11th of November, it seemed good to take some persons from amongst those at Rio de Mares, to bring to the Sovereigns, that they might learn our language, so as to be able to tell us what there is in their lands. Returning, they would be the mouthpieces of the Christians, and would adopt our customs and the things of the faith. "I saw and knew" (says the Admiral) "that these people are without any religion, not idolaters, but very gentle, not knowing what is evil, nor the sins of murder and theft, being without arms, and so timid that a hundred would fly before one Spaniard, although they joke with them.[1] They, however, believe and know that there is a God in heaven, and say that we have come from Heaven. At any prayer that we say, they repeat, and make the sign of the cross. Thus your Highnesses should resolve to make them Christians, for I believe that, if the work was begun, in a little time a multitude of nations would be converted to our faith, with the acquisition of great lordships, peoples, and riches for Spain. Without doubt, there is in these lands a vast quantity of gold, and the Indians I have on board do not speak without reason when they say that in these islands there are places where they dig out gold, and wear it on their necks, ears, arms, and legs, the rings being very large. There are also precious stones, pearls, and an infinity of spices. In this river of Mares, whence we departed to-night, there is undoubtedly a great quantity of mastic, and much more could be raised, because the trees may be planted, and will yield abundantly. The leaf and fruit are like the mastic, but the tree and leaf are larger. As Pliny describes it, I have seen it on the island of Chios in the Archipelago. I ordered many of these trees to be tapped, to see if any of them would yield resin; but, as it rained all the time I was in that river, I could not get any, except a very little, which I am bringing to your Highnesses. It may not be the right season for tapping, which is, I believe, when the trees come forth after winter and begin to flower. But when I was there the fruit was nearly ripe. Here also there is a great

---

[1] *I.e.*, although the Spaniards may be only fooling with them.

quantity of cotton, and 1 believe it would have a good sale here without sending it to Spain, but to the great cities of the Gran Can,[1] which will be discovered without doubt, and many others ruled over by other lords, who will be pleased to serve your Highnesses, and whither will be brought other commodities of Spain and of the Eastern lands; but these are to the west as regards us. There is also here a great yield of aloes,[2] though this is not a commodity that will yield great profit. The mastic, however, is important, for it is only obtained from the said island of Chios, and I believe the harvest is worth 50,000 ducats, if I remember right.[3] There is here, in the mouth of the river, the best port I have seen up to this time, wide, deep, and clear of rocks. It is an excellent site for a town and fort, for any ship could come close up to the walls; the land is high, with a temperate climate, and very good water.

"Yesterday a canoe came alongside the ship, with six youths in it. Five came on board, and I ordered them to be detained. They are now here. I afterwards sent to a house on the western side of the river, and seized seven women, old and young, and three children. I did this because the men would behave better in Spain if they had women of their own land, than without them. For on many occasions the men of Guinea have been brought to learn the language in Portugal, and afterwards, when they returned, and it was expected that

---

[1] An interesting forecast of the future which may be compared with John Cabot's; see one of the last pages of this volume.

[2] *Linaloe.* Lignaloes or agallochum, to be distinguished from the medicinal aloes. Both were highly prized articles of mediaeval Oriental trade. Lignaloes is mentioned by Marco Polo as one of the principal commodities exchanged in the market of Zaitun. It is also frequently mentioned in the Bible. *Cf.* Numbers xxiv. 6, or Psalm xlv. 8. The aloes of Columbus were probably the Barbadoes aloes of commerce, and the mastic the produce of the *Bursera gummifera.* The last did not prove to be a commercial resin like the mastic of Scio. See *Encyclopædia Britannica* under Aloes and Mastic, and Heyd, *Histoire du Commerce du Levant au Moyen Age*, II. 581, 633.

[3] The ducat being 9s. 2d. In the seventeenth century the value of the mastic exported from Chios (Scio) was 30,000 ducats. Chios belonged to Genoa from 1346 to 1566. (Markham.)

they would be useful in their land, owing to the good company they had enjoyed and the gifts they had received, they never appeared after arriving. Others may not act thus. But, having women, they have the wish to perform what they are required to do; besides, the women would teach our people their language, which is the same in all these islands, so that those who make voyages in their canoes are understood everywhere. On the other hand, there are a thousand different languages in Guinea, and one native does not understand another.

"The same night the husband of one of the women came alongside in a canoe, who was father of the three children — one boy and two girls. He asked me to let him come with them, and besought me much. They are now all consoled at being with one who is a relation of them all. He is a man of about 45 years of age." All these are the words of the Admiral. He also says that he had felt some cold, and that it would not be wise to continue discoveries in a northerly direction in the winter. On this Monday, until sunset, he steered a course E. b. S., making 18 leagues, and reaching a cape, to which he gave the name of Cabo de Cuba.

Tuesday, 13th of November

This night the ships were on a bowline, as the sailors say, beating to windward without making any progress. At sunset they began to see an opening in the mountains, where two very high peaks[1] were visible. It appeared that here was the division between the land of Cuba and that of Bohio, and this was affirmed by signs, by the Indians who were on board. As soon as the day had dawned, the Admiral made sail toward the land, passing a point which appeared at night to be distant two leagues. He then entered a large gulf, 5 leagues to the S.S.E., and there remained 5 more, to arrive at the point where, between two great mountains, there appeared to be an opening; but it could not be made out whether it was an inlet of the sea. As he desired to go to the island called Babeque,

---

[1] *Las Sierras del Cristal* and *Las Sierras de Moa*. (Navarrete.)

where, according to the information he had received, there was much gold; and as it bore east, and as no large town was in sight, the wind freshening more than ever, he resolved to put out to sea, and work to the east with a northerly wind. The ship made 8 miles an hour, and from ten in the forenoon, when that course was taken, until sunset, 56 miles, which is 14 leagues to the eastward from the Cabo de Cuba. The other land of Bohio was left to leeward. Commencing from the cape of the said gulf, he discovered, according to his reckoning, 80 miles, equal to 20 leagues, all that coast running E.S.E. and W.N.W.

Wednesday, 14th of November

All last night the Admiral was beating to windward (he said that it would be unreasonable to navigate among those islands during the night, until they had been explored), for the Indians said yesterday that it would take three days to go from Rio de Mares to the island of Babeque, by which should be understood days' journeys in their canoes equal to about 7 leagues. The wind fell, and, the course being east, she could not lay her course nearer than S.E., and, owing to other mischances, he was detained until the morning. At sunrise he determined to go in search of a port, because the wind had shifted from north to N.E., and, if a port could not be found, it would be necessary to go back to the ports in the island of Cuba, whence they came. The Admiral approached the shore, having gone over 28 miles E.S.E. that night. He steered south . . . miles to the land, where he saw many islets and openings. As the wind was high and the sea rough, he did not dare to risk an attempt to enter, but ran along the coast W.N.W., looking out for a port, and saw many, but none very clear of rocks. After having proceeded for 64 miles, he found a very deep opening, a quarter of a mile wide, with a good port and river. He ran in with her head S.S.W., afterwards south to S.E. The port[1] was spacious and very deep, and he saw so many islands that he could not count them

---

[1] Puerto de Taxamo, in Cuba. (Navarrete.)

all, with very high land covered with trees of many kinds, and an infinite number of palms. He was much astonished to see so many lofty islands; and assured the Sovereigns that the mountains and isles he had seen since yesterday seemed to him to be second to none in the world; so high and clear of clouds and snow, with the sea at their bases so deep. He believes that these islands are those innumerable ones that are depicted on the maps of the world in the Far East.[1] He believed that they yielded very great riches in precious stones and spices, and that they extend much further to the south, widening out in all directions. He gave the name of La Mar de Nuestra Señora, and to the haven, which is near the mouth of the entrance to these islands, Puerto del Principe. He did not enter it, but examined it from outside, until another time, on Saturday of the next week, as will there appear. He speaks highly of the fertility, beauty, and height of the islands which he found in this gulf, and he tells the Sovereigns not to wonder at his praise of them, for that he has not told them the hundredth part. Some of them seemed to reach to heaven, running up into peaks like diamonds. Others rising to a great height have a flat top like a table. At their bases the sea is of a great depth, with enough water for a very large carrack. All are covered with foliage and without rocks.

Thursday, 15th of November

The Admiral went to examine these islands in the ships' boats, and speaks marvels of them, how he found mastic, and aloes without end. Some of them were cultivated with the roots of which the Indians make bread; and he found that fires had been lighted in several places. He saw no fresh water. There were some natives, but they fled. In all parts of the sea where the vessels were navigated he found a depth of 15 or 16 fathoms, and all *basa*, by which he means that the ground

---

[1] *Cf.* Fra Mauro's Map (1457–1459), Bourne, *Spain in America*, 14, and Behaim's Globe, Winsor's *Columbus*, p. 186, or Fiske's *Discovery of America*, I. 422.

is sand, and not rocks; a thing much desired by sailors, for the rocks cut their anchor cables.

Friday, 16th of November

As in all parts, whether islands or mainlands, that he visited, the Admiral always left a cross; so, on this occasion, he went in a boat to the entrance of these havens, and found two very large trees on a point of land, one longer than the other. One being placed over the other, made a cross, and he said that a carpenter could not have made it better. He ordered a very large and high cross to be made out of these timbers. He found canes on the beach, and did not know where they had grown, but thought they must have been brought down by some river, and washed up on the beach (in which opinion he had reason). He went to a creek on the south-east side of the entrance to the port. Here, under a height of rock and stone like a cape, there was depth enough for the largest carrack in the world close in shore, and there was a corner where six ships might lie without anchors as in a room. It seemed to the Admiral that a fortress might be built here at small cost, if at any time any famous trade should arise in that sea of islands.

Returning to the ship, he found that the Indians who were on board had fished up very large shells found in those seas. He made the people examine them, to see if there was mother-o'-pearl, which is in the shells where pearls grow. They found a great deal, but no pearls, and their absence was attributed to its not being the season, which is May and June. The sailors found an animal which seemed to be a *taso*, or *taxo*.[1] They also fished with nets, and, among many others, caught a fish which was exactly like a pig, not like a tunny, but all covered with a very hard shell, without a soft place except the tail and the eyes, and a hole underneath to discharge its superfluities. It was ordered to be salted, to bring home for the Sovereigns to see.[2]

[1] Las Casas did not know the meaning of this word. In all probability it is the Italian *tasso*, badger. *Cf.* p. 139, note 1. The animal, Cuvier suggested, was probably the coati.

[2] Cuvier conjectured this to be the trunk fish.

Saturday, 17th of November

The Admiral got into the boat, and went to visit the islands he had not yet seen to the S.W. He saw many more very fertile and pleasant islands, with a great depth between them. Some of them had springs of fresh water, and he believed that the water of those streams came from some sources at the summits of the mountains. He went on, and found a beach bordering on very sweet water, which was very cold. There was a beautiful meadow, and many very tall palms. They found a large nut of the kind belonging to India, great rats,[1] and enormous crabs. He saw many birds, and there was a strong smell of musk, which made him think it must be there. This day the two eldest of the six youths brought from the Rio de Mares, who were on board the caravel *Niña*, made their escape.

Sunday, 18th of November

The Admiral again went away with the boats, accompanied by many of the sailors, to set up the cross which he had ordered to be made out of the two large trees at the entrance to the Puerto del Principe, on a fair site cleared of trees, whence there was an extensive and very beautiful view. He says that there is a greater rise and fall of the sea there than in any other port he has seen, and that this is no marvel, considering the numerous islands. The tide is the reverse of ours, because here, when the moon is S.S.W., it is low water in the port. He did not get under way, because it was Sunday.

Monday, 19th of November

The Admiral got under way before sunrise, in a calm. In the afternoon there was some wind from the east, and he shaped a N.N.E. course. At sunset the Puerto del Principe bore S.S.W. 7 leagues. He saw the island of Babeque bearing due east about 60 miles. He steered N.E. all that night,

---

[1] The agouti.

making 60 miles, and up to ten o'clock of Tuesday another
dozen; altogether 18 leagues N.E. b. W.

Tuesday, 20th of November

They left Babeque, or the islands of Babeque, to the
E.S.E., the wind being contrary; and, seeing that no progress
was being made, and the sea was getting rough, the Admiral
determined to return to the Puerto del Principe, whence he had
started, which was 25 leagues distant. He did not wish
to go to the island he had called Isabella, which was twelve
leagues off, and where he might have anchored that night, for
two reasons: one was that he had seen two islands to the south
which he wished to explore; the other, because the Indians he
brought with him, whom he had taken at the island of Guanahani, which he named San Salvador, eight leagues from
Isabella, might get away, and he said that he wanted them to
take to Spain. They thought that, when the Admiral had
found gold, he would let them return to their homes. He came
near the Puerto del Principe, but could not reach it, because it was night, and because the current drifted them to the
N.W. He turned her head to N.E. with a light wind. At
three o'clock in the morning the wind changed, and a course
was shaped E.N.E., the wind being S.S.W., and changing
at dawn to south and S.E. At sunset Puerto del Principe
bore nearly S.W. by W. 48 miles, which are 12 leagues.

Wednesday, 21st of November

At sunrise the Admiral steered east, with a southerly wind,
but made little progress, owing to a contrary sea. At vespers
he had gone 24 miles. Afterwards the wind changed to east,
and he steered S. b. E., at sunset having gone 12 miles. Here
he found himself forty-two degrees north of the equinoctial
line, as in the port of Mares, but he says that he kept the
result from the quadrant in suspense until he reached the shore,
that it might be adjusted (as it would seem that he thought
this distance was too great, and he had reason, it not being

possible, as these islands are only in . . . degrees).[1]   To believe the quadrant was right he was led by seeing the north star as high as in Castile. . . .   Reinforcing this was the great heat which he says he found there. . . .   From this heat which the Admiral says he endured there he argued that in these Indies and where he was going there must be much gold.[2]

This day Martin Alonso Pinzon parted company with the caravel *Pinta*, in disobedience to and against the wish of the Admiral, and out of avarice, thinking that an Indian who had been put on board his caravel could show him where there was much gold.   So he parted company, not owing to bad weather, but because he chose.   Here the Admiral says: "He had done and said many other things to me."

Thursday, 22nd of November

On Wednesday night the Admiral steered S.S.E., with the wind east, but it was nearly calm.   At 3 it began to blow from N.N.E.; and he continued to steer south to see the land he had seen in that quarter.   When the sun rose he was as far off as the day before, owing to adverse currents, the land being 40 miles off.   This night Martin Alonso shaped a course to the east, to go to the island of Babeque, where the Indians say there is much gold.   He did this in sight of the Admiral, from whom he was distant 16 miles.   The Admiral stood towards the land all night.   He shortened sail, and showed a lantern, because Pinzon would thus have an opportunity of joining him, the night being very clear, and the wind fair to come, if he had wished to do so.

---

[1] See p. 134, note 3.   The words following " Port of Mares " should be translated " but here he says that he has the quadrant hung up (or not in use) until he reaches land to repair it.   Since it seemed to him that this distance," etc.   Las Casas omitted to insert the number of degrees in his comment.

[2] The sentences omitted are comments of Las Casas on these reflections of Columbus.

Friday, 23rd of November

The Admiral stood towards the land all day, always steering south with little wind, but the current would never let them reach it, being as far off at sunset as in the morning. The wind was E.N.E., and they could shape a southerly course, but there was little of it. Beyond this cape there stretched out another land or cape, also trending east, which the Indians on board called Bohio. They said that it was very large, and that there were people in it who had one eye in their foreheads, and others who were cannibals, and of whom they were much afraid.[1] When they saw that this course was taken, they said that they could not talk to these people because they would be eaten, and that they were very well armed. The Admiral says that he well believes that there were such people, and that if they are armed they must have some ability. He thought that they may have captured some of the Indians, and because they did not return to their homes, the others believed that they had been eaten. They thought the same of the Christians and of the Admiral when some of them first saw the strangers.

Saturday, 24th of November

They navigated all night, and at 3[2] they reached the level island[3] at the very same point they had come to the week before, when they started for the island of Babeque. At first the Admiral did not dare to approach the shore, because it seemed that there would be a great surf in that mountain-girded bay. Finally he reached the sea of Nuestra Señora, where there are many islands, and entered a port near the mouth of the opening to the islands. He says that if he had known of this port before, he need not have occupied himself in exploring the islands, and it would not have been necessary to go back. He, however, considered that the time was well spent in examin-

[1] See p. 138, note 3.
[2] *A la hora de tercia*, about 9 A.M. See p. 118, note 1.
[3] Cayo de Moa. (Navarrete.)

ing the islands. On nearing the land he sent in the boat to sound, finding a good sandy bottom in 6 to 20 fathoms. He entered the haven, pointing the ship's head S.W. and then west, the flat island bearing north. This, with another island near it, forms a harbor which would hold all the ships of Spain safe from all winds. This entrance on the S.W. side is passed by steering S.S.W., the outlet being to the west very deep and wide. Thus a vessel can pass amidst these islands, and he who approaches from the north, with a knowledge of them, can pass along the coast. These islands are at the foot of a great mountain-chain running east and west, which is longer and higher than any others on this coast, where there are many. A reef of rocks outside runs parallel with the said mountains, like a bench, extending to the entrance. On the side of the flat island, and also to the S.E., there is another small reef, but between them there is great width and depth. Within the port, near the S.E. side of the entrance, they saw a large and very fine river,[1] with more volume than any they had yet met with, and fresh water could be taken from it as far as the sea. At the entrance there is a bar, but within it is very deep, 19 fathoms. The banks are lined with palms and many other trees.

Sunday, 25th of November

Before sunrise the Admiral got into the boat, and went to see a cape or point of land [2] to the S.E. of the flat island, about a league and a half distant, because there appeared to be a good river there. Presently, near to the S.E. side of the cape, at a distance of two cross-bow shots, he saw a large stream of beautiful water falling from the mountains [3] above, with a loud noise. He went to it, and saw some stones shining in its bed like gold.[4]

[1] Rio de Moa. (Navarrete.)
[2] Punta del Mangle or del Guarico. (Navarrete.)
[3] Sierras de Moa. (Navarrete.)
[4] "These must have been *margaseta* stones which look like gold in streams and of which there is an abundance in the rivers of these islands." Las Casas, I. 346.

He remembered that in the river Tagus, near its junction with
the sea, there was gold; so it seemed to him that this should
contain gold, and he ordered some of these stones to be collected, to be brought to the Sovereigns.   Just then the sailor
boys called out that they had found large pines.   The Admiral
looked up the hill, and saw that they were so wonderfully large
that he could not exaggerate their height and straightness,
like stout yet fine spindles.   He perceived that here there was
material for great store of planks and masts for the largest
ships in Spain.   He saw oaks and arbutus trees,[1] with a good
river, and the means of making water-power.[2]   The climate
was temperate, owing to the height of the mountains.   On the
beach he saw many other stones of the color of iron, and others
that some said were like silver ore, all brought down by the
river.   Here he obtained a new mast and yard for the mizzen
of the caravel *Niña*.   He came to the mouth of the river, and
entered a creek which was deep and wide, at the foot of that
S.E. part of the cape, which would accommodate a hundred
ships without any anchor or hawsers.   Eyes never beheld a
better harbor.   The mountains are very high, whence descend
many limpid streams, and all the hills are covered with pines,
and an infinity of diverse and beautiful trees.   Two or three
other rivers were not visited.

The Admiral described all this, in much detail, to the Sovereigns, and declared that he had derived unspeakable joy
and pleasure at seeing it, more especially the pines, because they
enable as many ships as is desired to be built here, bringing
out the rigging, but finding here abundant supplies of wood
and provisions.   He affirms that he has not enumerated a
hundredth part of what there is here, and that it pleased our
Lord always to show him one thing better than another, as
well on the ground and among the trees, herbs, fruits, and
flowers, as in the people, and always something different in
each place.   It had been the same as regards the havens and

[1] *Madroños.   Arbutus unedo* or the Strawberry tree.   The California
Madroña is the *Arbutus Menziesii.*
[2] Rather, "for making sawmills."

the waters. Finally, he says that if it caused him who saw it so much wonder, how much more will it affect those who hear about it; yet no one can believe until he sees it.

Monday, 26th of November

At sunrise the Admiral weighed the anchors in the haven of Santa Catalina, where he was behind the flat island, and steered along the coast in the direction of Cabo del Pico, which was S.E. He reached the cape late, because the wind failed, and then saw another cape, S.E. b. E. 60 miles, which, when 20 miles off, was named Cabo de Campana, but it could not be reached that day. They made good 32 miles during the day, which is 8 leagues. During this time the Admiral noted nine remarkable ports,[1] which all the sailors thought wonderfully good, and five large rivers; for they sailed close along the land, so as to see everything. All along the coast there are very high and beautiful mountains, not arid or rocky, but all accessible, and very lovely. The valleys, like the mountains, were full of tall and fine trees, so that it was a glory to look upon them, and there seemed to be many pines. Also, beyond the said Cabo de Pico to the S.E. there are two islets, each about two leagues round, and inside them three excellent havens and two large rivers. Along the whole coast no inhabited places were visible from the sea. There may have been some, and there were indications of them, for, when the men landed, they found signs of people and numerous remains of fires. The Admiral conjectured that the land he saw to-day S.E. of the Cabo de Campana was the island called by the Indians Bohio:[2] it looked as if this cape was separated from the mainland. The Admiral says that all the people he has hitherto met with have very great fear of those of Caniba or Canima. They affirm that they live in the island of Bohio, which must be very large, according to all accounts. The Admiral understood that those of Caniba come to take people from their homes, they being

---

[1] Among these were the Bay of Yamanique, and the ports of Jaragua, Taco, Cayaganueque, Nava, and Maravi. (Navarrete.)

[2] See p. 126, note 1.

very cowardly, and without knowledge of arms. For this cause it appears that these Indians do not settle on the sea-coast, owing to being near the land of Caniba. When the na-tives who were on board saw a course shaped for that land, they feared to speak, thinking they were going to be eaten; nor could they rid themselves of their fear. They declared that the Canibas [1] had only one eye and dogs' faces. The Admiral thought they lied, and was inclined to believe that it was peo-ple from the dominions of the Gran Can who took them into captivity.

Tuesday, 27th of November

Yesterday, at sunset, they arrived near a cape named Campana by the Admiral; and, as the sky was clear and the wind light, he did not wish to run in close to the land and anchor, although he had five or six singularly good havens under his lee. The Admiral was attracted on the one hand by the longing and delight he felt to gaze upon the beauty and freshness of those lands, and on the other by a desire to com-plete the work he had undertaken. For these reasons he re-mained close hauled, and stood off and on during the night. But, as the currents had set him more than 5 or 6 leagues to the S.E. beyond where he had been at nightfall, passing the land of Campana, he came in sight of a great opening beyond that cape, which seemed to divide one land from another, leaving an island between them. He decided to go back, with the wind S.E., steering to the point where the opening had appeared, where he found that it was only a large bay; [2] and at the end of it, on the S.E. side, there was a point of land on which was a high and square-cut hill, [3] which had looked like an island. A breeze sprang up from the north, and the Admiral continued on a S.E. course, to explore the coast and discover all that was there. Presently he saw, at the

[1] The original of the words Cannibal and Carib and Caribbean. *Cf.* also p. 138, note 3.

[2] The port of Baracoa. (Navarrete.)

[3] Monte del Yunque. (Navarrete.)

foot of the Cabo de Campana, a wonderfully good port,[1] and a large river, and, a quarter of a league on, another river, and a third, and a fourth to a seventh at similar distances, from the furthest one to Cabo de Campana being 20 miles S.E. Most of these rivers have wide and deep mouths, with excellent havens for large ships, without sandbanks or sunken rocks. Proceeding onwards from the last of these rivers, on a S.E. course, they came to the largest inhabited place they had yet seen, and a vast concourse of people came down to the beach with loud shouts, all naked, with their darts in their hands. The Admiral desired to have speech with them, so he furled sails and anchored. The boats of the ship and the caravel were sent on shore, with orders to do no harm whatever to the Indians, but to give them presents. The Indians made as if they would resist the landing, but, seeing that the boats of the Spaniards continued to advance without fear, they retired from the beach. Thinking that they would not be terrified if only two or three landed, three Christians were put on shore, who told them not to be afraid, in their own language, for they had been able to learn a little from the natives who were on board. But all ran away, neither great nor small remaining. The Christians went to the houses, which were of straw, and built like the others they had seen, but found no one in any of them. They returned to the ships, and made sail at noon in the direction of a fine cape[2] to the eastward, about 8 leagues distant. Having gone about half a league, the Admiral saw, on the south side of the same bay, a very remarkable harbor,[3] and to the S.E. some wonderfully beautiful country like a valley among the mountains, whence much smoke arose, indicating a large population, with signs of much cultivation. So he resolved to stop at this port, and see if he could have any speech or intercourse with the inhabitants. It was so that, if the Admiral had praised the other havens, he must praise this still more for its lands, climate, and people. He

---

[1] Port of Maravi.   (Navarrete.)
[2] Punta de Maici.   (*Id.*)
[3] Puerto de Baracoa.   (*Id.*)

tells marvels of the beauty of the country and of the trees, there being palms and pine trees; and also of the great valley which is not flat, but diversified by hill and dale, the most lovely scene in the world. Many streams flow from it, which fall from the mountains.

As soon as the ship was at anchor the Admiral jumped into the boat, to get soundings in the port, which is the shape of a hammer. When he was facing the entrance he found the mouth of a river on the south side of sufficient width for a galley to enter it, but so concealed that it is not visible until close to. Entering it for the length of the boat, there was a depth of from 5 to 8 fathoms. In passing up it the freshness and beauty of the trees, the clearness of the water, and the birds, made it all so delightful that he wished never to leave them. He said to the men who were with him that to give a true relation to the Sovereigns of the things they had seen, a thousand tongues would not suffice, nor his hand to write it, for that it was like a scene of enchantment. He desired that many other prudent and credible witnesses might see it, and he was sure that they would be as unable to exaggerate the scene as he was.

The Admiral also says: — "How great the benefit that is to be derived from this country would be, I cannot say. It is certain that where there are such lands there must be an infinite number of things that would be profitable. But I did not remain long in one port, because I wished to see as much of the country as possible, in order to make a report upon it to your Highnesses; and besides, I do not know the language, and these people neither understand me nor any other in my company; while the Indians I have on board often misunderstand. Moreover, I have not been able to see much of the natives, because they often take to flight. But now, if our Lord pleases, I will see as much as possible, and will proceed by little and little, learning and comprehending; and I will make some of my followers learn the language. For I have perceived that there is only one language up to this point. After they understand the advantages, I shall labor to make all these people Christians. They will become so readily, because they have no religion nor idolatry, and your Highnesses will send orders to build a city and fortress, and to convert the people. I assure your Highnesses that it does not appear to me that there can be a more fertile country nor a better climate under the sun, with abundant supplies of water. This is not like the rivers of Guinea, which are all pestilential. I thank our Lord that, up to this time, there has not been a person of my company who has had so much as a headache, or been in bed from illness, except an old man who has suffered from the stone all his life, and he was well again in two days. I speak of all three vessels. If it will please God that your Highnesses should send learned men out here, they will see the truth of all I have said. I have related already how good a place Rio de Mares would be for a town and fortress, and this is perfectly true; but it bears no comparison with this place, nor with the Mar de Nuestra Señora. For here there must be a large population, and very valuable productions, which I hope to discover before I return to Castile. I say that if Christendom will find profit among these people, how much more will Spain, to whom the whole country should be subject. Your Highnesses ought not to consent that any stranger should trade here, or put his foot in the country, except Catholic Christians, for this was the beginning and end of the undertaking; namely, the increase and glory of the Christian religion, and that no one should come to these parts who was not a good Christian." [1]

All the above are the Admiral's words. He ascended the river for some distance, examined some branches of it, and, returning to the mouth, he found some pleasant groves of trees, like a delightful orchard. Here he came upon a boat or

---

[1] With these suggestions for a colonial policy cf. Columbus's more detailed programme in his letter to Ferdinand and Isabella, pp. 273–277 below. In the Spanish policy of exclusion of foreigners from the colonies the religious motive, as here, was quite as influential as the spirit of trade monopoly. Las Casas, in making the same quotation from the Journal, remarks, I. 351: "All these are his exact words, although some of them are not perfect Castilian, since that was not the Admiral's mother tongue."

canoa, dug out of one tree, as big as a *fusta*[1] of twelve benches, fastened under a boat-house or bower made of wood, and thatched with palm-leaves, so that it could be neither injured by sun nor by the water. He says that here would be the proper site for a town and fort, by reason of the good port, good water, good land, and abundance of fuel.

Wednesday, 28th of November

The Admiral remained during this day, in consequence of the rain and thick weather, though he might have run along the coast, the wind being S.W., but he did not weigh, because he was unacquainted with the coast beyond, and did not know what danger there might be for the vessels. The sailors of the two vessels went on shore to wash their clothes, and some of them walked inland for a short distance. They found indications of a large population, but the houses were all empty, everyone having fled. They returned by the banks of another river, larger than that which they knew of, at the port.

Thursday, 29th of November

The rain and thick weather continuing, the Admiral did not get under way. Some of the Christians went to another village to the N.W., but found no one, and nothing in the houses. On the road they met an old man who could not run away, and caught him. They told him they did not wish to do him any harm, gave him a few presents, and let him go. The Admiral would have liked to have had speech with him, for he was exceedingly satisfied with the delights of that land, and wished that a settlement might be formed there, judging that it must support a large population. In one house they found a cake of wax,[2] which was taken to the Sovereigns, the

---

[1] The *fusta* was a long, low boat propelled by oars or a sail. It is represented in earlier English by "foist" and "fuste."

[2] Las Casas, I. 353, remarks, "This wax was never made in the island of Cuba, and this cake that was found came from the kingdom and provinces of Yucatan, where there is an immense amount of very good yellow wax." He supposes that it might have come from the wrecks of canoes engaged in trade along the coast of Yucatan.

M

Admiral saying that where there was wax there were also a thousand other good things. The sailors also found, in one house, the head of a man in a basket, covered with another basket, and fastened to a post of the house. They found the same things in another village. The Admiral believed that they must be the heads of some founder, or principal ancestor of a lineage, for the houses are built to contain a great number of people in each; and these should be relations, and descendants of a common ancestor.

Friday, 30th of November

They could not get under way to-day because the wind was east, and dead against them. The Admiral sent 8 men well armed, accompanied by two of the Indians he had on board, to examine the villages inland, and get speech with the people. They came to many houses, but found no one and nothing, all having fled. They saw four youths who were digging in their fields, but, as soon as they saw the Christians, they ran away, and could not be overtaken. They marched a long distance, and saw many villages and a most fertile land, with much cultivation and many streams of water. Near one river they saw a canoe dug out of a single tree, 95 *palmos*[1] long, and capable of carrying 150 persons.

Saturday, 1st of December

They did not depart, because there was still a foul wind, with much rain. The Admiral set up a cross at the entrance of this port, which he called Puerto Santo,[2] on some bare rocks. The point is that which is on the S.E. side of the entrance; but he who has to enter should make more over to the N.W.; for at the foot of both, near the rock, there are 12

[1] About 70 feet. Las Casas adds the words, "it was most beautiful," and continues, "it is no wonder for there are in that island very thick and very long and tall fragrant red cedars and commonly all their canoes are made from these valuable trees."

[2] Puerto de Baracoa. (Navarrete.)

fathoms and a very clean bottom.   At the entrance of the port, toward the S.E. point, there is a reef of rocks above water,[1] sufficiently far from the shore to enable one to pass between if it is necessary, for both on the side of the rock and the shore there is a depth of 12 to 15 fathoms; and, on entering, a ship's head should be turned S.W.

Sunday, 2nd of December

The wind was still contrary, and they could not depart. Every night the wind blows on the land, but no vessel need be alarmed at all the gales in the world, for they cannot blow home by reason of a reef of rocks at the opening to the haven, etc.   A sailor-boy found, at the mouth of the river, some stones which looked as if they contained gold; so they were taken to be shown to the Sovereigns.   The Admiral says that there are great rivers at the distance of a lombard shot.[2]

Monday, 3rd of December

By reason of the continuance of an easterly wind the Admiral did not leave this port.   He arranged to visit a very beautiful headland a quarter of a league to the S.E. of the anchorage.   He went with the boats and some armed men. At the foot of the cape there was the mouth of a fair river, and on entering it they found the width to be a hundred paces, with a depth of one fathom.   Inside they found 12, 5, 4, and 2 fathoms, so that it would hold all the ships there are in Spain. Leaving the river, they came to a cove in which were five very

[1] This reef actually exists on the S.E. side of the entrance to this port, which is described with great accuracy by Columbus.   (Navarrete.)

[2] *Lombarda* is the same as *bombarda*, bombard, the earliest type of cannon.   The name has nothing to do with Lombardy, but is simply the form which was used in Castile in the fifteenth century while *bombarda* was used elsewhere in the peninsula and in Europe.   The average-sized bombard was a twenty-five pounder.   *Diccionario Enciclopedico Hispano-Americano*, art. *lombardo*, based on Aráutegui, *Apuntes Históricos sobre la Artilleria Española en los Siglos XIV y XV*.

large canoes,[1] so well constructed that it was a pleasure to look at them. They were under spreading trees, and a path led from them to a very well-built boat-house, so thatched that neither sun nor rain could do any harm. Within it there was another canoe made out of a single tree like the others, like a *fusta* with 17 benches. It was a pleasant sight to look upon such goodly work. The Admiral ascended a mountain, and afterwards found the country level, and cultivated with many things of that land, including such calabashes, as it was a glory to look upon them.[2] In the middle there was a large village, and they came upon the people suddenly; but, as soon as they were seen, men and women took to flight. The Indian from on board, who was with the Admiral, cried out to them that they need not be afraid, as the strangers were good people. The Admiral made him give them bells, copper ornaments, and glass beads, green and yellow, with which they were well content. He saw that they had no gold nor any other precious thing, and that it would suffice to leave them in peace. The whole district was well peopled, the rest having fled from fear. The Admiral assures the Sovereigns that ten thousand of these men would run from ten, so cowardly and timid are they. No arms are carried by them, except wands,[3] on the point of which a short piece of wood is fixed, hardened by fire, and these they are very ready to exchange. Returning to where he had left the boats, he sent back some men up the hill, because he fancied he had seen a large apiary. Before those he had sent

---

[1] This line should be, "in which he saw five very large *almadias* [low, light boats] which the Indians call *canoas*, like *fustas*, very beautiful and so well constructed," etc. "Canoe" is one of the few Arawak-Indian words to have become familiar English.

[2] Rather, "He went up a mountain and then he found it all level and planted with many things of the country and gourds so that it was glorious to see it." De Candolle believes the calabash or gourd to have been introduced into America from Africa. *Cf.* his *Origin of Cultivated Plants*, pp. 245 ff. Oviedo, however, in his *Historia General y Natural de Indias*, lib. VIII., cap. VIII., says that the *calabaças* of the Indies were the same as those in Spain and were cultivated not to eat but to use the shells as vessels.

[3] Rather, "rods."

could return, they were joined by many Indians, and they went to the boats, where the Admiral was waiting with all his people. One of the natives advanced into the river near the stern of the boat, and made a long speech, which the Admiral did not understand. At intervals the other Indians raised their hands to Heaven, and shouted. The Admiral thought he was assuring him that he was pleased at his arrival; but he saw the Indian who came from the ship change the color of his face, and turn as yellow as wax, trembling much, and letting the Admiral know by signs that he should leave the river, as they were going to kill him. He pointed to a cross-bow which one of the Spaniards had, and showed it to the Indians, and the Admiral let it be understood that they would all be slain, because that cross-bow carried far and killed people. He also took a sword and drew it out of the sheath, showing it to them, and saying the same, which, when they had heard, they all took to flight; while the Indian from the ship still trembled from cowardice, though he was a tall, strong man. The Admiral did not want to leave the river, but pulled towards the place where the natives had assembled in great numbers, all painted, and as naked as when their mothers bore them. Some had tufts of feathers on their heads, and all had their bundles of darts.

The Admiral says: "I came to them, and gave them some mouthfuls of bread, asking for the darts, for which I gave in exchange copper ornaments, bells, and glass beads. This made them peaceable, so that they came to the boats again, and gave us what they had. The sailors had killed a turtle, and the shell was in the boat in pieces. The sailor-boys gave them some in exchange for a bundle of darts. These are like the other people we have seen, and with the same belief that we came from Heaven. They are ready to give whatever thing they have in exchange for any trifle without saying it is little; and I believe they would do the same with gold and spices if they had any. I saw a fine house, not very large, and with two doors, as all the rest have. On entering, I saw a marvellous work, there being rooms made in a peculiar way,

that I scarcely know how to describe it. Shells and other
things were fastened to the ceiling. I thought it was a temple,
and I called them and asked, by signs, whether prayers were
offered up there. They said that they were not, and one of
them climbed up and offered me all the things that were there,
of which I took some."

Tuesday, 4th of December

The Admiral made sail with little wind, and left that port,
which he called Puerto Santo. After going two leagues, he
saw the great river [1] of which he spoke yesterday. Passing
along the land, and beating to windward on S.E. and W.N.W.
courses, they reached Cabo Lindo,[2] which is E.S.E. 5 leagues
from Cabo del Monte. A league and a half from Cabo del
Monte there is an important but rather narrow river, which
seemed to have a good entrance, and to be deep. Three-
quarters of a league further on, the Admiral saw another very
large river, and he thought it must have its source at a great
distance. It had a hundred paces at its mouth, and no bar,
with a depth of 8 fathoms. The Admiral sent the boat in,
to take soundings, and they found the water fresh until it
enters the sea.

This river had great volume, and must have a large population on its banks. Beyond Cabo Lindo there is a great bay,
which would be open for navigation to E.N.E. and S.E.
and S.S.W.

Wednesday, 5th of December

All this night they were beating to windward off Cape
Lindo, to reach the land to the east, and at sunrise the Admiral
sighted another cape,[3] two and a half leagues to the east.
Having passed it, he saw that the land trended S. and S.W.,

[1] Rio Boma. (Navarrete.)
[2] Punta del Fraile. (Id.)
[3] Punta de los Azules. (Id.)

and presently saw a fine high cape in that direction, 7 leagues distant.[1] He would have wished to go there, but his object was to reach the island of Babeque, which, according to the Indians, bore N.E.; so he gave up the intention. He could not go to Babeque either, because the wind was N.E. Looking to the S.E., he saw land, which was a very large island, according to the information of the Indians, well peopled, and called by them Bohio.[2] The Admiral says that the inhabitants of Cuba, or Juana,[3] and of all the other islands, are much afraid of the inhabitants of Bohio, because they say that they eat people. The Indians relate other things, by signs, which are very wonderful; but the Admiral did not believe them. He only inferred that those of Bohio must have more cleverness and cunning to be able to capture the others, who, however, are very poor-spirited. The wind veered from N.E. to North, so the Admiral determined to leave Cuba, or Juana, which, up to this time, he had supposed to be the mainland, on account of its size, having coasted along it for 120 leagues.[4] He shaped a course S.E. b. E., the land he had sighted bearing S.E.; taking this precaution because the wind always veered from N. to N.E. again, and thence to east and S.E. The wind increased, and he made all sail, the current helping them; so that they were making 8 miles an hour from the morning until one in the afternoon (which is barely 6 hours, for they say that the nights were nearly 15 hours). Afterwards they went 10 miles an hour, making good 88 miles by sunset, equal to 22 leagues, all to the S.E. As night was coming on, the

[1] Las Casas, I. 359, says, "This high and beautiful cape whither he would have liked to go I believe was Point Maycí, which is the extreme end of Cuba toward the east." According to the modern maps of Cuba it must have been one of the capes to the southwest of Point Maicí.

[2] Cf. note 57. Las Casas, I. 359, remarks, "Its real name was Haytí, the last syllable long and accented." He thinks it possible that the cape first sighted may have been called Bohio.

[3] Columbus gave Cuba the name Juana "in memory of Prince Juan the heir of Castile." Historie, p. 83.

[4] "In leaving the cape or eastern point of Cuba he gave it the name Alpha and Omega, which means beginning and end, for he believed that this cape was the end of the mainland in the Orient." Las Casas, I. 360.

Admiral ordered the caravel *Niña*, being a good sailer, to proceed ahead, so as to sight a harbor at daylight. Arriving at
the entrance of a port which was like the Bay of Cadiz, while
it was still dark, a boat was sent in to take soundings, which
showed a light from a lantern. Before the Admiral could beat
up to where the caravel was, hoping that the boat would show
a leading-mark for entering the port, the candle in the lantern
went out. The caravel, not seeing the light, showed a light
to the Admiral, and, running down to him, related what had
happened. The boat's crew then showed another light, and
the caravel made for it; but the Admiral could not do so, and
was standing off and on all night.

Thursday, 6th of December

When daylight arrived the Admiral found himself four
leagues from the port, to which he gave the name of Puerto
Maria,[1] and to a fine cape bearing S.S.W. he gave the name of
Cabo de la Estrella.[2] It seemed to be the furthest point of the
island towards the south, distant 28 miles. Another point of
land, like an island, appeared about 40 miles to the east. To
another fine point, 54 miles to the east, he gave the name of
Cabo del Elefante,[3] and he called another, 28 miles to the S.E.,
Cabo de Cinquin. There was a great opening or bay, which
might be the mouth of a river,[4] distant 20 miles. It seemed
that between Cabo del Elefante and that of Cinquin there was
a great opening,[5] and some of the sailors said that it formed
an island, to which the name of Isla de la Tortuga[6] was given.
The island appeared to be very high land, not closed in with
mountains, but with beautiful valleys, well cultivated, the
crops appearing like the wheat on the plain of Cordova in May.

[1] The port of St. Nicholas Mole, in Hayti. (Navarrete.)
[2] Cape of St. Nicholas. (*Id.*)
[3] Punta Palmista. (*Id.*)
[4] Puerto Escudo. (*Id.*)
[5] The channel between Tortuga Island and the main.
[6] Tortoise.

That night they saw many fires, and much smoke, as if from workshops,[1] in the day time; it appeared to be a signal made by people who were at war. All the coast of this land trends to the east.

At the hour of vespers the Admiral reached this port, to which he gave the name of Puerto de San Nicolas, in honor of St. Nicholas, whose day it was;[2] and on entering it he was astonished at its beauty and excellence. Although he had given great praise to the ports of Cuba, he had no doubt that this one not only equalled, but excelled them, and none of them are like it. At the entrance it is a league and a half wide, and a vessel's head should be turned S.S.E., though, owing to the great width, she may be steered on any bearing that is convenient; proceeding on this course for two leagues.[3] On the south side of the entrance the coast forms a cape, and thence the course is almost the same as far as a point where there is a fine beach, and a plain covered with fruit-bearing trees of many kinds; so that the Admiral thought there must be nutmegs and other spices among them, but he did not know them, and they were not ripe. There is a river falling into the harbor, near the middle of the beach. The depth of this port is surprising, for, until reaching the land, for a distance of . . .[4] the lead did not reach the bottom at 40 fathoms; and up to this length there are 15 fathoms with a very clean bottom. Throughout the port there is a depth of 15 fathoms, with a clean bottom, at a short distance from the shore; and all along the coast there are soundings with clean bottom, and not a single sunken rock. Inside, at the length of a boat's oar from the land, there are 5 fathoms. Beyond the limit of the port to the S.S.E. a thousand carracks could beat up.

[1] *Atalayas,* "watchtowers."

[2] This method of giving names in honor of the saint on whose day a new cape or river was discovered was very commonly followed during the period of discoveries, and sometimes the date of a discovery, or the direction of a voyage, or other data can be verified by comparing the names given with the calendar.

[3] This clause should be " It extends in this manner to the south-south-east two leagues."

[4] A gap in the manuscript.

One branch of the port to the N.E. runs into the land for a long half league, and always the same width, as if it had been measured with a cord. Being in this creek, which is 25 paces wide, the principal entrance to the harbor is not in sight, so that it appears land-locked.[1] The depth of this creek is 11 fathoms throughout, all with clean bottom; and close to the land, where one might put the gangboards on the grass, there are eight fathoms.

The whole port is open to the air, and clear of trees. All the island appeared to be more rocky than any that had been discovered. The trees are smaller, and many of them of the same kinds as are found in Spain, such as the ilex, the arbutus, and others, and it is the same with the herbs. It is a very high country, all open and clear, with a very fine air, and no such cold has been met with elsewhere, though it cannot be called cold except by comparison. Towards the front of the haven there is a beautiful valley, watered by a river; and in that district there must be many inhabitants, judging from the number of large canoes, like galleys, with 15 benches. All the natives fled as soon as they saw the ships. The Indians who were on board had such a longing to return to their homes that the Admiral considered whether he should not take them back when he should depart from here. They were already suspicious, because he did not shape a course towards their country; whence he neither believed what they said, nor could he understand them, nor they him, properly. The Indians on board had the greatest fear in the world of the people of this island. In order to get speech of the people it would be necessary to remain some days in harbor; but the Admiral did not do so, because he had to continue his discoveries, and because he could not tell how long he might be detained. He trusted in our Lord that the Indians he brought with him would understand the language of the people of this island; and afterwards he would communicate with them, trusting that it might please God's Majesty that he might find trade in gold before he returned.

[1] This is the "Carenero," within the port of St. Nicholas. (Navarrete.)

Friday, 7th of December

At daybreak the Admiral got under way, made sail, and left the port of St. Nicholas. He went on with the wind in the west for two leagues, until he reached the point which forms the Carenero, when the angle in the coast bore S.E., and the Cabo de la Estrella was 24 miles to the S.W. Thence he steered along the coast eastward to Cabo Cinquin about 48 miles, 20 of them being on an E.N.E. coast. All the coast is very high, with a deep sea. Close in shore there are 20 to 30 fathoms, and at the distance of a lombard-shot there is no bottom; all which the Admiral discovered that day, as he sailed along the coast with the wind S.W., much to his satisfaction. The cape, which runs out in the port of St. Nicholas the length of a shot from a lombard, could be made an island by cutting across it, while to sail round it is a circuit of 3 or 4 miles. All that land is very high, not clothed with very high trees, but with ilex, arbutus, and others proper to the land of Castile. Before reaching Cape Cinquin by two leagues, the Admiral discovered a small roadstead[1] like an opening in the mountains, through which he could see a very large valley, covered with crops like barley, and he therefore judged that it must sustain a large population. Behind there was a high range of mountains. On reaching Cabo Cinquin, the Cabo de la Tortuga bore N.E. 32 miles.[2] Off Cabo Cinquin, at the distance of a lombard-shot, there is a high rock, which is a good landmark. The Admiral being there, he took the bearing of Cabo del Elefante, which was E.S.E. about 70 miles,[3] the intervening land being very high. At a distance of 6 leagues there was a conspicuous cape,[4] and he saw many large valleys and plains, and high mountains inland, all reminding him of Spain. After 8 leagues he came to a very deep but narrow river, though a carrack

[1] Accepting Navarrete's conjecture of *abrezuela* or *anglezuela* for the reading *agrezuela* of the text.

[2] It should be north 11 miles. (Navarrete.)

[3] This is an error. It should be 15 miles. (Navarrete.) The direction *al Leste cuarta del Sueste* is East by South.

[4] Puerto Escudo. (Navarrete.)

might easily enter it, and the mouth without bar or rocks.
After 16 miles there was a wide and deep harbor,[1] with on bottom at the entrance, nor, at 3 paces from the shore, less than
15 fathoms; and it runs inland a quarter of a league. It
being yet very early, only one o'clock in the afternoon, and the
wind being aft and blowing fresh, yet, as the sky threatened
much rain, and it was very thick, which is dangerous even on a
known coast, how much more in an unknown country, the
Admiral resolved to enter the port, which he called Puerto
de la Concepcion. He landed near a small river at the point
of the haven, flowing from valleys and plains, the beauty of
which was a marvel to behold. He took fishing-nets with him;
and, before he landed, a mullet, like those of Spain, jumped into
the boat, this being the first time they had seen fish resembling
the fish of Castile. The sailors caught and killed others
and soles and other fish like those of Castile. Walking a
short distance inland, the Admiral found much land under
cultivation, and heard the singing of nightingales and other
birds of Castile. Five men were seen, but they would not
stop, running away. The Admiral found myrtles and other
trees and plants, like those of Castile, and so also were the
land and mountains.[2]

Saturday, 8th of December

In this port there was heavy rain, with a fresh breeze from
the north. The harbor is protected from all winds except the
north; but even this can do no harm whatever, because there
is a great surf outside, which prevents such a sea within the
river as would make a ship work on her cables. After midnight
the wind veered to N.E., and then to east, from which winds
this port is well sheltered by the island of Tortuga, distant
36 miles.[3]

---

[1] Bahia Mosquito. (Navarrete.)
[2] Cuvier notes that neither the nightingale proper nor the Spanish
myrtle are found in America.
[3] It should be 11 miles. (Navarrete.)

Sunday, 9th of December

To-day it rained, and the weather was wintry, like October in Castile. No habitations had been seen except a very beautiful house in the Puerto de S. Nicolas, which was better built than any that had been in other parts. "The island is very large," says the Admiral: "it would not be much if it has a circumference of 200 leagues. All the parts he had seen were well cultivated. He believed that the villages must be at a distance from the sea, whither they went when the ships arrived; for they all took to flight, taking everything with them, and they made smoke-signals, like a people at war." This port has a width of a thousand paces at its entrance, equal to a quarter of a league. There is neither bank nor reef within, and there are scarcely soundings close in shore. Its length, running inland, is 3000 paces, all clean, and with a sandy bottom; so that any ship may anchor in it without fear, and enter it without precaution. At the upper end there are the mouths of two rivers, with the most beautiful champaign country, almost like the lands of Spain: these even have the advantage; for which reasons the Admiral gave the name of the said island Isla Española.[1]

Monday, 10th of December

It blew hard from the N.E., which made them drag their anchors half a cable's length. This surprised the Admiral,

---

[1] *I.e.*, Spanish Isle, not "Little Spain," which is sometimes erroneously given in explanation of the Latin Hispaniola. This last is a Latinized form of Española and not a diminutive. Las Casas, I. 367, in the corresponding passage, has "Seeing the greatness and beauty of this island and its resemblance to Spain although much superior and that they had caught fish in it like the fish of Castile and for other similar reasons he decided on December 9 when in the harbor of Concepcion to name this island Spanish Island."

At a period some time later than his first voyage Columbus decided that Española and Cipango were the same and also identical with the Ophir of the Bible. *Cf.* his marginal note to Landino's Italian translation of Pliny's *Natural History*, "la isola de Feyti, vel de Ofir, vel de Cipango, a la quale habio posto nome Spagnola." *Raccolta Colombiana*, pt. I., vol. II., p. 472.

who had seen that the anchors had taken good hold of the ground. As he saw that the wind was foul for the direction in which he wanted to steer, he sent six men on shore, well armed, to go two or three leagues inland, and endeavor to open communications with the natives. They came and returned without having seen either people or houses. But they found some hovels, wide roads, and some places where many fires had been made. They saw excellent lands, and many mastic trees, some specimens of which they took; but this is not the time for collecting it, as it does not coagulate.

Tuesday, 11th of December

The Admiral did not depart, because the wind was still east and S.E. In front of this port, as has been said, is the island of La Tortuga. It appears to be a large island, with the coast almost like that of Española, and the distance between them is about ten leagues.[1] It is well to know that from the Cabo de Cinquin, opposite Tortuga, the coast trends to the south. The Admiral had a great desire to see that channel between these two islands, and to examine the island of Española, which is the most beautiful thing in the world. According to what the Indians said who were on board, he would have to go to the island of Babeque. They declared that it was very large, with great mountains, rivers, and valleys; and that the island of Bohio was larger than Juana, which they call Cuba, and that it is not surrounded by water. They seem to imply that there is mainland behind Española, and they call it Caritaba, and say it is of vast extent. They have reason in saying that the inhabitants are a clever race, for all the people of these islands are in great fear of those of Caniba. So the Admiral repeats, what he has said before, that Caniba is nothing else but the Gran Can, who ought now to be very near. He sends ships to capture the islanders; and as they do not return, their countrymen believe that they have been eaten.

---

[1] The distance is 11 miles. (Navarrete.)

Each day we understand better what the Indians say, and they us, so that very often we are intelligible to each other. The Admiral sent people on shore, who found a great deal of mastic, but did not gather it. He says that the rains make it, and that in Chios they collect it in March. In these lands, being warmer, they might take it in January. They caught many fish like those of Castile — dace, salmon, hake, dory, gilt heads, mullets, *corbinas*, shrimps,[1] and they saw sardines. They found many aloes.[2]

Wednesday, 12th of December

The Admiral did not leave the port to-day, for the same reason: a contrary wind. He set up a great cross on the west side of the entrance, on a very picturesque height, "in sign," he says, "that your Highnesses hold this land for your own, but chiefly as a sign of our Lord Jesus Christ." This being done, three sailors strolled into the woods to see the trees and bushes. Suddenly they came upon a crowd of people, all naked like the rest. They called to them, and went towards them, but they ran away. At last they caught a woman; for I had ordered that some should be caught, that they might be treated well, and made to lose their fear. This would be a useful event, for it could scarcely be otherwise, considering the beauty of the country. So they took the woman, who was very young and beautiful, to the ship, where she talked to the Indians on board; for they all speak the same language. The Admiral caused her to be dressed, and gave her glass beads, hawks' bells, and brass ornaments; then he sent her back to the shore very courteously, according to his custom.

---

[1] *Camarones.*

[2] The proper English equivalents for these names in the original are hard to find. The *corbina* was a black fish and the name is found in both Spanish and Portuguese. *Pámpanos* is translated "giltheads," but the name is taken over into English as "pompano." It must be remembered that in many cases the names of European species were applied to American species which resembled them but which were really distinct species of the same genus.

He sent three of the crew with her, and three of the Indians he had on board, that they might open communications with her people. The sailors in the boat, who took her on shore, told the Admiral that she did not want to leave the ship, but would rather remain with the other women he had seized at the port of Mares, in the island of Juana or Cuba. The Indians who went to put the woman on shore said that the natives came in a canoe, which is their caravel, in which they navigate from one place to another; but when they came to the entrance of the harbor, and saw the ships, they turned back, left the canoe, and took the road to the village. The woman pointed out the position of the village. She had a piece of gold in her nose, which showed that there was gold in that island.

Thursday, 13th of December

The three men who had been sent by the Admiral with the woman returned at 3 o'clock in the morning, not having gone with her to the village, because the distance appeared to be long, or because they were afraid. They said that next day many people would come to the ships, as they would have been reassured by the news brought them by the woman. The Admiral, with the desire of ascertaining whether there were any profitable commodities in that land, being so beautiful and fertile, and of having some speech with the people, and being desirous of serving the Sovereigns, determined to send again to the village, trusting in the news brought by the woman that the Christians were good people. For this service he selected nine men well armed, and suited for such an enterprise, with whom an Indian went from those who were on board. They reached the village, which is $4\frac{1}{2}$ leagues to the S.E., and found that it was situated in a very large and open valley. As soon as the inhabitants saw the Christians coming they all fled inland, leaving all their goods behind them. The village consisted of a thousand houses, with over three thousand inhabitants. The Indian whom the Christians had brought with them ran after the fugitives, saying that they should have no fear, for the Christians did not come from Cariba, but were from Heaven, and that they gave many beautiful things to all the people they met. They were so impressed with what he said, that upwards of two thousand came close up to the Christians, putting their hands on their heads, which was a sign of great reverence and friendship; and they were all trembling until they were reassured. The Christians related that, as soon as the natives had cast off their fear, they all went to the houses, and each one brought what he had to eat, consisting of yams,[1] which are roots like large radishes, which they sow and cultivate in all their lands, and is their staple food. They make bread of it, and roast it. The yam has the smell of a chestnut, and anyone would think he was eating chestnuts. They gave their guests bread and fish, and all they had. As the Indians who came in the ship had understood that the Admiral wanted to have some parrots, one of those who accompanied the Spaniards mentioned this, and the natives brought out parrots, and gave them as many as they wanted, without asking anything for them. The natives asked the Spaniards not to go that night, and that they would give them many other things that they had in the mountains. While all these people were with the Spaniards, a great multitude was seen to come, with the husband of the woman whom the Admiral had honored and sent away. They wore hair over their shoulders, and came to give thanks to the Christians for the honor the Admiral had done them, and for the gifts. The Christians reported to the Admiral that this was a handsomer and finer people than any that had hitherto been met with. But the Admiral says that he does not see how they can be a finer people than the others, giving to understand that all those he had found in the other islands were very well conditioned. As regards beauty, the Christians said there was no comparison, both men and women, and that their skins are whiter than the others. They saw two girls whose skins were as white as any that could be seen in Spain. They also

---

[1] Rather, "bread of *niames*." *Cf.* note, p. 139.

N

said, with regard to the beauty of the country they saw, that the best land in Castile could not be compared with it. The Admiral also, comparing the lands they had seen before with these, said that there was no comparison between them, nor did the plain of Cordova come near them, the difference being as great as between night and day. They said that all these lands were cultivated, and that a very wide and large river passed through the centre of the valley, and could irrigate all the fields. All the trees were green and full of fruit, and the plants tall and covered with flowers. The roads were broad and good. The climate was like April in Castile; the nightingale and other birds sang as they do in Spain during that month, and it was the most pleasant place in the world. Some birds sing sweetly at night. The crickets and frogs are heard a good deal. The fish are like those of Spain. They saw much aloe and mastic, and cotton-fields. Gold was not found, and it is not wonderful that it should not have been found in so short a time.

Here the Admiral calculated the number of hours in the day and night, and from sunrise to sunset. He found that twenty half-hour glasses passed, though he says that here there may be a mistake, either because they were not turned with equal quickness, or because some sand may not have passed. He also observed with a quadrant, and found that he was 34 degrees from the equinoctial line.[1]

Friday, 14th of December

The Admiral left the Puerto de la Concepcion with the land-breeze, but soon afterwards it fell calm (and this is experienced every day by those who are on this coast). Later an east wind sprang up, so he steered N.N.E., and arrived at the island of Tortuga. He sighted a point which he named Punta Pierna, E.N.E. of the end of the island 12 miles; and from thence

---

[1] Las Casas, I. 373, says that at that season the length of the day in Española is somewhat over eleven hours. The correct latitude is 20°.

another point was seen and named Punta Lanzada, in the same N.E. direction 16 miles. Thus from the end of Tortuga to Punta Aguda the distance is 44 miles, which is 11 leagues E.N.E. Along this route there are several long stretches of beach. The island of Tortuga is very high, but not mountainous, and is very beautiful and populous, like Española, and the land is cultivated, so that it looked like the plain of Cordova. Seeing that the wind was foul, and that he could not steer for the island of Baneque,[1] he determined to return to the Puerto de la Concepcion whence he had come; but he could not fetch a river which is two leagues to the east of that port.

Saturday, 15th of December

Once more the Admiral left the Puerto de la Concepcion, but, on leaving the port, he was again met by a contrary east wind. He stood over to Tortuga, and then steered with the object of exploring the river he had been unable to reach yesterday; nor was he able to fetch the river this time, but he anchored half a league to leeward of it, where there was clean and good anchoring ground. As soon as the vessels were secured, he went with the boats to the river, entering an arm of the sea, which proved not to be the river. Returning, he found the mouth, there being only one, and the current very strong. He went in with the boats to find the villagers that had been seen the day before. He ordered a tow-rope to be got out and manned by the sailors, who hauled the boats up for a distance of two lombard-shots. They could not get further owing to the strength of the current. He saw some houses, and the large valley where the villages were, and he said that a more beautiful valley he had never seen, this river flowing through the centre of it. He also saw people at the entrance, but they all took to flight. He further says that these people must be much hunted, for they live in such a state of fear. When the ships arrived at any port, they pres-

[1] Elsewhere called Babeque. (Navarrete.)

ently made signals by fires on heights throughout the country;
and this is done more in this island of Española and in Tortuga, which is also a large island, than in the others that were
visited before.   He called this valley Valle del Paraiso,[1] and
the river Guadalquivir; because he says that it is the size of
the Guadalquivir at Cordova.   The banks consist of shingle,
suitable for walking.[2]

Sunday, 16th of December

At midnight the Admiral made sail with the land-breeze
to get clear of that gulf.   Passing along the coast of Española
on a bowline, for the wind had veered to the east, he met a
canoe in the middle of the gulf, with a single Indian in it.   The
Admiral was surprised how he could have kept afloat with such
a gale blowing.   Both the Indian and his canoe were taken on
board, and he was given glass beads, bells, and brass trinkets,
and taken in the ship, until she was off a village 17 miles from
the former anchorage, where the Admiral came to again.   The
village appeared to have been lately built, for all the houses
were new.   The Indian then went on shore in his canoe,
bringing the news that the Admiral and his companions were
good people; although the intelligence had already been conveyed to the village from the place where the natives had their
interview with the six Spaniards.   Presently more than five
hundred natives with their king came to the shore opposite
the ships, which were anchored very close to the land.   Presently one by one, then many by many, came to the ship without bringing anything with them, except that some had a few
grains of very fine gold in their ears and noses, which they
readily gave away.   The Admiral ordered them all to be well
treated; and he says: "for they are the best people in the
world, and the gentlest; and above all I entertain the hope
in our Lord that your Highnesses will make them all Christians,

---

[1] Paradise Valley.

[2] Rather, "There are on the edges or banks of the shore many beautiful
stones and it is all suitable for walking."   The Spanish text seems to be
defective.

and that they will be all your subjects, for as yours I hold them." He also saw that they all treated the king with respect, who was on the sea-shore. The Admiral sent him a present, which he received in great state. He was a youth of about 21 years of age, and he had with him an aged tutor, and other councillors who advised and answered him, but he uttered very few words. One of the Indians who had come in the Admiral's ship spoke to him, telling him how the Christians had come from Heaven, and how they came in search of gold, and wished to find the island of Baneque. He said that it was well, and that there was much gold in the said island. He explained to the alguazil of the Admiral [1] that the way they were going was the right way, and that in two days they would be there; adding, that if they wanted anything from the shore he would give it them with great pleasure. This king, and all the others, go naked as their mothers bore them, as do the women without any covering, and these were the most beautiful men and women that had yet been met with. They are fairly white, and if they were clothed and protected from the sun and air, they would be almost as fair as people in Spain. This land is cool, and the best that words can describe. It is very high, yet the top of the highest mountain could be ploughed with bullocks; and all is diversified with plains and valleys. In all Castile there is no land that can be compared with this for beauty and fertility. All this island, as well as the island of Tortuga, is cultivated like the plain of Cordova. They raise on these lands crops of yams,[2] which are small branches, at the foot of which grow roots like carrots, which serve as bread. They powder and knead them, and make them into bread; then they plant the same branch in another part, which again sends out four or five of the same roots, which are very nutritious, with the taste of chestnuts. Here they have the largest the Admiral had seen in any part of the world,

---

[1] Diego de Arana of Cordova, a near relation of Beatriz Henriquez, the mother of the Admiral's son Fernando. (Markham.) Alguazil means constable.

[2] *Ajes*. The same as *mames*. *Cf.* note, p. 139.

for he says that they have the same plant in Guinea. At this place they were as thick as a man's leg. All the people were stout and lusty, not thin, like the natives that had been seen before, and of a very pleasant manner, without religious belief. The trees were so luxuriant that the leaves left off being green, and were dark colored with verdure. It was a wonderful thing to see those valleys, and rivers of sweet water, and the cultivated fields, and land fit for cattle, though they have none, for orchards, and for anything in the world that a man could seek for.

In the afternoon the king came on board the ship, where the Admiral received him in due form, and caused him to be told that the ships belonged to the Sovereigns of Castile, who were the greatest princes in the world. But neither the Indians who were on board, who acted as interpreters, nor the king, believed a word of it. They maintained that the Spaniards came from Heaven, and that the Sovereigns of Castile must be in Heaven, and not in this world. They placed Spanish food before the king to eat, and he ate a mouthful, and gave the rest to his councillors and tutor, and to the rest who came with him.

"Your Highnesses may believe that these lands are so good and fertile, especially these of the island of Española, that there is no one who would know how to describe them, and no one who could believe if he had not seen them. And your Highnesses may believe that this island, and all the others, are as much yours as Castile. Here there is only wanting a settlement and the order to the people to do what is required. For I, with the force I have under me, which is not large, could march over all these islands without opposition. I have seen only three sailors land, without wishing to do harm, and a multitude of Indians fled before them. They have no arms, and are without warlike instincts; they all go naked, and are so timid that a thousand would not stand before three of our men. So that they are good to be ordered about, to work and sow, and do all that may be necessary, and to build towns, and they should be taught to go about clothed and to adopt our customs."

Monday, 17th of December

It blew very hard during the night from E.N.E., but there was not much sea, as this part of the coast is enclosed and sheltered by the island of Tortuga. The sailors were sent away to fish with nets. They had much intercourse with the natives, who brought them certain arrows of the Caniba or Canibales. They are made of reeds, pointed with sharp bits of wood hardened by fire, and are very long. They pointed out two men who wanted certain pieces of flesh on their bodies, giving to understand that the Canibales had eaten them by mouthfuls. The Admiral did not believe it. Some Christians were again sent to the village, and, in exchange for glass beads, obtained some pieces of gold beaten out into fine leaf. They saw one man, whom the Admiral supposed to be Governor of that province, called by them Cacique,[1] with a piece of gold leaf as large as a hand, and it appears that he wanted to barter with it. He went into his house, and the other remained in the open space outside. He cut the leaf into small pieces, and each time he came out he brought a piece and exchanged it. When he had no more left, he said by signs that he had sent for more, and that he would bring it another day. The Admiral says that all these things, and the manner of doing them, with their gentleness and the information they gave, showed these people to be more lively and intelligent than any that had hitherto been met with. In the afternoon a canoe arrived from the island of Tortuga with a crew of forty men; and when they arrived on the beach, all the people of the village sat down in sign of peace, and nearly all the crew came on shore. The cacique rose by himself, and, with words that appeared to be of a menacing character, made them go back to the canoe and shove off. He took up stones from the beach and threw them into the water, all having obediently gone back into the canoe. He also took a stone and put it in the hands of my Alguazil,[2] that he might throw it. He had been sent on shore

---

[1] This Indian word survives in modern Spanish with the meaning political boss.

[2] Diego de Arana.

with the Secretary [1] to see if the canoe had brought anything of value. The alguazil did not wish to throw the stone. That cacique showed that he was well disposed to the Admiral. Presently the canoe departed, and afterwards they said to the Admiral that there was more gold in Tortuga than in Española, because it is nearer to Baneque. The Admiral did not think that there were gold mines either in Española or Tortuga, but that the gold was brought from Baneque in small quantities, there being nothing to give in return. That land is so rich that there is no necessity to work much to sustain life, nor to clothe themselves, as they go naked. He believed that they were very near the source, and that our Lord would point out where the gold has its origin. He had information that from here to Baneque was four days' journey, about 34 leagues, which might be traversed with a fair wind in a single day.

Tuesday, 18th of December

The Admiral remained at the same anchorage, because there was no wind, and also because the cacique had said that he had sent for gold. The Admiral did not expect much from what might be brought, but he wanted to understand better whence it came. Presently he ordered the ship and caravel to be adorned with arms and dressed with flags, in honor of the feast of Santa Maria de la O,[2] or commemoration of the Annunciation, which was on that day, and many rounds were fired from the lombards. The king of that island of Española had got up very early and left his house, which is about five leagues away, reaching the village at three in the morning. There

---

[1] Rodrigo de Escobedo.

[2] In Spain in earlier times the Annunciation was celebrated on December 18 to avoid having it come in Lent. When the Roman usage in regard to Annunciation was adopted in Spain they instituted the Feast of our Lady's Expectation on December 18. It was called "The Feast of O because the first of the greater antiphons is said in the vespers of its vigil." Addis and Arnold, *Catholic Dictionary*, under "Mary." The series of anthems all begin with "O."

were several men from the ship in the village, who had been sent by the Admiral to see if any gold had arrived. They said that the king came with two hundred men; that he was carried in a litter by four men; and that he was a youth, as has already been said. To-day, when the Admiral was dining under the poop, the king came on board with all his people.

The Admiral says to the Sovereigns: "Without doubt, his state, and the reverence with which he is treated by all his people, would appear good to your Highnesses, though they all go naked. When he came on board, he found that I was dining at a table under the poop, and, at a quick walk, he came to sit down by me, and did not wish that I should give place by coming to receive him or rising from the table, but that I should go on with my dinner. I thought that he would like to eat of our viands, and ordered them to be brought for him to eat. When he came under the poop, he made signs with his hand that all the rest should remain outside, and so they did, with the greatest possible promptitude and reverence. They all sat on the deck, except the men of mature age, whom I believe to be his councillors and tutor, who came and sat at his feet. Of the viands which I put before him, he took of each as much as would serve to taste it, sending the rest to his people, who all partook of the dishes. The same thing in drinking: he just touched with his lips, giving the rest to his followers. They were all of fine presence and very few words. What they did say, so far as I could make out, was very clear and intelligent. The two at his feet watched his mouth, speaking to him and for him, and with much reverence. After dinner, an attendant brought a girdle, made like those of Castile, but of different material, which he took and gave to me, with pieces of worked gold, very thin. I believe they get very little here, but they say that they are very near the place where it is found, and where there is plenty. I saw that he was pleased with some drapery I had over my bed, so I gave it him, with some very good amber beads I wore on my neck, some colored shoes, and a bottle of orange-flower water. He was marvellously well content, and both he and his tutor and councillors were very sorry that they could not understand me, nor I them. However, I knew that they said that, if I wanted anything, the whole island was at my disposal. I sent for some beads of mine, with which, as a charm, I had a gold excelente,[1] on which your Highnesses were stamped. I showed it to him, and said, as I had done yesterday, that your Highnesses ruled the best part of the world, and that there were no princes so great. I also showed him the royal standards, and the others with a cross, of which he thought much. He said to his councillors what great lords your Highnesses must be to have sent me from so far, even from Heaven to this country, without fear. Many other things passed between them which I did not understand, except that it was easy to see that they held everything to be very wonderful."

When it got late, and the king wanted to go, the Admiral sent him on shore in his boat very honorably, and saluted him with many guns. Having landed, he got into his litter, and departed with his 200 men, his son being carried behind on the shoulders of an Indian, a man highly respected. All the sailors and people from the ships were given to eat, and treated with much honor wherever they liked to stop. One sailor said that he had stopped in the road and seen all the things given by the Admiral. A man carried each one before the king, and these men appeared to be among those who were most respected. His son came a good distance behind the king, with a similar number of attendants, and the same with a brother of the king, except that the brother went on foot, supported under the arms by two honored attendants. This brother came to the ship after the king, and the Admiral presented him with some of the things used for barter. It was then that the Admiral learnt that a king was called Cacique in their language. This day little gold was got by barter, but the Admiral heard from an old man that there were many neighboring islands, at a distance of a hundred leagues or more, as he understood, in which much gold is found; and there is even one island that was all gold. In the others there

---

[1] The excelente was worth two castellanos or about $6 in coin value.

was so much that it was said they gather it with sieves, and they fuse it and make bars, and work it in a thousand ways. They explained the work by signs. This old man pointed out to the Admiral the direction and position, and he determined to go there, saying that if the old man had not been a principal councillor of the king he would detain him, and make him go, too; or if he knew the language he would ask him, and he believed, as the old man was friendly with him and the other Christians, that he would go of his own accord. But as these people were now subjects of the King of Castile, and it would not be right to injure them, he decided upon leaving him. The Admiral set up a very large cross in the centre of the square of that village, the Indians giving much help; they made prayers and worshipped it, and, from the feeling they show, the Admiral trusted in our Lord that all the people of those islands would become Christians.

Wednesday, 19th of December

This night the Admiral got under way to leave the gulf formed between the islands of Tortuga and Española, but at dawn of day a breeze sprang up from the east, against which he was unable to get clear of the strait between the two islands during the whole day. At night he was unable to reach a port which was in sight.[1] He made out four points of land, and a great bay with a river, and beyond he saw a large bay,[2] where there was a village, with a valley behind it among high mountains covered with trees, which appeared to be pines. Over the Two Brothers there is a very high mountain-range running N.E. and S.W., and E.S.E. from the Cabo de Torres is a small island to which the Admiral gave the name of Santo Tomas, because to-morrow was his vigil. The whole circuit of this island alternates with capes and excellent harbors, so far as could be judged from the sea. Before coming to the island on

---

[1] El Puerto de la Granja. (Navarrete.)
[2] The bay of Puerto Margot. (Id.)

the west side, there is a cape which runs far into the sea, in part high, the rest low; and for this reason the Admiral named it Cabo Alto y Bajo.[1] From the road[2] of Torres East by South 60 miles, there is a mountain higher than any that reaches the sea,[3] and from a distance it looks like an island, owing to a depression on the land side. It was named Monte Caribata, because that province was called Caribata. It is very beautiful, and covered with green trees, without snow or clouds. The weather was then, as regards the air and temperature, like March in Castile, and as regards vegetation, like May. The nights lasted 14 hours.[4]

Thursday, 20th of December

At sunrise they entered a port between the island of Santo Tomas and the Cabo de Carabata,[5] and anchored. This port is very beautiful, and would hold all the ships in Christendom. The entrance appears impossible from the sea to those who have never entered, owing to some reefs of rocks which run from the mountainous cape almost to the island. They are not placed in a row, but one here, another there, some towards the sea, others near the land. It is therefore necessary to keep a good look-out for the entrances, which are wide and with a depth of 7 fathoms, so that they can be used without fear. Inside the reefs there is a depth of 12 fathoms. A ship can lie with a cable made fast, against any wind that blows. At the entrance of this port there is a channel on the west side of a sandy islet with 7 fathoms, and many trees on its shore. But there are many sunken rocks in that direction, and a look-out should be kept up until the port is reached. Afterwards there is no need to fear the greatest storm in the world. From this port a very beautiful cultivated valley is in sight, descending from the S.E.,

---

[1] Point and Island of Margot. (Navarrete.)
[2] *Camino* for *Cabo* (?). (Markham.)
[3] Mountain over Guarico. (Navarrete.)
[4] *Cf.* p. 178, note.
[5] Bahia de Acúl. (Navarrete.)

surrounded by such lofty mountains that they appear to reach the sky, and covered with green trees. Without doubt there are mountains here which are higher than the island of Tenerife, in the Canaries, which is held to be the highest yet known.[1] On this side of the island of Santo Tomas, at a distance of a league, there is another islet, and beyond it another, forming wonderful harbors; though a good look-out must be kept for sunken rocks. The Admiral also saw villages, and smoke made by them.

Friday, 21st of December

To-day the Admiral went with the ship's boats to examine this port, which he found to be such that it could not be equalled by any he had yet seen; but, having praised the others so much, he knew not how to express himself, fearing that he will be looked upon as one who goes beyond the truth. He therefore contents himself with saying that he had old sailors with him who say the same. All the praises he has bestowed on the other ports are true, and that this is better than any of them is equally true. He further says: "I have traversed the sea for 23 years,[2] without leaving it for any time worth counting, and I saw all the east and the west, going on the route of the north, which is England, and I have been to Guinea, but in all those parts there will not be found the perfection of harbors . . .[3] always found . . .[4] better than another, that I, with good care, saw written; and I again affirm it was well written, that this one is better than all others, and will hold all the ships of the world, secured with the

---

[1] This conjecture proved to be wrong. The Peak of Teneriffe is over 12,000 ft. high, while 10,300 ft. (Mt. Tina) is the highest elevation in Santo Domingo.

[2] This is one of the passages used to determine the date of Columbus's birth. By combining his statement quoted in the *Historie* of Ferdinand, ch. IV., that he went to sea at 14, and this assertion that he followed the sea steadily for 23 years, we find that he was 37 years old in 1484 or 1485, when he left Portugal and ceased sea-faring till 1492.

[3] A gap of a line and a half in the manuscript.

[4] Another gap in the manuscript.

oldest cables."[1]   From the entrance to the end is a distance of
five leagues.[2]   The Admiral saw some very well cultivated
lands, although they are all so, and he sent two of the boat's
crew to the top of a hill to see if any village was near, for none
could be seen from the sea.   At about ten o'clock that night,
certain Indians came in a canoe to see the Admiral and the
Christians, and they were given presents, with which they were
much pleased.   The two men returned, and reported that they
had seen a very large village at a short distance from the sea.[3]
The Admiral ordered the boat to row towards the place where
the village was until they came near the land, when he saw two
Indians, who came to the shore apparently in a state of fear.
So he ordered the boats to stop, and the Indians that were
with the Admiral were told to assure the two natives that no
harm whatever was intended to them.   Then they came nearer
the sea, and the Admiral nearer the land.   As soon as the
natives had got rid of their fear, so many came that they
covered the ground, with women and children, giving a thousand thanks.   They ran hither and thither to bring us bread
made of *niames*, which they call *ajes*, which is very white and
good, and water in calabashes, and in earthen jars made like
those of Spain, and everything else they had and that they
thought the Admiral could want, and all so willingly and
cheerfully that it was wonderful.   "It cannot be said that,
because what they gave was worth little, therefore they gave
liberally, because those who had pieces of gold gave as freely
as those who had a calabash of water; and it is easy to know
when a thing is given with a hearty desire to give."   These
are the Admiral's words.   "These people have no spears nor
any other arms, nor have any of the inhabitants of the whole

---

[1] The mutilation of the text makes this passage difficult.   The third line
literally is, "and I saw all the east [or perhaps better the Levant, *el Levante*]
and the west which means the way to England," etc.   After the second gap
read: "better than the other which I with proper caution tried to describe."
After "world," read: "and [is] enclosed so that the oldest cable of the ship
would hold it fast."

[2] The distance is six miles.   (Navarrete.)

[3] Acúl.   (*Id.*)

island, which I believe to be very large. They go naked as
when their mothers bore them, both men and women. In
Juana and the other islands the women wear a small clout of
cotton in front, with which to cover their private parts, as large
as the flap of a man's breeches, especially after they have passed
the age of twelve years, but here neither old nor young do so.
Also, the men in the other islands jealously hide their women
from the Christians, but here they do not." The women
have very beautiful bodies, and they were the first to come
and give thanks to Heaven, and to bring what they had,
especially things to eat, such as bread of *ajes*, nuts,[1]
and four or five kinds of fruits, some of which the Admiral
ordered to be preserved, to be taken to the Sovereigns. He
says that the women did not do less in other ports before they
were hidden; and he always gave orders that none of his
people should annoy them; that nothing should be taken
against their wills, and that everything that was taken should
be paid for. Finally, he says that no one could believe that
there could be such good-hearted people, so free to give,
anxious to let the Christians have all they wanted, and, when
visitors arrived, running to bring everything to them.

Afterwards the Admiral sent six Christians to the village
to see what it was like, and the natives showed them all the
honor they could devise, and gave them all they had; for no
doubt was any longer entertained that the Admiral and all his
people had come from Heaven; and the same was believed by
the Indians who were brought from the other islands, although
they had now been told what they ought to think. When the
six Christians had gone, some *canoas* came with people to ask
the Admiral to come to their village when he left the place
where he was. *Canoa* is a boat in which they navigate, some
large and others small. Seeing that this village of the chief
was on the road, and that many people were waiting there
for him, the Admiral went there; but, before he could depart,
an enormous crowd came to the shore, men, women, and chil-

[1] *Gonze avellanada.* The interpretation of the French translators is
followed. The word *gonze* is not given in the dictionaries.

dren, crying out to him not to go, but to stay with them. The
messengers from the other chief, who had come to invite him,
were waiting with their canoes, that he might not go away,
but come to see their chief, and so he did. On arriving where
the chief was waiting for him with many things to eat, he ordered that all the people should sit down, and that the food
should be taken to the boats, where the Admiral was, on the
sea-shore. When he saw that the Admiral had received what
he sent, all or most of the Indians ran to the village, which
was near, to bring more food, parrots, and other things they
had, with such frankness of heart that it was marvellous. The
Admiral gave them glass beads, brass trinkets, and bells: not
because they asked for anything in return, but because it
seemed right, and, above all, because he now looked upon them
as future Christians, and subjects of the Sovereigns, as much
as the people of Castile. He further says that they want
nothing except to know the language and be under governance;
for all they may be told to do will be done without any contra-
diction. The Admiral left this place to go to the ships, and
the people, men, women, and children, cried out to him not
to go, but remain with them. After the boats departed,
several canoes full of people followed after them to the ship,
who were received with much honor, and given to eat. There
had also come before another chief from the west, and many
people even came swimming, the ship being over a good half-
league from the shore. I sent certain persons to the chief,
who had gone back, to ask him about these islands. He
received them very well, and took them to his village, to give
them some large pieces of gold. They arrived at a large river,
which the Indians crossed by swimming. The Christians
were unable, so they turned back. In all this district there
are very high mountains which seem to reach the sky, so that
the mountain in the island of Tenerife appears as nothing
in height and beauty, and they are all green with trees. Between them there are very delicious valleys, and at the end
of this port, to the south, there is a valley so large that the end
of it is not visible, though no mountains intervene, so that it

seems to be 15 or 20 leagues long. A river flows through it, and it is all inhabited and cultivated, and as green as Castile in May or June; but the night contains 14 hours, the land being so far north. This port is very good for all the winds that can blow, being enclosed and deep, and the shores peopled by a good and gentle race without arms or evil designs. Any ship may lie within it without fear that other ships will enter at night to attack her, because, although the entrance is over two leagues wide, it is protected by reefs of rocks which are barely awash; and there is only a very narrow channel through the reef, which looks as if it had been artificially made, leaving an open door by which ships may enter. In the entrance there are 7 fathoms of depth up to the shore of a small flat island, which has a beach fringed with trees. The entrance is on the west side, and a ship can come without fear until she is close to the rock. On the N.W. side there are three islands, and a great river a league from the cape on one side of the port. It is the best harbor in the world, and the Admiral gave it the name of Puerto de la Mar de Santo Tomas, because to-day it was that Saint's day. The Admiral called it a sea, owing to its size.

Saturday, 22nd of December

At dawn the Admiral made sail to shape a course in search of the islands which the Indians had told him contained much gold, some of them having more gold than earth. But the weather was not favorable, so he anchored again, and sent away the boat to fish with a net. The lord of that land,[1] who had a place near there, sent a large canoe full of people, including one of his principal attendants, to invite the Admiral to come with the ships to his land, where he would give him all he wanted. The chief sent, by this servant, a girdle which, in-

---

[1] "This king was the great lord and king Guacanagarí, one of the five great kings and lordships of this island." Las Casas, I. 389.

o

stead of a purse,[1] had attached to it a mask with two large ears made of beaten gold, the tongue, and the nose. These people are very open-hearted, and whatever they are asked for they give most willingly; while, when they themselves ask for anything, they do so as if receiving a great favor. So says the Admiral. They brought the canoe alongside the boat, and gave the girdle to a boy; then they came on board with their mission. It took a good part of the day before they could be understood. Not even the Indians who were on board understood them well, because they have some differences of words for the names of things. At last their invitation was understood by signs. The Admiral determined to start to-morrow, although he did not usually sail on a Sunday, owing to a devout feeling, and not on account of any superstition whatever. But in the hope that these people would become Christians through the willingness they show, and that they will be subjects of the Sovereigns of Castile, and because he now holds them to be so, and that they may serve with love, he wished and endeavored to please them. Before leaving, to-day, the Admiral sent six men to a large village three leagues to the westward, because the chief had come the day before and said that he had some pieces of gold. When the Christians arrived, the secretary of the Admiral, who was one of them, took the chief by the hand. The Admiral had sent him, to prevent the others from imposing upon the Indians. As the Indians are so simple, and the Spaniards so avaricious and grasping, it does not suffice that the Indians should give them all they want in exchange for a bead or a bit of glass, but the Spaniards would take everything without any return at all. The Admiral always prohibits this, although, with the exception of gold, the things given by the Indians are of little value. But the Admiral, seeing the simplicity of the Indians,

---

[1] "This girdle was of fine jewellery work, like misshapen pearls, made of fish-bones white and colored interspersed, like embroidery, so sewed with a thread of cotton and by such delicate skill that on the reverse side it looked like delicate embroidery, although all white, which it was a pleasure to see." Las Casas, I. 389. From this we learn that wampum belts were in use among the Indians of Española.

and that they will give a piece of gold in exchange for six beads, gave the order that nothing should be received from them unless something had been given in exchange. Thus the chief took the secretary by the hand and led him to his house, followed by the whole village, which was very large. He made his guests eat, and the Indians brought them many cotton fabrics, and spun-cotton in skeins. In the afternoon the chief gave them three very fat geese and some small pieces of gold. A great number of people went back with them, carrying all the things they had got by barter, and they also carried the Spaniards themselves across streams and muddy places. The Admiral ordered some things to be given to the chief, and both he and his people were very well satisfied, truly believing that the Christians had come from Heaven, so that they considered themselves fortunate in beholding them. On this day more than 120 canoes came to the ships, all full of people, and all bringing something, especially their bread and fish, and fresh water in earthen jars. They also brought seeds of good kinds, and there was a grain which they put into a porringer of water and drank it. The Indians who were on board said that this was very wholesome.

Sunday, 23rd of December

The Admiral could not go with the ships to that land whither he had been invited by the chief, because there was no wind. But he sent, with the three messengers who were waiting for the boats, some people, including the secretary. While they were gone, he sent two of the Indians he had on board with him to the villages which were near the anchorage. They returned to the ship with a chief, who brought the news that there was a great quantity of gold in that island of Española, and that people from other parts came to buy it. They said that here the Admiral would find as much as he wanted. Others came, who confirmed the statement that there was much gold in the island, and explained the way it was collected.

The Admiral understood all this with much difficulty; nevertheless, he concluded that there was a very great quantity in those parts, and that, if he could find the place whence it was got, there would be abundance; and, if not, there would be nothing. He believed there must be a great deal, because, during the three days that he had been in that port, he had got several pieces of gold, and he could not believe that it was brought from another land. "Our Lord, who holds all things in his hands, look upon me, and grant what shall be for his service." These are the Admiral's words. He says that, according to his reckoning, a thousand people had visited the ship, all of them bringing something. Before they come alongside, at a distance of a crossbow-shot, they stand up in the canoe with what they bring in their hands, crying out, "Take it! take it!" He also reckoned that 500 came to the ship swimming, because they had no canoes, the ship being near a league from the shore. Among the visitors, five chiefs had come, sons of chiefs, with all their families of wives and children, to see the Christians. The Admiral ordered something to be given to all, because such gifts were all well employed. "May our Lord favor me by his clemency, that I may find this gold, I mean the mine of gold, which I hold to be here, many saying that they know it." These are his words. The boats arrived at night, and said that there was a grand road as far as they went, and they found many canoes, with people who went to see the Admiral and the Christians, at the mountain of Caribatan. They held it for certain that, if the Christmas festival was kept in that port,[1] all the people of the island would come, which they calculated to be larger than England.[2] All the people went with them to the village,[3] which they said was the largest, and the best laid out with streets, of any they had seen. The Admiral says it is part of the Punta Santa,[4] almost three leagues S.E. The canoes go

---

[1] Port of Guarico. (Navarrete.)

[2] This estimate was far too great. The island is about one-third the size of Great Britain and one-half the size of England.

[3] Guarico.

[4] It is now called San Honorato. (Navarrete.)

very fast with paddles; so they went ahead to apprise the *Cacique*, as they call the chief. Up to that time the Admiral had not been able to understand whether Cacique meant king or governor. They also have another name for a great man — *Nitayno;* [1] but it was not clear whether they used it for lord, or governor, or judge. At last the cacique came to them, and joined them in the square, which was clean-swept, as was all the village. The population numbered over 2,000 men. This king did great honor to the people from the ship, and every inhabitant brought them something to eat and drink. Afterwards the king gave each of them cotton cloths such as women wear, with parrots for the Admiral, and some pieces of gold. The people also gave cloths and other things from their houses to the sailors; and as for the trifles they got in return, they seemed to look upon them as relics. When they wanted to return in the afternoon, he asked them to stay until the next day, and all the people did the same. When they saw that the Spaniards were determined to go, they accompanied them most of the way, carrying the gifts of the cacique on their backs as far as the boats, which had been left at the mouth of the river.

Monday, 24th of December

Before sunrise the Admiral got under way with the land-breeze. Among the numerous Indians who had come to the ship yesterday, and had made signs that there was gold in the island, naming the places whence it was collected, the Admiral noticed one who seemed more fully informed, or who spoke with more willingness, so he asked him to come with the Christians and show them the position of the gold mines. This Indian has a companion or relation with him, and among other places they mentioned where gold was found, they named Cipango, which they called Civao.[2] Here they said that there

---

[1] "The fact is that *Cacique* was the word for king, and *Nitayno* for knight and principal lord." Las Casas, I. 394.

[2] The similarity between the names and the report of gold made Columbus particularly confident of the identification.

was a great quantity of gold, and that the cacique carried banners of beaten gold. But they added that it was very far off to the eastward.

Here the Admiral addresses the following words to the Sovereigns: "Your Highnesses may believe that there is no better nor gentler people in the world. Your Highnesses ought to rejoice that they will soon become Christians, and that they will be taught the good customs of your kingdom. A better race there cannot be, and both the people and the lands are in such quantity that I know not how to write it. I have spoken in the superlative degree of the country and people of Juana, which they call Cuba, but there is as much difference between them and this island and people as between day and night. I believe that no one who should see them could say less than I have said, and I repeat that the things and the great villages of this island of Española, which they call Bohio, are wonderful. All here have a loving manner and gentle speech, unlike the others, who seem to be menacing when they speak. Both men and women are of good stature, and not black. It is true that they all paint, some with black, others with other colors, but most with red. I know that they are tanned by the sun, but this does not affect them much. Their houses and villages are pretty, each with a chief, who acts as their judge, and who is obeyed by them. All these lords use few words, and have excellent manners. Most of their orders are given by a sign with the hand, which is understood with surprising quickness." All these are the words of the Admiral.

He who would enter the sea of Santo Tomé [1] ought to stand for a good league across the mouth to a flat island in the middle, which was named La Amiga, [2] pointing her head towards it. When the ship is within a stone's-throw of it the course should be altered to make for the eastern shore, leaving the west side, and this shore, and not the other, should be kept on board, because a great reef runs out from the west, and even beyond that there are three sunken rocks. This reef comes within a

[1] Entrance of the Bay of Acúl. (Navarrete.)
[2] Isla de Ratos. (*Id.*)

lombard-shot of the Amiga island. Between them there are seven fathoms at least, with a gravelly bottom. Within, a harbor will be found large enough for all the ships in the world, which would be there without need of cables. There is another reef, with sunken rocks, on the east side of the island of Amiga, which are extensive and run out to sea, reaching within two leagues of the cape. But it appeared that between them there was an entrance, within two lombard-shots of Amiga, on the west side of Monte Caribatan, where there was a good and very large port.[1]

Tuesday, 25th of December. Christmas

Navigating yesterday, with little wind, from Santo Tomé to Punta Santa, and being a league from it, at about eleven o'clock at night the Admiral went down to get some sleep, for he had not had any rest for two days and a night. As it was calm, the sailor who steered the ship thought he would go to sleep, leaving the tiller in charge of a boy.[2] The Admiral had forbidden this throughout the voyage, whether it was blowing or whether it was calm. The boys were never to be entrusted with the helm. The Admiral had no anxiety respecting sand-banks and rocks, because, when he sent the boats to that king on Sunday, they had passed to the east of Punta Santa at least three leagues and a half, and the sailors had seen all the coast, and the rocks there are from Punta Santa, for a distance of three leagues to the E.S.E. They saw the course that should be taken, which had not been the case before, during this voyage. It pleased our Lord that, at twelve o'clock at night, when the Admiral had retired to rest, and when all had fallen asleep, seeing that it was a dead calm and the sea like glass, the tiller being in the hands of a boy, the current carried the ship on one of the sand-banks. If it had not been night the bank could have been seen, and the surf on it could be heard for a good league. But the ship ran upon

---

[1] Puerto Frances. (Navarrete.)
[2] Perhaps better "a young common sailor."

it so gently that it could scarcely be felt. The boy, who felt
the helm and heard the rush of the sea, cried out. The Admiral at once came up, and so quickly that no one had felt that
the ship was aground. Presently the master of the ship,[1]
whose watch it was, came on deck. The Admiral ordered him
and others to launch the boat, which was on the poop, and lay
out an anchor astern. The master, with several others, got
into the boat, and the Admiral thought that they did so with
the object of obeying his orders. But they did so in order to
take refuge with the caravel, which was half a league to leeward. The caravel would not allow them to come on board,
acting judiciously, and they therefore returned to the ship;
but the caravel's boat arrived first. When the Admiral saw
that his own people fled in this way, the water rising and the
ship being across the sea, seeing no other course, he ordered
the masts to be cut away and the ship to be lightened as much
as possible, to see if she would come off. But, as the water
continued to rise, nothing more could be done. Her side fell
over across the sea, but it was nearly calm. Then the timbers
opened, and the ship was lost.[2] The Admiral went to the caravel to arrange about the reception of the ship's crew, and as a
light breeze was blowing from the land, and continued during
the greater part of the night, while it was unknown how far
the bank extended, he hove her to until daylight. He then
went back to the ship, inside the reef; first having sent a boat
on shore with Diego de Arana of Cordova, alguazil of the fleet,
and Pedro Gutierrez, gentleman of the king's bedchamber,
to inform the king, who had invited the ships to come on the
previous Saturday. His town was about a league and a half
from the sand-bank. They reported that he wept when he

---

[1] The master, who was also the owner, of the Admiral's ship was Juan
de la Cosa of Santoña, afterwards well known as a draughtsman and pilot.
(Markham.)

[2] Rather, "Then the seams opened but not the ship." That is, the ship
was not stove. The word translated "seams" is *conventos*, which Las Casas,
I. 398, defines as *los vagos que hay entre costillas y costillas*. In this passage
he is using *costillas* not in the technical sense of *costillas de nao*, "ribs," but
in the sense of "planks," as in *costillas de cuba*, "barrel staves."

heard the news, and he sent all his people with large canoes to unload the ship. This was done, and they landed all there was between decks in a very short time. Such was the great promptitude and diligence shown by that king. He himself, with brothers and relations, was actively assisting as well in the ship as in the care of the property when it was landed, that all might be properly guarded. Now and then he sent one of his relations weeping to the Admiral, to console him, saying that he must not feel sorrow or annoyance, for he would supply all that was needed. The Admiral assured the Sovereigns that there could not have been such good watch kept in any part of Castile, for that there was not even a needle missing. He ordered that all the property should be placed by some houses which the king placed at his disposal, until they were emptied, when everything would be stowed and guarded in them. Armed men were placed round the stores to watch all night. "The king and all his people wept [says the Admiral]. They are a loving people, without covetousness, and fit for anything; and I assure your Highnesses that there is no better land nor people. They love their neighbors as themselves, and their speech is the sweetest and gentlest in the world, and always with a smile. Men and women go as naked as when their mothers bore them. Your Highnesses should believe that they have very good customs among themselves. The king is a man of remarkable presence, and with a certain self-contained manner that is a pleasure to see. They have good memories, wish to see everything, and ask the use of what they see." All this is written by the Admiral.

Wednesday, 26th of December

To-day, at sunrise, the king of that land came to the caravel *Niña*, where the Admiral was, and said to him, almost weeping, that he need not be sorry, for that he would give him all he had; that he had placed two large houses at the disposal of the Christians who were on shore, and that he would give more if they were required, and as many canoes as could load from the ship and discharge on shore, with as many people as

were wanted. This had all been done yesterday, without so
much as a needle being missed. "So honest are they," says the
Admiral, "without any covetousness for the goods of others,
and so above all was that virtuous king." While the Admiral
was talking to him, another canoe arrived from a different place,
bringing some pieces of gold, which the people in the canoe
wanted to exchange for a hawk's bell; for there was nothing
they desired more than these bells. They had scarcely come
alongside when they called and held up the gold, saying *Chuq
chuq* for the bells, for they are quite mad about them. After
the king had seen this, and when the canoes which came from
other places had departed, he called the Admiral and asked him
to give orders that one of the bells was to be kept for another
day, when he would bring four pieces of gold the size of a man's
hand. The Admiral rejoiced to hear this, and afterwards a
sailor, who came from the shore, told him that it was wonderful what pieces of gold the men on shore were getting in exchange for next to nothing. For a needle they got a piece of
gold worth two *castellanos*, and that this was nothing to what
it would be within a month. The king rejoiced much when he
saw that the Admiral was pleased. He understood that his
friend wanted much gold, and he said, by signs, that he knew
where there was, in the vicinity, a very large quantity; so
that he must be in good heart, for he should have as much as he
wanted. He gave some account of it, especially saying that in
Cipango, which they call Cibao,[1] it is so abundant that it is of
no value, and that they will bring it, although there is also
much more in the island of Española, which they call Bohio,
and in the province of Caritaba. The king dined on board the
caravel with the Admiral and afterwards went on shore, where
he received the Admiral with much honor. He gave him a
collation consisting of three or four kinds of *ajes*, with shrimps
and game, and other viands they have, besides the bread
they call *cazavi*.[2] He then took the Admiral to see some groves

---

[1] In reality Cibao was a part of Española.
[2] Made from the manioc roots or *ajes*. Cassava biscuit can be got to-day
at fancy grocery stores. It is rather insipid.

of trees near the houses, and they were accompanied by at least a thousand people, all naked. The lord had on a shirt and a pair of gloves, given to him by the Admiral, and he was more delighted with the gloves than with anything else. In his manner of eating, both as regards the high-bred air and the peculiar cleanliness he clearly showed his nobility. After he had eaten, he remained some time at table, and they brought him certain herbs, with which he rubbed his hands. The Admiral thought that this was done to make them soft, and they also gave him water for his hands. After the meal he took the Admiral to the beach. The Admiral then sent for a Turkish bow and a quiver of arrows, and took a shot at a man of his company, who had been warned. The chief, who knew nothing about arms, as they neither have them nor use them, thought this a wonderful thing. He, however, began to talk of those of Caniba, whom they call Caribes. They come to capture the natives, and have bows and arrows without iron, of which there is no memory in any of these lands, nor of steel, nor any other metal except gold and copper. Of copper the Admiral had only seen very little. The Admiral said, by signs, that the Sovereigns of Castile would order the Caribs to be destroyed, and that all should be taken with their hands tied together. He ordered a lombard and a hand-gun to be fired off, and seeing the effect caused by its force and what the shots penetrated, the king was astonished. When his people heard the explosion they all fell on the ground. They brought the Admiral a large mask, which had pieces of gold for the eyes and ears and in other parts, and this they gave, with other trinkets of gold that the same king had put on the head and round the neck of the Admiral, and of other Christians, to whom they also gave many pieces. The Admiral received much pleasure and consolation from these things, which tempered the anxiety and sorrow he felt at the loss of the ship. He knew our Lord had caused the ship to stop here, that a settlement might be formed. "From this," he says, "originated so many things that, in truth, the disaster was really a piece of good fortune. For it is certain that, if I had not lost the ship, I should have gone on without anchoring in this place, which is within a great bay, having two or three reefs of rock. I should not have left people in the country during this voyage, nor even, if I had desired to leave them, should I have been able to obtain so much information, nor such supplies and provisions for a fortress. And true it is that many people had asked me to give them leave to remain. Now I have given orders for a tower and a fort, both well built, and a large cellar, not because I believe that such defences will be necessary. I believe that with the force I have with me I could subjugate the whole island, which I believe to be larger than Portugal, and the population double.[1] But they are naked and without arms, and hopelessly timid. Still, it is advisable to build this tower, being so far from your Highnesses. The people may thus know the skill of the subjects of your Highnesses, and what they can do; and will obey them with love and fear. So they make preparations to build the fortress, with provision of bread and wine for more than a year, with seeds for sowing, the ship's boat, a caulker and carpenter, a gunner and cooper. Many among these men have a great desire to serve your Highnesses and to please me, by finding out where the mine is whence the gold is brought. Thus everything is got in readiness to begin the work. Above all, it was so calm that there was scarcely wind or wave when the ship ran aground." This is what the Admiral says; and he adds more to show that it was great good luck, and the settled design of God, that the ship should be lost in order that people might be left behind. If it had not been for the treachery of the master and his boat's crew, who were all or mostly his countrymen,[2] in neglecting to lay out the anchor so as to haul the ship off in obedience to the Admiral's orders, she would have been saved. In that case, the same knowledge of the land as has been gained in these days would not have been secured, for the Admiral always proceeded with

---

[1] In reality, three-quarters the size of Portugal.

[2] Juan de la Cosa, the master, was a native of Santoña, on the north coast of Spain. There were two other Santoña men on board, and several from the north coast. (Markham.)

the object of discovering, and never intended to stop more than a day at any one place, unless he was detained by the wind. Still, the ship was very heavy and unsuited for discovery. It was the people of Palos who obliged him to take such a ship, by not complying "with what they had promised to the King and Queen, namely, to supply suitable vessels for this expedition. This they did not do. Of all that there was on board the ship, not a needle, nor a board, nor a nail was lost, for she remained as whole as when she sailed, except that it was necessary to cut away and level down in order to get out the jars and merchandise, which were landed and carefully guarded." He trusted in God that, when he returned from Spain, according to his intention, he would find a tun of gold collected by barter by those he was to leave behind, and that they would have found the mine, and spices in such quantities that the Sovereigns would, in three years, be able to undertake and fit out an expedition to go and conquer the Holy Sepulchre. "With this in view," he says, "I protested to your Highnesses that all the profits of this my enterprise should be spent in the conquest of Jerusalem, and your Highnesses laughed and said that it pleased them, and that, without this, they entertained that desire." These are the Admiral's words.

Thursday, 27th of December

The king of that land came alongside the caravel at sunrise, and said that he had sent for gold, and that he would collect all he could before the Admiral departed; but he begged him not to go. The king and one of his brothers, with another very intimate relation, dined with the Admiral, and the two latter said they wished to go to Castile with him. At this time the news came that the caravel *Pinta* was in a river at the end of this island. Presently the cacique sent a canoe there, and the Admiral sent a sailor in it. For it was wonderful how devoted the cacique was to the Admiral. The necessity was now evident of hurrying on preparations for the return to Castile.

Friday, 28th of December

The Admiral went on shore to give orders and hurry on the work of building the fort, and to settle what men should remain behind.[1] The king, it would seem, had watched him getting into the boat, and quickly went into his house, dissimulating, sending one of his brothers to receive the Admiral, and conduct him to one of the houses that had been set aside for the Spaniards, which was the largest and best in the town. In it there was a couch made of palm matting, where they sat down. Afterward the brother sent an attendant to say that the Admiral was there, as if the king did not know that he had come. The Admiral, however, believed that this was a feint in order to do him honor more. The attendant gave the message, and the cacique came in great haste, and put a large soft piece of gold he had in his hand round the Admiral's neck. They remained together until the evening, arranging what had to be done.

Saturday, 29th of December

A very youthful nephew of the king came to the caravel at sunrise, who showed a good understanding and disposition. As the Admiral was always working to find out the origin of the gold, he asked everyone, for he could now understand somewhat by signs. This youth told him that, at a distance of four days' journey, there was an island to the eastward called Guarionex, and others called Macorix, Mayonic, Fuma, Cibao, and Coroay,[2] in which there was plenty of gold. The Admiral

[1] "He ordered then all his people to make great haste and the king ordered his vassals to help him and as an immense number joined with the Christians they managed so well and with such diligence that in a matter of ten days our stronghold was well made and as far as could be then constructed. He named it the City of Christmas (Villa de la Navidad) because he had arrived there on that day, and so to-day that harbor is called Navidad, although there is no memory that there even has been a fort or any building there, since it is overgrown with trees as large and tall as if fifty years had passed, and I have seen them." Las Casas, I. 408.

[2] These were not islands, but districts whose chiefs were called by the same names. Cf. Las Casas, I. 410.

wrote these names down, and now understood what had been said by a brother of the king, who was annoyed with him, as the Admiral understood. At other times the Admiral had suspected that the king had worked against his knowing where the gold had its origin and was collected, that he might not go away to barter in another part of the island. For there are such a number of places in this same island that it is wonderful. After nightfall the king sent a large mask of gold, and asked for a washhand basin and jug. The Admiral thought he wanted them for patterns to copy from, and therefore sent them.

Sunday, 30th of December

The Admiral went on shore to dinner, and came at a time when five kings had arrived, all with their crowns, who were subject to this king, named Guacanagari. They represented a very good state of affairs, and the Admiral says to the Sovereigns that it would have given them pleasure to see the manner of their arrival. On landing, the Admiral was received by the king, who led him by the arms to the same house where he was yesterday, where there were chairs, and a couch on which the Admiral sat. Presently the king took the crown off his head and put it on the Admiral's head, and the Admiral took from his neck a collar of beautiful beads of several different colors, which looked very well in all its parts, and put it on the king. He also took off a cloak of fine material, in which he had dressed himself that day, and dressed the king in it, and sent for some colored boots, which he put on his feet, and he put a large silver ring on his finger, because he had heard that he had admired greatly a silver ornament worn by one of the sailors. The king was highly delighted and well satisfied, and two of those kings who were with him came with him to where the Admiral was, and each gave him a piece of gold. At this time an Indian came and reported that it was two days since he left the caravel *Pinta* in a port to the eastward. The Admiral returned to the caravel, and Vicente Anes,[1] the cap-

---

[1] For Yañez. Vicente Yañez Pinzon.

tain, said that he had seen the rhubarb plant, and that they had it on the island Amiga, which is at the entrance of the sea of Santo Tomé, six leagues off, and that he had recognized the branches and roots.   They say that rhubarb forms small branches above ground, and fruit like green mulberries, almost dry, and the stalk, near the root, is as yellow and delicate as the best color for painting, and underground the root grows like a large pear.

Monday, 31st of December

To-day the Admiral was occupied in seeing that water and fuel were taken on board for the voyage to Spain, to give early notice to the Sovereigns, that they might despatch ships to complete the discoveries.   For now the business appeared to be so great and important that the Admiral was astonished.[1] He did not wish to go until he had examined all the land to the eastward, and explored the coast, so as to know the route to Castile, with a view to sending sheep and cattle.[2]   But as he had been left with only a single vessel, it did not appear prudent to encounter the dangers that are inevitable in making discoveries.   He complained that all this inconvenience had been caused by the caravel *Pinta* having parted company.

Tuesday, 1st of January, 1493

At midnight the Admiral sent a boat to the island Amiga to bring the rhubarb.   It returned at vespers with a bundle of it.   They did not bring more because they had no spade to dig it up with; it was taken to be shown to the Sovereigns. The king of that land said that he had sent many canoes for gold.   The canoe returned that had been sent for tidings of the *Pinta*, without having found her.   The sailor who went in

---

[1] Rather, "For now the business appeared to be so great and important that it was wonderful (said the Admiral) and he said he did not wish," etc.

[2] The first suggestion of systematic colonization in the New World.

the canoe said that twenty leagues from there he had seen a king who wore two large plates of gold on his head, but when the Indians in the canoe spoke to him he took them off. He also saw much gold on other people. The Admiral considered that the King Guacanagari ought to have prohibited his people from selling gold to the Christians, in order that it might all pass through his hands. But the king knew the places, as before stated, where there was such a quantity that it was not valued. The supply of spices also is extensive, and is worth more than pepper or manegueta.[1] He left instructions to those who wished to remain that they were to collect as much as they could.

Wednesday, 2nd of January

In the morning the Admiral went on shore to take leave of the King Guacanagari, and to depart from him in the name of the Lord. He gave him one of his shirts. In order to show him the force of the lombards, and what effect they had, he ordered one to be loaded and fired into the side of the ship that was on shore, for this was apposite to the conversation respecting the Caribs, with whom Guacanagari was at war. The king saw whence the lombard-shot came, and how it passed through the side of the ship and went far away over the sea. The Admiral also ordered a skirmish of the crews of the ships, fully armed, saying to the cacique that he need have no fear of the Caribs even if they should come. All this was done that the king might look upon the men who were left behind as friends, and that he might also have a proper fear of them. The king took the Admiral to dinner at the house where he was established, and the others who came with him. The Admiral strongly recommended to his friendship Diego de Arana, Pedro Gutierrez, and Rodrigo Escovedo, whom he left jointly as his lieutenants over the people who remained behind, that all might be well regulated and governed for the service of their Highnesses. The cacique showed much

---

[1] See note 2 under Jan. 9, p. 218.

P

love for the Admiral, and great sorrow at his departure, especially when he saw him go on board. A relation of that king said to the Admiral that he had ordered a statue of pure gold to be made, as big as the Admiral, and that it would be brought within ten days. The Admiral embarked with the intention of sailing presently, but there was no wind.

He left on that island of Española, which the Indians called Bohio, 39 men [1] with the fortress, and he says that they were great friends of Guacanagari. The lieutenants placed over them were Diego de Arana of Cordova, Pedro Gutierrez, keeper of the king's drawing-room, and servant of the chief butler, and Rodrigo de Escovedo, a native of Segovia, nephew of Fray Rodrigo Perez, with all the powers he himself received from the Sovereigns. He left behind all the merchandise which had been provided for bartering, which was much, that they might trade for gold. He also left the ship's boat, that they, most of them being sailors, might go, when the time seemed convenient, to discover the gold mine, in order that the Admiral, on his return, might find much gold. They were also to find a good site for a town, for this was not altogether a desirable port; especially as the gold the natives brought came from the east; also, the farther to the east the nearer to Spain. He also left seeds for sowing, and his officers, the alguazil and secretary, as well as a ship's carpenter, a caulker, a good gunner familiar with engineering (*que sabe bien de ingenios*), a cooper, a physician, and a tailor, all being seamen as well. [2]

Thursday, 3rd of January

The Admiral did not go to-day, because three of the Indians whom he had brought from the islands, and who had staid behind, arrived, and said that the others with their women

---

[1] The actual number was 44, according to the official list given in a document printed by Navarrete, which is a notice to the next of kin to apply for wages due, dated Burgos, December 20, 1507. Markham reproduces this list in his edition of Columbus's Journal.

[2] Las Casas gives the farewell speech of the Admiral to those who were left behind at Navidad. I. 415. It is translated in Thacher's *Columbus*, I. 632.

would be there at sunrise.[1] The sea also was rather rough, so that they could not land from the boat. He determined to depart to-morrow, with the grace of God. The Admiral said that if he had the caravel *Pinta* with him he could make sure of shipping a tun of gold, because he could then follow the coasts of these islands, which he would not do alone, for fear some accident might impede his return to Castile, and prevent him from reporting all he had discovered to the Sovereigns. If it was certain that the caravel *Pinta* would arrive safely in Spain with Martin Alonso Pinzon, he would not hesitate to act as he desired; but as he had no certain tidings of him, and as he might return and tell lies to the Sovereigns, that he might not receive the punishment he deserved for having done so much harm in having parted company without permission, and impeded the good service that might have been done, the Admiral could only trust in our Lord that he would grant favorable weather, and remedy all things.

Friday, 4th of January

At sunrise the Admiral weighed the anchor, with little wind, and turned her head N.W. to get clear of the reef, by another channel wider than the one by which he entered, which, with others, is very good for coming in front of the Villa de la Navidad, in all which the least depth is from 3 to 9 fathoms. These two channels run N.W. and S.E., and the reefs are long, extending from the Cabo Santo to the Cabo de Sierpe for more than six leagues, and then a good three leagues out to sea. At a league outside Cabo Santo there are not more than 8 fathoms of depth, and inside that cape, on the east side, there are many sunken rocks, and channels to enter between them. All this coast trends N.W. and S.E., and it is all beach, with the land very level for about a quarter of a league inland.

[1] "It is not known how many he took from this island but I believe he took some, and altogether he carried ten or twelve Indians to Castile according to the Portuguese History [Barros] and I saw them in Seville yet I did not notice nor do I recollect that I counted them." Las Casas, I. 419.

After that distance there are very high mountains, and the whole is peopled with a very good race, as they showed themselves to the Christians.   Thus the Admiral navigated to the east, shaping a course for a very high mountain, which looked like an island, but is not one, being joined to the mainland by a very low neck.   The mountain has the shape of a very beautiful tent.   He gave it the name of Monte Cristi.   It is due east of Cabo Santo, at a distance of 18 leagues.[1]   That day, owing to the light wind, they could not reach within six leagues of Monte Cristi.   He discovered four very low and sandy islets,[2] with a reef extending N.W. and S.E.   Inside, there is a large gulf,[3] which extends from this mountain to the S.E. at least twenty leagues,[4] which must all be shallow, with many sandbanks, and inside numerous rivers which are not navigable. At the same time the sailor who was sent in the canoe to get tidings of the *Pinta* reported that he saw a river [5] into which ships might enter.   The Admiral anchored at a distance of 6 leagues [6] from Monte Cristi, in 19 fathoms, and so kept clear of many rocks and reefs.   Here he remained for the night. The Admiral gives notice to those who would go to the Villa de la Navidad that, to make Monte Cristi, he should stand off the land two leagues, etc.   (But as the coast is now known it is not given here.)   The Admiral concluded that Cipango was in that island, and that it contained much gold, spices, mastic, and rhubarb.

Saturday, 5th of January

At sunrise the Admiral made sail with the land-breeze, and saw that to the S.S.E.[7] of Monte Cristi, between it and an

---

[1] It is N. 80° E. 70 leagues.   (Navarrete.)
[2] Los siete Hermanos.   (*Id.*)
[3] Bahia de Manzanillo.   (*Id.*)
[4] Should be S.W. three leagues.
[5] Rio Tapion, in the Bahia de Manzanillo.   (***Id.***)
[6] A mistake for three leagues.   (*Id.*)
[7] Should be W.S.W.   (*Id.*)

island, there seemed to be a good port to anchor in that night. He shaped an E.S.E. course, afterward S.S.E., for six leagues round the high land, and found a depth of 17 fathoms, with a very clean bottom, going on for three leagues with the same soundings. Afterwards it shallowed to 12 fathoms up to the promontory of the mountain, and off the promontory, at one league, the depth of 9 fathoms was found, the bottom clean, and all fine sand. The Admiral followed the same course until he came between the mountain and the island,[1] where he found $3\frac{1}{2}$ fathoms at low water, a very good port, and here he anchored.[2] He went in the boat to the islet, where he found remains of fire and footmarks, showing that fishermen had been there. Here they saw many stones painted in colors, or a quarry of such stones, very beautifully worked by nature, suited for the building of a church or other public work, like those he found on the island of San Salvador. On this islet he also found many plants of mastic. He says that this Monte Cristi is very fine and high, but accessible, and of a very beautiful shape, all the land round it being low, a very fine plain, from which the height rises, looking at a distance like an island disunited from other land. Beyond the mountain, to the east, he saw a cape at a distance of 24 miles, which he named Cabo del Becerro,[3] whence to the mountain for two leagues there are reefs of rocks, though it appeared as if there were navigable channels between them. It would, however, be advisable to approach in daylight, and to send a boat ahead to sound. From the mountain eastward to Cabo del Becerro, for four leagues, there is a beach, and the land is low, but the rest is very high, with beautiful mountains and some cultivation. Inland, a chain of mountains runs N.E. and S.W., the most beautiful he had seen, appearing like the hills of Cordova. Some other very lofty mountains appear in the distance toward the south and S.E., and very extensive green valleys with large rivers: all this in such quantity that he did not believe

---

[1] Isla Cabra.   (Navarrete.)
[2] Anchorage of Monte Cristi.   (*Id.*)
[3] Punta Rucia.   (*Id.*)

he had exaggerated a thousandth part. Afterwards he saw, to the eastward of the mountain, a land which appeared like that of Monte Cristi in size and beauty. Further to the east and N.E. there is land which is not so high, extending for some hundred miles or near it.

Sunday, 6th of January

That port is sheltered from all winds, except north and N.W., and these winds seldom blow in this region. Even when the wind is from those quarters, shelter may be found near the islet in 3 or 4 fathoms. At sunrise the Admiral made sail to proceed along the coast, the course being east, except that it is necessary to look out for several reefs of stone and sand, within which there are good anchorages, with channels leading to them. After noon it blew fresh from the east. The Admiral ordered a sailor to go to the mast-head to look out for reefs, and he saw the caravel *Pinta* coming, with the wind aft, and she joined the Admiral.[1] As there was no place to anchor, owing to the rocky bottom, the Admiral returned for ten leagues to Monte Cristi, with the *Pinta* in company. Martin Alonso Pinzon came on board the caravel *Niña*, where the Admiral was, and excused himself by saying that he had parted company against his will, giving reasons for it. But the Admiral says that they were all false; and that on the night when Pinzon parted company he was influenced by pride and covetousness. He could not understand whence had come the insolence and disloyalty with which Pinzon had treated him during the voyage. The Admiral had taken no notice, because he did not wish to give place to the evil works of Satan, who desired to impede the voyage. It appeared that one of the Indians, who had been put on board the caravel by the Admiral with others, had said that there was much gold in an island called Baneque, and, as Pinzon's vessel was light and swift, he determined to go there, parting company with

[1] Martin Alonso Pinzon had slipped away during the night of November 21.

the Admiral, who wished to remain and explore the coasts of Juana and Española, with an easterly course. When Martin Alonso arrived at the island of Baneque[1] he found no gold. He then went to the coast of Española, on information from the Indians that there was a great quantity of gold and many mines in that island of Española, which the Indians call Bohio. He thus arrived near the Villa de Navidad, about 15 leagues from it, having then been absent more than twenty days, so that the news brought by the Indians was correct, on account of which the King Guacanagari sent a canoe, and the Admiral put a sailor on board; but the *Pinta* must have gone before the canoe arrived. The Admiral says that the *Pinta* obtained much gold by barter, receiving large pieces the size of two fingers in exchange for a needle. Martin Alonso took half, dividing the other half among the crew. The Admiral then says: "Thus I am convinced that our Lord miraculously caused that vessel to remain here, this being the best place in the whole island to form a settlement, and the nearest to the gold mines." He also says that he knew of another great island, to the south of the island of Juana, in which there is more gold than in this island, so that they collect it in bits the size of beans, while in Española they find the pieces the size of grains of wheat. They call that island Yamaye.[2] The Admiral also heard of an island further east, in which there were only women, having been told this by many people.[3] He was also informed that Yamaye and the island of Española were ten days' journey in a canoe from the mainland, which would be about 70 or 80 leagues, and that there the people wore clothes.[4]

---

[1] Here probably the island of Iguana Grande.

[2] Jamaica.

[3] On this myth see below under January 15.

[4] It is remarkable that this report, which refers probably to Yucatan and to the relatively high state of culture of the Mayas, drew no further comment from Columbus. From our point of view it ought to have made a much greater impression than we have evidence that it did; from his point of view that he was off Asia it was just what was to be expected and so is recorded without comment.

Monday, 7th of January

This day the Admiral took the opportunity of calking the caravel, and the sailors were sent to cut wood. They found mastic and aloes in abundance.

Tuesday, 8th of January

As the wind was blowing fresh from the east and S.E., the Admiral did not get under way this morning. He ordered the caravel to be filled up with wood and water and with all other necessaries for the voyage. He wished to explore all the coast of Española in this direction. But those he appointed to the caravels as captains were brothers, namely, Martin Alonso Pinzon and Vicente Anes. They also had followers who were filled with pride and avarice, considering that all now belonged to them, and unmindful of the honor the Admiral had done them. They had not and did not obey his orders, but did and said many unworthy things against him; while Martin Alonso had deserted him from the 21st of November until the 6th of January without cause or reason, but from disaffection. All these things had been endured in silence by the Admiral in order to secure a good end to the voyage. He determined to return as quickly as possible, to get rid of such an evil company, with whom he thought it necessary to dissimulate, although they were a mutinous set, and though he also had with him many good men; for it was not a fitting time for dealing out punishment.

The Admiral got into the boat and went up the river [1] which is near, toward the S.S.W. of Monte Cristi, a good league. This is where the sailors went to get fresh water for the ships. He found that the sand at the mouth of the river, which is very large and deep, was full of very fine gold, and in astonishing quantity. The Admiral thought that it was pul-

---

[1] This is the large river Yaqui, which contains much gold in its sand. It was afterwards called the Santiago. (Navarrete.)

verized in the drift down the river, but in a short time he found
many grains as large as lentils, while there was a great deal of
the fine powder.

As the fresh water mixed with the salt when it entered the
sea, he ordered the boat to go up for the distance of a stone's-
throw. They filled the casks from the boat, and when they
went back to the caravel they found small bits of gold stick-
ing to the hoops of the casks and of the barrel. The Admiral
gave the name of Rio del Oro to the river.[1] Inside the bar it
is very deep, though the mouth is shallow and very wide.
The distance to the Villa de la Navidad is 17 leagues,[2] and there
are several large rivers on the intervening coast, especially
three which probably contain much more gold than this one,
because they are larger. This river is nearly the size of the
Guadalquivir at Cordova, and from it to the gold mines the
distance is not more than 20 leagues.[3] The Admiral further
says that he did not care to take the sand containing gold,
because their Highnesses would have it all as their property
at their town of Navidad; and because his first object was now
to bring the news and to get rid of the evil company that was
with him, whom he had always said were a mutinous set.

Wednesday, 9th of January

The Admiral made sail at midnight, with the wind S.E.,
and shaped an E.N.E. course, arriving at a point named
Punta Roja,[4] which is 60 miles[5] east of Monte Cristi, and anchored under its lee three hours before nightfall. He did not
venture to go out at night, because there are many reefs, until
they are known. Afterwards, if, as will probably be the case,
channels are found between them, the anchorage, which is

[1] Afterwards called the Rio de Santiago. (Navarrete.)
[2] This should be 8 leagues. (Id.)
[3] Las Casas, I. 429, says the distance to the mines was not 4 leagues.
[4] Punta Isabelica. (Id.)
[5] The distance is 10½ leagues, or 42 of the Italian miles used by Columbus.
(Id.)

good and well sheltered, will be profitable. The country between Monte Cristi and this point where the Admiral anchored
is very high land, with beautiful plains, the range running east
and west, all green and cultivated, with numerous streams of
water, so that it is wonderful to see such beauty. In all this
country there are many turtles, and the sailors took several
when they came on shore to lay their eggs at Monte Cristi,
as large as a great wooden buckler.

On the previous day, when the Admiral went to the Rio
del Oro, he saw three mermaids,[1] which rose well out of the sea;
but they are not so beautiful as they are painted, though to
some extent they have the form of a human face. The Admiral says that he had seen some, at other times, in Guinea,
on the coast of the Manequeta.[2]

The Admiral says that this night, in the name of our Lord,
he would set out on his homeward voyage without any further
delay whatever, for he had found what he sought, and he did
not wish to have further cause of offence with Martin Alonso
until their Highnesses should know the news of the voyage
and what had been done. Afterwards he says, "I will not
suffer the deeds of evil-disposed persons, with little worth,
who, without respect for him to whom they owe their positions, presume to set up their own wills with little ceremony."

[1] The mermaids [Spanish, "sirens"] of Columbus are the *manatis*, or
sea-cows, of the Caribbean Sea and great South American rivers. They are
now scarcely ever seen out at sea. Their resemblance to human beings,
when rising in the water, must have been very striking. They have small
rounded heads, and cervical vertebrae which form a neck, enabling the
animal to turn its head about. The fore limbs also, instead of being pectoral
fins, have the character of the arm and hand of the higher mammalia. These
peculiarities, and their very human way of suckling their young, holding
it by the forearm, which is movable at the elbow-joint, suggested the idea
of mermaids. The congener of the *manati*, which had been seen by Columbus on the coast of Guinea, is the *dugong*. (Markham.)

[2] Las Casas has "on the coast of Guinea where manequeta is gathered"
(I. 430). *Amomum Melequeta*, an herbaceous, reedlike plant, three to
five feet high, is found along the coast of Africa, from Sierra Leone to the
Congo. Its seeds were called "Grains of Paradise," or *maniguetta*, and the
coast alluded to by Columbus, between Liberia and Cape Palmas, was hence
called the Grain Coast. The grains were used as a condiment, like pepper,
and in making the spiced wine called *hippocras*. (Markham.)

Thursday, 10th of January

He departed from the place where he had anchored, and at sunset he reached a river, to which he gave the name of Rio de Gracia, three leagues to the S.E. He came to at the mouth,[1] where there is good anchorage on the east side. There is a bar with no more than two fathoms of water, and very narrow across the entrance. It is a good and well-sheltered port, except that there are many shipworms,[2] owing to which the caravel *Pinta*, under Martin Alonso, received a good deal of damage. He had been here bartering for 16 days, and got much gold, which was what Martin Alonso wanted. As soon as he heard from the Indians that the Admiral was on the coast of the same island of Española, and that he could not avoid him, Pinzon came to him. He wanted all the people of the ship to swear that he had not been there more than six days. But his treachery was so public that it could not be concealed. He had made a law that half of all the gold that was collected was his. When he left this port he took four men and two girls by force. But the Admiral ordered that they should be clothed and put on shore to return to their homes. "This," the Admiral says, "is a service of your Highnesses. For all the men and women are subjects of your Highnesses, as well in this island as in the others. Here, where your Highnesses already have a settlement, the people ought to be treated with honor and favor, seeing that this island has so much gold and such good spice-yielding lands."

Friday, 11th of January

At midnight the Admiral left the Rio de Gracia with the land-breeze, and steered eastward until he came to a cape

---

[1] Rio Chuzona chica. (Navarrete.)

[2] Reading *broma* ("shipworm") for *bruma* ("mist") in the sentence : *sino que tiene mucha bruma*. De la Roquette in the French translation gives *bruma* the meaning of "shipworm," supposing it to be a variant form of *broma*. The Italian translator of the letter on the fourth voyage took *broma* to be *bruma*, translated it *pruina e bruma*, and consequently had Columbus's ship injured by frost near Panama in April ! *Cf.* Thacher, *Christopher Columbus*, II. 625, 790.

named Belprado, at a distance of four leagues. To the S.E. is the mountain to which he gave the name of Monte de Plata,[1] eight leagues distant. Thence from the cape Belprado to E.S.E. is the point named Angel, eighteen leagues distant; and from this point to the Monte de Plata there is a gulf, with the most beautiful lands in the world, all high and fine lands which extend far inland. Beyond there is a range of high mountains running east and west, very grand and beautiful. At the foot of this mountain there is a very good port,[2] with 14 fathoms in the entrance. The mountain is very high and beautiful, and all the country is well peopled. The Admiral believed there must be fine rivers and much gold. At a distance of 4 leagues E.S.E. of Cabo del Angel there is a cape named Punta del Hierro,[3] and on the same course, 4 more leagues, a point is reached named Punta Seca.[4] Thence, 6 leagues further on, is Cabo Redondo,[5] and further on Cabo Frances, where a large bay [6] is formed, but there did not appear to be anchorage in it. A league further on is Cabo del Buen Tiempo, and thence, a good league S.S.E., is Cabo Tajado.[7] Thence, to the south, another cape was sighted at a distance of about 15 leagues. To-day great progress was made, as wind and tide were favorable. The Admiral did not venture to anchor for fear of the rocks, so he was hove-to all night.

Saturday, 12th of January

Towards dawn the Admiral filled and shaped a course to the east with a fresh wind, running 20 miles before daylight,

[1] So called because the summit is always covered with white or silver clouds. Las Casas, I. 432. A monastery of Dominicans was afterwards built on Monte de Plata, in which Las Casas began to write his history of the Indies in the year 1527. Las Casas, IV. 254. (Markham.)

[2] Puerto de Plata, where a flourishing seaport town was afterwards established; founded by Ovando in 1502. It had fallen to decay in 1606. (Markham.)

[3] Punta Macuris. The distance is 3, not 4 leagues. (Navarrete.)

[4] Punta Sesua. The distance is only one league. (Id.)

[5] Cabo de la Roca. It should be 5, not 6 leagues. (Id.)

[6] Bahia Escocesa. (Id.)

[7] Las Casas says that none of these names remained even in his time. I. 432.

and in two hours afterwards 24 miles. Thence he saw land to the south,[1] and steered towards it, distant 48 miles. During the night he must have run 28 miles N.N.E., to keep the vessels out of danger. When he saw the land, he named one cape that he saw Cabo de Padre y Hijo, because at the east point there are two rocks, one larger than the other.[2] Afterwards, at two leagues to the eastward, he saw a very fine bay between two grand mountains. He saw that it was a very large port with a very good approach; but, as it was very early in the morning, and as the greater part of the time it was blowing from the east, and then they had a N.N.W. breeze, he did not wish to delay any more. He continued his course to the east as far as a very high and beautiful cape, all of scarped rock, to which he gave the name of Cabo del Enamorado,[3] which was 32 miles to the east of the port named Puerto Sacro.[4] On rounding the cape, another finer and loftier point came in sight,[5] like Cape St. Vincent in Portugal, 12 miles east of Cabo del Enamorado. As soon as he was abreast of the Cabo del Enamorado, the Admiral saw that there was a great bay[6] between this and the next point, three leagues across, and in the middle of it a small island.[7] The depth is great at the entrance close to the land. He anchored here in twelve fathoms, and sent the boat on shore for water, and to see if intercourse could be opened with the natives, but they all fled. He also anchored to ascertain whether this was all one land with the island of Española, and to make sure that this was a gulf and not a channel, forming another island. He remained astonished at the great size of Española.

[1] This was the Peninsula of Samana. (Navarrete.)

[2] Isla Yazual. (*Id.*)

[3] Cabo Cabron, or Lover's Cape; the extreme N.E. point of the island, rising nearly 2000 feet above the sea. (Markham.)

[4] Puerto Yaqueron. (Navarrete.)

[5] Cabo Samana; called Cabo de San Theramo afterwards by Columbus. (Markham.)

[6] The Bay of Samana. (Navarrete.)

[7] Cayo de Levantados. (*Id.*)

Sunday, 13th of January

The Admiral did not leave the port, because there was no land-breeze with which to go out. He wished to shift to another better port, because this was rather exposed. He also wanted to wait, in that haven, the conjunction of the sun and moon, which would take place on the 17th of this month, and the opposition of the moon with Jupiter and conjunction with Mercury, the sun being in opposition to Jupiter, which is the cause of high winds. He sent the boat on shore to a beautiful beach to obtain yams for food. They found some men with bows and arrows, with whom they stopped to speak, buying two bows and many arrows from them. They asked one of them to come on board the caravel and see the Admiral; who says that he was very wanting in reverence, more so than any native he had yet seen.[1] His face was all stained with charcoal,[2] but in all parts there is the custom of painting the body different colors. He wore his hair very long, brought together and fastened behind, and put into a small net of parrots' feathers. He was naked, like all the others. The Admiral supposed that he belonged to the Caribs, who eat men,[3] and that the gulf he had seen yesterday formed this part of the land into an island by itself. The Admiral asked about the Caribs, and he pointed to the east, near at hand, which means that he saw the Admiral yesterday before he entered the bay. The Indian said there was much gold to the east, pointing to the poop of the caravel, which was a good size, meaning that there were pieces as large. He called gold *tuob*, and did not understand *caona*, as they call it in the first part of the island that was visited, nor *nozay*, the name in San Salvador and the other islands. Copper or a base gold is

---

[1] This should be, "who says that he was very ugly of countenance, more so than the others that he had seen."

[2] Las Casas says, I. 433, "Not charcoal but a certain dye they make from a certain fruit."

[3] Las Casas, I. 434, says there never were any cannibals in Española.

called *tuob* in Española.[1]   Of the island of Matinino this
Indian said that it was peopled by women without men,[2] and
that in it there was much *tuob*, which is gold or copper, and
that it is more to the east of Carib.[3]   He also spoke of the
island of Goanin,[4] where there was much *tuob*.   The Admiral
says that he had received notices of these islands from many
persons; that in the other islands the natives were in great
fear of the Caribs, called by some of them Caniba, but in Española Carib.   He thought they must be an audacious race,
for they go to all these islands and eat the people they can
capture.   He understood a few words, and the Indians who
were on board comprehended more, there being a difference
in the languages owing to the great distance between the
various islands.   The Admiral ordered that the Indian should
be fed, and given pieces of green and red cloth, and glass beads,
which they like very much, and then sent on shore.   He was
told to bring gold if he had any, and it was believed that he
had, from some small things he brought with him.   When the
boat reached the shore there were fifty-five men behind the
trees, naked, and with very long hair, as the women wear it
in Castile.   Behind the head they wore plumes of feathers
of parrots and other birds, and each man carried a bow.   The
Indian landed, and signed to the others to put down their
bows and arrows, and a piece of a staff, which is like . . .,[5]

[1] Las Casas, I. 434, says that a section in the northeastern part
of Española "was inhabited by a tribe which called themselves *Mazariges*
and others *Ciguayos* and that they spoke different languages from the
rest of the island. I do not remember if they differed from each other
in speech since so many years have passed, and to-day there is no one
to inquire of, although I have talked many times with both genera-
tions; but more than fifty years have gone by."   The Ciguayos, he adds,
were called so because they wore their hair long as women do in Castile.   This passage shows that Las Casas was writing this part of his
history a half-century after he went first to Española, which was in 1502,
with Ovando.

[2] See p. 226, note 4, under Jan. 15.

[3] Porto Rico.   (Navarrete.)

[4] Las Casas, I. 434, says that Guanin was not the name of an island, but
the word for a kind of base gold.

[5] A gap in the original manuscript.

very heavy, carried instead of a sword.[1] As soon as they came
to the boat the crew landed, and began to buy the bows and
arrows and other arms, in accordance with an order of the
Admiral. Having sold two bows, they did not want to give
more, but began to attack the Spaniards, and to take hold of
them. They were running back to pick up their bows and
arrows where they had laid them aside, and took cords in
their hands to bind the boat's crew. Seeing them rushing
down, and being prepared — for the Admiral always warned
them to be on their guard — the Spaniards attacked the
Indians, and gave one a slash with a knife in the buttocks,
wounding another in the breast with an arrow. Seeing that
they could gain little, although the Christians were only seven
and they numbered over fifty, they fled, so that none were
left, throwing bows and arrows away.[2] The Christians
would have killed many, if the pilot, who was in command,
had not prevented them. The Spaniards presently returned
to the caravel with the boat. The Admiral regretted the affair
for one reason, and was pleased for another. They would
have fear of the Christians, and they were no doubt an ill-
conditioned people, probably Caribs, who eat men. But the
Admiral felt alarm lest they should do some harm to the 39
men left in the fortress and town of Navidad, in the event
of their coming here in their boat. Even if they are not
Caribs, they are a neighboring people, with similar habits,
and fearless, unlike the other inhabitants of the island, who are
timid, and without arms. The Admiral says all this, and adds
that he would have liked to have captured some of them.
He says that they lighted many smoke signals, as is the custom
in this island of Española.

[1] Las Casas, I. 435, has, "and as word of a palm-tree board which is very
hard and very heavy, not sharp but blunt, about two fingers thick everywhere, with which as it is hard and heavy like iron, although a man has a
helmet on his head they will crush his skull to the brain with one blow."
[2] "This was the first fight that there was in all the Indies and when
the blood of the Indians was shed." Las Casas, I. 436.

Monday, 14th of January

This evening the Admiral wished to find the houses of the Indians and to capture some of them, believing them to be Caribs. For, owing to the strong east and north-east winds and the heavy sea, he had remained during the day. Many Indians were seen on shore. The Admiral, therefore, ordered the boat to be sent on shore, with the crew well armed. Presently the Indians came to the stern of the boat, including the man who had been on board the day before, and had received presents from the Admiral. With him there came a king, who had given to the said Indian some beads in token of safety and peace for the boat's crew. This king, with three of his followers, went on board the boat and came to the caravel. The Admiral ordered them to be given biscuit and treacle to eat, and gave the chief a red cap, some beads, and a piece of red cloth. The others were also given pieces of cloth. The chief said that next day he would bring a mask made of gold, affirming that there was much here, and in Carib [1] and Matinino.[2] They afterwards went on shore well satisfied.

The Admiral here says that the caravels were making much water, which entered by the keel; and he complains of the caulkers at Palos, who caulked the vessels very badly, and ran away when they saw that the Admiral had detected the badness of their work, and intended to oblige them to repair the defect. But, notwithstanding that the caravels were making much water, he trusted in the favor and mercy of our Lord, for his high Majesty well knew how much controversy there was before the expedition could be despatched from Castile, that no one was in the Admiral's favor save Him alone who knew his heart, and after God came your Highnesses, while all others were against him without any reason. He further says: "And this has been the cause that the royal crown of your Highnesses has not a hundred millions of revenue more

---

[1] Porto Rico. Navarrete says it is certain that the Indians called Porto Rico Isla de Carib.

[2] Probably Martinique or Guadeloupe. (Navarrete.)

Q

than after I entered your service, which is seven years ago in
this very month, the 20th of January.[1]   The increase will take
place from now onwards.   For the almighty God will remedy
all things." [2]   These are his words.

Tuesday, 15th of January

The Admiral now wished to depart, for there was nothing
to be gained by further delay, after these occurrences and the
tumult with the Indians.   To-day he had heard that all the
gold was in the district of the town of Navidad, belonging to
their Highnesses; and that in the island of Carib [3] there was
much copper, as well as in Matinino.   The intercourse at Carib
would, however, be difficult, because the natives are said to
eat human flesh.   Their island would be in sight from thence,
and the Admiral determined to go there, as it was on the route,
and thence to Matinino, which was said to be entirely peopled
by women, without men.[4]   He would thus see both islands, and

---

[1] By this calculation the Admiral entered the service of the Catholic
Sovereigns on January 20, 1486.   (Navarrete.)

[2] "What would he have said if he had seen the millions and millions
(*cuentos y millones*) that the sovereigns have received from his labors since
his death?"   Las Casas, I. 437.

[3] Porto Rico.

[4] Columbus had read in Marco Polo of the islands of MASCULIA and FEMI-
NINA in the Indian Seas and noted the passage in his copy.   See ch. XXXIII.
of pt. III. of Marco Polo.   On the other hand there is evidence for an indigenous Amazon myth in the New World.   The earliest sketch of American folk-lore ever made, that of the Friar Ramon Pane in 1497, preserved
in Ferdinand Columbus's *Historie* and in a condensed form in Peter
Martyr's *De Rebus Oceanicis* (Dec. I., lib. IX.), tells the story of the culture-
hero Guagugiona, who set forth from the cave, up to that time the home of
mankind, "with all the women in search of other lands and he came to
Matinino, where at once he left the women and went away to another country," etc., *Historie* (London ed., 1867), p. 188.   Ramon's name is erroneously given as Roman in the *Historie*.   On the Amazons in Venezuela, see
Oviedo, lib. XXV., cap. XIV.   It may be accepted that the Amazon myth
as given by Oviedo, from which the great river derived its name, River of
the Amazons, is a composite of an Arawak folk-tale like that preserved by
Ramon Pane overlaid with the details of the Marco Polo myth, which in
turn derives from the classical myth.

might take some of the natives. The Admiral sent the boat on shore, but the king of that district had not come, for his village was distant. He, however, sent his crown of gold, as he had promised; and many other natives came with cotton, and bread made from yams, all with their bows and arrows. After the bartering was finished, four youths came to the caravel. They appeared to the Admiral to give such a clear account of the islands to the eastward, on the same route as the Admiral would have to take, that he determined to take them to Castile with him. He says that they had no iron nor other metals; at least none was seen, but it was impossible to know much of the land in so short a time, owing to the difficulty with the language, which the Admiral could not understand except by guessing, nor could they know what was said to them, in such a few days. The bows of these people are as large as those of France or England. The arrows are similar to the darts of the natives who have been met with previously, which are made of young canes, which grow very straight, and a yard and a half or two yards in length. They point them with a piece of sharp wood, a span and a half long, and at the end some of them fix a fish's tooth, but most of them anoint it with an herb.[1] They do not shoot as in other parts, but in a certain way which cannot do much harm. Here they have a great deal of fine and long cotton, and plenty of mastic. The bows appeared to be of yew, and there is gold and copper. There is also plenty of *aji*,[2] which is their pepper, which is more valuable than pepper, and all the people eat nothing else, it being very wholesome. Fifty caravels might be annually loaded with it from Española. The Admiral says that he found a great deal of weed in this bay, the same as was met with at sea when he came on this discovery. He therefore

---

[1] *Y los mas le ponen allí yerba,* " and the most of them put on poison." The description of these arrows corresponds exactly with that given by Sir E. im Thurn of the poisoned arrows of the Indians of Guiana, which still have " adjustable wooden tips smeared with poison, which are inserted in the socket at the end of a reed shaft." *Among the Indians of Guiana,* p. 242.

[2] Capsicum. (Markham.)

supposed that there were islands to the eastward, in the direction of the position where he began to meet with it; for he considers it certain that this weed has its origin in shallow water near the land, and, if this is the case, these Indies must be very near the Canary Islands. For this reason he thought the distance must be less than 400 leagues.

Wednesday, 16th of January

They got under way three hours before daylight, and left the gulf, which was named Golfo de las Flechas,[1] with the land-breeze. Afterwards there was a west wind, which was fair to go to the island of Carib on an E.N.E. course. This was where the people live of whom all the natives of the other islands are so frightened, because they roam over the sea in canoes without number, and eat the men they can capture. The Admiral steered the course indicated by one of the four Indians he took yesterday in the Puerto de las Flechas. After having sailed about 64 miles, the Indians made signs that the island was to the S.E.[2] The Admiral ordered the sails to be trimmed for that course, but, after having proceeded on it for two leagues, the wind freshened from a quarter which was very favorable for the voyage to Spain. The Admiral had noticed that the crew were downhearted when he deviated from the direct route home, reflecting that both caravels were leaking badly, and that there was no help but in God. He therefore gave up the course leading to the islands, and shaped a direct course for Spain E.N.E. He sailed on this course, making 48 miles, which is 12 leagues, by sunset. The Indians said that by that route they would fall in with the island of Matinino, peopled entirely by women without men, and the Admiral wanted very much to take five or six of them to the Sovereigns. But he doubted whether the Indians understood

[1] Gulf of the Arrows. This was the Bay of Samana, into which the river Yuna flows. (Navarrete.)

[2] Porto Rico. It would have been distant about 30 leagues. (Navarrete.)

the route well, and he could not afford to delay, by reason of
the leaky condition of the caravels. He, however, believed the
story, and that, at certain seasons, men came to them from
the island of Carib, distant ten or twelve leagues. If males
were born, they were sent to the island of the men; and if
females, they remained with their mothers.[1] The Admiral
says that these two islands cannot have been more than 15
or 20 leagues to the S.E. from where he altered course, the
Indians not understanding how to point out the direction.
After losing sight of the cape, which was named San Theramo,[2]
which was left 16 leagues to the west, they went for 12 leagues
E.N.E. The weather was very fine.

Thursday, 17th of January

The wind went down at sunset yesterday, the caravels
having sailed 14 glasses, each a little less than half-an-hour.
at 4 miles an hour, making 28 miles. Afterwards the wind
freshened, and they ran all that watch, which was 10 glasses.
Then another six until sunrise at 8 miles an hour, thus making
altogether 84 miles, equal to 21 leagues, to the E.N.E., and
until sunset 44 miles, or 11 leagues, to the east. Here a
booby[3] came to the caravel, and afterwards another. The
Admiral saw a great deal of gulf-weed.

Friday, 18th of January

During the night they steered E.S.E., with little wind, for
40 miles, equal to 10 leagues, and then 30 miles, or 7½ leagues,
until sunrise. All day they proceeded with little wind to
E.N.E. and N.E. by E., more or less, her head being sometimes

---

[1] "The sons remain with their mothers till the age of fourteen when they
go to join their fathers in their separate abode." Marco Polo, pt. iii.,
ch. xxxiii. Cf. p. 226, note 4.

[2] Now called Cabod el Engaño, the extreme eastern point of Española.
It had the same name when Las Casas wrote. (Markham.)

[3] Alcatraz.

north and at others N.N.E., and, counting one with the other, they made 60 miles, or 15 leagues. There was little weed, but yesterday and to-day the sea appeared to be full of tunnies. The Admiral believed that from there they must go to the tunny-fisheries of the Duke, of Conil and Cadiz.[1] He also thought they were near some islands, because a frigate-bird [2] flew round the caravel, and afterwards went away to the S.S.E. He said that to the S.E. of the island of Española were the islands of Carib, Matinino, and many others.

Saturday, 19th of January

During the night they made good 56 miles N.N.E., and 64 N.E. by N. After sunrise they steered N.E. with the wind fresh from S.W., and afterwards W.S.W. 84 miles, equal to 21 leagues. The sea was again full of small tunnies. There were boobies, frigate-birds, and terns.[3]

Sunday, 20th of January

It was calm during the night, with occasional slants of wind, and they only made 20 miles to the N.E. After sunrise they went 11 miles S.E., and then 36 miles N.N.E., equal to 9 leagues. They saw an immense quantity of small tunnies, the air very soft and pleasant, like Seville in April or May,

---

[1] The *almadrabas*, or tunny fisheries of Rota, near Cadiz, were inherited by the Duke, as well as those of Conil, a little fishing town 6 leagues east of Cadiz. (Markham.)

[2] *Un pescado* (a fish), called the *rabiforcado*. For *un pescado*, we should probably read *una ave pescadora*, and translate : a fishing bird, called *rabiforcado*. See entry for September 29 and note.

[3] *Alcatraces, rabos de juncos*, and *rabiforcados* : boobies, boatswain-birds, and frigate-birds. The translator has not been consistent in selecting English equivalents for these names. In the entry of January 18 *rabiforcado* is frigate-bird; in that of January 19 *rabo de junco* is frigate-bird; in that of January 21 *rabo de junco* is boatswain-bird. September 14 *garjao* is the tern, while on January 19 the *rabiforcado* is the tern. On these birds, see notes 11, 12, 13, and 20. See also Oviedo, *Historia General y natural de las Indias*, lib. XIV., cap. I., for descriptions of these birds.

and the sea, for which God be given many thanks, always very smooth. Frigate-birds, sandpipers,[1] and other birds were seen.

Monday, 21st of January

Yesterday, before sunset, they steered N.E. b. E., with the wind east, at the rate of 8 miles an hour until midnight, equal to 56 miles. Afterwards they steered N.N.E. 8 miles an hour, so that they made 104 miles, or 26 leagues, during the night N.E. by N. After sunrise they steered N.N.E. with the same wind, which at times veered to N.E., and they made good 88 miles in the eleven hours of daylight, or 21 leagues: except one that was lost by delay caused by closing with the *Pinta* to communicate. The air was colder, and it seemed to get colder as they went further north, and also that the nights grew longer owing to the narrowing of the sphere. Many *boatswain-birds* and terns [2] were seen, as well as other birds but not so many fish, perhaps owing to the water being colder. Much weed was seen.

Tuesday, 22nd of January

Yesterday, after sunset, they steered N.N.E. with an east wind. They made 8 miles an hour during five glasses, and three before the watch began, making eight glasses, equal to 72 miles, or 18 leagues. Afterwards they went N.E. by N. for six glasses, which would be another 18 miles. Then, during four glasses of the second watch N.E. at six miles an hour, or three leagues. From that time to sunset, for eleven glasses, E.N.E. at 6 leagues an hour,[3] equal to seven leagues. Then

---

[1] *Rabiforcados y pardelas.* Las Casas, I. 440, has *aves pardelas.* Talhausen, *Neues Spanisch-deutsches Wörterbuch*, defines *pardelas* as *Peters-vogel*, *i.e.*, petrel.

[2] *Rabos de juncos y pardelas.* The translator vacillates between sandpipers and terns in rendering *pardelas*. *Cf.* January 28 and 31, but as has just been noted "petrels" is the proper word.

[3] An error of the transcriber for miles. Each glass being half-an-hour, going six miles an hour, they would have made 33 miles or 8¼ leagues in five hours and a half. (Navarrete.)

E.N.E. until 11 o'clock, 32 miles. Then the wind fell, and they made no more during that day. The Indians swam about. They saw boatswain-birds and much weed.

Wednesday, 23rd of January

To-night the wind was very changeable, but, making the allowances applied by good sailors, they made 84 miles, or 21 leagues, N.E. by N. Many times the caravel *Niña* had to wait for the *Pinta*, because she sailed badly when on a bowline, the mizzen being of little use owing to the weakness of the mast. He says that if her captain, that is, Martin Alonso Pinzon, had taken the precaution to provide her with a good mast in the Indies, where there are so many and such excellent spars, instead of deserting his commander from motives of avarice, he would have done better. They saw many boatswain-birds and much weed. The heavens have been clouded over during these last days, but there has been no rain. The sea has been as smooth as a river, for which many thanks be given to God. After sunrise they went free, and made 30 miles, or 7½ leagues N.E. During the rest of the day E.N.E. another 30 miles.

Thursday, 24th of January

They made 44 miles, or 11 leagues, during the night, allowing for many changes in the wind, which was generally N.E. After sunrise until sunset E.N.E. 14 leagues.

Friday, 25th of January

They steered during part of the night E.N.E. for 13 glasses, making 9½ leagues. Then N.N.E. 6 miles. The wind fell, and during the day they only made 28 miles E.N.E., or 7 leagues. The sailors killed a tunny and a very large shark, which was very welcome, as they now had nothing but bread and wine, and some yams from the Indies.

Saturday, 26th of January

This night they made 56 miles, or 14 leagues, E.S.E. After sunrise they steered E.S.E., and sometimes S.E., making 40 miles up to 11 o'clock. Afterwards they went on another tack, and then on a bowline, 24 miles, or 6 leagues, to the north, until night.

Sunday, 27th of January

Yesterday, after sunset, they steered N.E. and N.E. by N. at the rate of five miles an hour, which in thirteen hours would be 65 miles, or 16½ leagues. After sunrise they steered N.E. 24 miles, or 6 leagues, until noon, and from that time until sunset 3 leagues E.N.E.

Monday, 28th of January

All night they steered E.N.E. 36 miles, or 9 leagues. After sunrise until sunset E.N.E. 20 miles, or 5 leagues. The weather was temperate and pleasant. They saw boatswain-birds, sandpipers,[1] and much weed.

Tuesday, 29th of January

They steered E.N.E. 39 miles, or 9½ leagues, and during the whole day 8 leagues. The air was very pleasant, like April in Castile, the sea smooth, and fish they call *dorados*[2] came on board.

[1] Petrels.
[2] The English equivalent is dory, or gilthead.

Wednesday, 30th of January

All this night they made 6 leagues E.N.E., and in the day
S.E. by S. 13½ leagues. Boatswain-birds, much weed, and
many tunnies.

Thursday, 31st of January

This night they steered N.E. by N. 30 miles, and afterwards N.E. 35 miles, or 16 leagues. From sunrise to night
E.N.E. 13½ leagues. They saw boatswain-birds and terns.[1]

Friday, 1st of February

They made 16½ leagues E.N.E. during the night, and went
on the same course during the day 29¼ leagues. The sea very
smooth, thanks be to God.

Saturday, 2nd of February

They made 40 miles, or 10 leagues, E.N.E. this night. In
the daytime, with the same wind aft, they went 7 miles an
hour, so that in eleven hours they had gone 77 miles, or 9¼
leagues. The sea was very smooth, thanks be to God, and the
air very soft. They saw the sea so covered with weed that,
if they had not known about it before, they would have been
fearful of sunken rocks. They saw terns.[1]

Sunday, 3rd of February

This night, the wind being aft and the sea very smooth,
thanks be to God, they made 29 leagues. The North Star
appeared very high, as it does off Cape St. Vincent. The

[1] Petrels.

Admiral was unable to take the altitude, either with the astrolabe or with the quadrant, because the rolling caused by the waves prevented it. That day he steered his course E.N.E., going 10 miles an hour, so that in eleven hours he made 27 leagues.

Monday, 4th of February

During the night the course was N.E. by E., going twelve miles an hour part of the time, and the rest ten miles. Thus they made 130 miles, or 32 leagues and a half. The sky was very threatening and rainy, and it was rather cold, by which they knew that they had not yet reached the Azores. After sunrise the course was altered to east. During the whole day they made 77 miles, or 19¼ leagues.

Tuesday, 5th of February

This night they steered east, and made 55 miles, or 13½ leagues. In the day they were going ten miles an hour, and in eleven hours made 110 miles, or 27½ leagues. They saw sandpipers, and some small sticks, a sign that they were near land.

Wednesday, 6th of February

They steered east during the night, going at the rate of eleven miles an hour, so that in the thirteen hours of the night they made 143 miles, or 35¼ leagues. They saw many birds. In the day they went 14 miles an hour, and made 154 miles, or 38½ leagues; so that, including night and day, they made 74 leagues, more or less. Vicente Anes [1] said that they had left the island of Flores to the north and Madeira to the east. Roldan [2] said that the island of Fayal, or San Gregorio, was

---

[1] Vicente Yañez Pinzon.
[2] Later a rich citizen of the city of Santo Domingo, Española, where he was known as Roldan the pilot. Las Casas, I. 443.

to the N.N.E. and Puerto Santo to east. There was much weed.

Thursday, 7th of February

This night they steered east, going ten miles an hour, so that in thirteen hours they made 130 miles, or 32½ leagues. In the daytime the rate was eight miles an hour, in eleven hours 88 miles, or 22 leagues. This morning the Admiral found himself 65 leagues south of the island of Flores, and the pilot Pedro Alonso,[1] being further north, according to his reckoning, passed between Terceira and Santa Maria to the east, passing to windward of the island of Madeira, twelve leagues further north. The sailors saw a new kind of weed, of which there is plenty in the islands of the Azores.

Friday, 8th of February

They went three miles an hour to the eastward for some time during the night, and afterwards E.S.E., going twelve miles an hour. From sunrise to noon they made 27 miles, and the same distance from noon till sunset, equal to 13 leagues S.S.E.

Saturday, 9th of February

For part of this night they went 3 leagues S.S.E., and afterwards S. by E., then N.E. 5 leagues until ten o'clock in the forenoon, then 9 leagues east until dark.

Sunday, 10th of February

From sunset they steered east all night, making 130 miles, or 32½ leagues. During the day they went at the rate of nine

---

[1] The name is also written Peralonso Niño. He made one of the first voyages to the mainland of South America after the third voyage of Columbus. See Irving, *Companions of Columbus.* Bourne, *Spain in America,* p. 69.

waves, or she would otherwise have been swamped. An E.N.E. course was steered, and afterwards N.E. by E. for six hours, making 7½ leagues. The Admiral ordered that a pilgrimage should be made to Our Lady of Guadalupe,[1] carrying a candle of 6 lbs. of weight in wax, and that all the crew should take an oath that the pilgrimage should be made by the man on whom the lot fell. As many chick-peas were got as there were persons on board, and on one a cross was cut with a knife. They were then put into a cap and shaken up. The first who put in his hand was the Admiral, and he drew out the chick-pea with a cross, so the lot fell on him; and he was bound to go on the pilgrimage and fulfil the vow. Another lot was drawn, to go on pilgrimage to Our Lady of Loreto, which is in the march of Ancona, in the Papal territory, a house where Our Lady works many and great miracles.[2] The lot fell on a sailor of the port of Santa Maria, named Pedro de Villa, and the Admiral promised to pay his travelling expenses. Another pilgrimage was agreed upon, to watch for one night in Santa Clara at Moguer,[3] and have a mass said, for which they again used the chick-peas, including the one with a cross. The lot again fell on the Admiral. After this the Admiral and all the crew made a vow that, on arriving at the first land, they would all go in procession, in their shirts, to say their prayers in a church dedicated to Our Lady.

Besides these general vows made in common, each sailor made a special vow; for no one expected to escape, holding themselves for lost, owing to the fearful weather from which they were suffering. The want of ballast increased the danger of the ship, which had become light, owing to the consumption of the provisions and water. On account of the favorable

---

[1] The Virgin of Guadalupe was the patroness of Estremadura. As many of the early colonists went from Estremadura there came to be a good number of her shrines in Mexico. *Cf.* R. Ford, *Handbook for Spain,* index under "Guadalupe."

[2] A full account of the shrine at Loreto may be found in Addis and Arnold, *Catholic Dictionary,* under "Loreto."

[3] "This is the house where the sailors of the country particularly have their devotions." Las Casas, I. 446. Moguer was a village near Palos.

weather enjoyed among the islands, the Admiral had omitted to make provision for this need, thinking that ballast might be taken on board at the island inhabited by women, which he had intended to visit. The only thing to do was to fill the barrels that had contained wine or fresh water with water from the sea, and this supplied a remedy.

Here the Admiral writes of the causes which made him fear that he would perish, and of others that gave him hope that God would work his salvation, in order that such news as he was bringing to the Sovereigns might not be lost. It seemed to him that the strong desire he felt to bring such great news, and to show that all he had said and offered to discover had turned out true, suggested the fear that he would not be able to do so, and that each stinging insect would be able to thwart and impede the work. He attributes this fear to his little faith, and to his want of confidence in Divine Providence.

He was comforted, on the other hand, by the mercies of God in having vouchsafed him such a victory, in the discoveries he had made, and in that God had complied with all his desires in Castile, after much adversity and many misfortunes. As he had before put all his trust in God, who had heard him and granted all he sought, he ought now to believe that God would permit the completion of what had been begun, and ordain that he should be saved. Especially as he had freed him on the voyage out, when he had still greater reason to fear, from the trouble caused by the sailors and people of his company, who all with one voice declared their intention to return, and protested that they would rise against him.[1] But the eternal God gave him force and valor to withstand them all, and in many other marvellous ways had God shown his will in this voyage besides those known to their Highnesses. Thus he ought not to fear the present tempest, though his weakness and anxiety prevent him from giving tranquillity to his mind. He says further that it gave him great sorrow to think of the two sons he had left at their studies in Cordova, who would be left orphans,

[1] See page 108, note 1, and entry for October 10.

without father or mother,[1] in a strange land; while the Sovereigns would not know of the services he had performed in this voyage, nor would they receive the prosperous news which would move them to help the orphans. To remedy this, and that their Highnesses might know how our Lord had granted a victory in all that could be desired respecting the Indies,[2] and that they might understand that there were no storms in those parts, which may be known by the herbs and trees which grow even within the sea;[3] also that the Sovereigns might still have information, even if he perished in the storm, he took a parchment and wrote on it as good an account as he could of all he had discovered, entreating any one who might pick it up to deliver it to the Sovereigns. He rolled this parchment up in waxed cloth, fastened it very securely, ordered a large wooden barrel to be brought, and put it inside, so that no one else knew what it was. They thought that it was some act of devotion, and so he ordered the barrel to be thrown into the sea. Afterwards, in the showers and squalls, the wind veered to the west, and they went before it, only with the foresail, in a very confused sea, for five hours. They made 2½ leagues N.E. They had taken in the reefed mainsail, for fear some wave of the sea should carry all away.[4]

[1] As Beatriz Enriquez, the mother of Ferdinand, was still living, this passage has occasioned much perplexity. A glance at the corresponding passage, quoted in direct discourse from this entry in the Journal, in the *Historie* of Ferdinand, shows that the words "orphans without father or mother" were not in the original Journal, if we can trust this transcript. On the other hand, Las Casas, in his *Historia*, I. 447, where he used the original Journal and not the abridgment that has come down to us, has the words "*huerfanos de padre y madre en tierra estraña.*" It may be that Ferdinand noted the error of the original Journal and quietly corrected it.

[2] In Ferdinand's text nothing is said explicitly about the Indies.

[3] There is nothing corresponding to this in Ferdinand's extract from the Journal. Was this omission also a case of pious revision?

The Admiral thought that there could be no great storms in the countries he had discovered, because trees (mangroves) actually grew with their roots in the sea. The herbage on the beach nearly reached the waves, which does not happen when the sea is rough. (Markham.)

[4] Ferdinand Columbus has preserved in his life of his father the exact words of the Journal for the last two pages of the entry for February 14. The extract is given here to illustrate the character of the work of the epito-

Friday, 15th of February

Last night, after sunset, the sky began to clear towards the west, showing that the wind was inclined to come from

mizer who prepared the text of the Journal as it has come down to us. "I should have borne this fortune with less distress if my life alone had been in peril, since I am aware that I am in debt to the Most High Creator for my life and because at other times I have found myself so near to death that almost nothing remained but to suffer it. But what caused me boundless grief and trouble was the reflection that, now that Our Lord had been pleased to enlighten me with the faith and with the certainty of this undertaking in which he had already given me the victory, that just now, when our gainsayers were to be convinced and your Highnesses were to receive from me glory and enlargement of your high estate, the Divine Majesty should will to block it with my death. This last would have been more endurable if it did not involve that of the people I brought with me with the promise of a very prosperous issue. They seeing themselves in such a plight not only cursed their coming but even the fear or the restraint which after my persuasions prevented them from turning back from the way as many times they were resolved to do. And above all this my grief was redoubled at the vision before my eyes and at the recollection of two little sons that I had left at their studies in Cordova without succor in a strange land and without my having rendered (or at least without its being made manifest) the service for which one might trust that your Highnesses would remember them.

" And although on the one hand I was comforted by the faith that I had that Our Lord would never suffer a work which would highly exalt his Church, which at length after so much opposition and such labors I had brought to the last stage, to remain unaccomplished and that I should be broken; on the other hand, I thought that, either on account of my demerits or to prevent my enjoying so much glory in this world, it was his pleasure to take it away from me, and so while thus in perplexity I bethought myself of the venture of your Highnesses who even if I should die and the ship be lost, might find means of not losing a victory already achieved and that it might be possible in some way for the news of the success of my voyage to come to your ears; wherefore I wrote on a parchment with the brevity that the time demanded how I had discovered the lands that I had promised to, and in how many days; and the route I had followed; and the goodness of the countries, and the quality of their inhabitants and how they were the vassals of your Highnesses who had possession of all that had been found by me. This writing folded and sealed I directed to your Highnesses with the superscription or promise of a thousand ducats to him who should deliver it thus unopened, in order that, if some foreigners should find it, the truth of this superscription might prevent them from disposing of the information which was inside. And I straightway had a large cask brought and having wrapped the writing in a waxed cloth and put it into a kind of tart or cake of wax I placed it in the barrel which, stoutly hooped, I then threw into the sea. All believed that it was some act of devotion. Then because I thought it might

that quarter. The admiral added the bonnet [1] to the mainsail.
The sea was still very high, although it had gone down slightly.
They steered E.N.E., and went four miles an hour, which made
13 leagues during the eleven hours of the night. After sunrise
they sighted land. It appeared from the bows to bear E.N.E.
Some said it was the island of Madeira, others that it was the
rock of Cintra, in Portugal, near Lisbon. Presently the wind
headed to E.N.E., and a heavy sea came from the west, the
caravel being 5 leagues from the land. The Admiral found by
his reckoning that he was close to the Azores, and believed
that this was one of them. The pilots and sailors thought
it was the land of Castile.[2]

Saturday, 16th of February

All that night the Admiral was standing off and on to keep
clear of the land, which they now knew to be an island, sometimes standing N.E., at others N.N.E., until sunrise, when they
tacked to the south to reach the island, which was now concealed by a great mist. Another island was in sight from
the poop, at a distance of eight leagues. Afterwards, from
sunrise until dark, they were tacking to reach the land
against a strong wind and head-sea. At the time of repeat-
ing the Salve, which is just before dark, some of the men
saw a light to leeward, and it seemed that it must be on the
island they first saw yesterday. All night they were beating
to windward, and going as near as they could, so as to see some
way to the island at sunrise. That night the Admiral got a little
rest, for he had not slept nor been able to sleep since Wednesday, and he had lost the use of his legs from long exposure

not arrive safely and the ships were all the while approaching Castile I made
another package like that and placed it on the upper part of the poop in
order that if the ship should sink the barrel might float at the will of fate."

[1] The bonnet was a small sail usually cut to a third the size of the mizzen,
or a fourth of the mainsail. It was secured through eyelet-holes to the leech
of the mainsail, in the manner of a studding sail. (Navarrete.)

[2] On this day the Admiral dated the letter to Santangel, the escribano de
racion, which is given below on pp. 263–272.

to the wet and cold. At sunrise [1] he steered S.S.W., and reached the island at night, but could not make out what island it was, owing to the thick weather.

Monday, 18th of February

Yesterday, after sunset, the Admiral was sailing round the island, to see where he could anchor and open communications. He let go one anchor, which he presently lost, and then stood off and on all night.   After sunrise he again reached the north side of the island, where he anchored, and sent the boat on shore.   They had speech with the people, and found that it was the island of Santa Maria, one of the Azores.   They pointed out the port [2] to which the caravel should go.   They said that they had never seen such stormy weather as there had been for the last fifteen days, and they wondered how the caravel could have escaped.   They gave many thanks to God, and showed great joy at the news that the Admiral had discovered the Indies.   The Admiral says that his navigation had been very certain, and that he had laid his route down on the chart.   Many thanks were due to our Lord, although there had been some delay.   But he was sure that he was in the region of the Azores, and that this was one of them.   He pretended to have gone over more ground, to mislead the pilots and mariners who pricked off the charts, in order that he might remain master of that route to the Indies, as, in fact, he did. For none of the others kept an accurate reckoning, so that no one but himself could be sure of the route to the Indies.

Tuesday, 19th of February

After sunset three natives of the island came to the beach and hailed. The Admiral sent the boat, which returned with fowls and fresh bread.   It was carnival time, and they brought

---

[1] This was on Sunday, 17th of February.   (Navarrete.)
[2] The port of San Lorenzo.   (*Id.*)

other things which were sent by the captain of the island, named Juan de Castañeda, saying that he knew the Admiral very well, and that he did not come to see him because it was night, but that at dawn he would come with more refreshments, bringing with him three men of the boat's crew, whom he did not send back owing to the great pleasure he derived from hearing their account of the voyage. The Admiral ordered much respect to be shown to the messengers, and that they should be given beds to sleep in that night, because it was late, and the town was far off. As on the previous Thursday, when they were in the midst of the storm, they had made a vow to go in procession to a church of Our Lady as soon as they came to land, the Admiral arranged that half the crew should go to comply with their obligation to a small chapel, like a hermitage, near the shore; and that he would himself go afterwards with the rest. Believing that it was a peaceful land, and confiding in the offers of the captain of the island, and in the peace that existed between Spain and Portugal, he asked the three men to go to the town and arrange for a priest to come and say mass. The half of the crew then went in their shirts, in compliance with their vow. While they were at their prayers, all the people of the town, horse and foot, with the captain at their head, came and took them all prisoners. The Admiral, suspecting nothing, was waiting for the boat to take him and the rest to accomplish the vow. At 11 o'clock, seeing that they did not come back, he feared that they had been detained, or that the boat had been swamped, all the island being surrounded by high rocks. He could not see what had taken place, because the hermitage was round a point. He got up the anchor, and made sail until he was in full view of the hermitage, and he saw many of the horsemen dismount and get into the boat with arms. They came to the caravel to seize the Admiral. The captain stood up in the boat, and asked for an assurance of safety from the Admiral, who replied that he granted it; but, what outrage was this, that he saw none of his people in the boat? The Admiral added that they might come on board, and that he would do all that might be proper. The Admiral tried, with fair words, to get hold of this captain, that he might recover his own people, not considering that he broke faith by giving him security, because he had offered peace and security, and had then broken his word. The captain, as he came with an evil intention, would not come on board. Seeing that he did not come alongside, the Admiral asked that he might be told the reason for the detention of his men, an act which would displease the King of Portugal, because the Portuguese received much honor in the territories of the King of Castile, and were as safe as if they were in Lisbon. He further said that the Sovereigns had given him letters of recommendation to all the Lords and Princes of the world, which he would show the captain if he would come on board; that he was the Admiral of the Ocean Sea, and Viceroy of the Indies, which belonged to their Highnesses,[1] and that he would show the commissions signed with their signatures, and attested by their seals, which he held up from a distance. He added that his Sovereigns were in friendship and amity with the King of Portugal, and had ordered that all honor should be shown to ships that came from Portugal. Further, that if the captain did not surrender his people, he would still go on to Castile, as he had quite sufficient to navigate as far as Seville, in which case the captain and his followers would be severely punished for their offence. Then the captain and those with him replied that they did not know the King and Queen of Castile there, nor their letters, nor were they afraid of them, and they would give the Admiral to understand that this was Portugal, almost menacing him. On hearing this the Admiral was much moved, thinking that some cause of disagreement might have arisen between the two kingdoms during his absence, yet he could not endure that they should not be answered reasonably. Afterwards he turned to the captain,

---

[1] The incredulity of the Portuguese governor as to these assertions was natural. The title Admiral of the Ocean Sea was novel and this was the first time it was announced that Spain or any other European power had possessions in the Indies.

and said that he should go to the port with the caravel, and that all that had been done would be reported to the King his Lord. The Admiral made those who were in the caravel bear witness to what he said, calling to the captain and all the others, and promising that he would not leave the caravel until a hundred Portuguese had been taken to Castile, and all that island had been laid waste. He then returned to anchor in the port where he was first, the wind being very unfavorable for doing anything else.

Wednesday, 20th of February

The Admiral ordered the ship to be repaired, and the casks to be filled alongside for ballast. This was a very bad port, and he feared he might have to cut the cables. This was so, and he made sail for the island of San Miguel; but there is no good port in any of the Azores for the weather they then experienced, and there was no other remedy but to go to sea.

Thursday, 21st of February

Yesterday the Admiral left that island of Santa Maria for that of San Miguel, to see if a port could be found to shelter his vessel from the bad weather. There was much wind and a high sea, and he was sailing until night without being able to see either one land or the other, owing to the thick weather caused by wind and sea. The Admiral says he was in much anxiety, because he only had three sailors who knew their business, the rest knowing nothing of seamanship.[1] He was lying-to all that night, in great danger and trouble. Our Lord showed him mercy in that the waves came in one direction, for if there had been a cross sea they would have suffered much more. After sunrise the island of San Miguel was not in sight, so the Admiral determined to return to Santa Maria, to see if he could recover his people and boat, and the anchors and cables he had left there.

[1] Half the crew were still detained on shore.

The Admiral says that he was astonished at the bad weather he encountered in the region of these islands. In the Indies he had navigated throughout the winter without the necessity for anchoring, and always had fine weather, never having seen the sea for a single hour in such a state that it could not be navigated easily. But among these islands he had suffered from such terrible storms. The same had happened in going out as far as the Canary Islands, but as soon as they were passed there was always fine weather, both in sea and air. In concluding these remarks, he observes that the sacred theologians and wise men[1] said well when they placed the terrestrial paradise in the Far East, because it is a most temperate region. Hence these lands that he had now discovered must, he says, be in the extreme East.

Friday, 22nd of February

Yesterday the Admiral anchored off Santa Maria, in the place or port where he had first anchored. Presently a man came down to some rocks at the edge of the beach, signalling that they were not to go away. Soon afterwards the boat came with five sailors, two priests, and a scrivener. They asked for safety, and when it was granted by the Admiral, they came on board, and as it was night they slept on board, the Admiral showing them all the civility he could. In the morning they asked to be shown the authority of the Sovereigns of Castile, by which the voyage had been made. The Admiral felt that they did this to give some color of right to what they had done, and to show that they had right on their side. As they were unable to secure the person of the Admiral, whom they intended to get into their power when they came with the boat armed, they now feared that their game might not turn out so well, thinking, with some fear, of what the Admiral had threatened, and which he proposed to put into

---

[1] That the site of the Garden of Eden was to be found in the Orient was a common belief in the Middle Ages and later. *Cf.* the *Book of Sir John Mandeville*, ch. xxx.

execution. In order to get his people released, the Admiral displayed the general letter of the Sovereigns to all Princes and Lords, and other documents, and having given them of what he had, the Portuguese went on shore satisfied, and presently released all the crew and the boat. The Admiral heard from them that if he had been captured also, they never would have been released, for the captain said that those were the orders of the King his Lord.

Saturday, 23rd of February

Yesterday the weather began to improve, and the Admiral got under way to seek a better anchorage, where he could take in wood and stones for ballast; but he did not find one until the hour of compline.[1]

Sunday, 24th of February

He anchored yesterday in the afternoon, to take in wood and stones, but the sea was so rough that they could not land from the boat, and during the first watch it came on to blow from the west and S.W. He ordered sail to be made, owing to the great danger there is off these islands in being at anchor with a southerly gale, and as the wind was S.W. it would go round to south. As it was a good wind for Castile, he gave up his intention of taking in wood and stones, and shaped an easterly course until sunset, going seven miles an hour for six hours and a half, equal to 45½ miles. After sunset he made six miles an hour, or 66 miles in eleven hours, altogether 111 miles, equal to 28 leagues.

Monday, 25th of February

Yesterday, after sunset, the caravel went at the rate of five miles an hour on an easterly course, and in the eleven

[1] The last of the canonical hours of prayer, about nine in the evening.

hours of the night she made 65 miles, equal to $16\frac{1}{4}$ leagues. From sunrise to sunset they made another $16\frac{1}{2}$ leagues with a smooth sea, thanks be to God. A very large bird, like an eagle, came to the caravel.

Tuesday, 26th of February

Yesterday night the caravel steered her course in a smooth sea, thanks be to God. Most of the time she was going eight miles an hour, and made a hundred miles, equal to 25 leagues. After sunrise there was little wind and some rain-showers. They made about 8 leagues E.N.E.

Wednesday, 27th of February

During the night and day she was off her course, owing to contrary winds and a heavy sea. She was found to be 125 leagues from Cape St. Vincent, and 80 from the island of Madeira, 106 from Santa Maria. It was very troublesome to have such bad weather just when they were at the very door of their home.

Thursday, 28th of February

The same weather during the night, with the wind from south and S.E., sometimes shifting to N.E. and E.N.E., and it was the same all day.

Friday, 1st of March

To-night the course was E.N.E., and they made twelve leagues. During the day, $23\frac{1}{2}$ leagues on the same course.

Saturday, 2nd of March

The course was E.N.E., and distance made good 28 leagues during the night, and 20 in the day.

Sunday, 3rd of March

After sunset the course was east; but a squall came down, split all the sails, and the vessel was in great danger; but God was pleased to deliver them. They drew lots for sending a pilgrim in a shirt to Santa Maria de la Cinta at Huelva, and the lot fell on the Admiral. The whole crew also made a vow to fast on bread and water during the first Saturday after their arrival in port. They had made 60 miles before the sails were split. Afterwards they ran under bare poles, owing to the force of the gale and the heavy sea. They saw signs of the neighborhood of land, finding themselves near Lisbon.

Monday, 4th of March

During the night they were exposed to a terrible storm, expecting to be overwhelmed by the cross-seas, while the wind seemed to raise the caravel into the air, and there was rain and lightning in several directions. The Admiral prayed to our Lord to preserve them, and in the first watch it pleased our Lord to show land, which was reported by the sailors. As it was advisable not to reach it before it was known whether there was any port to which he could run for shelter, the Admiral set the mainsail, as there was no other course but to proceed, though in great danger. Thus God preserved them until daylight, though all the time they were in infinite fear and trouble. When it was light, the Admiral knew the land, which was the rock of Cintra, near the river of Lisbon, and he resolved to run in because there was nothing else to be done. So terrible was the storm, that in the village of Cascaes, at the mouth of the river, the people were praying for the little vessel all that morning. After they were inside, the people came off, looking upon their escape as a miracle. At the third hour they passed Rastelo, within the river of Lisbon, where they were told that such a winter, with so many storms, had never before been known, and that 25 ships had been lost in

Flanders, while others had been wind-bound in the river for four months. Presently the Admiral wrote to the king of Portugal, who was then at a distance of nine leagues, to state that the Sovereigns of Castile had ordered him to enter the ports of his Highness, and ask for what he required for payment, and requesting that the king would give permission for the caravel to come to Lisbon, because some ruffians, hearing that he had much gold on board, might attempt a robbery in an unfrequented port, knowing that they did not come from Guinea, but from the Indies.[1]

Tuesday, 5th of March

To-day the great ship of the King of Portugal was also at anchor off Rastelo, with the best provision of artillery and arms that the Admiral had ever seen. The master of her, named Bartolomé Diaz, of Lisbon, came in an armed boat to the caravel, and ordered the Admiral to get into the boat, to go and give an account of himself to the agents of the king and to the captain of that ship. The Admiral replied that he was the Admiral of the Sovereigns of Castile, and that he would not give an account to any such persons, nor would he leave the ship except by force, as he had not the power to resist. The master replied that he must then send the master of the caravel. The Admiral answered that neither the master nor any other person should go except by force, for if he allowed anyone to go, it would be as if he went himself; and that such was the custom of the Admirals of the Sovereigns of Castile, rather to die than to submit, or to let any of their people submit. The master then moderated his tone, and told the Admiral that if that was his determination he might do as he pleased. He, however, requested that he might be shown the letters of the Kings of Castile, if they were on board. The Admiral readily showed them, and the master returned to the

---

[1] On this day the Admiral probably wrote the postscript to his letter to Santangel written at sea on February 15.

ship and reported what had happened to the captain, named
Alvaro Dama. That officer, making great festival with
trumpets and drums, came to the caravel to visit the Admiral,
and offered to do all that he might require.[1]

Wednesday, 6th of March

As soon as it was known that the Admiral came from the
Indies, it was wonderful how many people came from Lisbon
to see him and the Indians, giving thanks to our Lord, and
saying that the heavenly Majesty had given all this to the
Sovereigns of Castile as a reward for their faith and their
great desire to serve God.

Thursday, 7th of March

To-day an immense number of people came to the caravel,
including many knights, and amongst them the agents of the
king, and all gave infinite thanks to our Lord for so wide an
increase of Christianity granted by our Lord to the Sovereigns of Castile; and they said that they received it because
their Highnesses had worked and labored for the increase of
the religion of Christ.

Friday, 8th of March

To-day the Admiral received a letter from the king of
Portugal,[2] brought by Don Martin de Noroña, asking him to

[1] Modern scholars have too hastily identified this Bartolomé Diaz with
the discoverer of the Cape of Good Hope. There is no evidence for this except
the identity of the name. Against the supposition are the facts that neither
Columbus, Las Casas, nor Ferdinand remark upon this meeting with the
most eminent Portuguese navigator of the time, and that this Diaz is a subordinate officer on this ship who is sent to summon Columbus to report to the
captain. That the great admiral of 1486–1487 would in 1493 be a simple
Patron on a single ship is incredible.

[2] João II.

visit him where he was, as the weather was not suitable for the departure of the caravel. He complied, to prevent suspicion, although he did not wish to go, and went to pass the night at Sacanben. The king had given orders to his officers that all that the Admiral, his crew, and the caravel were in need of should be given without payment, and that all the Admiral wanted should be complied with.

Saturday, 9th of March

To-day the Admiral left Sacanben, to go where the king was residing, which was at Valparaiso, nine leagues from Lisbon. Owing to the rain, he did not arrive until night. The king caused him to be received very honorably by the principal officers of his household; and the king himself received the Admiral with great favor, making him sit down, and talking very pleasantly. He offered to give orders that everything should be done for the service of the Sovereigns of Castile, and said that the successful termination of the voyage had given him great pleasure. He said further that he understood that, in the capitulation between the Sovereigns and himself, that conquest belonged to him.[1] The Admiral replied that he had not seen the capitulation, nor knew more than that the Sovereigns had ordered him not to go either to La Mina[2] or to any other port of Guinea, and that this had been ordered to be proclaimed in all the ports of Andalusia before he sailed. The king graciously replied that he held it for certain that there would be no necessity for any arbitrators. The Admiral was assigned as a guest to the Prior of Clato, who was the

[1] The treaty of Alcaçovas signed by Portugal September 8, 1479, and by Spain March 6, 1480. In it Ferdinand and Isabella relinquished all rights to make discoveries along the coast of Africa and retained of the African islands only the Canaries. The Spanish text is printed in *Alguns Documentos da Torre do Tombo* (Lisbon, 1892), pp. 45–46. See also Vignaud, *Toscanelli and Columbus*, pp. 61–64.

[2] "The Mine," more commonly El Mina, a station established on the Gold Coast by Diogo de Azambuja in 1482. The full name in Portuguese was S. Jorge da Mina, St. George of the Mine.

principal person in that place, and from whom he received many favors and civilities.

Sunday, 10th of March

To-day, after mass, the king repeated that if the Admiral wanted anything he should have it. He conversed much with the Admiral respecting his voyage, always ordering him to sit down, and treating him with great favor.

Monday, 11th of March

To-day the Admiral took leave of the king, who entrusted him with some messages to the Sovereigns, and always treating him with much friendliness.[1] He departed after dinner, Don

[1] The Portuguese historian Ruide Pina, in his *Cronica D'El Rey João*, gives an account of Columbus's meeting with the king which is contemporary. From his official position as chief chronicler and head of the national archives and from the details which he mentions it is safe to conclude that he was an eye-witness.

"In the following year, 1493, while the king was in the place of the Val do Paraiso which is above the Monastery of Sancta Maria das Vertudes, on account of the great pestilences which prevailed in the principal places in this district, on the sixth of March there arrived at Restello in Lisbon Christovam Colombo, an Italian who came from the discovery of the islands of Cipango and Antilia which he had accomplished by the command of the sovereigns of Castile from which land he brought with him the first specimens of the people, gold and some other things that they have; and he was entitled Admiral of them. And the king being informed of this, commanded him to come before him and he showed that he felt disgusted and grieved because he believed that this discovery was made within the seas and bounds of his lordship of Guinea which was prohibited and likewise because the said Admiral was somewhat raised from his condition and in the account of his affairs always went beyond the bounds of the truth and made this thing in gold, silver, and riches much greater than it was. The king was accused of negligence in withdrawing from him for not giving him credit and authority in regard to this discovery for which he had first come to make request of him. And although the king was urged to consent to have him slain there, since with his death the prosecution of this enterprise so far as the sovereigns of Castile were concerned would cease on account of the decease of the discoverer ; and that this could be done without suspicion if he consented and

Martin de Noroña being sent with him, and all the knights set
out with him, and went with him some distance, to do him
honor.   Afterwards he came to a monastery of San Antonio,
near a place called Villafranca, where the Queen was residing.
The Admiral went to do her reverence and to kiss her hand,
because she had sent to say that he was not to go without
seeing her.   The Duke [1] and the Marquis were with her, and
the Admiral was received with much honor.   He departed at
night, and went to sleep at Llandra.

Tuesday, 12th of March

To-day, as he was leaving Llandra to return to the caravel,
an esquire of the king arrived, with an offer that if he desired
to go to Castile by land, that he should be supplied with
lodgings, and beasts, and all that was necessary.   When the
Admiral took leave of him, he ordered a mule to be supplied
to him, and another for his pilot, who was with him, and he
says that the pilot received a present of twenty *espadines*.[2]
He said this that the Sovereigns might know all that was done.
He arrived on board the caravel that night.

ordered it, since as he was discourteous and greatly elated they could get
involved with him in such a way that each one of these his faults would
seem to be the true cause of his death; yet the king like a most God-fearing
prince not only forbade this but on the contrary did him honor and showed
him kindness and therewith sent him away."   *Collecçaõ de Livros Ineditos de
Historia Portugueza*, II. 178–179.   It will be noted that according to this
account Columbus said he had discovered Cipango and Antilia, a mythical
island which is represented on the maps of the fifteenth century, and that
Columbus is called Colombo his Italian name, and not Colom or Colon.

[1] This may have been her brother, the Duke of Bejar, afterwards King
Manoel.

[2] *Espadim :* a Portuguese gold piece coined by João II.   Las Casas,
I. 466, says: " 20 *Espadinos*, a matter of 20 ducats."   The Espadim contained 58 to 65 grains of gold.   W. C. Hazlitt, *Coinage of European Nations*,
sub voce.   King João II. gave Columbus's pilot almost exactly the sum
which Henry VII. gave to John Cabot, which was £10.   In the French
translation and the translation in J. B. Thacher's *Christopher Columbus*
the word *espadines* is erroneously taken to be Spanish and rendered
" *Épées*," and " small short swords."

Wednesday, 13th of March

To-day, at 8 o'clock, with the flood tide, and the wind N.N.W., the Admiral got under way and made sail for Seville.

Thursday, 14th of March

Yesterday, after sunset, a southerly course was steered, and before sunrise they were off Cape St. Vincent, which is in Portugal. Afterwards he shaped a course to the east for Saltes, and went on all day with little wind, " until now that the ship is off Furon."

Friday, 15th of March

Yesterday, after sunset, she went on her course with little wind, and at sunrise she was off Saltes. At noon, with the tide rising, they crossed the bar of Saltes, and reached the port which they had left on the 3rd of August of the year before.[1] The Admiral says that so ends this journal, unless it becomes necessary to go to Barcelona by sea, having received news that their Highnesses are in that city, to give an account of all his voyage which our Lord had permitted him to make, and saw fit to set forth in him. For, assuredly, he held with a firm and strong knowledge that His High Majesty made all things good, and that all is good except sin. Nor can he value or think of anything being done without His consent. "I know respecting this voyage," says the Admiral, "that he has miraculously shown his will, as may be seen from this journal, setting forth the numerous miracles that have been displayed in the voyage, and in me who was so long at the court of your Highnesses, working in opposition to and against the opinions of so many chief persons of your household, who were all

---

[1] Having been absent 225 days.

s

against me, looking upon this enterprise as folly. But I hope, in our Lord, that it will be a great benefit to Christianity, for so it has ever appeared." These are the final words of the Admiral Don Cristoval Colon respecting his first voyage to the Indies and their discovery.

LETTER FROM COLUMBUS TO LUIS DE SANTANGEL

INTRODUCTION

THIS letter, the earliest published narrative of Columbus's first voyage, was issued in Barcelona in April, 1493, not far from the time when the discoverer was received in state by the King and Queen. The *Escribano de Racion*, to whom it was addressed, was Luis de Santangel, who had deeply interested himself in the project of Columbus and had advanced money to enable Queen Isabella to meet the expenses of the voyage. He, no doubt, placed a copy in the hands of the printer. Only two printed copies of this Spanish letter, as it is called, have come down to us. One is a folio of the first imprint, discovered and reproduced in 1889. Of this the unique copy is in the Lenox Library in New York; its first page is reproduced in facsimile in this volume, by courteous permission of the authorities of the library. The other is a quarto of the second and slightly corrected imprint, first made known in 1852 and first reproduced in 1866. Facsimiles of both are given in Thacher's *Christopher Columbus*, II. 17–20 and 33–40.

Columbus sent a duplicate of this letter with some slight changes to Gabriel Sanxis (Spanish form, Sanchez), the treasurer of Aragon, from whose hands a copy came into the possession of Leander de Cosco, who translated it into Latin, April 29, 1493.

This Latin version was published in Rome, probably in May, 1493, and this issue was rapidly followed by reprints in Rome, Basel, Paris, and Antwerp. It is to this Latin version that the European world outside of Spain was indebted for its first knowledge of the new discoveries.

A poetical paraphrase in Italian by Giuliano Dati was published in Rome in June, 1493. This is reprinted in Major's *Select Letters of Columbus*. The first German edition of the letter was published in Strassburg in 1497.

In the years 1493–1497 the Santangel letter was printed twice in Spanish, and the duplicate of it, the Sanchez letter, was printed nine times in Latin, five times in Dati's Italian paraphrase, and once in German. Until the publication in 1571 of the *Historie*, the Italian translation of Ferdinand Columbus's biography of his father, which contains an abridgment of Columbus's *Journal*, these letters and the account in Peter Martyr's *Decades de Rebus Oceanicis*, were the only sources of information in regard to the first voyage accessible to the world at large. The translation here given is that contained in Quaritch's *The Spanish Letter of Columbus* (London, 1893), with a few minor changes in the wording. An English translation of the Latin or Sanchez letter may be found in the first edition of Major's *Select Letters of Columbus* (London, 1847). This version is reprinted in P. L. Ford's *Writings of Christopher Columbus*, New York, 1892. By an error in the title of the first edition, Rome, 1493, Sanchez's Christian name is given as Raphael.

The text of the Santangel letter published by Navarrete in 1825 was derived from a manuscript preserved in the Spanish Archives at Simancas. In 1858 the Brazilian scholar Varnhagen published an edition of the Sanchez letter from a manuscript discovered by him in Valencia. Neither of these manuscripts, however, has the authority of the first printed editions.

E. G. B.

Facsimile of the first page of the folio (first) edition of the Spanish text of Columbus's letter to Santangel, describing his first voyage, dated February 15, 1493. From the original (unique) in the New York Public Library (Lenox Building).

LETTER FROM COLUMBUS TO LUIS DE SANTANGEL

Sir: As I know that you will have pleasure from the great victory which our Lord hath given me in my voyage, I write you this, by which you shall know that in thirty-three days I passed over to the Indies with the fleet which the most illustrious King and Queen, our Lords, gave me; where I found very many islands peopled with inhabitants beyond number. And, of them all, I have taken possession for their Highnesses, with proclamation and the royal standard displayed; and I was not gainsaid. To the first which I found, I gave the name Sant Salvador, in commemoration of His High Majesty, who marvellously hath given all this: the Indians call it Guanaham.[1] The second I named the Island of Santa Maria de Concepcion, the third Ferrandina, the fourth, Fair Island,[2] the fifth La Isla Juana; and so for each one a new name. When I reached Juana, I followed its coast westwardly, and found it so large that I thought it might be mainland, the province of Cathay. And as I did not thus find any towns and villages on the sea-coast, save small hamlets with the people whereof I could not get speech, because they all fled away forthwith, I went on further in the same direction, thinking I should not miss of great cities or towns. And at the end of many leagues, seeing that there was no change, and that the coast was bearing me northwards, whereunto my desire was contrary, since the winter was already confronting us, I formed the purpose of making from thence to the South, and as the wind also blew against me, I determined not to wait for other weather and turned back as far as a port agreed

[1] Guanahani in the Journal; see entry covering October 11 and 12.
[2] The original text has Isla bella, which was a misprint for Isabella. *Cf.* Journal, October 20.

upon; from which I sent two men into the country to learn if there were a king, or any great cities. They travelled for three days, and found innumerable small villages and a numberless population, but nought of ruling authority; wherefore they returned.[1]   I understood sufficiently from other Indians whom I had already taken, that this land, in its continuousness, was an island;[2] and so I followed its coast eastwardly for a hundred and seven leagues as far as where it terminated; from which headland I saw another island to the east, eighteen leagues distant from this, to which I at once gave the name La Spañola.[3]   And I proceeded thither, and followed the northern coast, as with La Juana, eastwardly for a hundred and eighty-eight great leagues in a direct easterly course, as with La Juana. The which, and all the others, are most fertile to an excessive degree, and this extremely so.   In it, there are many havens on the sea-coast, incomparable with any others that I know in Christendom, and plenty of rivers so good and great that it is a marvel. The lands thereof are high, and in it are very many ranges of hills, and most lofty mountains incomparably beyond the island of Tenerife,[4] all most beautiful in a thousand shapes, and all accessible, and full of trees of a thousand kinds, so lofty that they seem to reach the sky. And I am assured that they never lose their foliage; as may be imagined, since I saw them as green and as beautiful as they are in Spain during May. And some of them were in flower, some in fruit, some in another stage according to their kind.   And the nightingale was singing, and other birds of a thousand sorts, in the month of November, there where I was going. There are palm-trees of six or eight species, wondrous to see for their beautiful variety; but so are the other trees, and fruits, and plants therein. There are wonderful pine-groves, and very large plains of verdure, and there is honey, and many kinds of birds, and many various fruits.   In the earth there are

---

[1] Cf. Journal, November 2 and 6.
[2] Cf. Journal, November 1, for Columbus's strong inclination to regard Cuba as mainland.
[3] Cf. Journal, December 9.
[4] Cf. Journal, December 20 and note.

many mines of metals; and there is a population of incalculable number.[1] Española is a marvel; the mountains and hills,
and plains, and fields, and the soil, so beautiful and rich for
planting and sowing, for breeding cattle of all sorts, for building of towns and villages. There could be no believing, without seeing, such harbors as are here, as well as the many and
great rivers, and excellent waters, most of which contain gold.
In the trees and fruits and plants, there are great diversities
from those of Juana. In this, there are many spiceries, and
great mines of gold and other metals. The people of this
island, and of all the others that I have found and seen, or not
seen, all go naked, men and women, just as their mothers
bring them forth; although some women cover a single place
with the leaf of a plant, or a cotton something which they make
for that purpose. They have no iron or steel, nor any weapons;
nor are they fit thereunto; not because they be not a well-
formed people and of fair stature, but that they are most won-
drously timorous. They have no other weapons than the
stems of reeds in their seeding state, on the end of which they
fix little sharpened stakes. Even these, they dare not use;
for many times has it happened that I sent two or three men
ashore to some village to parley, and countless numbers of them
sallied forth, but as soon as they saw those approach, they
fled away in such wise that even a father would not wait for
his son. And this was not because any hurt had ever been
done to any of them: — on the contrary, at every headland
where I have gone and been able to hold speech with them, I
gave them of everything which I had, as well cloth as many
other things, without accepting aught therefor; — but such they
are, incurably timid. It is true that since they have become
more assured, and are losing that terror, they are artless and
generous with what they have, to such a degree as no one would

[1] The prevalent Spanish estimate of the population of Española at
the time of the first colonization was 1,100,000. The modern ethnologist
and critical historian, Oscar Peschel, placed it at less than 300,000 and more
than 200,000. The estimates of Indian population by the early writers
were almost invariably greatly exaggerated. *Cf.* Bourne, *Spain in
America*, pp. 213–214, and notes.

believe but him who had seen it. Of anything they have, if it
be asked for, they never say no, but do rather invite the person to accept it, and show as much lovingness as though they
would give their hearts. And whether it be a thing of value,
or one of little worth, they are straightways content with whatsoever trifle of whatsoever kind may be given them in return
for it. I forbade that anything so worthless as fragments of
broken platters, and pieces of broken glass, and strap buckles,[1]
should be given them; although when they were able to get
such things, they seemed to think they had the best jewel in
the world, for it was the hap of a sailor to get, in exchange for
a strap,[1] gold to the weight of two and a half castellanos,[2] and
others much more for other things of far less value; while
for new blancas [3] they gave everything they had, even though
it were [the worth of] two or three gold castellanos, or one or
two arrobas of spun [4] cotton. They took even pieces of broken
barrel-hoops, and gave whatever they had, like senseless brutes;
insomuch that it seemed to me bad. I forbade it, and I gave
gratuitously a thousand useful things that I carried, in order
that they may conceive affection, and furthermore may become Christians; for they are inclined to the love and service
of their Highnesses and of all the Castilian nation, and they
strive to combine in giving us things which they have in abundance, and of which we are in need. And they knew no sect,
nor idolatry; save that they all believe that power and goodness are in the sky, and they believed very firmly that I,
with these ships and crews, came from the sky; and in such
opinion, they received me at every place where I landed,
after they had lost their terror. And this comes not because
they are ignorant: on the contrary, they are men of very
subtle wit, who navigate all those seas, and who give a marvellously good account of everything, but because they never

[1] *Cabos de agugetas*.   Rather the metallic tips of lacings or straps. *Agugeta*
is a leather lacing or strap. The contemporary Latin translator used
bingulae, shoe-straps, shoe-latchets.

[2] The *castellano* was one-sixth of an ounce of gold.

[3] *Blancas* were little coins worth about one-third of a cent.

[4] The *arroba* was 25 pounds.

saw men wearing clothes nor the like of our ships. And as soon as I arrived in the Indies, in the first island that I found, I took some of them by force, to the intent that they should learn [our speech] and give me information of what there was in those parts. And so it was, that very soon they understood [us] and we them, what by speech or what by signs; and those [Indians] have been of much service. To this day I carry them [with me] who are still of the opinion that I come from Heaven [as appears] from much conversation which they have had with me. And they were the first to proclaim it wherever I arrived; and the others went running from house to house and to the neighboring villages, with loud cries of "Come! come to see the people from Heaven!" Then, as soon as their minds were reassured about us, every one came, men as well as women, so that there remained none behind, big or little; and they all brought something to eat and drink, which they gave with wondrous lovingness. They have in all the islands very many *canoas*,[1] after the manner of rowing-galleys,[2] some larger, some smaller; and a good many are larger than a galley of eighteen benches. They are not so wide, because they are made of a single log of timber, but a galley could not keep up with them in rowing, for their motion is a thing beyond belief. And with these, they navigate through all those islands, which are numberless, and ply their traffic. I have seen some of those *canoas* with seventy and eighty men in them, each one with his oar. In all those islands, I saw not much diversity in the looks of the people, nor in their manners and language; but they all understand each other, which is a thing of singular advantage for what I hope their Highnesses will decide upon for converting them to our holy faith, unto which they are well disposed. I have already told how I had gone a hundred and seven leagues, in a straight line from West to East, along the sea-coast of the Island of Juana; according to which itinerary, I can declare that that island is larger than England and Scotland com-

---

[1] The first appearance of this West Indian word in Europe.
[2] *Fustas de remo.*

bined;[1] as, over and above those hundred and seven leagues,
there remain for me, on the western side, two provinces whereto
I did not go — one of which they call Avan, where the people
are born with tails [2] — which provinces cannot be less in
length than fifty or sixty leagues, according to what may be
understood from the Indians with me, who know all the islands.
This other, Española, has a greater circumference than the
whole of Spain from Col[ibre in Catal]unya, by the sea-coast,
as far as Fuente Ravia in Biscay; since, along one of its four
sides, I went for a hundred and eighty-eight great leagues in
a straight line from west to east.[3] This is [a land] to be desired, — and once seen, never to be relinquished — in which
(although, indeed, I have taken possession of them all for
their Highnesses, and all are more richly endowed than I
have skill and power to say, and I hold them all in the name
of their Highnesses who can dispose thereof as much and as
completely as of the kingdoms of Castile) in this Española,
in the place most suitable and best for its proximity to the
gold mines, and for traffic with the mainland both on this
side and with that over there belonging to the Great Can,[4]
where there will be great commerce and profit, I took possession of a large town which I named the city of Navidad.[5]
And I have made fortification there, and a fort (which by this

[1] Cf. Journal, December 23, and note. The reader will observe the tone
of exaggeration in the letter as compared with the Journal.

[2] Marco Polo reported that in the kingdom of Lambri in Sumatra "there
are men who have tails like dogs, larger than a palm, and who are covered
with hair." Marco Polo, pt. III., ch. XIV. See Yule's note on the legend
of men with tails, Yule's Marco Polo, II. 284. The name Avan (Anan in
the Latin letter) does not occur in the Journal. Bernaldez, Historia de las
Reyes Catolicos, II. 19, gives Albao as one of the provinces of Española. As
this name is not found in his chief source, Dr. Chanca's letter, he may have
got it from Columbus and through a lapse of memory transferred it from
Cuba to Española.

[3] The area of Spain is about 191,000 square miles; that of Española or
Hayti is 28,000. The extreme length of Hayti is 407 miles.

[4] That is, with the mainland of Europe on this side of the Atlantic and
with the mainland on that side of the ocean belonging to the Great Can, i.e.,
China.

[5] I.e., Nativity, Christmas, because the wreck occurred on that day.
Cf. Journal, December 25 and January 4, and note to entry of December 28.

time will have been completely finished) and I have left therein
men enough for such a purpose, with arms and artillery, and
provisions for more than a year, and a boat, and a [man who
is] master of all seacraft for making others; and great friendship with the king of that land, to such a degree that he prided
himself on calling and holding me as his brother. And even
though his mind might change towards attacking those men,
neither he nor his people know what arms are, and go naked.
As I have already said, they are the most timorous creatures
there are in the world, so that the men who remain there are
alone sufficient to destroy all that land, and the island is
without personal danger for them if they know how to behave
themselves. It seems to me that in all those islands, the men
are all content with a single wife; and to their chief or king
they give as many as twenty. The women, it appears to me,
do more work than the men. Nor have I been able to learn
whether they held personal property, for it seemed to me
that whatever one had, they all took share of, especially of
eatable things. Down to the present, I have not found in
those islands any monstrous men, as many expected,[1] but on
the contrary all the people are very comely; nor are they black
like those in Guinea, but have flowing hair; and they are not
begotten where there is an excessive violence of the rays of
the sun. It is true that the sun is there very strong, although
it is twenty-six degrees distant from the equinoctial line.[2]
In those islands, where there are lofty mountains, the cold
was very keen there, this winter; but they endure it by
being accustomed thereto, and by the help of the meats which
they eat with many and inordinately hot spices. Thus I
have not found, nor had any information of monsters, except

[1] Columbus had read in the *Imago Mundi* of Pierre d'Ailly and noted in
the margin the passage which says that in the ends of the earth there "were
monsters of such a horrid aspect that it were hard to say whether they were
men or beasts." *Raccolta Colombiana*, pt. I., vol. II., p. 468. *Cf.* also the
stories in the *Book of Sir John Mandeville*, chs. XXVII. and XXVIII.

[2] Columbus apparently revised his estimate of the latitude on the return,
without, however, correcting his Journal; *cf.* entries for October 30 and
November 21.

of an island which is here the second in the approach to the
Indies, which is inhabited by a people whom, in all the islands,
they regard as very ferocious, who eat human flesh. These
have many canoes with which they run through all the
islands of India, and plunder and take as much as they can.
They are no more ill-shaped than the others, but have the
custom of wearing their hair long, like women; and they use
bows and arrows of the same reed stems, with a point of wood
at the top, for lack of iron which they have not. Amongst
those other tribes who are excessively cowardly, these are
ferocious; but I hold them as nothing more than the others.
These are they who have to do with the women of Matinino [1]
— which is the first island that is encountered in the passage
from Spain to the Indies — in which there are no men. Those
women practise no female usages, but have bows and arrows of
reed such as above mentioned; and they arm and cover themselves with plates of copper of which they have much. In
another island, which they assure me is larger than Española,
the people have no hair. In this there is incalculable gold;
and concerning these and the rest I bring Indians with me as
witnesses. And in conclusion, to speak only of what has been
done in this voyage, which has been so hastily performed, their
Highnesses may see that I shall give them as much gold as
they may need, with very little aid which their Highnesses
will give me; spices and cotton at once, as much as their
Highnesses will order to be shipped, and as much as they
shall order to be shipped of mastic, — which till now has never
been found except in Greece, in the island of Xio,[2] and the
Seignory sells it for what it likes; and aloe-wood as much
as they shall order to be shipped; and slaves as many
as they shall order to be shipped, — and these shall be from
idolators. And I believe that I have discovered rhubarb
and cinnamon, and I shall find that the men whom I am leav-

---

[1] See Journal, January 15, and note. The island is identified with Martinique.
[2] See Journal, November 12, and note. The Seignory was the government of Genoa to which Chios [Scio] belonged at this time.

ing there will have discovered a thousand other things of value; as I made no delay at any point, so long as the wind gave me an opportunity of sailing, except only in the town of Navidad till I had left things safely arranged and well established. And in truth I should have done much more if the ships had served me as well as might reasonably have been expected. This is enough; and [thanks to] Eternal God our Lord who gives to all those who walk His way, victory over things which seem impossible; and this was signally one such, for although men have talked or written of those lands,[1] it was all by conjecture, without confirmation from eyesight, amounting only to this much that the hearers for the most part listened and judged that there was more fable in it than anything actual, however trifling. Since thus our Redeemer has given to our most illustrious King and Queen, and to their famous kingdoms, this victory in so high a matter, Christendom should have rejoicing therein and make great festivals, and give solemn thanks to the Holy Trinity for the great exaltation they shall have by the conversion of so many peoples to our holy faith; and next for the temporal benefit which will bring hither refreshment and profit, not only to Spain, but to all Christians. This briefly, in accordance with the facts. Dated, on the caravel, off the Canary Islands,[2] the 15 February of the year 1493.

At your command,

THE ADMIRAL.

POSTSCRIPT WHICH CAME WITHIN THE LETTER

After having written this letter, and being in the sea of Castile, there rose upon me so much wind, South and South-

---

[1] Such writers, for example, as Pierre d'Ailly, Marco Polo, and the author of the *Book of Sir John Mandeville*, from whom Columbus had derived most of his preconceptions which often biassed or misled him in interpreting the signs of the natives.

[2] According to the Journal, Columbus thought he was off the Azores, February 15.

east,[1] that it has caused me to lighten the vessels; however, I ran hither to-day into this port of Lisbon, which was the greatest wonder in the world; where I decided to write to their Highnesses. I have always found the seasons like May in all the Indies, whither I passed in thirty-three days, and returned in twenty-eight, but that these storms have delayed me twenty-three days running about this sea.[2] All the seamen say here that there never has been so bad a winter, nor so many shipwrecks.

Dated the 14th of March.[3]

Colom sent this letter to the Escrivano de Racion.[4] Of the islands found in the Indies. Received with another for their Highnesses.[5]

[1] The storm of March 3d; see Journal.

[2] The time of the return voyage, like that of the outgoing voyage, is reckoned as that consumed in making the Atlantic passage from the last island left on one side to the first one reached on the other. Just how the twenty-three days is to be explained is not altogether clear. The editor of Quaritch's *The Spanish Letter of Columbus* supposed Columbus to refer to the time which elapsed from February 16, when he arrived at the Azores, to March 13, when he left Lisbon.

[3] Columbus arrived at Lisbon March 4, and he is supposed by R. H. Major to have written the postscript there, but not to have despatched the letter until he reached Seville, March 15, when he redated it March 14.

[4] The *Escrivano de Racion* in the kingdom of Aragon was the high steward or controller of the king's household expenditures. In Castile the corresponding official was the *contador mayor*, chief auditor or steward. Navarrete, I. 167.

[5] No longer extant. These lines are a memorandum appended to the text by Santangel or the printer, and might have been used as a title, as the similar memorandum was used in the publication of the Latin letter. The Admiral's name is spelled as in the Articles of Agreement "Colom."

LETTER FROM COLUMBUS TO FERDINAND AND ISABELLA CONCERNING THE COLONIZATION AND COMMERCE OF ESPAÑOLA [1]

MOST HIGH AND POWERFUL LORDS: In obedience to what your Highnesses command me, I shall state what occurs to me for the peopling and management of the Spanish Island [2] and of all others, whether already discovered or hereafter to be discovered, submitting myself, however, to any better opinion.

[1] The original text of this letter will be most accessible in Thacher, *Christopher Columbus*, III. 100–113. It is there accompanied by a facsimile of the original manuscript and an English translation. The translation here given is a revision of that made by Dr. José Ignacio Rodriguez of Washington and printed in the *Report of the American Historical Association*, 1894, pp. 452–455, as part of a paper by W. E. Curtis on *Autographs of Christopher Columbus*. The text was first printed by Justo Zaragoza in his *Cartas de Indias*, etc. (Madrid, 1877). It was first translated by George Dexter in the *Proceedings of the Massachusetts Historical Society*, Vol. XVI. This translation, which contains some errors which seriously affect the meaning, is also to be found in P. L. Ford, *Writings of Christopher Columbus*, pp. 67–74. Zaragoza placed the date of this letter in 1497. It is the opinion of the present editor that it should be placed between the first and the second voyage. The arguments advanced by Lollis in favor of 1493 are conclusive. See *Raccolta Colombiana*, parte I., tomo I., pp. lxxv–lxxx.

The letter is of great importance as the first draft of a systematic colonial policy for the newly discovered islands. Several of its suggestions were incorporated in the letter of instructions which the Sovereigns gave Columbus May 29, 1493, for the second voyage. See Navarrete, *Viages*, II. 66–72. It was supplemented in 1494 by the memorandum which the Admiral sent back to the sovereigns by Antonio de Torres and the two together entitle Columbus to be considered the pioneer lawgiver as well as the discoverer of the New World. *Cf.* Bourne, *Spain in America*, pp. 204–206.

[2] *La ysla Española.* So translated, for so it would sound to the Sovereigns. There had not been time for Española to sound like a proper name.

In the first place, in regard to the Spanish Island: that there should go there settlers up to the number of two thousand [1] who may want to go so as to render the possession of the country safer and cause it to be more profitable and helpful in the intercourse and traffic with the neighboring islands.

Likewise, that in the said island three or four towns be founded at convenient places, and the settlers be properly distributed among said places and towns.

Likewise, in order to secure the better and prompter settlement of the said island, that the privilege of getting gold be granted exclusively to those who actually settle and build dwelling-houses in the settlement where they may be, in order that all may live close to each other and more safely.

Likewise, that in each place and settlement there be a mayor [2] or mayors and a clerk [3] according to the use and custom of Castile.

Likewise, that a church be built, and that priests or friars be sent there for the administration of the sacraments, and for divine worship and the conversion of the Indians.

Likewise, that no settler be allowed to go and gather gold unless with a permit from the governor or mayor of the town in which he lives, to be given only upon his promising under oath to return to the place of his residence and faithfully report all the gold which he may have gathered, this to be done once a month, or once a week, as the time may be assigned to him, the said report to be entered on the proper registry by the clerk of the town in the presence of the mayor, and if so deemed advisable, in the presence of a friar or priest selected for the purpose.

Likewise, that all the gold so gathered be melted forthwith, and stamped with such a stamp as the town may have devised and selected, and that it be weighed and that the share of that gold which belongs to your Highnesses be given and deliv-

---

[1] See Bourne, *Spain in America*, pp. 34–35, for the actual equipment of the second voyage.

[2] Alcalde.

[3] *Escribano del pueblo.*

ered to the mayor of the town, the proper record thereof being made by the clerk and by the priest or friar, so that it may not pass through only one hand and may so render the concealing of the truth impossible.

Likewise, that all the gold which may be found without the mark or seal aforesaid in the possession of any one who formerly had reported once as aforesaid, be forfeited and divided by halves, one for the informer and the other for your Highnesses.

Likewise, that one per cent. of all the gold gathered be set apart and appropriated for building churches, and providing for their proper furnishing and ornamentation, and to the support of the priests or friars having them in their charge, and, if so deemed advisable, for the payment of some compensation to the mayors and clerks of the respective towns, so as to cause them to fulfil their duties faithfully, and that the balance be delivered to the governor and treasurer sent there by your Highnesses.

Likewise, in regard to the division of the gold and of the share which belongs to your Highnesses, I am of the opinion that it should be entrusted to the said governor and treasurer, because the amount of the gold found may sometimes be large and sometimes small, and, if so deemed advisable, that the share of your Highnesses be established for one year to be one-half, the other half going to the gatherers, reserving for a future time to make some other and better provision, if necessary.

Likewise, that if the mayors and clerks commit any fraud or consent to it, the proper punishment be inflicted upon them, and that a penalty be likewise imposed upon those settlers who do not report in full the whole amount of the gold which is in their possession.

Likewise, that there be a treasurer [1] in the said island, who

[1] As the King and Queen on May 7, 1493, appointed Gomez Tello to go with Columbus on the second voyage to act as receiver of the royal dues, Thacher argues strongly, on the ground that this recommendation presumably antedates the appointment of a treasurer, that this letter of Columbus's was written earlier than May 7, 1493.

shall receive all the gold belonging to your Highnesses, and shall have a clerk to make and keep the proper record of the receipts, and that the mayors and clerks of the respective towns be given the proper vouchers for everything which they may deliver to the said treasurer.

Likewise, that whereas the extreme anxiety of the colonists to gather gold may induce them to neglect all other business and occupations, it seems to me that prohibition should be made to them to engage in the search of gold during some season of the year, so as to give all other business, profitable to the island, an opportunity to be established and carried on.

Likewise, that as far as the business of discovering other lands is concerned,[1] it is my opinion that permission to do so should be given to everyone who desires to embark in it, and that some liberality should be shown in reducing the fifth to be given away, so as to encourage as many as possible for entering into such undertakings.

And now I shall set forth my opinion as to the manner of sending vessels to the said Spanish Island, and the regulation of this subject which must be made, which is as follows: That no vessels should be allowed to unload their cargoes except at one or two ports designated for that purpose, and that a record should be made of all that they carry and unload; and that no vessels should be allowed either to leave the island except from the same ports, after a record has been made also of all that they have taken on board, so that nothing can be concealed.

Likewise, in regard to the gold to be brought from the island to Castile, that the whole of it, whether belonging to your Highnesses or to some private individual, must be kept in a chest, with two keys, one to be kept by the master of the vessel and the other by some person chosen by the governor and the treasurer, and that an official record must be made of every-

---

[1] Such an authorization was given by the sovereigns, April 10, 1495, reserving Columbus's rights to one-eighth of the trade. Navarrete, II. 166–167. The Admiral protested that this authorization led to infringement of his rights and it was in so far revoked, June 2, 1497.

thing put in the said chest, in order that each one may have what is his, and that any other gold, much or little, found outside of the said chest in any manner be forfeited to the benefit of your Highnesses, so as to cause the transaction to be made faithfully.

Likewise, that all vessels coming from the said island must come to unload to the port of Cadiz, and that no person shall be allowed to leave the vessels or get in them until such person or persons of the said city as may be appointed for this purpose by your Highnesses go on board the same vessels, to whom the masters must declare all that they have brought, and show the statement of everything they have in the cargoes, so that it may be seen and proved whether the said ships have brought anything hidden and not declared in the manifests at the time of shipment.

Likewise, that in the presence of the Justice of the said city of Cadiz and of whosoever may be deputed for the purpose by your Highnesses, the said chest shall be opened in which the gold is to be brought and that to each one be given what belongs to him.[1]

May your Highnesses keep me in their minds, while I, on my part, shall ever pray to God our Lord to preserve the lives of your Highnesses and enlarge their dominions.

S.

S.A.S.

X.M.Y.

Xpo Ferens.[2]

Sent by the admiral.

[1] On the development of the fiscal and commercial regulations of the Spanish colonial administration, see Bourne, *Spain in America*, pp. 282–301 and 337; Moses, *Establishment of Spanish Rule in America*, pp. 27–67.

[2] The formal signature of Columbus which he enjoined upon his heir in his deed of entail, February 28, 1498. See P. L. Ford, *Writings of Christopher Columbus*, p. 90. If this letter was written, as is supposed, in 1493, this is the earliest use of this monogram. Its meaning has never been determined. The various conjectures are presented by Thacher, *Christopher Columbus*, III. 454–458.

LETTER OF DR. CHANCA ON THE SECOND VOYAGE OF COLUMBUS

INTRODUCTION

Dr. Chanca of Seville volunteered to go to the Indies, and on May 23, 1493, the King and Queen appointed him surgeon (Navarrete, *Viages*, II. 54). This letter was written to the cabildo or town council of Seville and is the first narrative of one of Columbus's voyages that we have exactly as it was written by a private observer. It is also the first description of the natives that we have from an observer of scientific training. The original text was first printed by Navarrete in his *Viages* in 1825. The original manuscript or a copy came into the possession of the historian Bernaldez, who embodied it with a few trifling changes and omissions in his *Historia de Los Reyes Catolicos*, chs. cxix., cxx. (Seville ed., 1870), Vol. II., pp. 5–36.

Columbus kept a journal on this voyage which is no longer extant. Abridgments of it are preserved to us in the *Historie* of Ferdinand Columbus and in the *Historia de las Indias* of Las Casas. There are other contemporary narratives of the voyage from private hands, but they are either made up from conversations with those who went on the voyage, like the letters of Simone Verde, printed in Harrisse, *Christophe Colomb*, II. 68–78, or the account in Books ii. and iii. of the first decade of Peter Martyr's *De Rebus Oceanicis*, or a literary embellishment of some private letters like the translation into Latin by Nicolo Syllacio of some letters he received from Guillelmo Coma who went on the voyage. The Syllacio-Coma letter and Peter Martyr's account in its earliest published form, the Venetian *Libretto de tutta la Navigatione de Re de Spagna de le Isole et Terreni novamente Trovati*, are accessible in English in Thacher, *Christopher Columbus*, II. 243–262, 489–502. These two narratives gave the European public its first knowledge of the second voyage. The Syllacio-Coma letter was published late in 1494 or early in 1495, and the *Libretto* in Venice in 1504.

The translation of Dr. Chanca's letter given here is that of R. H. Major. It has been carefully revised to bring it into closer conformity to the original. Any noteworthy changes will be indicated. Attention may be called to a somewhat important correction of the text on p. 304.

Of Dr. Chanca personally little or nothing is known beyond what has been mentioned except that he devoted himself with zeal and self-sacrifice to his duties. In the report of the Second Voyage which Columbus prepared January 30, 1494, and sent off by Antonio de Torres February 2, he charged Torres as follows in regard to Dr. Chanca. "You will inform their Highnesses of the labor that Dr. Chanca is performing on account of the many that are ill and the lack of supplies and that with all this he is conducting himself with great diligence and kindness in everything that concerns his duties," etc. Major, *Select Letters of Columbus*, pp. 93, 94.

E. G. B.

LETTER OF DR. CHANCA ON THE SECOND VOYAGE OF COLUMBUS

A letter addressed to the Town Council of Seville by Dr. Chanca, a native of that city, and physician to the fleet of Columbus, on his second voyage to the Indies, describing the principal events which occurred during that voyage

Most noble Lord: —

SINCE the occurrences which I relate in private letters to other persons are not of such general interest as those which are contained in this epistle, I have resolved to give you a distinct narrative of the events of our voyage, as well as to treat of the other matters which form the subject of my petition to your Lordship. The news I have to communicate are as follows: The expedition which their Catholic Majesties sent, by Divine permission, from Spain to the Indies, under the command of Christopher Columbus, Admiral of the Ocean, left Cadiz on the twenty-fifth of September, of the year [1493, with seventeen ships well equipped and with 1200 fighting men or a little less,][1] with wind and weather favorable for the voyage. This weather lasted two days, during which time we managed to make nearly fifty leagues; the weather then changing, we made little or no progress for the next two days; it pleased God, however, after this, to restore us fine weather, so that in two days more we reached the Great Canary. Here we put into harbor, which we were obliged to do, to repair one of the ships which made a great deal of water; we remained all that day, and on the following set sail again, but were several times becalmed, so that we were four or five days

---

[1] There is a gap here in the text of the original which has been filled by taking the corresponding words in Bernaldez's text.

before we reached Gomera. We had to remain at Gomera some days [1] to lay in our stores of meat, wood, and as much water as we could stow, preparatory to the long voyage which we expected to make without seeing land: thus through the delay at these two ports, and being calmed one day after leaving Gomera, we were nineteen or twenty days before we arrived at the island of Ferro. After this we had, by the goodness of God, a return of fine weather, more continuous than any fleet ever enjoyed during so long a voyage, so that leaving Ferro on the thirteenth of October, within twenty days we came in sight of land; and we should have seen it in fourteen or fifteen days, if the ship *Capitana* [2] had been as good a sailer as the other vessels; for many times the others had to shorten sail, because they were leaving us much behind. During all this time we had great good fortune, for throughout the voyage we encountered no storm, with the exception of one on St. Simon's eve, [3] which for four hours put us in considerable jeopardy.

On the first Sunday after All Saints, namely the third of November, about dawn, a pilot of the flagship cried out, "The reward, I see the land!"

The joy of the people was so great, that it was wonderful to hear their cries and exclamations of pleasure; and they had good reason to be delighted; for they had become so wearied of bad living, and of working the water out of the ships, that all sighed most anxiously for land. The pilots of the fleet reckoned on that day, that between leaving Ferro and first reaching land, we had made eight hundred leagues; others said seven hundred and eighty (so that the difference was not great), and three hundred more between Ferro and Cadiz, making in all eleven hundred leagues; I do not therefore feel

---

[1] Major here translated *algun dia* "one day." It should be "some days." Bernaldez has *algunos dias,* and Coma says the tarry at Gomera was nearly six days.

[2] *La nao Capitana* means the flagship. The name of the flagship on the second voyage was *Marigalante.* *Historie* of Ferdinand Columbus, cap. XLV. (London, ed. 1867), p. 137.

[3] October 27.

as one who had not seen enough of the water.   On the morning
of the aforesaid Sunday, we saw lying before us an island, and
soon on the right hand another appeared: the first [1] was high
and mountainous, on the side nearest to us; the other [2]
flat, and very thickly wooded. As soon as it became lighter,
other islands began to appear on both sides; so that on that
day, there were six islands to be seen lying in different directions, and most of them of considerable size.   We directed
our course towards that which we had first seen, and reaching
the coast, we proceeded more than a league in search of a
port where we might anchor, but without finding one; all
that part of the island which met our view, appeared mountainous, very beautiful, and green even up to the water, which
was delightful to see, for at that season, there is scarcely any
thing green in our own country.   When we found that there
was no harbor there, the Admiral decided that we should go
to the other island, which appeared on the right, and which
was at four or five leagues distance; one vessel however still
remained on the first island all that day seeking for a harbor,
in case it should be necessary to return thither.   At length,
having found a good one, where they saw both people and
dwellings, they returned that night to the fleet, which had put
into harbor at the other island,[3] and there the Admiral, accompanied by a great number of men, landed with the royal banner
in his hands, and took formal possession on behalf of their
Majesties.   This island was filled with an astonishingly thick
growth of wood; the variety of unknown trees, some bearing
fruit and some flowers, was surprising, and indeed every spot
was covered with verdure.   We found there a tree whose leaf
had the finest smell of cloves that I have ever met with; it was
like a laurel leaf, but not so large: but I think it was a species of
laurel.   There were wild fruits of various kinds, some of which
our men, not very prudently, tasted; and upon only touching

[1] The island of Dominica, which is so called from having been discovered
on a Sunday.   *Historie,* p. 137.

[2] The island Marigalante, which was so called from the name of the ship
in which Columbus sailed.   *Historie, ibid.*

[3] Marigalante.

them with their tongues, their countenances became inflamed,[1] and such great heat and pain followed, that they seemed to be mad, and were obliged to resort to refrigerants to cure themselves. We found no signs of any people in this island, and concluded it was uninhabited; we remained only two hours, for it was very late when we landed, and on the following morning we left for another very large island,[2] situated below this at the distance of seven or eight leagues. We approached it under the side of a great mountain, that seemed almost to reach the skies, in the middle of which rose a peak, higher than all the rest of the mountain, whence many streams diverged into different channels, especially towards the part at which we arrived. At three leagues distance, we could see a fall of water as broad as an ox, which discharged itself from such a height that it appeared to fall from the sky; it was seen from so great a distance that it occasioned many wagers to be laid on board the ships, some maintaining that it was but a series of white rocks, and others that it was water. When we came nearer to it, it showed itself distinctly, and it was the most beautiful thing in the world to see from how great a height and from what a small space so large a fall of water was discharged. As soon as we neared the island the Admiral ordered a light caravel to run along the coast to search for a harbor; the captain put into land in a boat, and seeing some houses, leapt on shore and went up to them, the inhabitants fleeing at sight of our men; he then went into the houses and there found various household articles that had been left unremoved, from which he took two parrots, very large and quite different from any we had before seen; he found a great quantity of cotton, both spun and prepared for spinning, and articles of food, of all of which he brought away a portion; besides these, he also brought away four or five bones of human arms and legs. On seeing these we suspected that

---

[1] One would infer from this that it was the fruit of the *manzanillo*, which produces similar effects. (Navarrete.) On the Manzanillo (Manchineel), see Oviedo, lib. ix., cap. xii. He says the Caribs used it in making their arrow poisons.

[2] Guadeloupe.

we were amongst the Caribbee islands, whose inhabitants eat
human flesh; for the Admiral, guided by the information respecting their situation which he had received from the
Indians of the islands discovered in his former voyage, had
directed his course with a view to their discovery, both because they were the nearest to Spain, and because this was
the direct track for the island of Española, where he had left
some of his people. Thither, by the goodness of God and the
wise management of the Admiral, we came in as straight a
track as if we had sailed by a well known and frequented
route. This island is very large, and on the side where we
arrived it seemed to us to be twenty-five leagues in length.
We sailed more than two leagues along the shore in search of
a harbor; on the part towards which we moved appeared
very high mountains, and on that which we left extensive
plains; on the sea-coast there were a few small villages, whose
inhabitants fled as soon as they saw the sails: at length after
proceeding two leagues we found a port late in the evening.
That night the Admiral resolved that some of the men should
land at break of day in order to confer with the natives, and
learn what sort of people they were; although it was suspected, from the appearance of those who had fled at our
approach, that they were naked, like those whom the Admiral
had seen in his former voyage. That morning certain captains
started out; one of them arrived at the dinner hour, and
brought away a boy of about fourteen years of age, as it afterwards appeared, who said that he was one of the prisoners
taken by these people. The others divided themselves, and
one party took a little boy whom a man was leading by the
hand, but who left him and fled; this boy they sent on board
immediately with some of our men; others remained, and took
certain women, natives of the island, together with other women
from among the captives who came of their own accord. One
captain of this last company, not knowing that any intelligence of the people had been obtained, advanced farther into
the island and lost himself, with the six men who accompanied
him: they could not find their way back until after four days,

when they lighted upon the sea-shore, and following the line
of coast returned to the fleet.[1] We had already looked upon
them as killed and eaten by the people that are called Caribbees; for we could not account for their long absence in any
other way, since they had among them some pilots who by
their knowledge of the stars could navigate either to or from
Spain, so that we imagined that they could not lose themselves
in so small a space. On this first day of our landing several
men and women came on the beach up to the water's edge,
and gazed at the ships in astonishment at so novel a sight;
and when a boat pushed on shore in order to speak with them,
they cried out, "tayno, tayno," [2] which is as much as to say,
"good, good," and waited for the landing of the sailors,
standing by the boat in such a manner that they might escape
when they pleased. The result was, that none of the men
could be persuaded to join us, and only two were taken by
force, who were secured and led away. More than twenty
women of the captives were taken with their own consent,
and other women, natives of the island, were surprised and
carried off; several of the boys, who were captives, came to
us fleeing from the natives of the island who had taken them
prisoners. We remained eight days in this port in conse-
quence of the loss of the aforesaid captain, and went many
times on shore, passing amongst the dwellings and villages
which were on the coast; we found a vast number of human
bones and skulls hung up about the houses, like vessels in-

---

[1] It was Diego Marquez, the inspector, who with eight other men went
on shore into the interior of the island, without permission from the Admiral,
who caused him to be sought for by parties of men with trumpets, but
without success. One of those who were sent out with this object was
Alonzo Ojeda, who took with him forty men, and on their return they reported that they had found many aromatic plants, a variety of birds, and
some considerable rivers. The wanderers were not able to find their way
to the ships until the 8th of November. [Navarrete, condensed from Las
Casas, *Historia de las Indias*, II. 7–8.]

[2] Tayno was also the tribal name of these people, who differentiated themselves from the Caribs. Peter Martyr reports the assertions of the followers
of Guacamari that they were Taynos not Caribs: "Se Tainos, id est, nobiles
esse, non Canibales, inclamitant." *De Rebus Oceanicis*, Dec. i., lib. ii.,
p. 25. (Cologne ed. of 1574.)

tended for holding various things.[1] There were very few men to be seen here, and the women informed us that this was in consequence of ten canoes having gone to make an attack upon other islands. These islanders appeared to us to be more civilized than those that we had hitherto seen; for although all the Indians have houses of straw, yet the houses of these people are constructed in a much superior fashion, are better stocked with provisions, and exhibit more evidences of industry, both on the part of the men and the women. They had a considerable quantity of cotton, both spun and prepared for spinning, and many cotton sheets, so well woven as to be no way inferior to those of our country. We inquired of the women, who were prisoners in the island, what people these islanders were ; they replied that they were Caribbees. As soon as they learned that we abhorred such people,[2] on account of their evil practice of eating human flesh, they were much delighted; and, after that, if they brought forward any woman or man of the Caribbees, they informed us (but secretly) that they were such, still evincing by their dread of their conquerors, that they belonged to a vanquished nation, though they knew them all to be in our power.

We were enabled to distinguish which of the women were Caribbees, and which were not, by the Caribbees wearing on each leg two bands of woven cotton, the one fastened round the knee, and the other round the ankle; by this means they make the calves of their legs large, and the above-mentioned parts very small, which I imagine that they regard as a mark of elegance: by this peculiarity we distinguished them.[3]

[1] Las Casas, *Historia de las Indias*, II. 8, remarks of these bones, "They must have belonged to lords or persons whom they loved since it is not probable that they belonged to those they ate, because if they ate as many as some say, the cabins would not hold all the bones and skulls, and it seems that after having eaten them there would be no object in keeping the skulls and bones for relics unless they belonged to some very notable enemies. The whole matter is a puzzle."

[2] The name *Caribe* here obviously has begun to have the meaning " cannibal," which is in origin the same word.

[3] This practice still survives among the Caribs. Im Thurn describes it in almost the same words as Dr. Chanca. See *Among the Indians of Guiana*, p. 192.

U

The habits of these Caribbees are brutal. There are three islands: this is called Turuqueira; the other, which was the first that we saw, is called Ceyre; the third is called Ayay: [1] all these are alike as if they were of one race, who do no injury to each other; but each and all of them wage war against the other neighboring islands, and for the purpose of attacking them, make voyages of a hundred and fifty leagues at sea, with their numerous canoes, which are a small kind of craft with one mast. Their arms are arrows, in the place of iron weapons, and as they have no iron, some of them point their arrows with tortoise-shell, and others make their arrow-heads of fish spines, which are naturally barbed like coarse saws: these prove dangerous weapons to a naked people like the Indians, and may cause death or severe injury, but to men of our nation, are not very formidable. In their attacks upon the neighboring islands, these people capture as many of the women as they can, especially those who are young and beautiful, and keep them for servants and to have as concubines; and so great a number do they carry off, that in fifty houses no men were to be seen; and out of the number of the captives, more than twenty were young girls. These women also say that the Caribbees use them with such cruelty as would scarcely be believed; and that they eat the children which they bear to them, and only bring up those which they have by their native wives. Such of their male enemies as they can take alive, they bring to their houses to slaughter them, and those who are killed they devour at once. They say that man's flesh is so good, that there is nothing like it in the world; and this is pretty evident, for of the bones which we found in their houses, they had gnawed everything that could be gnawed, so that nothing remained of them, but what from its great hardness, could not be eaten: in one of the houses we found the neck of a man, cooking in a pot. When they take any boys prisoners, they cut off their member and make use

[1] These are the native names for Dominica (Ceyre) and Guadeloupe (Turuqueira and Ayay), which consists of two islands separated by a narrow channel.

of them as servants until they grow up to manhood, and then when they wish to make a feast they kill and eat them; for they say that the flesh of boys and women is not good to eat. Three of these boys came fleeing to us thus mutilated.

At the end of four days arrived the captain who had lost himself with his companions, of whose return we had by this time given up all hope; for other parties had been twice sent out to seek him, one of which came back on the same day that he rejoined us, without having gained any information respecting the wanderers; we rejoiced at their arrival, regarding it as a new accession to our numbers. The captain and the men who accompanied him brought back some women and boys, ten in number. Neither this party, nor those who went out to seek them, had seen any of the men of the island, which must have arisen either from their having fled, or possibly from there being but very few men in that locality; for, as the women informed us, ten canoes had gone away to make an attack upon the neighboring islands. The wanderers had returned from the mountains in such an emaciated condition, that it was distressing to see them; when we asked them how it was that they lost themselves, they said that the trees were so thick and close that they could not see the sky; some of them who were mariners had climbed the trees to get a sight of the stars, but could never see them, and if they had not found their way to the sea-coast, it would have been impossible to have returned to the fleet. We left this island eight days after our arrival.[1] The next day at noon we saw another island, not very large,[2] at about twelve leagues distance from the one we were leaving; the greater part of the first day of our departure we were kept close in to the coast of this island by a calm, but as the Indian women whom we brought with us said that it was not inhabited, but had been dispeopled by the Caribbees, we made no stay in it. On that evening we saw another island;[3] and in the night finding there were

---

[1] They left on Sunday, the 10th of November. Las Casas, *Historia*, II. 9.

[2] The island Montserrat. Las Casas, *ibid.*

[3] The island of St. Martin. Las Casas, *ibid.*

some sandbanks near, we dropped anchor, not venturing to proceed until the morning. On the morrow another island appeared, of considerable size, but we touched at none of these because we were anxious to convey consolation to our people who had been left in Española; but it did not please God to grant us our desire, as will hereafter appear. Another day at the dinner hour we arrived at an island which seemed to be worth the finding, for judging by the extent of cultivation in it, it appeared very populous. We went thither and put into harbor, when the Admiral immediately sent on shore a well manned barge to hold speech with the Indians, in order to ascertain what race they were, and also because we considered it necessary to gain some information respecting our course; although it afterwards plainly appeared that the Admiral, who had never made that passage before, had taken a very correct route. But as matters of doubt should always be brought to as great a certainty as possible by inquiry, he wished that communication should be held with the natives at once, and some of the men who went in the barge leapt on shore and went up to a village, whence the inhabitants had already withdrawn and hidden themselves. They took in this island five or six women and some boys, most of whom were captives, like those in the other island; we learned from the women whom we had brought with us, that the natives of this place also were Caribbees. As this barge was about to return to the ships with the capture which they had made, a canoe came along the coast containing four men, two women, and a boy; and when they saw the fleet they were so stupefied with amazement, that for a good hour they remained motionless at the distance of nearly two cannon shots from the ships. In this position they were seen by those who were in the barge and also by all the fleet. Meanwhile those in the barge moved towards the canoe, but so close in shore, that the Indians, in their perplexity and astonishment as to what all this could mean, never saw them, until they were so near that escape was impossible; for our men pressed on them so rapidly that they could not get away, although they made considerable effort to do so.

When the Caribbees saw that all attempt at flight was useless, they most courageously took to their bows, both women and men; I say most courageously, because they were only four men and two women, and our people were twenty-five in number. Two of our men were wounded by the Indians, one with two arrow-shots in his breast, and another with one in his side, and if it had not happened that they carried shields and wooden bucklers, and that they soon got near them with the barge and upset their canoe, most of them would have been killed with their arrows. After their canoe was upset, they remained in the water swimming and occasionally wading (for there were shallows in that part), still using their bows as much as they could, so that our men had enough to do to take them; and after all there was one of them whom they were unable to secure till he had received a mortal wound with a lance, and whom thus wounded they took to the ships. The difference between these Caribbees and the other Indians, with respect to dress, consists in their wearing their hair very long, while the latter have it clipt and paint their heads with crosses and a hundred thousand different devices, each according to his fancy; which they do with sharpened reeds. All of them, both the Caribbees and the others, are beardless, so that it is a rare thing to find a man with a beard: the Caribbees whom we took had their eyes and eyebrows stained, which I imagine they do from ostentation and to give them a more frightful appearance. One of these captives said, that in an island belonging to them called Cayre [1] (which is the first we saw, though we did not go to it), there is a great quantity of gold; and that if we were to take them nails and tools with which to make their canoes, we might bring away as much gold as we liked. On the same day we left that island, having been there no more than six or seven hours; and steering for another point of land [2] which appeared to lie in our intended course, we reached it by night. On the morning of the following day we coasted along it, and

[1] Dominica.
[2] Santa Cruz. November 14. Las Casas, *ibid.*

found it to be a large extent of country, but not continuous, for it was divided into more than forty islets.[1]   The land was very high and most of it barren, an appearance which we have never observed in any of the islands visited by us before or since: the surface of the ground seemed to suggest the probability of its containing metals. None of us went on shore here, but a small latteen caravel went up to one of the islets and found in it some fishermen's huts; the Indian women whom we brought with us said they were not inhabited. We proceeded along the coast the greater part of that day, and on the evening of the next we discovered another island called Burenquen,[2] which we judged to be thirty leagues in length, for we were coasting along it the whole of one day.   This island is very beautiful and apparently fertile; hither the Caribbees come with the view of subduing the inhabitants, and often carry away many of the people. These islanders have no boats nor any knowledge of navigation; but, as our captives inform us, they use bows as well as the Caribbees, and if by chance when they are attacked they succeed in taking any of their invaders, they will eat them in like manner as the Caribbees themselves in the contrary event would devour them. We remained two days in this island, and a great number of our men went on shore, but could never get speech of the natives, who had all fled, from fear of the Caribbees. All the above-mentioned islands were discovered in this voyage, the Admiral having seen nothing of them in his former voyage; they are all very beautiful and possess a most luxuriant soil, but this last island appeared to exceed all the others in beauty. Here terminated the islands, which on the side towards Spain had not been seen before by the Admiral, although we regard it as a matter of certainty that there is land more than forty leagues beyond the foremost of these newly discovered islands, on the side nearest to Spain.   We believe this to be the case,

---

[1] The Admiral named the largest of these islands St. Ursula, and all the others The Eleven Thousand Virgins. Las Casas, *Historia*, II. 10.

[2] The island of Porto Rico, to which the Admiral "gave the name of St. John the Baptist, which we now call Sant Juan and which the Indians called Boriquen." Las Casas, II. 10.

because two days before we saw land we observed some birds
called rabihorcados,[1] marine birds of prey which do not sit
or sleep upon the water, making circumvolutions in the air
at the close of evening previous to taking their flight towards
land for the night. These birds could not be going to settle
at more than twelve or fifteen leagues distance, because it
was late in the evening, and this was on our right hand on
the side towards Spain; from which we all judged that there
was land there still undiscovered; but we did not go in search
of it, because it would have taken us round out of our intended
route. I hope that in a few voyages it will be discovered.
It was at dawn that we left the before-mentioned island of
Burenquen,[2] and on that day before nightfall we caught sight
of land, which though not recognized by any of those who had
come hither in the former voyage, we believed to be Española,
from the information given us by the Indian women whom
we had with us; and in this island we remain at present.[3]
Between this island and Burenquen another island appeared
at a distance, but of no great size. When we reached Española
the land, at the part where we approached it, was low and very
flat,[4] on seeing which, a general doubt arose as to its identity;
for neither the Admiral nor his companions, on the previous
voyage, had seen it on this side.

The island being large, is divided into provinces; the part
which we first touched at, is called Hayti; another province
adjoining it, they call Xamaná;[5] and the next province is
named Bohio,[6] where we now are. These provinces are again
subdivided, for they are of great extent. Those who have
seen the length of its coast, state that it is two hundred leagues
long, and I myself should judge it not to be less than a hun-

[1] See note to Journal, September 29. Frigate-bird is the accepted
English name; a species of pelican.

[2] Porto Rico.

[3] On Friday, the 22d of November, the Admiral first caught sight of the
island of Española. Las Casas, II. 10.

[4] Cape Engaño, in the island of Española. (Navarrete.)

[5] Preserved in the Bay of Samana.

[6] See Journal, October 21, and note.

dred and fifty leagues: as to its breadth, nothing is hitherto known; it is now forty days since a caravel left us with the view of circumnavigating it,[1] and is not yet returned. The country is very remarkable, and contains a vast number of large rivers, and extensive chains of mountains, with broad open valleys, and the mountains are very high; it does not appear that the grass is ever cut throughout the year. I do not think they have any winter in this part, for at Christmas were found many birds-nests, some containing the young birds, and others containing eggs. No four-footed animal has ever been seen in this or any of the other islands, except some dogs of various colors, as in our own country, but in shape like large house-dogs;[2] and also some little animals, in color and fur like a rabbit, and the size of a young rabbit, with long tails, and feet like those of a rat; these animals climb up the trees, and many who have tasted them, say they are very good to eat:[3] there are not any wild beasts.

There are great numbers of small snakes, and some lizards, but not many; for the Indians consider them as great a luxury as we do pheasants; they are of the same size as ours, but different in shape. In a small adjacent island[4] (close by a harbor called Monte Cristo, where we stayed several days), our men saw an enormous kind of lizard, which

---

[1] Of this voyage of exploration there seems to be no record. Our natural sources, the *Historie* and Las Casas, are silent. Columbus suspended his writing in his Journal from December 11, 1493, till March 12, 1494. Antonio de Torres sailed for Spain February 2, 1494, when Dr. Chanca sent off his letter. Probably this exploration was begun about December 20.

[2] *Unos gosques grandes.* The French translation has *gros carlins*, "large pug-dogs." Bernaldez calls these dogs, *gozcos pequeños*, "small curs." "Cur" is the common meaning for *gozque* or *gosque.* See Oviedo, lib. xii., cap. v., for a description of these native dogs which soon became extinct.

[3] Bernaldez, II. 34, supplies the native name, *Utia.* Oviedo, lib. xii., cap. i., describes the *hutia.* When he wrote it had become so scarce as to be seen only on rare occasions. It was extinct in Du Tertre's time, a century later. Of the four allied species described by Oviedo, the *hutia*, the *quemi*, the *mohuy*, and the *cori* (agouti), only the last has survived to the present day.

[4] Cabra, or Goat Island, between Puerto de Plata and Cas Rouge Point. (Major.)

they said was as large round as a calf, with a tail as long as a lance, which they often went out to kill: but bulky as it was, it got into the sea, so that they could not catch it.[1] There are, both in this and the other islands, an infinite number of birds like those in our own country, and many others such as we had never seen. No kind of domestic fowl has been seen here, with the exception of some ducks in the houses in Zuruquia; these ducks were larger than those of Spain, though smaller than geese, — very pretty, with flat crests on their heads, most of them as white as snow, but some black.

We ran along the coast of this island nearly a hundred leagues, concluding, that within this range we should find the spot where the Admiral had left some of his men, and which we supposed to be about the middle of the coast. As we passed by the province called Xamaná, we sent on shore one of the Indians, who had been taken in the previous voyage, clothed, and carrying some trifles, which the Admiral had ordered to be given him. On that day died one of our sailors, a Biscayan, who had been wounded in the affray with the Caribbees, when they were captured, as I have already described, through their want of caution. As we were proceeding along the coast, an opportunity was afforded for a boat to go on shore to bury him, the boat being accompanied by two caravels to protect it. When they reached the shore, a great number of Indians came out to the boat, some of them wearing necklaces and ear-rings of gold, and expressed a wish to accompany the Spaniards to the ships; but our men refused to take them, because they had not received permission from the Admiral. When the Indians found that they would not take them, two of them got into a small canoe, and went up to one of the caravels that had put in to shore; they were received on board with great kindness, and taken to the Admiral's ship, where, through the medium of an interpreter, they related that a certain king had sent them to ascertain who we were, and to invite us to land, adding that they had plenty of gold, and also of provisions, to which we should be welcome.

---

[1] Apparently the cayman or South American alligator.

The Admiral desired that shirts, and caps, and other trifles,
should be given to each of them, and said that as he was going
to the place where Guacamari dwelt, he would not stop then,
but that another time there would be an opportunity of seeing him, and with that they departed. We continued our
route till we came to an harbor called Monte Cristi, where we
remained two days, in order to observe the character of the
land; for the Admiral had an objection to the spot where his
men had been left with the view of making a settlement. We
went on shore therefore to see the character of the land: there
was a large river of excellent water close by; [1] but the ground
was inundated, and very ill-calculated for habitation. As
we went on making our observations on the river and the land,
some of our men found two dead bodies by the river's side,
one with a rope round his neck, and the other with one round
his foot; this was on the first day of our landing. On the
following day they found two other corpses farther on, and
one of these was observed to have a great quantity of beard;
this was regarded as a very suspicious circumstance by many
of our people, because, as I have already said, all the Indians
are beardless. This harbor is twelve leagues [2] from the place
where the Spaniards had been left under the protection of
Guacamari, [3] the king of that province, whom I suppose to be
one of the chief men of the island. After two days we set sail
for that spot, but as it was late when we arrived there, [4] and
there were some shoals, where the Admiral's ship had been lost,
we did not venture to put in close to the shore, but remained
that night at a little less than a league from the coast, waiting
until the morning, when we might enter securely. On that
evening, a canoe, containing five or six Indians, came out at a

[1] The river Yaque.

[2] It is only seven leagues.   (Navarrete.)

[3] This chief's name is Guacanagari in Las Casas, *Historia de las Indias*,
and in the *Historie* of Ferdinand Columbus, Goathanari in the Syllacio-
Coma letter, Guacanari in Bernaldez and Guaccanarillus in Peter Martyr's
De Rebus Oceanicis.

[4] The admiral anchored at the entrance of the harbor of Navidad, on
Wednesday, the 27th of November, towards midnight. Las Casas,
II. 11.

considerable distance from where we were, and approached us with great celerity. The Admiral believing that he insured our safety by keeping the sails set, would not wait for them; they, however, perseveringly rowed up to us within a cannon shot [1] and then stopped to look at us; but when they saw that we did not wait for them, they put back and went away. After we had anchored that night at the spot in question,[2] the Admiral ordered two cannons to be fired, to see if the Spaniards, who had remained with Guacamari, would fire in return, for they also had cannons with them; but when we received no reply, and could not perceive any fires, nor the slightest symptom of habitations on the spot, the spirits of our people became much depressed, and they began to entertain the suspicion which the circumstances were naturally calculated to excite. While all were in this desponding mood, and when four or five hours of the night had passed away, the same canoe which we had seen in the evening, came up, and the Indians with a loud voice addressed the captain of the caravel, which they first approached, inquiring for the Admiral; [3] they were conducted to the Admiral's vessel, but would not go on board till he had spoken to them, and they had asked for a light, in order to assure themselves that it was he who conversed with them. One of them was a cousin of Guacamari, who had been sent by him once before: it appeared, that after they had turned back the previous evening, they had been charged by Guacamari with two masks of gold as a present; one for the Admiral, the other for a captain who had accompanied him on the former voyage. They remained on board for three hours, talking with the Admiral in the presence of all of us, he showing much pleasure in their conversation, and inquiring respecting the welfare of the Spaniards whom he had left behind. Guacamari's cousin replied, that those who remained were all well, but that some of them

[1] See Journal of First Voyage, December 25.

[2] The Bay of Caracol, four leagues west of Fort Dauphin. (Major.)

[3] "Toward midnight a canoe came full of Indians and reached the ship of the Admiral, and they called for him saying 'Almirante, Almirante.'" Las Casas, II. 11.

had died of disease, and others had been killed in quarrels that had arisen amongst them; and that Guacamari was at some distance, lying ill of a wound in his leg, which was the occasion of his not appearing, but that he would come on the next day. He said also that two kings named Caonabó and Mayreni, had come to fight with him and that they had burned the village. The Indians then departed, saying they would return on the following day with the said Guacamari, and left us consoled for that night. On the morning of the next day, we were expecting that Guacamari would come; and, in the meantime, some of our men landed by command of the Admiral, and went to the spot where the Spaniards had formerly been: they found the building which they had inhabited, and which they had in some degree fortified with a palisade, burnt and levelled with the ground; they found also some cloaks and clothing which the Indians had brought to throw upon the house. They observed too that the Indians who were seen near the spot, looked very shy, and dared not approach, but, on the contrary, fled from them. This appeared strange to us, for the Admiral had told us that in the former voyage, when he arrived at this place, so many came in canoes to see us, that there was no keeping them off; and as we now saw that they were suspicious of us, it gave us a very unfavorable impression. We threw trifles, such as hawk bells [1] and beads, towards them, in order to conciliate them, but only four, a relation of Guacamari's and three others, took courage to enter the boat, and were rowed on board. When they were asked concerning the Spaniards, they replied that all of them were dead; we had been told this already by one of the Indians whom we had brought from Spain, and who had conversed with the two Indians that on the former occasion came on board with their canoe, but we had not believed it. Guacamari's kinsman was asked who had killed them; he replied that the king of Caonabó and king Mayreni had made an attack upon them, and burnt the buildings on the spot, that

---

[1] The hawk bell was a small open bell used in hawking. The discoverers used hawk bells as a small measure as of gold dust.

many were wounded in the affray, and among them Guacamari, who had received a wound in his thigh, and had retired to some distance. He also stated that he wished to go and fetch him; upon which some trifles were given to him, and he took his departure for the place of Guacamari's abode. All that day we remained in expectation of them, and when we saw that they did not come, many suspected that the Indians who had been on board the night before, had been drowned; for they had had wine given them two or three times, and they had come in a small canoe that might be easily upset. The next morning the Admiral went on shore, taking some of us with him; we went to the spot where the settlement had been, and found it utterly destroyed by fire, and the clothes of the Spaniards lying about upon the grass, but on that occasion we saw no dead body. There were many different opinions amongst us; some suspecting that Guacamari himself was concerned in the betrayal and death of the Christians; others thought not, because his own residence was burnt: so that it remained a very doubtful question. The Admiral ordered all the ground which had been occupied by the fortifications of the Spaniards to be searched, for he had left orders with them to bury all the gold that they might get. While this was being done, the Admiral wished to examine a spot at about a league's distance, which seemed to be suitable for building a town, for it was already time to do so; — and some of us went thither with him, making our observations of the land as we went along the coast, until we reached a village of seven or eight houses, which the Indians forsook when they saw us approach, carrying away what they could, and leaving the things which they could not remove, hidden amongst the grass, around the houses. These people are so like beasts that they have not even the sense to select a fitting place to live in; those who dwell on the shore, build for themselves the most miserable hovels that can be imagined, and all the houses are so covered with grass and dampness, that I am amazed at the way they live. In these houses we found many things belonging to the Spaniards, which it could not be supposed they

would have bartered; such as a very handsome Moorish mantle,
which had not been unfolded since it was brought from Spain,
stockings and pieces of cloth, also an anchor belonging to the
ship which the Admiral had lost here on the previous voyage;
with other articles, which the more confirmed our suspicions.
On examining some things which had been put away to keep
in a basket, closely woven and very secure, we found a man's
head kept with great care; this we judged might be the
head of a father, or mother, or of some person whom they
much regarded:[1] I have since heard that many were found in
the same state, which makes me believe that our first impression was the true one. After this we returned. We went
on the same day to the site of the settlement; and when we
arrived, we found many Indians, who had regained their
courage, bartering gold with our men: they had bartered to
the extent of a mark;[2] we also learned that they had shown
where the bodies of eleven of the dead Spaniards were laid,
which were already covered with the grass that had grown
over them; and they all with one voice asserted that Caonabó
and Mayreni had killed them; but notwithstanding all this,
we began to hear complaints that one of the Spaniards had
taken three women to himself, and another four; from whence
we drew the inference that jealousy was the cause of the misfortune that had occurred. On the next morning, as no spot
in that vicinity appeared suitable for our making a settlement, the Admiral ordered a caravel to go in one direction to
look for a convenient locality, while some of us went with him
another way. In the course of our explorations, we discovered a harbor, of great security, and a very favorable situation
for a settlement; but as it was far from where we wanted to
have the gold mine, the Admiral decided to settle only in some
spot which would give us greater certainty of attaining that
object, provided the position of the land should prove equally

[1] See above, p. 289, note 1.
[2] The mark was a weight of eight ounces, two-thirds of a Troy pound.
The mark of gold in Spain was equivalent to 50 castellanos, or in bullion
value to-day about $150.

convenient. On our return, we found the other caravel arrived, in which Melchior [1] and four or five other trustworthy
men had been exploring with a similar object. They reported
that as they went along the coast, a canoe came out to them
in which were two Indians, one of whom was the brother of
Guacamari, and was recognized by a pilot who was in the
caravel. When he asked them "who goes there," they replied that Guacamari sent to beg the Spaniards to come on
shore, as he had his settlement near, with nearly fifty houses.
The chief men of the party then went on shore in the boat,
proceeded to the place where Guacamari was, and found him
stretched on his bed, complaining of a severe wound. They
conferred with him, and inquired respecting the Spaniards;
his reply was, in accordance with the account already given
by the others, viz. — that they had been killed by Caonabó
and Mayreni, who also had wounded him in the thigh; which
he showed to them bandaged up: on seeing which, they concluded that his statement was correct. At their departure
he gave to each of them a jewel of gold, according to his estimation of their respective merits. The Indians beat the gold
into very thin plates, in order to make masks of it, and to be
able to set it in bitumen; if it were not so prepared it could not
be mounted; other ornaments they make of it, to wear on the
head and to hang in the ears and nostrils, for these also they
require it to be thin; since they set no store by it as wealth
but only for adornment. Guacamari desired them by signs
and as well as he was able, to tell the Admiral that as he was
thus wounded, he prayed him to have the goodness to come
to see him. The sailors told this to the Admiral when he
arrived. The next morning he resolved to go thither, for the
spot could be reached in three hours, being scarcely three
leagues distance from the place where we were; but as it
would be the dinner-hour when we arrived, we dined before
we went on shore. After dinner, the Admiral gave orders that

[1] Melchior Maldonado, apparently the Melchiorius from whom Peter
Martyr derived some of his material for his account of the second voyage.
See his *De Rebus Oceanicis*, ed. 1574, p. 26.

all the captains should come with their barges to proceed to
the shore, for already on that morning, previous to our departure, the aforesaid brother of Guacamari had come to speak
with the Admiral to urge him to come to the place where Guacamari was.   Then the Admiral went on shore accompanied
by all the principal officers, so richly dressed that they would
have made a fine appearance even in any of our chief cities.
He took with him some articles as presents, having already
received from Guacamari a certain quantity of gold, and it
was reasonable that he should make a commensurate response
to his acts and expressions of good-will: Guacamari had also
provided himself with a present.   When we arrived, we found
him stretched upon his bed, which was made of cotton net-
work, and, according to their custom, suspended.[1]   He did not
arise, but made from his bed the best gesture of courtesy of
which he was capable.   He showed much feeling with tears
in his eyes for the death of the Spaniards, and began speaking
on the subject, with explaining to the best of his power, how
some died of disease, others had gone to Caonabó in search of
the mine of gold, and had there been killed, and that the rest
had been attacked and slain in their own town.   According
to the appearance of the dead bodies, it was not two months
since this had happened.   Then he presented the Admiral
with eight marks and a half of gold and five or six belts worked
with stones [2] of various colors, and a cap of similar jewel-work,
which I think they must value very highly, because in it was

[1] The familiar hammock.

[2] The original reads "cinco o seiscientos labrados de pedreria," which
Major translated "five or six hundred pieces of jewellery," and Thacher
"five or six hundred cut stones."   The dictionaries recognize *labrado* as
a noun only in the plural *labrados*, "tilled lands."   Turning to Bernaldez,
Historia de los Reyes Catolicos, in which Dr. Chanca's letter was copied almost
bodily, we find, II. 27, "cinco ó seis labrados de pedrería," which presents
the same difficulty.   The omission of *cientos* is notable, however.   I think the
original text of Dr. Chanca's letter read "cinco ó seis cintos labrados de
pedreria," *i.e.*, five or six belts worked with jewellery.   *Cintos* being written
blindly was copied *cientos* by Antonio de Aspa, from whom our text of Dr.
Chanca's letter has come down (Navarrete, I. 224), and was omitted perhaps
accidentally in Bernaldez's copy.   This conjecture is rendered almost certain
by the *Historie*, where it is recorded that "the Cacique gave the Admiral

a jewel, which was presented to him with great reverence. It appears to me that these people put more value upon copper than gold. The surgeon of the fleet and myself being present, the Admiral told Guacamari that we were skilled in the treatment of human disorders, and wished that he would shew us his wound; he replied that he was willing; upon which I said it would be necessary that he should, if possible, go out of the house, because we could not see well on account of the place being darkened by the crowd of people; to this he consented, I think more from timidity than inclination, and left the house leaning on the arm of the Admiral. After he was seated, the surgeon approached him and began to untie the bandage; then he told the Admiral that the wound was made with a *ciba*, by which he meant with a stone. When the wound was uncovered, we went up to examine it: it is certain that there was no more wound on that leg than on the other, although he cunningly pretended that it pained him much. Ignorant as we were of the facts, it was impossible to come to a definite conclusion. There were certainly many proofs of an invasion by a hostile people, so that the Admiral was at a loss what to do; he with many others thought, however, that for the present, and until they could ascertain the truth, they ought to conceal their distrust; for after ascertaining it, they would be able to claim whatever indemnity they thought proper. That evening Guacamari accompanied the Admiral to the ships, and when they showed him the horses and other objects of interest, their novelty struck him with the greatest amazement;[1] he took supper on board, and returned that

eight belts worked with small beads made of white, green, and red stones," p. 148, London ed. of 1867. This passage enables us to correct the text of Las Casas, II. 14, changing "ochocientas cuentas menudas de piedra," "eight hundred small beads of stone," to "ocho cintos de cuentas menudas," etc., "eight belts of small beads," and again, *ciento de oro* to *cinto de oro*. In the Syllacio-Coma letter the gift is *balteos duodecim*, "twelve belts." Thacher, *Columbus*, II. 235. *Cf.* Las Casas's description of the girdle or belt that this chief wore when Columbus first saw him, Dec. 22, above, p. 194.

[1] These were not only the first horses seen in the New World since the extinction of the prehistoric varieties, but the first large quadrupeds the West Indians had seen.

x

evening to his house. The Admiral told him that he wished
to settle there and to build houses; to which he assented, but
said that the place was not wholesome, because it was very
damp: and so it most certainly was.

All this passed through the interpretation of two of the
Indians who had gone to Spain in the last voyage, and who
were the sole survivors of seven who had embarked with us;
five died on the voyage, and these but narrowly escaped.
The next day we anchored in that port: Guacamari sent to
know when the Admiral intended leaving, and was told that he
would do so on the morrow. The same day Guacamari's
brother, and others with him, came on board, bringing gold
to barter: on the day of our departure also they bartered a
great quantity of gold. There were ten women on board, of
those who had been taken in the Caribbee islands, principally
from Boriquen, and it was observed that the brother of Guacamari spoke with them; we think that he told them to make
an effort to escape that night; for certainly during our first
sleep they dropped themselves quietly into the water, and
went on shore, so that by the time they were missed they had
reached such a distance that only four could be taken by the
boats which went in pursuit, and these were secured when just
leaving the water: they had to swim considerably more than
half a league. The next morning the Admiral sent to desire
that Guacamari would cause search to be made for the women
who had escaped in the night, and that he would send them
back to the ships. When the messengers arrived they found
the place forsaken and not a soul there; this made many
openly declare their suspicions, but others said they might
have removed to another village, as was their custom. That
day we remained quiet, because the weather was unfavorable
for our departure. On the next morning the Admiral resolved
that as the wind was adverse, it would be well to go with the
boats to inspect a harbor on the coast at two leagues distance
further up,[1] to see if the formation of the land was favorable
for a settlement; and we went thither with all the ship's boats,

[1] Port Dauphin. (Navarrete.)

leaving the ships in the harbor. As we moved along the coast the people manifested a sense of insecurity, and when we reached the spot to which we were bound all the natives had fled. While we were walking about this place we found an Indian stretched on the hill-side, close by the houses, with a gaping wound in his shoulder caused by a dart, so that he had been disabled from fleeing any further. The natives of this island fight with sharp darts, which they shoot with straps in the same manner as boys in Spain shoot their little darts, and with these they shoot with considerable skill to a great distance; and certainly upon an unarmed people these weapons are calculated to do serious injury. The man told us that Caonabó and his people had wounded him and burnt the houses of Guacamari. Thus we are still kept in uncertainty respecting the death of our people, on account of the paucity of information on which to form an opinion, and the conflicting and equivocal character of the evidence we have obtained. We did not find the position of the land in this port favorable for healthy habitation, and the Admiral resolved upon return- ing along the upper coast by which we had come from Spain, because we had had tidings of gold in that direction. But the weather was so adverse that it cost more labor to sail thirty leagues in a backward direction than the whole voyage from Spain; so that, what with the contrary wind and the length of the passage, three months had elapsed when we landed.[1] It pleased God, however, that through the check upon our progress caused by contrary winds, we succeeded in finding the best and most suitable spot that we could have selected for a settlement, where there was an excellent harbor [2] and abun- dance of fish, an article of which we stand in great need from the scarcity of meat. The fish caught here are very singular and more wholesome than those of Spain. The climate does

[1] That is, three months from the time the fleet left Spain, September 25, 1493. Neither the *Historie* nor Las Casas mentions the date of landing. In the Syllacio-Coma letter the date is given as "eight days from Christmas." See Thacher, *Columbus*, II. 236, 257.

[2] Port Isabelique, or Isabella, ten leagues to the east of Monte Cristi. (Navarrete.)

not allow the fish to be kept from one day to another, for it is hot and moist, so that all animal food [1] spoils very quickly.

The land is very rich for all purposes; near the harbor there are two rivers: one large,[2] and another of moderate breadth somewhat near it; the water is of a very remarkable quality. On the bank of it is being built a city called Marta,[3] one side of which is bounded by the water with a ravine of cleft rock, so that at that part there is no need of fortification; the other half is girt with a plantation of trees so thick that a rabbit could scarcely pass through it; and so green that fire will never be able to burn it. A channel has been commenced for a branch of the river, which the managers say they will lead through the middle of the settlement, and will place on it grist-mills and saw-mills and mills of other kinds requiring to be worked by water. Great quantities of vegetables have been planted, which certainly attain a more luxuriant growth here in eight days than they would in Spain in twenty. We are frequently visited by numbers of Indians, among whom are some of their *caciques* or chiefs, and many women. They all come loaded with *ages*,[4] which are like turnips, very excellent for food, which we dressed in various ways. This food was so nutritious as to prove a great support to all of us after the privations we endured when at sea, which were more severe than ever were suffered by man; for as we could not tell what weather it would please God to send us on our voyage, we were obliged

---

[1] *Cosas introfatibles* in the Spanish. The translation follows the French version. The text perhaps is corrupt. The word *introfatibles* is not found in any of the Spanish dictionaries nor is it a learned compound whose meaning is apparent from its etymology. Professor H. R. Lang suggests that *cosas corruptibles* may be the proper reading. The sentence is omitted in the corresponding passage in Bernaldez, II. 30.

[2] The river Isabella.

[3] I can offer no explanation for this name, which is found only in Dr. Chanca's letter. Bernaldez, who copied Dr. Chanca, gives Isabela as the name of the city, II. 30, and the *Historie* and Las Casas, who preserve for us the gist of Columbus's own narrative, both say that "he named the city Isabela in memory of Queen Isabela." Las Casas, II. 21. *Historie*, p. 150.

[4] Yams, the *Dioscorea sativa*. Columbus had seen the yam in Guinea and applied the African negro name, *igname*, *ñame*, whence the English, yam. See note to Journal, November 4.

to limit ourselves most rigorously with regard to food, in order that, at all events, we might at least have the means of supporting life. This *age* the Caribbees call *nabi*, and the Indians *hage*.[1] The Indians barter gold, provisions, and everything they bring with them, for tips of lacings, beads, and pins, and pieces of porringers and dishes. They all, as I have said, go naked as they were born, except the women of this island, who have their private parts covered, some with a covering of cotton, which they bind round their hips, while others use grass and leaves of trees.[2] When they wish to adorn themselves, both men and women paint themselves, some black, others white, and various colors, in so many devices that the effect is very laughable;[3] they shave some parts of their heads, and in others wear long tufts of matted hair, which have an indescribably ridiculous appearance: in short, whatever would be looked upon in our country as characteristic of a madman, is here regarded by the highest of the Indians as a mark of distinction.

In our present position, we are in the neighborhood of many mines of gold, not one of which, we are told, is more than twenty or twenty-five leagues off: the Indians say that some of them are in Niti, in the possession of Caonabó, who killed the Christians; the others are in another place called Cibao, which, if it please God, we shall see with our eyes before many days are over; indeed we should go there at once, but that we have so many things to provide that we are not equal to it at present. One third of our people have fallen sick within the last four or five days, which I think has principally arisen from the toil and privations of the journey; another cause has been the variableness of the climate; but I hope in our Lord that all will be restored to health. My idea of this people is, that if we could converse with them,

---

[1] By the Indians Dr. Chanca means the Tainos, the native inhabitants of Española.

[2] "Every woman wears a tiny apron called a *queyu*, suspended by tying its strings around her waist." Im Thurn, *Among the Indians of Guiana*, 194.

[3] On this body painting, see Im Thurn, *ibid.*

they would all become converted, for they do whatever they see us do, making genuflections before the altars at the *Ave Maria* and the other parts of the devotional service, and making the sign of the cross. They all say that they wish to be Christians, although in truth they are idolaters, for in their houses they have many kinds of figures; when asked what such a figure was, they would reply it is a thing of *Turey*, by which they meant "of Heaven." I made a pretence of throwing them on the fire, which grieved them so that they began to weep: they believe that everything we bring comes from Heaven, and therefore call it *Turey*, which, as I have already said, means heaven in their language. The first day that I went on shore to sleep, was the Lord's day. The little time that we have spent on land, has been so much occupied in seeking for a fitting spot for the settlement, and in providing necessaries, that we have had little opportunity of becoming acquainted with the products of the soil, yet although the time has been so short, many marvellous things have been seen. We have met with trees bearing wool, of a sufficiently fine quality (according to the opinion of those who are acquainted with the art) to be woven into good cloth; there are so many of these trees that we might load the caravels with wool, although it is troublesome to collect, for the trees are very thorny,[1] but some means may be easily found of overcoming this difficulty. There are also cotton trees, perennials, as large as peach trees, which produce cotton in the greatest abundance.[2] We found trees producing wax as good both in color and smell as bees-wax and equally useful for burning; indeed there is no great difference between them.[3] There are vast numbers of trees which yield surprisingly fine turpentine;

---

[1] A species of the *N.O. Bombaceae;* perhaps the *Eriodendron anfractuosum.* (Major.) The English name is silk-cotton tree. The fibre, however, cannot be woven. Von Martius suggests the *Bombax ceiba.*

[2] *Cf.* Hazard, *Santo Domingo,* p. 350, "the cotton plant which instead of being a simple bush planted from the seed each year, is here a tree, growing two or three years, which needs only to be trimmed and pruned to produce a large yield of the finest cotton."

[3] Probably the so-called Carnauba wax or perhaps palm-tree wax. *Cf.* the *Encyclopædia Britannica,* art. "Wax."

and there is also a great abundance of tragacanth, also very good. We found other trees which I think bear nutmegs, because the bark tastes and smells like that spice, but at present there is no fruit on them; I saw one root of ginger, which an Indian wore hanging round his neck. There are also aloes; not like those which we have hitherto seen in Spain, but no doubt they are one of the species used by us doctors.[1] A sort of cinnamon also has been found; but, to tell the truth, it is not so fine as that with which we are already acquainted in Spain. I do not know whether this arises from ignorance of the proper season to gather it, or whether the soil does not produce better. We have also seen some lemon-colored myrobolans; at this season they are all lying under the trees, and have a bitter flavor, arising, I think, from the rottenness occasioned by the moisture of the ground; but the taste of such parts as have remained sound, is that of the genuine myrobolan.[2] There is also very good mastic.[3] None of the natives of these islands, as far as we have yet seen, possess any iron; they have, however, many tools, such as axes and adzes, made of stone, which are so handsome and well finished, that it is wonderful how they contrive to make them without the use of iron. Their food consists of bread, made of the roots of a vegetable which is between a tree and a vegetable, and the *age*,[4] which I have already described as being like the turnip, and very good food; they use, to season it, a spice called *agi*,[5] which they also eat with fish, and such

---

[1] The Spanish here is *linaloe*, but the reference seems to be to the medicinal aloes and not to lign aloes. On lign aloes, see Columbus's Journal, November 12, and note.

[2] The myrobolan is an East Indian fruit with a stone, of the prune genus. Crude or preserved myrobolans were a more important article of commerce in the Middle Ages than now. There were five varieties, one of which, the *Mirobalani citrini*, were so named because they were lemon-colored. Heyd, *Histoire du Commerce du Levant au Moyen-Age*, II. 641. A species of myrobolan grows in South America.

[3] The product of the *Bursera gummifera*.

[4] *Cf.* Columbus's Journal, November 4, and note.

[5] *Agi*, also written *Axi*, is the *Capsicum annuum* or Spanish pepper. Most of the cayenne or red pepper of commerce comes from the allied species,

birds as they can catch of the many kinds which abound in the island. They have, besides, a kind of grain like hazel-nuts, very good to eat. They eat all the snakes, and lizards, and spiders, and worms, that they find upon the ground;[1] so that, to my fancy, their bestiality is greater than that of any beast upon the face of the earth. The Admiral had at one time determined to leave the search for the mines until he had first despatched the ships which were to return to Spain, on account of the great sickness which had prevailed among the men,[2] but afterwards he resolved upon sending two bands under the command of two captains, the one to Cibao, and the other to Niti, where, as I have already said, Caonabó lived. These parties went, one of them returning on the twentieth, and the other on the twenty-first of January. The party that went to Cibao saw gold in so many places as to seem almost incredible, for in truth they found it in more than fifty streamlets and rivers, as well as upon their banks; so that, the captain said they had only to seek throughout that province, and they would find as much as they wished. He brought specimens from the different parts, namely, from

---

Capsicum frutescens. In Mexico the name of this indigenous pepper plant was Quauhchilli, *Chili* tree. *Chili* was taken over into Spanish as the common name for capsicum and has come down in English in the familiar Chili sauce. See Peschel, *Zeitalter der Entdeckungen*, p. 139; De Candolle, *Origin of Cultivated Plants*, pp. 289–290. *Encyclopædia Britannica*, art. "Cayenne Pepper."

[1] *Cf.* Im Thurn, *Among the Indians of Guiana*, 266.

[2] The Admiral, "having described the country at length and the condition in which he was and where he had settled for the Catholic sovereigns and sending them the specimen of gold which Guacanagari had given him and that which Hojeda had brought, and informing them of all that he saw to be needed, despatched the twelve ships before mentioned, placing in command of them all Antonio de Torres, brother of the nurse of the prince Don Juan, to whom he intrusted the gold and all his despatches. They made sail the 2d of February, 1494." Las Casas, *Historia de las Indias*, II. 25–26. Columbus's letter to Ferdinand and Isabella mentioned here has not been preserved. That part of it which related to future needs was apparently duplicated in the "memorial" which he gave to Torres. This document is given in English in Thacher, *Christopher Columbus*, II. 297–308, and Major, *Select Letters of Christopher Columbus*, ed. 1870, pp. 72–107. See p. 73, *ibid.*, for a reference to letters of the Admiral no longer extant.

the sand of the rivers and small springs. It is thought, that by digging, it will be found in greater pieces, for the Indians neither know how to dig nor have the means of digging more than a hand's depth. The other captain, who went to Niti, returned also with news of a great quantity of gold in three or four places; of which he likewise brought specimens.[1]

Thus, surely, their Highnesses the King and Queen may henceforth regard themselves as the most prosperous and wealthy sovereigns in the world; never yet, since the creation, has such a thing been seen or read of; for on the return of the ships from their next voyage, they will be able to carry back such a quantity of gold as will fill with amazement all who hear of it. Here I think I shall do well to break off my narrative. I think those who do not know me, who hear these things, may consider me prolix, and a man who has exaggerated somewhat, but God is my witness, that I have not exceeded, by one tittle, the bounds of truth.[2]

[1] Alonso de Hojeda was sent to explore the region of Cibao with fifteen men. He found Cibao to be fifteen or twenty leagues from Isabella. The other exploring party was headed by Gines de Gorbalan. Further details of these expeditions are given in the Syllacio-Coma letter. Thacher, *Columbus*, II. 258–260. According to Coma, or his translator Syllacio, Cibao was identified with the Sheba of the Bible. Columbus, on the other hand, identified Cibao and Cipango. *Cf.*, *e.g.*, Peter Martyr, *De Rebus Oceanicis*, ed. 1574, p. 31.

[2] "The preceding is the transcript of that part of Doctor Chanca's letter, which refers to intelligence respecting the Indies. The remainder of the letter does not bear upon the subject, but treats of private matters, in which Doctor Chanca requests the interference and support of the Town Council of Seville (of which city he was a native), in behalf of his family and property, which he had left in the said city. This letter reached Seville in the month of [March] in the year fourteen hundred and ninety-three [four]." This note is no doubt from the hand of Friar Antonio de Aspa, who formed the collection of papers in which Navarrete found the text of Dr. Chanca's letter. The collection was made about the middle of the sixteenth century. See Navarrete, II. 224. The returning fleet arrived at Cadiz in March, 1494. Bernaldez, *Historia de los Reyes Catolicos*, (ed. 1870), II. 37.

NARRATIVE OF THE THIRD VOYAGE OF COLUMBUS AS CONTAINED IN LAS CASAS'S HISTORY

INTRODUCTION

THE narrative given here of the third voyage of Columbus in which he discovered the mainland of South America is taken from the *Historia de las Indias* of Las Casas. In preparing his History Las Casas had the use of a larger body of Columbus's papers than has come down to us. Among these papers was a journal of this third voyage which was incorporated in a condensed form by Las Casas in his History, just as he did in the case of the journals of the first and second voyages. This narrative is found in the second volume of the *Historia de las Indias*, pp. 220–317. The translation is, as is mentioned in the preface to this volume, that given in John Boyd Thacher's *Christopher Columbus*.

In certain places the text differs slightly from that in the printed edition of Las Casas, as Mr. Thacher followed the critical text of Cesare de Lollis prepared for the *Raccolta Colombiana* by a collation of the manuscript in the Archives at Madrid with the recently discovered autograph manuscript of Las Casas. Mr. Thacher, following Lollis, omitted passages that were obviously comments on the text by Las Casas. These have been supplied either from Mr. Thacher's notes or translated by the editor from the printed text. The editor has gone over the whole translation and can testify to its exceptional accuracy. A few slight changes have been made in the wording for the sake of greater clearness or exactness.

Columbus described this voyage in a letter to Ferdinand and Isabella. This letter is included in Major's *Select Letters of Columbus* and in P. L. Ford's *Writings of Columbus*. This letter is of great importance in the study of Columbus's geographical ideas. Other contemporary accounts of this voyage are contained in Ferdinand Columbus's *Historie*, the life of his father, where the journal abridged by Las Casas is still further condensed, in Peter Martyr's *De Rebus Oceanicis*, Dec. I., lib. VI., and in the letter of Simone Verde and the three letters of Angelo Trivigiano which will be found in Harrisse, *Christophe Colomb*, II. 95–98 and 119–123.

E. G. B.

NARRATIVE OF THE THIRD VOYAGE OF COLUMBUS AS CONTAINED IN LAS CASAS'S HISTORY

May 30–August 31, 1498

HE started then (our First Admiral),[1] "in the name of the Most Holy Trinity" (as he says and as he was always accustomed to say) from the port of San Lucar de Barrameda, Wednesday, May 30, 1498, with the intention of discovering new land not yet discovered, with his six ships, "greatly fatigued," he says, "with my voyage, since as I was hoping for some quietude, when I left the Indies, I experienced double hardships;" they being the result of the labors, new obstacles and difficulties with which he obtained the funds for his starting upon the expedition and the annoyances in connection therewith received from the royal officials and the hindrance and the evil reports the people around about the Sovereigns gave concerning the affairs in the Indies, wherefore it appeared to him that what he already had done was not sufficient but that he must renew his labors to gain new credit. And because war had then broken out with France,[2] he had news of a French fleet which was waiting for the Admiral beyond the Cape of St. Vincent, to capture him. On this

---

[1] *I.e.*, the first Admiral of the Ocean and the Indies where Las Casas was when he was writing.

[2] This clause is probably an explanatory remark by Las Casas. It is misleading. The war in Naples growing out of the invasion of Italy by Charles VIII. of France, in which Ferdinand had taken an active part against the French, had been brought to a close so far as concerned France and Spain by a truce in March, 1497. The treaty of peace was signed August 5, 1498.

account he decided to steal away as they say and make a detour, directing his course straight to the island of Madeira.

He arrived at the island of Puerto Sancto, Thursday, June 7, where he stopped to take wood, water and supplies and to hear mass, and he found all the island disturbed and all the farms, goods and flocks guarded, fearing that the new-comers might be French; and then that night he left for the island of Madeira and arrived there the following Sunday, June 10. He was very well received in the town [1] and with much rejoicing, because he was well known there, having been a citizen thereof during some time.[2] He remained there six days, providing himself fully with water and wood and the other necessities for his journey.

Saturday, June 16, he left the island of Madeira with his six ships and arrived at the island of Gomera [3] the following Tuesday. At this island he found a French corsair with a French vessel and two large ships which the corsair had taken from the Castilians, and when the Frenchman saw the six vessels of the Admiral he left his anchors and one vessel and fled with the other vessel. The Admiral sent a ship after him and when the six Spaniards who were being carried away on the captured ship saw this ship coming to their aid, they attacked six Frenchmen who were guarding them and by force they placed them below decks and thus brought them back.

Here in the island of Gomera the Admiral determined to send three ships directly to the island of Española, so that, if he should be detained here, they might give news of him and cheer and console the Christians with the supplies: and principally that they might give joy to his brothers, the Adelan-

---

[1] Funchal.

[2] This positive assertion that Columbus had lived in Funchal, Madeira, has been overlooked by Vignaud and Harrisse. Vignaud, *Études Critiques sur la Vie de Colomb avant ses Découvertes* (Paris, 1905), p. 443, note 9, rejects as unauthenticated the tradition that Columbus lived in Madeira, without adequate grounds it seems to me. Diego Columbus told Las Casas in 1519 that he was born in the neighboring island of Puerto Santo and that his father had lived there. Las Casas, *Historia de las Indias*, I. 54. This passage is not noted by Vignaud.

[3] One of the Canary Islands.

tado [1] and Don Diego, who were very desirous of hearing from him. He named Pedro de Arana, a native of Cordova, as captain of one ship, — a very honorable and prudent man, whom I knew very well, brother of the mother of Don Ferdinand Columbus,[2] the second son of the Admiral, and cousin of that Arana who remained in the fortress with the 38 men whom the Admiral on his return found dead. The other captain of the second ship was called Alonso Sanchez de Carvajal, governor of the city of Baçea, an honorable gentleman. The third captain for the remaining ship was Juan Antonio Columbo,[3] a Genoese, a relation of the Admiral, a very capable and prudent man and one of authority, with whom I had frequent conversation.

He gave them suitable instructions, in which instructions he ordered that, one week one captain, and another week another, each by turns should be captain-general of all the ships, as regarded the navigation and the placing of the night lantern, which is a lighted lantern placed in the stern of the ship in order that the other ships may know and follow where the captain guides. He ordered them to go to the west, quarter south-west,[4] for 850 leagues and told them that then they would arrive at the island of Dominica. From Dominica they should go west-north-west and they would then reach the island of Sant Juan,[5] and it would be the southern part of it, because that was the direct way to go to the New Isabella,[6]

---

[1] The Adelantado was Bartholomew Columbus. The title Adelantado was given in Spain to the military and political governors of border provinces. In this use it was transplanted to America in the earlier days. *Cf.* Moses, *The Establishment of Spanish Rule in America*, pp. 68–69.

[2] Beatrix Enriquez.

[3] This Juan Antonio Columbo seems to have been a first cousin of the admiral. *Cf.* Markham, *Christopher Columbus*, pp. 2 and 187. It is to be noted that he retained in Spain his family name and did not follow the discoverer in changing his name to Colon. On this change of name, see above, p. 77, note 2.

[4] *I.e.*, west by south.

[5] Porto Rico.

[6] Founded in the summer of 1496 by Bartholomew Columbus in accordance with the directions of the Admiral to establish a new settlement on the south side of the island. Las Casas, II. 136.

which now is Santo Domingo. Having passed the island of Sant Juan, they should leave the island of Mona to the north and from there they should make for the point of this Española,[1] which he called Sant Raphael, which now is the Cabo del Engaño, from there to Saona, which he says makes a good harbor between it and this Española. Seven leagues farther there is another island, which is called Santa Catherina, and from there to the New Isabella, which is the port of Santo Domingo, the distance is 25 leagues. And he told the captains that wherever they should arrive and land they should purchase all that they needed by barter and that for the little they might give the Indians, although they might be the canibales,[2] who are said to eat human flesh, they would obtain what they wished and the Indians would give them all that they had; and if they should undertake to procure things by force, the Indians would conceal themselves and remain hostile. He says further in the instructions that he was going by the Cape Verde Islands (which he says were called in ancient times Gorgodes[3] or according to others Hesperides) and that he was going in the name of the Holy Trinity with the intention of navigating to the south of these islands so as to arrive below the equinoctial line and to follow the course to the west until this island of Española should lie to the northwest, to see if there are islands or lands. "Our Lord," he says, "guides me and gives me things which may serve Him and the King and Queen, our Lords, and which may be for the honor of the Christians, for I believe that no

---

[1] "This Española," so frequently repeated, is one of the indications that Las Casas was writing in Española.

[2] *Canibales*, here used still as a tribal name equivalent to Caribbees.

[3] The correct form of this name is Gargades. Columbus's knowledge of them was derived indirectly from Pliny's *Natural History*, book VI., ch. XXXVII., through Cardinal d'Ailly's *Imago Mundi*. *Cf.* Columbus's marginal note to ch. XXXXI. of that work: "*De situ Gorgodum insule nunc de Capite Viride vel Antonii dicitur.*" *Raccolta Colombiana*, parte I., vol. II., p. 395. According to Pliny's location of them they were probably the Canaries. Pliny's knowledge of the location of the Hesperides is naturally vague, but his text would support their identification with the Cape Verde Islands.

one has ever gone this way and that this sea is entirely unknown." [1] And here the Admiral finished his instructions.

Having then taken water and wood and other provisions, especially cheese, of which there are many and good ones there, the Admiral made sail with his six ships on Thursday, June 21, towards the island of Hierro,[2] which is distant from Gomera about fifteen leagues, and of the seven Canaries is the one farthest to the west. Passing it, the Admiral took his course with one ship and two caravels for the islands of Cape Verde, and dismissed the other three ships in the name of the Holy Trinity; and he says that he entreated the Holy Trinity to care for him and for all of them; and at the setting of the sun they separated and the three ships took their course for this island. Here the Admiral makes mention to the Sovereigns of the agreement they had made with the King of Portugal that the Portuguese should not go to the westward of the Azores and Cape Verde Islands, and also mentions how the Sovereigns sent for him that he should be present at the meetings in regard to the partition,[3] and that he could not go on account of the grave illness which he had incurred in the discovery of the mainland of the Indies, that is to say of Cuba, which he always regarded as the mainland even until the present time as he could not circumnavigate it. He adds further that then occurred the death of Don Juan, before he could carry out the matter.[4]

[1] In this Columbus was mistaken, although he had no means of knowing it in 1498. Vasco da Gama had sailed in that sea the preceding summer. Cf. Bourne, *Spain in America*, p. 72.

[2] Ferro.

[3] August 16, 1494, the sovereigns included in the letter despatched to Columbus by Torres the essential articles of the Treaty of Tordesillas, signed June 7, 1494, and asked him if he could not co-operate in locating the Demarcation Line. Navarrete, *Coleccion de Viages*, II. 155; Harrisse, *Diplomatic History of America*, pp. 80–81.

[4] Columbus's illness began in September, 1494, and it was five months before he was fully recovered. Ferdinand Columbus, *Historie*, ed. 1867, p. 177. The death of Prince John took place October 4, 1497. No actual scientific conference to locate the line took place till that at Badajoz in 1524. See Bourne, *Essays in Historical Criticism*, pp. 205–211.

Then the Admiral continuing on his way arrived at the Cape Verde Islands, which according to what he says, have a false name, because he never saw anything green but all things dry and sterile.   The first thing he saw was the island of La Sal, Wednesday, June 27: and it is a small island. From there he went to another which is called Buenavista and is very sterile, where he anchored in a bay, and near it is a very small island. To this island come all the lepers of Portugal to be cured and there are not more than six or seven houses on it. The Admiral ordered the boats to go to land to provide themselves with salt and flesh, because there are a great number of goats on the island.   There came to the ships a steward [1] to whom that island belonged, named Roderigo Alonso, notary public of the exchequer [2] of the King of Portugal, who offered to the Admiral what there was on the island of which he might be in need. The Admiral thanked him and ordered that he should be given some supplies from Castile, which he enjoyed very much.

Here he relates how the lepers came there to be cured because of the great abundance of turtles on that island, which commonly are as large as shields. By eating the flesh and constantly bathing in the blood of these turtles, the lepers become cured.[3] The turtles in infinite number come there three months in the year, June, July, and August, from the mainland, which is Ethiopia,[4] to lay eggs in the sand and with the claws and legs they scratch places in the sand and spawn

[1] *Mayordomo.*

[2] *Escribano de la hacienda.* In 1497 Rodrigo Affonso, a member of the king's council, was granted the northern of the two captaincies into which São Thiago was divided and also the wild cattle on the island of Boavista (Buenavista in Spanish). D'Avezac, *Iles de l'Afrique* (Paris, 1848), p. 218. The word *mayordomo*, translated "steward," here stands for the high Portuguese title of honor *Mordomo môr da Casa Real*, a title in its origin similar to the *majores domus* or mayors of the palace of the early French kings. *Escribano de la hacienda del Rey* means rather the king's treasurer.

[3] This account of Boavista and its lepers is not noticed in the histories of the Cape Verde Islands so far as I know.

[4] From Pliny's time through the Middle Ages the name Ethiopia embraced all tropical Africa. He calls the Atlantic in the tropics the "Ethiopian Sea." Pliny's *Natural History*, book vi., chs. xxxv. and xxxvi.

more than five hundred eggs, as large as those of a hen except that they have not a hard shell but a tender membrane which covers the yolk, like the membrane which covers the yolk of the hen's egg after taking off the hard shell. They cover the eggs in the sand as a person would do, and there the sun hatches them, and the little live turtles come out and then run in search of the sea as if they had come out of it alive. They take the turtles there in this manner: At night with lights which are torches of dry wood, they go searching for the track of the turtle which is easily traced, and find the turtle tired and sleeping. They come up quickly and turn it over with the belly up and leave it, sure that it cannot turn itself back, and go in search of another. And the Indians do the same in the sea; if they come upon one asleep and turn it over it remains safe for them to take it whenever they wish. The Indians, however, have another greater device for taking them on the sea, which will be explained God willing when we give a description of Cuba.[1]

The healthy persons on that island of Buenavista who lead a laborious life were six or seven residents who have no water except brackish water from wells and whose employment is to kill the big goats and salt the skins and send them to Portugal in the caravels which come there for them, of which in one year they kill so many and send so many skins that they are worth 2000 ducats to the notary public, to whom the island belonged. Such a great multitude of goats, male and female, have been grown there, from only eight original head. Those who live there neither eat bread nor drink wine during four or five months, nor anything else except goat flesh or fish or turtles. All this they told to the Admiral.

He left there Saturday, June 30, at night for the island of Santiago, where he arrived on Sunday at the hour of vespers, because it is distant 28 leagues: and this is the principal one of the Cape Verde Islands. He wished to take from this island a herd of black cattle in order to carry them to Española as

---

[1] A remark by Las Casas, of which many are interspersed with the material from Columbus's Journal of this voyage.

the Sovereigns had ordered, and he was there eight days and could not get them; and because the island is very unhealthy since men are burned with heat there and his people commenced to fall ill, he decided to leave it. The Admiral says again that he wishes to go to the south, because he intends with the aid of the Most Holy Trinity, to find islands and lands, that God may be served and their Highnesses and Christianity may have pleasure, and that he wishes to see what was the idea of King Don Juan of Portugal, who said that there was mainland to the south: and because of this, he says that he had a contention with the Sovereigns of Castile, and finally the Admiral says that it was concluded that the King of Portugal should have 370 leagues to the west from the islands of the Azores [1] and Cape Verde, from north to south, from pole to pole. And the Admiral says further that the said King Don Juan was certain that within those limits famous lands and things must be found.[2] Certain principal inhabitants of the island of Santiago came to see them and they said that to the south-west of the island of Huego, which is one of the Cape Verde Islands distant 12 leagues from this, may be seen an island, and that the King Don Juan was greatly inclined to send to make discoveries to the south-west, and that canoes had been found which start from the coast of Guinea and navigate to the west with merchandise. Here the Admiral says again as if he was speaking with the Sovereigns, — "He that is Three and One guides me by His pity and mercy that I may serve Him and give great pleasure to your Highnesses and to all Christianity, as was done in the discovery of the Indies which resounded throughout all the world."

[1] The Tordesillas line was 370 leagues west of the Cape Verde Islands alone.

[2] This reason for the desire of King John of Portugal to have the Demarcation Line moved further west has escaped all the writers on the subject. If Columbus reported the king's ideas correctly, we may have here a clew to one of the reasons why Cabral went so far to the southwest in 1500 that he discovered Brazil when on his voyage to India, and perhaps also one of the reasons why Vasco da Gama struck off so boldly into the South Atlantic. *Cf.* Bourne, *Spain in America*, pp. 72, 74.

Wednesday, July 4, he ordered sail made from that island in which he says that since he arrived there he never saw the sun or the stars, but that the heavens were covered with such a thick mist that it seemed they could cut it with a knife and the heat was so very intense that they were tormented, and he ordered the course laid to the way of the south-west, which is the route leading from these islands to the south, in the name, he says, of the Holy and Indivisible Trinity, because then he would be on a parallel with the land of the sierra of Loa[1] and cape of Sancta Ana in Guinea, which is below the equinoctial line, where he says that below that line of the world are found more gold and things of value; and that after, he would navigate, the Lord pleasing, to the west, and from there would go to this Española, in which route he would prove the theory of the King John aforesaid; and that he thought to investigate the report of the Indians of this Española who said that there had come to Española from the south and south-east, a black people who have the tops of their spears made of a metal which they call *guanin*, of which he had sent samples to the Sovereigns to have them assayed, when it was found that of 32 parts, 18 were of gold, 6 of silver and 8 of copper.

Following this course to the south-west he commenced to find grasses like those encountered in the direct way to these Indies; and the Admiral says here that after having gone 480 miles which make 120 leagues, that at nightfall he took the latitude and found that the North Star was in five degrees. Yet it seems to me that he must have gone more than 200 leagues, and that the text is in error because it is necessary to traverse more than 200 leagues on that course from the Cape Verde Islands and Santiago whence he started to put a ship within five degrees of the equator, as any sailor will observe who will judge it by the map and by the latitude. And he says that there, Friday, July 13, the wind deserted him and he entered into heat so great and so ardent that he feared the ships would take fire and the people perish. The ceasing

[1] Sierra Leone.

of the wind and coming of the excessive and consuming heat was so unexpected and sudden that there was no person who dared to descend below to care for the butts of wine and water, which swelled, breaking the hoops of the casks; the wheat burned like fire; the pork and salted meat roasted and putrefied. This ardent heat lasted eight days. The first day was clear with a sun which burned them. God sent them less suffering because the seven following days it rained and was clouded; however with all this, they could not find any hope of saving themselves from perishing and from being burned, and if the other seven days had been like the first, clear and with the sun, the Admiral says here that it would have been impossible for a man of them to have escaped alive. And thus they were divinely succored by the coming of some showers and by the days being cloudy. He determined from this, if God should give him wind in order to escape from this suffering, to run to the west some days, and then if he found himself in any moderation of temperature to return to the south, which was the way he desired to follow. "May our Lord," says he, "guide me and give me grace that I may serve Him, and bring pleasing news to your Highnesses." He says he remembered, being in this burning latitude, that when he came to the Indies in the past voyages, always when he reached 100 leagues toward the west from the Azores Islands he found a change in the temperature from north to south, and for this he wished to go to the west to reach the said place.

The Admiral must have been on that same parallel or rather meridian, on which Hanno the Carthaginian was with his fleet, who departing from Cadiz and going out into the Ocean to the left[1] of Lybia or Ethiopia after thirty days' voyaging toward the south, among other distresses that he suffered the heat and fire were so intense that it seemed as if they were roasting; they heard such thundering and lightning that their ears pained them and their eyes were blinded and it appeared no otherwise than as if flames of fire fell from heaven. Amianus

---

[1] As one faces north.

narrates this — a Greek historian, a follower of the truth, and very famous — in the *History of India* near the end, and Ludovico Celio quotes it in Book I., ch. XXII., of the *Lectiones Antiguas*.[1] Returning to these days of toil: —

Saturday, which they counted July 14, the Guards[2] being on the left hand, he says the *North* was in seven degrees: he saw black and white jays,[3] which are birds that do not go far from land, and from this he considered it a sign of land. He was sick at this point of the journey, from gout and from not sleeping; but because of this he did not cease to watch and work with great care and diligence.

Sunday and Monday, they saw the same birds and more swallows, and some fish appeared which they called *botos*,[4] which are little smaller than great calves, and which have the head very blunt. The Admiral says here incidentally that the Azores Islands which in ancient times were called Caseterides,[5] were situated at the end of the fifth clime.[6]

Thursday, July 19, there was such intense and ardent heat that they thought the men and ships would burn, but as our Lord at sight of the afflictions which He gives is accustomed

---

[1] On Hanno's voyage see *Encyclopædia Britannica* under his name. There was no Greek historian Amianus; the name should be Arrianus, who wrote the history of Alexander the Great's expedition to India and a history of India. The reference is to the latter work, ch. XLIII., sects. 11, 12.

Ludovico Celio: Ludovico Ricchieri, born about 1450. He was for a time a professor in the Academy at Milan. He took the Latin name Rhodiginus from his birthplace Rovigo, and sometimes his name appears in full as Ludovicus Coelius Richerius Rhodiginus. His *Antiquarum Lectionum Libri XVI.* was published at Venice in 1516, at Paris in 1517, and in an extended form at Basel, 1542. It is a collection of passages from the classical authors relating to all branches of knowledge, with a critical commentary.

[2] The Guards, "the two brightest stars in Ursa Minor." (Tolhausen.)

[3] *Grajos.* The meaning given in the dictionaries for *grajo* is "daw."

[4] This word, as a name of a fish, is Portuguese. It means "blunted."

[5] See Pliny, *Natural History*, book IV., ch. XXXVI. The Cassiterides are commonly identified with the Scilly Islands.

[6] The fifth clime or climate is a term in Ptolemy's geographical system. The fifth climate was a strip 255 Roman miles in width lying between 41° and 45° north latitude. *Cf. Raccolta Columbiana*, Parte I., Tomo 2, p. 293. The latitude of the Azores is about 37°–40°.

by interfering to the contrary to alleviate them, He succored
him by His mercy at the end of seven or eight days, giving
him very good weather to get away from that fire; with
which good weather he navigated towards the west 17
days, always intending to return to the south, and place himself, as above said, in such a region, that this Española should
be to the north or *septentrion*, where he thought he must find
land before or beyond the said place: and thus he intended
to repair the ships which were already opening from the past
heat, and the supplies, of which he had a large quantity, because of the necessity of taking them to this island and the
great difficulty in getting them from Castile, and which were
becoming worthless and damaged.

Sunday, July 22, in the afternoon, as they were going with
good weather, they saw innumerable birds pass from the west-
south-west to the north-east: he says that they were a great
sign of land. They saw the same the Monday following and
the days after, on one of which days a pelican came to the
ship of the Admiral, and many others appeared another day,
and there were other birds which are called "frigate pelicans."[1]

On the seventeenth day of the good weather which they
were experiencing, the Admiral was hoping to see land, because of the said signs of the birds, and as he did not see it
Monday, or the next day, Tuesday, July 31, as they lacked
water, he decided to change his route, and this was to the west,
and to go to the right, and make for the island of Dominica,
or some of the islands of the Canibales, which to-day are called
the Caribes, and thus he ordered the course to the north,
quarter north-east, and went that way until midday. "But
as His Divine Majesty," he says, "has always used mercy
with me, a sailor from Guelva,[2] my servant, who was called
Alonso Pérez, by chance and conjecture ascended to the
round top and saw land to the west, and he was 15 leagues
from it, and that part which appeared were three rocks or

---

[1] The names are *alcatraz* and *rabihorcado*. See above, note to Journal of
First Voyage, p. 98, note 1, and p. 103, note 1.

[2] Huelva, near Palos.

mountains." These are his words. He named this land "The Island of the Trinity,"[1] because he had determined that the first land he discovered should be named thus. "And it pleased our Lord," he says, "by His Exalted Majesty, that the first lands seen were three rocks all united at the base, I say three mountains, all at one time and in one glance." "His High Power by His pity guides me," he says, "in such a manner, that He may have much service, and your Highnesses much pleasure: as it is certain that the discovery of this land in this place was as great a miracle as the discovery of the first voyage." These are his words. He gave infinite thanks to God as was his custom, and all praised the divine goodness, and with great rejoicings and merriment the *Salve Regina*[2] was sung with other devout songs which contain praises of God and our Lady, according to the custom of sailors, at least our sailors of Spain, who in tribulations and rejoicings are accustomed to say them.

Here he makes a digression and recapitulation of the services he has rendered the Sovereigns, and of the will he always had keen to serve them, "not as false tongues," says he, "and as false witnesses from envy said."[3] And surely, I believe that such as these God took for instruments to chasten him because he loved him since many without cause and without object maligned him and disturbed these efforts, and brought it about that the Sovereigns grew lukewarm and wearied of expense and of keeping up their attachment and expectation that these Indies were likely to be of profit, at least that it should be more than the expenses with increase that came to them. He repeats a mention of the heat he suffered, and how they were nevertheless now going by the same parallel, except they had drawn near to the land when he ordered the course directed to the west, because the land emits coolness from its

---

[1] Trinidad.

[2] Salve Regina, one of the great hymns to the Virgin in the Catholic service. "The antiphon said after Lauds and Compline from Trinity Sunday to Advent." Addis and Arnold, *Catholic Dictionary.*

[3] *I.e.,* that his will was not to serve the sovereigns but to advance himself.

fountains and rivers, and by its waters causes moderation and softness; and because of this he says the Portuguese who go to Guinea which is below the equinoctial line are able to navigate because they go along the coast.   He says further, that now he was in the same parallel from which the King of Portugal brought gold, from which he believed that whoever would search those seas would find things of value.   He confesses here that there is no man in the world for whom God has shown so much grace, and entreats Him that He will furnish something from which their Highnesses and Christianity may receive great pleasure; and he says that, although he should not find any other thing of benefit except these beautiful lands, which are so green and full of groves and palms, that they are superior to the gardens of Valencia in May, they would deserve to be highly valued.   And in this he speaks the truth and later on he will place a still higher value on it with much reason.   He says that it is a miraculous thing that the Sovereigns of Castile should have lands so near the equinoctial as 6 degrees, Ysabela being distant from the said line 24 degrees.

Having seen the land then to the great consolation of all, he left the course which he desired to follow in search of some of the islands of the Canibales in order to provide himself with water, of which he was greatly in need, and made a short excursion towards the land which he had seen, towards a cape which appeared to be to the west, which he called "Cabo de la Galera," [1] from a great rock which it had, which from a distance appeared like a galley sailing.   They arrived there at the hour of compline.[2]   They saw a good harbor but it was not deep, and the Admiral regretted that they could not enter it.   He pursued his course to the point he had seen, which was seven leagues toward the south.   He did not find a harbor.   On all the coast he found that the groves reached to the sea, the most beautiful coast that eyes ever saw.   He says that this island must be large; a canoe appeared at a distance

---

[1] Cape of the Galley.   To-day, Cape Galeota.
[2] The last of the canonical hours of prayer, after sunset or early evening.

filled with people who must have been fishing, and made towards the land to some houses which appeared there. The land was very cultivated and high and beautiful.

Wednesday, August 1, he ran down the coast toward the west, five leagues, and arrived at a point, where he anchored with all three ships, and took water from fountains and streams. They found signs of people, instruments for fishing, signs of goats, but they were only of deer of which there are many in those lands. He says that they found aloes and great groves of palms, and very beautiful lands: "for which infinite thanks may be given to the Holy Trinity." These are his words. He saw much tilled land along the coast and many settlements. He saw from there towards the south, another island, which is distant more than 20 leagues. (And he might well say five hundred since this is the mainland which, as he saw a part of it, seemed to him to be an island); to this he gave the name of "Ysla Sancta." He says here that he would not take any Indians in order not to disturb the land. From the Cape of Galera to the point where he took the water, which I believed he named "Punta de la Playa," he says that having been a great way, and running east-west (he should say that he went from east to west) there was no port in all that way, but the land was well populated and tilled, and with many trees and thick groves, the most beautiful thing in the world, the trees reaching to the sea. Here it may be remarked that when the trees of the country grow down to the water's edge it indicates that such a coast is not exposed to high seas, because when the coast is so exposed trees do not grow down to the water, but there is an open sandy shore. The current, *surgente*, which is that which comes down, and the *montante*, which is that which ascends from below, he says appear to be great. The island which lies to the south he says is very large, because he was already going along with the mainland in sight although he did not think so, but that it was an island.

He says that he came to search for a harbor along the island of Trinidad, Thursday, August 2, and arrived at the cape of the island of Trinidad, which is a point, to which he gave the name "Punta del Arenal,"[1] which is to the west: so that he had in a sense already entered in the gulf which he called "de la Ballena,"[2] where he underwent great danger of losing his ships, and he as yet did not know that he was becoming encircled by land as will be seen. This gulf is a wonderful thing and dangerous on account of the very great river that flows into it which is called the Yuyapari,[3] the last syllable long. It comes from more than 300 and I believe more than 400 leagues, and it has been traversed for 300 leagues up stream partly with a ship, partly with brigantines and partly with large canoes. And since the force of the water is very great at all times and particularly so in this season of July and August in which the Admiral was there, which is the season of high water as in Castile in October and November, and since it wants naturally to get to the sea, and the sea with its great mass under the same natural impulse wants to break upon the land, and since this gulf is enclosed by the mainland on one side and on the other by the island of Trinidad, and since it is very narrow for such a violent force of contrary waters, it must needs be that when they meet a terrific struggle takes place and a conflict most perilous for those that find themselves in that place.

He says here that the island of Trinidad is large, because from the Cape of Galera to the Point of Arenal, where he was at the present time, he says it is 35 leagues. I say that it is more than 45, as he that desires may see by the charts, although now those names are not written on the charts as they have been forgotten, and to understand the matter they must consider the course the Admiral pursued until he arrived there, and at what point he first saw land, and from there where he went till he stopped, and in that way, one will find out what he called the Cape of Galera and what the Point

[1] Sandy Point.

[2] Of the whale.

[3] One of the native names of the Orinoco, here referring to one of the northern branch mouths. A detailed map of the region is given in Winsor's *Columbus*, p. 353.

of Arenal. It is not a matter of surprise that the Admiral did
not make an accurate estimate of the leagues of the island
because he went along it piece by piece.

He ordered that his people should land on this Point of
Arenal, the end of the island toward the west, to enjoy themselves and obtain recreation, because they had become wearied
and fatigued; who found the land very much trampled by
deer, although they believed they were goats. This Thursday,
August 2, a large canoe came from towards the east, in which
came twenty-five men, and having arrived at the distance of a
lombard shot, they ceased to row, and cried out many words.
The Admiral believed, and I also believe, that they were asking what people they were, as the others of the Indies were
accustomed to do, to which they did not respond in words,
but by showing them certain small boxes of brass and other
shining things, in order that they should come to the ship,
coaxing them with motions of the body and signs. They approached somewhat, and afterwards became terrified by the
ship; and as they would not approach, the Admiral ordered
a tambourine player to come up to the poop deck of the ship
and that the young boys of the ship should dance, thinking
to please them. But they did not understand it thus, but
rather, as they saw dancing and playing, taking it for a signal
of war, they distrusted them. They left all their oars and
laid hold of their bows and arrows; and each one embracing
his wooden shield, they commenced to shoot a great cloud of
arrows. Having seen this, the Admiral ordered the playing
and dancing to cease, and that some cross-bows should be
drawn on deck and two of them shot off at them, nothing
more than to frighten them. The Indians then, having shot
the arrows, went to one of the two caravels, and suddenly,
without fear, placed themselves below the poop, and the pilot
of the caravel, also without any fear, glided down from the
poop and entered with them in the canoe with some things
which he gave them; and when he was with them he gave
a smock frock and a bonnet to one of them who appeared to
be the principal man. They took them and as if in gratitude

for what had been given them, by signs said to him that he should go to land with them, and there they would give him what they had. He accepted and they went away to land. The pilot entered the boat and went to beg permission of the Admiral on the ship, and when they saw that he did not go directly with him, they did not expect him longer, and so they went away and neither the Admiral nor any other ever saw them more. From the sudden change in their bearing because ·of the playing on the tambourine and the dancing, it appears that this must be considered among them a sign of hostility.

A servant of the Admiral, called Bernaldo de Ibarro, who was on this voyage with him, told me and gave it to me in writing and I have this writing in my possession to-day, that a cacique came to the ship of the Admiral and was wearing upon his head a diadem of gold; and he went to the Admiral who was wearing a scarlet cap and greeted him and kissed his own diadem, and with the other hand he removed the cap of the Admiral and placed upon him the diadem, and he himself put upon his own head the scarlet cap, appearing very content and pleased.

The Admiral says here that these were all youths and very well shaped and adorned, although I do not believe they wore much silk or brocade, with which, also, I believe the Spaniards and the Admiral might be more pleased; but they came armed with bows and arrows and wooden shields. They were not as short as others he had seen in the Indies and they were whiter, and of very good movements and handsome bodies, the hair long and smooth and cut in the manner of Castile. They had the head tied with a large handkerchief of cotton, symmetrically woven in colors, which the Admiral believed to be the *almaiçar;*[1] he says that others had this cloth around them, and they covered themselves with it in

---

[1] "A sort of veil, or head attire used by the Moorish women, made of thin silk, striped of several colors, and shagged at the ends, which hangs down on the back." John Stevens, *A New Dictionary, Spanish and English*, etc. (London, 1726.)

place of trousers. He says that they are not black although they are near the equinoctial,[1] but of an Indian color like all the others he has found. They are of very fine stature, go naked, are warlike, wear the hair very long like the women in Castile, carry bows and arrows with plumes, and at the end of the arrows a sharp bone with a point like a fish-hook, and they carry wooden shields, which he had not seen before; and according to the signs and gestures which they made, he says he could understand from them that they believed the Admiral came from the south, from which he judged that there must be great lands toward the south, and he said well since the mainland is so large that it occupies a large part of the south.

The temperature of this land, he says, is very high, and according to him this causes the color of the people, and the hair which is all flowing, and the very thick groves which abound everywhere. He says it must be believed that when once the boundary is passed, 100 leagues to the west of the Azores, that many times he has said that there is a change in the sky and the sea and the temperature, "and this," he says, "is manifest," because here where he was, so near to the equinoctial line, each morning, he says, it was cool and the sun was in Leo. What he says is very true, since I who write this have been there and required a robe nights and mornings especially at Navidad.[2]

The waters were running toward the west with a current stronger than the river of Seville; the water of the sea rose and fell 65 paces and more, as in Barrameda so that they are able to beach carracks;[3] he says that the current flows very

---

[1] The exploration of the west coast of Africa, the only equatorial regions then known to Europeans, had led to the conclusion that black was the natural color of the inhabitants of the tropics.

[2] The Navidad referred to by Las Casas was near the Gulf of Paria. (Thacher.)

[3] *Poner á monte carracas. Poner á monte* is not given in the Spanish dictionaries, and is apparently a sea phrase identical with the Portuguese "pôr um navio a monte," to beach or ground a vessel. The translator went entirely astray in this passage. See Thacher's *Columbus*, II. 388. The figure here given and the use of word *pasos*, normally, a land measure of

z

strongly going between these two islands, Trinidad and that
one which he called Sancta, and the land which afterwards
and farther on he called Isla de Gracia. And he calls the
mainland an island, since he was already between the two
which are two leagues apart which [*i.e.*, the channel] is like
a river as it appears on the map. They found fruits[1] like
those of this Española, and the trees and the soil, and the
temperature of the sky. In this Española they found few
fruits native to the soil. The temperature of that country is
much higher than it is in this Española, except in the mines of
Cibao and in some other districts, as has been said above.

They found *hostias* or oysters, very large, infinite fish,
parrots as large as hens, he says. In this land and in all the
mainland the parrots are larger than any of those in these
islands and are green, the color being very light, but those of
the islands are of a green somewhat darker. Those of the
mainland have the yellow with spots and the upper part of
the wings with reddish spots, and some are of yellow plumage;
those of the islands have no yellow, the neck being red with
spots. The parrots of Española have a little white over the
back; those of Cuba have that part red and they are very
pretty. Those of the island of San Juan I believe are similar
to those of this island [Española] and I have not observed
this feature in those of Jamaica. Finally it appears that
those of each island are somewhat different. In this mainland where the Admiral is now, there is a species of parrots
which I believe are found nowhere else, very large, not much

---

length, instead of *braza*, "fathom," would seem to indicate that the 65
paces refers to the extent of shore laid bare, and not to the height of the
tide. The corresponding passage in the *Historie* reads: "so that it seemed
a rapid river both day and night and at all hours, notwithstanding the
fact that the water rose and fell along the shore (*per la spiaggia*) more
than sixty paces between the waves (*alle marette*) as it is wont to do in
San Lucar di Barrameda where the waters [of the river] are high since
although the water rises and falls it never ceases to run toward the
sea," *Historie* (London ed.), p. 229. In this passage *maree*, "tides," should
be read instead of *marette*.

[1] Accepting the emendation of de Lollis which substitutes *fructas* for
fuentes, "springs."

smaller than hens, reddish with blue and black feathers in the wings. These never speak nor are attractive except in appearance. They are called by the Indians *guacamayas*. It is marvellous how all the other kinds can speak except the smallest, which are called *xaxaues*.

Being at this Point of Arenal, which is the end of the island of Trinidad, they saw toward the north, quarter northeast,[1] a distance of 15 leagues, a cape or point of the same mainland, and this is that which is called Paria. The Admiral believing that it was another distinct island named it "Isla de Gracia": which island he says goes to the west [Oeste] which is the west [*poniente*], and that it is a very high land. And he says truly, for through all that land run great chains of very high mountains.

Saturday, August 4, he determined to go to the said island of Gracia and raised the anchors and made sail from the said Point of Arenal, where he was anchored; and because that strait by which he entered into the Gulf of Ballena was not more than two leagues wide between Trinidad on one side and the mainland on the other, the fresh water came out very swiftly. There came from the direction of the Arenal, on the island of Trinidad, such a great current from the south, like a mighty flood (and it was because of the great force of the river Yuyaparí which is toward the south and which he had not yet seen), with such great thundering and noise, that all were frightened and did not think to escape from it, and when the water of the sea withstood it, coming in opposition, the sea was raised making a great and very high swell[2] of water which raised the ship and placed it on top of the swell, a thing which was never heard of nor seen, and raised the anchors of the other ship which must have been already cast and forced it toward the sea, and the Admiral made sail to get away from the said slope. "It pleased God not to injure us," says the Admiral here, and when he wrote this thing to the Sovereigns he said, "even to-day I feel the fear in my body which I felt

---

[1] *I.e.*, north by east.   [2] *Loma.*

lest it should upset the ship when it came under her." [1]   For this great danger, he named the mouth "Boca de la Sierpe." [2]

Having reached that land which he saw in that direction and believed was an island, he saw near that cape two small islands in the middle of another channel which is made by that cape which he called Cabo de Lapa and another cape of the Trinidad which he called Cabo Boto, because of being thick and blunt, — the one island he named El Caracol, the other El Delfin. [3]   It is only five leagues in this strait between the Point of Paria and Cape Boto of Trinidad, and the said islands are in the middle of the strait.   The impetus of the great river Yuyaparí and the tempestuous waves of the sea make the entrance and exit by this strait greatly dangerous, and because the Admiral experienced this difficulty and also danger, he called that difficult entrance Boca del Drago [4] and thus it is called to this day.   He went along the coast of the mainland of Paria, [5] which he believed to be an island, and named it Isla de Gracia, towards the west in search of a harbor.   From the point of the Arenal, which is one cape of Trinidad as has been said, and is towards the south, as far as the other Cape Boto, which is of the same island and is towards the sea, the Admiral says it is 26 large leagues, and this part appears to be the width of the island, and these two said capes are north and south.   There were great currents, the one against the other; there came many showers as it was the rainy season, as aforesaid.   The Isla de Gracia is, as has been said, mainland. The Admiral says that it is a very high land and all full of trees which reach to the sea; this is because the gulf being surrounded by land, there is no surf and no waves which break on the land as where the shores are uncovered.   He says that, being at the point or end of it, he saw an island of very high

---

[1] Las Casas here quotes Columbus's letter to Ferdinand and Isabella on this voyage.   See Major, *Select Letters of Columbus*, p. 123.

[2] Serpent's mouth.   The name is still retained.

[3] *Lapa* means barnacle; *caracol*, periwinkle; and *delfin*, dolphin.

[4] Dragon's mouth.   The name is still retained.

[5] *I.e.*, along the south shore of the peninsula of Paria in the Gulf of Paria.

land to the north-east, which might be 26 leagues from there. He named it "Belaforma," because it must have looked very well from a distance, yet all this is the mainland, which, as the ships changed their position from one side to the other within the gulf enclosed by land, some inlets appeared as if they separated lands which might be detached, and these the Admiral called islands; for such was his opinion.[1]

He navigated Sunday, August 5, five leagues from the point of the Cape of Lapa, which is the eastern end of the island of Gracia. He saw very good harbors adjacent to each other, and almost all this sea he says is a harbor, because it is surrounded by islands and there are no waves. He called the parts of the mainland which disclosed themselves to him "islands," but there are only the island of Trinidad and the mainland, which inclose the gulf which he now calls the sea. He sent the boats to land and found fish and fire, and traces of people, and a great house visible to the view. From there he went eight leagues where he found good harbors. This part of this island of Gracia he says is very high land, and there are many valleys, and "all must be populated," says he, because he saw it all cultivated. There are many rivers because each valley has its own from league to league; they found many fruits, and grapes like [our] grapes and of good taste, and myrobolans[2] very good, and others like apples, and others, he says, like oranges, and the inside is like figs. They found numberless monkeys.[3] The waters, he says, are the best that they saw. "This island," he says, "is all full of harbors, this sea is fresh, although not wholly so, but brackish like that of Carthagena"; farther down he says that it is fresh like the river of Seville, and this was caused when it encountered some current of water from the sea, which made that of the river salty.

[1] The grammatical form of this sentence follows the original, which is irregular.

[2] See p. 311, note 2.

[3] *Gatos paules* (Cat-Pauls). A species of African monkey was so called in Spain. The name occurs in Marco Polo. On its history and meaning, see Yule's *Marco Polo*, II. 372.

He sailed to a small port Monday, August 6, five leagues, from whence he went out and saw people, and then a canoe with four men came to the caravel which was nearest the land, and the pilot called the Indians as if he wished to go to land with them, and in drawing near and entering he submerged the canoe, and they commenced swimming; he caught them and brought them to the Admiral. He says that they are of the color of all the others of the Indies. They wear the hair (some of them) very long, others as with us; none of them have the hair cut as in Española and in the other lands. They are of very fine stature and all well grown; they have the genital member tied and covered, and the women all go naked as their mothers gave them birth. This is what the Admiral says, but I have been, as I said above, within 30 leagues of this land yet I never saw women that did not have their private parts, at least, covered.[1] The Admiral must have meant that they went as their mothers bore them as to the rest of the body.

"To these Indians," says the Admiral, "as soon as they were here, I gave hawks' bells and beads and sugar, and sent them to land, where there was a great battle among them, and after they knew the good treatment, all wished to come to the ships. Those who had canoes came and they were many, and to all we gave a good welcome and held friendly conversation with them, giving them the things which pleased them." The Admiral asked them questions and they replied, but they did not understand each other. They brought them bread and water and some beverage like new wine; they are very much adorned with bows and arrows and wooden shields, and they almost all carry arrows poisoned.

Tuesday, August 7, there came an infinite number of Indians by land and by sea and all brought with them bread and maize and things to eat and pitchers of beverages, some white, like milk, tasting like wine, some green, and some of different colors; he believes that all are made from fruits. Most or

[1] Im Thurn, *Among the Indians of Guiana,* p. 193, says, " Indians after babyhood are never seen perfectly naked."

all of it is made from maize but as the maize itself is white
or violet and reddish, it causes the wine to be of different colors.
I do not know of what the green wine is made. They all
brought their bows and poisoned arrows, very pointed;[1]
they gave nothing for beads, but would give as much as they
had for hawks' bells, and asked nothing else. They gave a
great deal for brass. It is certain that they hold this in high
estimation and they gave in this Española for a little brass
as much gold as any one would ask, and I believe that in the
beginning it was always thus in all these Indies. They
called it *turey* as if it came from Heaven because they called
Heaven *hureyo*.[2] They find in it I do not know what odor,
but one which is agreeable to them. Here the Admiral says
whatever they gave them from Castile they smelled it as soon
as it was given them. They brought parrots of two or three
kinds, especially the very large ones like those in the island of
Guadeloupe, he says, with the large tail. They brought
handkerchiefs of cotton very symmetrically woven and worked
in colors like those brought from Guinea, from the rivers of
the Sierra Leona and of no difference, and he says that they
cannot communicate with the latter, because from where he
now is to Guinea the distance is more than 800 leagues; below
he says that these handkerchiefs resemble *almayzars*.[3] He
desired, he says, to take a half-dozen Indians, in order to carry
them with him, and says that he could not take them because
they all went away from the ships before nightfall.

But Wednesday, August 8, a canoe came with 12 men to
the caravel and they took them all, and brought them to the
ship of the Admiral, and from them he chose six and sent the
others to land. From this it appears that the Admiral did it

---

[1] *Flechas con hierba muy á punto*, literally, arrows with grass very sharp.
Gaffarel, *Histoire de la Découverte de l'Amérique*, II. 196, interprets this to
mean arrows feathered with grass; but *hierba* used in connection with
arrows usually means poison. *Cf.* Oviedo, lib. IX., title of cap. XII., " *Del
árbol ó mançanillo con cuya fructa los indios caribes flecheros haçen la
hierba con que tiran é pélean.*"

[2] *Hureyos* is *Tureyos* in the printed edition of Las Casas, an obvious correction of the manuscript reading. On *turey*, see above, p. 310.

[3] See above, p. 336, note 1.

without scruple as he did many other times in the first navigation, it not appearing to him that it was an injustice and an offence against God and his neighbor to take free men against their will, separating fathers from their sons and wives from their husbands and [not reflecting] that according to natural law they were married, and that other men could not take these women, or those men other women, without sin and perhaps a mortal sin of which the Admiral was the efficient cause — and there was the further circumstance that these people came to the ships under tacit security and promised confidence which should have been observed toward them; and beyond this, the scandal and the hatred of the Christians not only there, but in all the earth and among the peoples that should hear of this.

He made sail then towards a point which he calls "de l'Aguja," [1] he does not say when he gave it this name, and from there he says that he discovered the most beautiful lands that have been seen and the most populated, and arriving at one place which for its beauty he called Jardines,[2] where there were an infinite number of houses and people, and those whom he had taken told him there were people who were clothed, for which reason he decided to anchor, and infinite canoes came to the ships. These are his words. Each one, he says, wore his cloth so woven in colors, that it appeared an *almayzar*, with one tied on the head and the other covering the rest, as has been already explained. Of these people who now came to the ships, some he says wore gold leaf [3] on the breast, and one of the Indians he had taken told him there was much gold there, and that they made large mirrors of it, and they showed how they gathered it. He says mirrors, wherefore the Admiral must have given some mirrors and the Indian must have said by signs that of the gold they made those things, for they did not understand the language. He says that, as he was going hastily along there, because he was

---

[1] Needle.   Alcatrazes, to-day.   (Navarrete.)   [2] Gardens.

[3] *Ojas de oro*.   The translator took *ojas* (*hojas*) for *ojos* and rendered it "eyes of gold."   See Thacher, *Columbus*, II. 393.

losing the supplies which it had cost him so much labor to
obtain, and this island Española is more than 300 leagues
from there, he did not tarry, which he would have wished very
much in order to discover much more land, and says that it
is all full of very beautiful islands, much populated, and very
high lands and valleys and plains, and all are very large.
The people are much more politic than those of Española
and warlike, and there are handsome houses. If the Admiral
had seen the kingdom of Xaraguá as did his brother the
Adelantado and the court of the King Behechio [1] he would not
have made so absolute a statement.

Arriving at the point of Aguja, he says that he saw another
island to the south 15 leagues which ran south-east and
north-west, very large, and very high land, and he called it
Sabeta, and in the afternoon he saw another to the west, very
high land. All these islands I understand to be pieces of the
mainland which by reason of the inlets and valleys that separate them seem to be distinct islands notwithstanding that he
went clear inside the gulf which he called Ballena enclosed as
is said by land; and this seems clear since when one is, as he
was, within the said gulf no land bears off to the south, except
the mainland; next, the islands which he mentioned were not
islands but pieces of the mainland which he judged to be
islands.

He anchored at the place he had named the Jardines, and
then there came an infinite number of canoes, large and small,
full of people, according to what he says. Afterwards in the
afternoon there came more from all the territory, many of
whom wore at the neck pieces of gold of the size of horseshoes.
It appeared that they had a great deal of it: but they gave it
all for hawks' bells and he did not take it. And this is strange
that a man as provident as the Admiral and desiring to make
discoveries should not have seized this opportunity for trading, as he did on his first voyage. Yet he had some specimens
from them and it was of very poor quality so that it appeared
plated. They said, as well as he could understand by signs,

[1] *I.e.*, in Española.

that there were some islands there where there was much of that gold, but that the people were canibales, and the Admiral says here that this word "Canibales" every one there held as a cause for enmity, or perhaps they said so because they did not wish the Christians to go yonder, but that they should remain there all their life. The Christians saw one Indian with a grain of gold as large as an apple.

Another time there came an infinite number of canoes loaded with people, and all wore gold and necklaces, and beads of infinite kinds, and had handkerchiefs tied on their heads as they had hair well cut, and they appeared very well. It rained a great deal, and for this reason the people ceased to go and come. Some women came who wore on the arms strings of beads, and mingled with them were pearls or *aljofars*,[1] very fine, not like the colored ones which were found on the islands of Babueca; they traded for some of them, and he says that he would send them to their Highnesses.

I never knew of these pearls that were found in the islands of Babueca, which are near Puerto de Plata, in this Española; and these besides are low under the water and not islands, and they are very dangerous to ships that pass that way if they are not aware of them; and so they have the name Abre el Ojo.[2]

The Admiral asked the Indians where they found them or fished them, and they showed him some mother-of-pearl where they are formed; and they replied to him by very clear signs, that they grow and are gathered towards the west, behind that island, which was the Cape of Lapa, the Point of Paria and mainland, which he believed to be an island, but it was the mainland. He sent the boats to land to know if there was any new thing which he had not seen, and they found the people so tractable, says the Admiral, that, "although the sailors did not go intending to land, there came two principal persons with all the village, who induced them to descend and who took them to a large house, built near two streams

---

[1] Irregularly shaped pearls, seed pearls.
[2] "Keep your eyes open."

and not round, like a camp-tent, in the manner of the houses of the islands, where they received them very well and made them a feast and gave them a collation, bread and fruit of many kinds; and the drink was a white beverage which had a great value, which every one brought there, at this time, and some of it is tinted and better than the other, as the wine with us. The men were all together at one end of the house and the women at the other. Having taken the collation at the house of the older man, the younger conducted them to the other house, where they went through the same function. It appeared that one must be the cacique and lord, and the other must be his son. Afterwards the sailors returned to the boats and with them went back to the ships, very pleased with this people." These are all the words of the Admiral. He says further: "They are of very handsome stature, and all uniformly large," and whiter than any other he had seen in these Indies, and that yesterday he saw many as white as we are, and with better hair and well cut, and of very good speech. "No lands in the world can be more green and beautiful or more populated; moreover the temperature since I have been in this island," says he, "is, I say, cool enough each morning for a lined gown, although it is so near the equinoctial line; the sea is however fresh. They called the island Paria." All are the words of the Admiral. He called the mainland an island, however, because so he believed it to be.

Friday, August 10, he ordered sail to be made and went to the west of that which he thought to be an island, and travelled five leagues and anchored. For fear of not finding bottom, he went to search for an opening [mouth] by which to get out of that gulf, within which he was going, encircled by mainland and islands, although he did not believe it to be mainland, and he says it is certain that that was an island, because the Indians said thus, and thus it appears he did not understand them. From there he saw another island facing the south, which he called Ysabeta,[1] which extends from the south-east to north-west, afterwards another which he called

---

[1] Isabela in the printed text.

La Tramontana,[1] a high land and very beautiful, and it seemed that it ran from north to south. It appeared very large. This was the mainland. The Indians whom he had taken said — according to what he understood — that the people there were *Canibales* and that yonder was where the gold was found and that the pearls which they had given the Admiral they had sought and found on the northern part of Paria toward the west. The water of that sea he says was as fresh as that of the river of Seville and in the same manner muddy. He would have wished to go to those islands except for turning backward because of the haste he felt in order not to lose the supplies that he was taking for the Christians of Española, which with so much labor, difficulty and fatigue he had gathered for them; and as being a thing for the sake of which he had suffered much, he repeats this about the provisions or supplies many times. He says he believes that in those islands he had seen, there must be things of value because they are all large and high lands with valleys and plains and with many waters and very well cultivated and populated and the people of very good speech, as their gestures showed. These are the words of the Admiral.

He says also that if the pearls are born as Pliny [2] says from the dew which falls in the oysters while they are open, there is good reason for having them there because much dew falls in that place and there are an infinite number of oysters and very large ones and because there are no tempests there, but the sea is always calm, a sign of which is that the trees enter into the sea, which shows there is never a storm there, and every branch of the trees which were in the water (and there are also roots of certain trees in the sea, which according to the language of this Española are called *mangles* [3]), was full of an infinite number of oysters so that breaking a branch, it comes out full of oysters attached to it. They are white

[1] The north wind.

[2] Pliny, *Natural History*, book IX., ch. LIV.

[3] The name is still used. It is the *Rhicopharia mangle*. See the description of it in Thompson's Alcedo's *Geographical and Historical Dictionary of America and the West Indies*, Appendix.

within, and their flesh also, and very savory, not salt but fresh and they require some salt, and he says that they do not know or spring from mother-of-pearl. Wherever the pearls are generated, he says, they are extremely fine and they pierce them as in Venice. As for this that the Admiral says that the branches were full of oysters there, we say that those oysters that he saw and that are on the branches above the water and a little under the water are not those that produce pearls, but another species; because those that bear pearls are more careful from their natural instinct to hide themselves as much further under water as they can than those he saw on the branches. . . .[1]

Returning to where I dropped the thread of the history, at this place the Admiral mentions many points of land and islands and the names he had given them, but it does not appear when. In this and elsewhere the Admiral shows himself to be a native of another country and of another tongue, because he does not apprehend all the signification of the Castilian words nor the manner of using them. He gave names to the Punta Seca, the Ysla Ysabeta, the Ysla Tramontana, the Punta Llana, Punta Sara, assuming them to be known, although he has said nothing of them or of any of them. He says that all that sea is fresh, and he does not know from whence it proceeds, because it did not appear to have the flow from great rivers, and that, if it had them, he says it would not cease to be a marvel. But he was mistaken in thinking there were no rivers, since the river Yuyaparí furnished so great a flow of fresh water, as well as others which come from near there.

Desiring to get out of this Gulf of Ballena, where he was encircled by mainland and La Trinidad, as already said, in going to the west by that coast of the mainland, which he called "de Gracia" towards the point Seca, although he does not say where it was, he found two fathoms of water, no more. He sent the small caravel to see if there was an outlet to the

---

[1] Las Casas here inserts a long disquisition on pearls which is omitted. It covers pp. 246–252 of the printed edition, Vol. II.

north, because, in front of the mainland and of the other
which he called Ysabeta, to the west, there appeared a very
high and beautiful island. The caravel returned, and said
that they found a great gulf, and in it four great openings which
appeared small gulfs, and at the end of each one a river. This
gulf he named Golpho de las Perlas, although I believe there
are no pearls there. It appears that this was the inside corner
of all this great gulf,[1] in which the Admiral was going enclosed
by the mainland and the island of Trinidad; those four bays
or openings, the Admiral believed were four islands, and that
there did not appear to be a sign of a river, which would make
all that gulf, of 40 leagues of sea, all fresh; but the sailors
affirmed that those openings were mouths of rivers. And
they say true, at least in regard to two of these openings,
because by one comes the great river Yuyaparí and by the
other comes another great river which to-day is called the
river of Camarí.[2]

The Admiral would have liked very much to find out the
truth of this secret, which was the cause of this great gulf
being 40 leagues in length by 26 in width, containing fresh
water, which was a thing, he says, for wonder, (and he was
certainly right), and also to penetrate the secrets of those lands,
where he did not believe it to be possible that there were
not things of value, or that they were not in the Indies, especially from having found there traces of gold and pearls and
the news of them, and discovered such lands, so many and such
people in them; from which the things there and their riches
might easily be known; but because the supplies he was
carrying for the people who were in this Española, and which
he carried that they who were in the mines gathering gold
might have food, were being lost, which food and supplies he
had gathered with great difficulty and fatigue, he did not
allow himself to be detained, and he says that, if he had the

---

[1] *I.e.*, the western end of the Gulf of Paria.

[2] These mouths of the Orinoco supplied the fresh water, but they can
hardly be the streams referred to by the sailors who explored the western
end of the Gulf of Paria. Las Casas had no good map of this region.

hope of having more as quickly, he would postpone delivering them, in order to discover more lands and see the secrets of them; and finally he resolves to follow that which is most sure, and come to this island, and send from it moneys to Castile to bring supplies and people under hire, and at the earliest opportunity to send also his brother, the Adelantado, to prosecute his discovery and find great things, as he hoped they would be found, to serve our Lord and the Sovereigns.

Yet, just at the best time, the thread was cut, as will appear, of these his good desires, and he says thus: "Our Lord guides me by His pity and presents me things with which He may be served, and your Highnesses may have great pleasure, and certainly they ought to have pleasure, because here they have such a noble thing and so royal for great princes. And it is a great error to believe any one who speaks evil to them of this undertaking, but to abhor them, because there is not to be found a prince who has had so much grace from our Lord, and so much victory from a thing so signal and of so much honor to their high estate and realms, and by which God may receive endlessly more services and the people of Spain more refreshment and gains. Because it has been seen that there are infinite things of value, and although now this that I say may not be known, the time will come when it will be accounted of great excellence, and to the great reproach of those persons who oppose this project to your Highnesses; and although they may have expended something in this matter, it has been in a cause more noble and of greater account than any undertaking of any other prince until now, nor was it proper to withdraw from it hastily, but to proceed and give me aid and favor; because the Sovereigns of Portugal spent and had courage to spend in Guinea, for four or five years, money and people, before they received any benefit, and afterward God gave them advantages and gold. For certainly, if the people of the kingdom of Portugal be counted, and those of them who died in this undertaking of Guinea be enumerated, it would be found that they are more than half

of the kingdom;[1] and certainly, it would be the greatest thing
to have in Spain a revenue which would come from this undertaking. Your Highnesses would leave nothing of greater
memory; and they may examine, and discover that no prince
of Castile may be found, and I have not found such by history
or by tradition, — who has ever gained land outside of Spain.
And your Highnesses will gain these lands, so very great,
which are another world,[2] and where Christianity will have
so great pleasure, and our faith in time so great an increase.[3]
All this I say with very honest intention, and because I desire
that Your Highnesses may be the greatest Lords in the world,[4]
I say Lords of it all; and that it may all be with great service
and contentment of the Holy Trinity, for which at the end of
their days they may have the glory of Paradise, and not for
that which concerns me myself, whose hope is in His High Majesty, that Your Highnesses will soon see the truth of it, and

---

[1] Columbus elaborated this point in his letter to Ferdinand and Isabella.
Major, *Select Letters of Columbus*, p. 113. Columbus's estimate of the
sacrifice of lives in the exploration of the west coast of Africa must be considered a most gross exaggeration. The contemporary narratives of those
explorations give no such impression.

[2] *Cf.* Columbus's letter to the sovereigns, "Your Highnesses have here
another world." Major, *Select Letters of Columbus*, p. 148, and the letter to
the nurse of Prince John, p. 381, *post*. "I have placed under the dominion
of the King and Queen our sovereigns another world." These passages
clearly show that Columbus during and after this voyage realized that he
accomplished something quite different from merely reaching Asia by a
western route. He had found a hitherto unknown portion of the world,
unknown to the ancients or to Marco Polo, but not for that reason necessarily
physically detached from the known Asia. For a fuller discussion of the
meaning of the phrase "*another world*," "*New World*," and of Columbus's
ideas of what he had done, see Bourne, *Spain in America*, pp. 94–98, and the
facsimile of the Bartholomew Columbus map, opposite p. 96.

[3] A noteworthy prediction. In fact the discovery of the New World has
effected a most momentous change in the relative strength and range of
Christianity among the world-religions. During the Middle Ages Christianity
lost more ground territorially than it gained. Since the discovery of America
its gain has been steady.

[4] Such in fact their Highnesses' grandson, Charles I. (V. as Emperor),
was during his long reign, and such during a part of his reign if not the
whole, was their great-grandson Philip II. See Oviedo's reflections upon
Columbus's career. Bourne, *Spain in America*, p. 82.

this is my ardent desire." All these are the actual words of the Admiral. . . .[1]

So, in order to get out of this gulf, within which he was surrounded by land on all parts, with the intention already told of saving the supplies which he carried, which were being lost, in coming to this island of Española, — Saturday, August 11, at the appearance of the moon, he raised the anchors, spread the sails, and navigated toward the east (*el leste*), that is towards the place where the sun rises,[2] because he was in the corner of the gulf where was the river Yuyaparí as was said above, in order to go out between the Point of Paria and the mainland, which he called the Punta or Cabo de Lapa, and the land he named Ysla de Gracia, and between the cape which he called Cabo Boto of the island of Trinidad.

He arrived at a very good harbor, which he called Puerto de Gatos,[3] which is connected with the mouth where are the two little islands of the Caracol and Delfin, between the capes of Lapa and Cape Boto. And this occurred Sunday, August 12.

He anchored near the said harbor, in order to go out by the said mouth in the morning. He found another port near there, to examine which he sent a boat. It was very good. They found certain houses of fishermen, and much water and very fresh. He named it Puerto de las Cabañas.[4] They found, he says, myrobolans on the land: near the sea, infinite oysters attached to the branches of the trees which enter into the sea, the mouths open to receive the dew which drops from the leaves and which engenders the pearls, as Pliny says and as is alleged in the vocabulary which is called *Catholicon*.[5]

[1] Las Casas here comments at some length on these remarks of Columbus and the great significance of his discoveries. The passage omitted takes up pp. 255 (line six from bottom) to 258.

[2] Las Casas explains *leste*, which would seem to have been either peculiar to sailors or at least not in common usage then for "east."

[3] Probably *gatos* in the sense of *gatos paules*, monkeys, noted above, p. 341, as very plentiful.   [4] Port of the Cabins.

[5] The *Catholicon* was one of the earliest Latin lexicons of modern times and the first to be printed. It was compiled by Johannes de Janua (Giovanni Balbi of Genoa) toward the end of the thirteenth century and first printed at Mainz in 1460, and very frequently later.

2 A

Monday, August 13, at the rising of the moon, he weighed anchor from where he was, and came towards the Cape of Lapa, which is Paria, in order to go to the north by the mouth called Del Drago, for the following cause and danger in which he saw himself there; the Mouth of the Dragon, he says, is a strait which is between the Point of Lapa, the end of the island of Gracia, which is at the east end of the land of Paria and between Cape Boto which is the western end of the island of Trinidad. He says it is about a league and a half between the two capes. This must be after having passed four little islands which he says lie in the centre of the channel, although now we do not really see more than two, by which he could not go out, and there remained of the strait only a league and a half in the passage. From the Punta de la Lapa to the Cabo de Boto it is five leagues. Arriving at the said mouth at the hour of tierce,[1] he found a great struggle between the fresh water striving to go out to the sea and the salt water of the sea striving to enter into the gulf, and it was so strong and fearful, that it raised a great swell, like a very high hill, and with this, both waters made a noise and thundering, from east to west, very great and fearful, with currents of water, and after one came four great waves one after the other, which made contending currents; here they thought to perish, no less than in the other mouth of the Sierpe by the Cape of Arenal when they entered into the gulf. This danger was doubly more than the other, because the wind with which they hoped to get out died away, and they wished to anchor, because there was no remedy other than that, although it was not without danger from the fierceness of the waters, but they did not find bottom, because the sea was very deep there. They feared that the wind having calmed, the fresh or salt water might throw them on the rocks with their currents, when there would be no help. It is related that the Admiral here said, although I did not find it written with his own hand as I found the above, that if they escaped from that place they

---

[1] The third of the canonical hours of prayer, about nine o'clock in the morning.

could report that they escaped from the mouth of the dragon, and for this reason that name was given to it and with reason.

It pleased the goodness of God that from the same danger safety and deliverance came to them and the current of the fresh water overcame the current of the salt water and carried the ships safely out, and thus they were placed in security; because when God wills that one or many shall be kept alive, water is a remedy for them.[1] Thus they went out, Monday, August 13, from the said dangerous Gulf and Mouth of the Dragon. He says that there are 48 leagues from the first land of La Trinidad to the gulf which the sailors discovered whom he sent in the caravel, where they saw the rivers and he did not believe them, which gulf he called "de las Perlas," and this is the interior angle of all the large gulf, which he called "de la Ballena," where he travelled so many days encircled by land. I add that it is a good 50 leagues, as appears from the chart.

Having gone out of the gulf and the Boca del Drago and having passed his danger, he decides to go to the west by the coast below[2] of the mainland, believing yet that it was the island of Gracia, in order to get abreast, on the right, of the said Gulf of the Pearls, north and south, and to go around it,[3] and see whence comes so great abundance of water, and to see if it proceeded from rivers, as the sailors affirmed and which he says he did not believe because he had not heard that either the Ganges, the Nile or the Euphrates[4] carried so much fresh

---

[1] *El agua les es medicina, i.e.,* a means of curing the ill.

[2] *Abajo.* Las Casas views the mainland as extending up from the sea. Columbus was going west along the north shore of the peninsula of Paria.

[3] *I.e.,* to go west along the north shore of this supposed island until looking south he was to the right of it and abreast of the Gulf of Pearls.

[4] Three of the greatest known rivers, each of which drained a vast range of territory. This narrative reveals the gradual dawning upon Columbus of the fact that he had discovered a hitherto unknown continental mass. In his letter to the sovereigns his conviction is settled and his efforts to adjust it with previous knowledge and the geographical traditions of the ages are most interesting. See Major, *Select Letters of Columbus*, pp. 134 *et seqq.* "Ptolemy," he says, on p. 136, "and the others who have written upon the globe had no information respecting this part of the world, for it was most unknown."

water. The reason which moved him was because he did not
see lands large enough to give birth to such great rivers,
"unless indeed," he says, "that this is mainland."   These are
his words.   So that he was already beginning to suspect that
the land of Gracia which he believed to be an island is mainland,
which it certainly was and is, and the sailors had been right,
from which land there came such a quantity of water from
the rivers, Yuyaparí and the other which flows out near it,
which we now call Camarí, and others which must empty there,
so that, going in search of that Gulf of the Pearls, where the
said rivers empty, thinking to find it surrounded by land,
considering it an island and to see if there was an entrance
there, or an outlet to the south, and if he did not find
it, he says he would affirm then that it was a river, and
that both were a great wonder, — he went down the coast
that Monday until the setting of the sun.

He saw that the coast was filled with good harbors and a
very high land; by that lower coast he saw many islands
toward the north and many capes on the mainland, to all of
which he gave names: to one, Cabo de Conchas; to another,
Cabo Luengo; to another, Cabo de Sabor; to another, Cabo
Rico.   A high and very beautiful land.   He says that on that
way there are many harbors and very large gulfs which must
be populated, and the farther he went to the west he saw the
land more level and more beautiful.   On going out of the
mouth, he saw an island to the north, which might be 26
leagues from the north, and named it La Isla de la Asuncion;
he saw another island and named it La Concepcion, and three
other small islands together he called Los Testigos.[1]   They are
called this to-day.   Another near them he called El Romero,
and three other little small islands he called Las Guardias.
Afterwards he arrived near the Isla Margarita, and called it
Margarita, and another near it he named El Martinet.

This Margarita is an island 15 leagues long, and 5 or 6
wide, and is very green and beautiful on the coast and is very
good within, for which reason it is inhabited; it has near it

---

[1] The Witnesses.

extending lengthwise east and west, three small islands, and two behind them extending north and south. The Admiral did not see more than the three, as he was going along the southern part of Margarita. It is six or seven leagues from the mainland, and this makes a small gulf between it and the mainland, and in the middle of the gulf are two small islands, east and west, beside each other: the one is called Coche, which means deer, and the other Cubagua, which is the one we have described in chapter 136, and said that there are an infinite quantity of pearls gathered there. So that the Admiral, although he did not know that the pearls were formed in this gulf, appears to have divined that fact in naming it Margarita; he was very near it, although he does not express it, because he says he was nine leagues from the island of Martinet, which he says was near Margarita, on the northern part, and he says near it, because as he was going along the southern part of Margarita, it appeared to be near, although it was eight or nine leagues away; and this is the small island to the north, near Margarita, which is now called Blanca, and is distant eight or nine leagues from Margarita as I said. For here it seems that the Admiral must have been close to or near Margarita and I believe that he anchored because the wind failed him. Finally of all the names that he gave to the islands and capes of the mainland which he took for the island of Gracia none have lasted or are used to-day except Trinidad, Boca del Drago, Los Testigos, and Margarita.

There the eyes of the Admiral became very bad from not sleeping. Because always, as he was in so many dangers sailing among islands, it was his custom himself to watch on deck, and whoever takes ships with cargo should for the most part do that very thing, like the pilots, and he says that he found himself more fatigued here than when he discovered the other mainland, which is the island of Cuba, (which he regarded as mainland even until now), because his eyes were bloodshot; and thus his labors on the sea were incomparable. For this reason he was in bed this night, and therefore he found himself farther out in the sea than he would have been if he had himself watched, from which he did not trust himself to the sailors, nor should any one who is a diligent and perfect pilot trust to anybody, because dependent on him and on his head are all those who go in the ship, and that which is most necessary and proper to his office is to watch and not sleep all the time while he navigates.

The Admiral appears to have gone down the coast after he came out of the Mouth of the Dragon, yesterday Monday and to-day Tuesday, 30 or 40 leagues at least, although he does not say so, as he complains that he did not write all that he had to write, as he could not on account of his being so ill here. And as he saw that the land was becoming very extended below to the west, and appeared more level and more beautiful, and the Gulf of the Pearls which was in the back part of the gulf, or fresh-water sea, whence the river of Yuyaparí flowed, in the search of which he was going, had no outlet, which he hoped to see, believing that this mainland was an island, he now became conscious that a land so great was not an island, but mainland, and as if speaking with the Sovereigns, he says here: "I believe that this is mainland, very great, which until to-day has not been known. And reason aids me greatly because of this being such a great river and because of this sea which is fresh, and next the saying of Esdras aids me, in the 4th book, chapter 6th, which says that the six parts of the world are of dry land and the one of water.[1] Which book St. Ambrose approves in his Examenon [2] and St. Augustine on the passage, 'Morietur filius meus Christus,'

---

[1] The reference is to *II. Esdras*, VI. 42, in the Apocrypha of the English Bible. The Apocryphal books of I. and II. Esdras were known as III. and IV. Esdras in the Middle Ages, and the canonical books in the Vulgate called I. and II. Esdras are called Ezra and Nehemiah in the English Bible. II. Esdras is an apocalyptic work and dates from the close of the first century A.D. The passage to which Columbus referred reads as follows: "Upon the third day thou didst command that the waters should be gathered in the seventh part of the earth; six parts hast thou dried up, and kept them, to the intent that of these some being planted of God and tilled might serve thee."

[2] The reference is wrong, as Las Casas points out two or three pages further on (II. 266); it should be to the treatise *De Bono Mortis*, cap. 10.

as Francisco de Mayrones alleges.[1]   And further, I am supported by the sayings of many Canibales Indians, whom I
took at other times, who said that to the south of them was
mainland, and at that time I was on the island of Guadeloupe,
and also I heard it from others of the island of Sancta Cruz
and of Sant Juan, and they said that in it there was much gold,
and, as your Highnesses know, a very short time ago, there
was no other land known than that which Ptolemy wrote of,
and there was not in my time any one who would believe that
one could navigate from Spain to the Indies; about which
matter I was seven years in your Court, and there were few
who understood it; and finally the very great courage of your
Highnesses caused it to be tried, against the opinion of those
who contradicted it.   And now the truth appears, and it
will appear before long, much greater; and if this is mainland,
it is a thing of wonder, and it will be so among all the learned,
since so great a river flows out that it makes a fresh-water sea
of 48 leagues."   These are his words. . . .[2]

Having finished this digression let us return then to our
history and to what the Admiral resolved to do in the place
where he was, and that is, going as fast as possible, he wished
to come to this Española, for some reasons which impelled
him greatly: one, because he was going with great anxiety

---

[1] Francis de Mayrones was an eminent Scotist philosopher. He died in
1327.   Columbus here quotes from his *Theologicae Veritates* (Venice, 1493).
See *Raccolta Colombiana*, Parte I., tomo II., p. 377.   Las Casas (II. 266)
was unable to verify the citation from St. Augustine.

[2] The passage omitted, Las Casas, II. 265–307, consists first, pp. 265–267,
of his comments on these words of Columbus, and second, pp. 268–274, of
a criticism of Vespucci's claim to have made a voyage in 1497 to this region
of Paria, and of his narratives and the naming of America from him.   This
criticism is translated with Las Casas's other trenchant criticisms of Vespucci's
work and claims by Sir Clements R. Markham in his *Letters of Amerigo
Vespucci* (London, 1894), pp. 68 *et seq*.   These passages are very interesting as perhaps the earliest piece of detailed critical work relating to the
discoveries, and they still constitute the cornerstone of the case against
Vespucci.   The third portion of the omitted passage, pp. 275–306, is a long
essay on the location of the earthly paradise which Columbus placed in this
new mainland he had just discovered.   *Cf.* Columbus's letter on the Third
Voyage.   Major, *Select Letters of Columbus*, pp. 140–146.

and affliction, as he had not had news of the condition of this island for so many days; and it would seem that he had some premonition of the disorder and the losses and the travail which with the rising of Francisco Roldan[1] all this land and his brothers were suffering; the other in order to despatch immediately the Adelantado, his brother, with three ships, to continue his discovery of the mainland which he had already begun to explore; and it is certain that if Francisco Roldan with his rebellion and shamelessness had not prevented him, the Admiral or his brother for him would have discovered the mainland as far as New Spain; but, according to the decree of Divine Providence, the hour of its discovery had not come, nor was the permission recalled[2] by which many were being enabled to distinguish themselves in unjust works under color of making discoveries.

The third cause which hastened him in coming to this island, was from seeing that the supplies were spoiling and being lost, of which he had such great need for the relief of those who were here, which made him weep again, considering that he had obtained them with great difficulties and fatigues, and he says that, if they are lost, he has no hope of getting others, from the great opposition he always encountered from those who counselled the Sovereigns, "who," he says here, "are not friends nor desire the honor of the high condition of their Highnesses, the persons who have spoken evil to them of such a noble undertaking. Nor was the cost so great that it should not be expended, although benefits might not be had quickly to recompense it, since the service was very great which was rendered our Lord in spreading His Holy Name through un-

[1] On the Roldan revolt, see Irving, *Christopher Columbus*, II. 199 *et seqq.*
[2] April 10, 1495, the sovereigns authorized independent exploring expeditions. Columbus protested that such expeditions infringed upon his rights, and so, June 2, 1497, the sovereigns modified their ordinance and prohibited any infringements. Apparently Las Casas is in error in saying the permission had not been recalled in 1498, but the independent voyages of Hojeda and Pinzon, who first explored the northern coast of South America (Paria) in 1499–1500, may have led him to conclude that the authorization had not been recalled.

known lands. And besides this, it would be a much greater
memorial than any Prince had left, spiritual and temporal."
And the Admiral says further, "And for this the revenue of
a good bishopric or archbishopric would be well secured, and
I say," says he, "as good as the best in Spain, since there
are here so many resources and as yet no priesthood. They
may have heard that here there are infinite peoples, which
may have determined the sending here of learned and intelligent persons and friends of Christ to try and make them
Christians and commence the work; the establishment of
which bishopric I am very sure will be made, please our Lord,
and the revenues will soon come from here and be carried
there." These are his words. How much truth he spoke and
how clear a case there was of inattention and remissness and
lukewarmness of charity in the men of that day, spiritual or
ecclesiastical and temporal, who held the power and resources,
not to make provision for the healing and conversion of these
peoples, so disposed and ready to receive the faith, the day of
universal judgment will reveal.

The fourth cause for coming to this island and not stopping
to discover more, which he would have very much wished, as
he says, was because the seamen did not come prepared to
make discoveries, since he says that he did not dare to say in
Castile that he came with intention to make discoveries, because they would have placed some impediments in his way,
or would have demanded more money of him than he had,
and he says that the people were becoming very tired. The
fifth cause, was because the ships he had were large for making
discoveries, as the one was of more than 100 tons and
the other more than 70, and only smaller ones are needed
to make discoveries; and because of the ship which he took
on his first voyage being large, he lost it in the harbor of
Navidad, kingdom of the King Guacanagarí.[1] Also the sixth
reason which very much constrained him to leave the discoveries and come to this island, was because of having his
eyes almost lost from not sleeping, from the long and continued

[1] See Journal of First Voyage, December 25.

watches or vigils he had had; and in this place he says thus: "May it please our Lord to free me from this malady," he says. "He well knows that I did not suffer these fatigues in order to find treasures for myself, since surely I recognize that all is vanity which is done in this age, save that which is for the honor and service of God, which is not to amass pomps or riches, nor the many other things we use in this world, in which we are more inclined than to the things which can save us." These are his words.

Truly this man had a good Christian purpose and was very contented with his own estate and desired in a moderate degree to maintain himself in it, and to rest from such sore travail, which he fully merited; yet the result of his sweat and toil was to impose a greater burden on the Sovereigns, and I do not know what greater was necessary than had already fallen to them, and even he had imposed obligations on them, except that he kept seeing that little importance was made of his distinguished services that he had performed, and that all at once the estimation of these Indies which was held at first was declining and coming to naught, through those that had the ears of the Sovereigns, so that he feared each day greater disfavors and that the Sovereigns might give up the whole business and thus his sweat and travail be entirely lost.

Having determined, then, to come as quickly as he could to this island, Wednesday, August 15, which was the day of the Assumption of Our Lady, after the rising of the sun, he ordered the anchors weighed from where he was anchored, which must have been within the small gulf which Margarita and the other islands make with the mainland (and he must have been near Margarita as we said above, ch. 139), and sailed on the way to this island; and, pursuing his way, he saw very clearly Margarita and the little islands which were there, and also, the farther away he went, he discovered more high land of the continent. And he went that day from sunrise to sunset 63 leagues, because of the great currents which supplemented the wind. . . .[1]

[1] The passage omitted, II. 309-313, of the printed edition, gives an

Let us return to the voyage of the Admiral, whom we left started from the neighborhood of the island of Margarita, and he went that day, Wednesday, 63 leagues from sun to sun, as they say. The next day, Thursday, August 16, he navigated to the north-west, quarter of the north,[1] 26 leagues, with the sea calm, "thanks be to God," as he always said. He tells here a wonderful thing, that when he left the Canaries for this Española, having gone 300 leagues to the west, then the needles declined to the north-west [2] one quarter, and the North Star did not rise but 5 degrees, and now in this voyage it has not declined to the north-west [2] until last night, when it declined more than a quarter and a half, and some needles declined a half wind which are two quarters; [3] and this happened suddenly last night. And he says each night he was marvelling at such a change in the heavens, and of the temperature there, so near the equinoctial line, which he experienced in all this voyage, after having found land; especially the sun being in Leo, where, as has been told, in the mornings a loose gown was worn, and where the people of that place — Gracia — were actually whiter than the people who have been seen in the Indies. He also found in the place where he now came, that the North Star was in 14 degrees when the Guardians [4] had passed from the head after two hours and a half. Here he again exhorted the Sovereigns to esteem this affair highly, since he had shown them that there was in this land gold, and he had seen in it minerals without number, which will have to be extracted with intelligence, industry and labor, since even the iron, as much as there is, cannot be taken out without these sacrifices; and he has taken them a nugget of

account of the voyage and arrival of the vessels which came to Española directly from the Canaries.

[1] Northwest by north.

[2] Northeast in the printed text.

[3] The circle of the horizon, represented by the compass card, was conceived of as divided into eight winds and each wind into halves and quarters, the quarters corresponding to the modern points of the compass, which are thirty-two in number. The declination observed was two points of the compass, or 22° 30'.

[4] See above, p. 329, note 2.

20 ounces and many others, and where this is, it must be
believed there is plenty, and he took their Highnesses a lump
of copper originally of six *arrobas*,[1] lapis-lazuli, gum-lac, amber,
cotton, pepper, cinnamon, a great quantity of Brazil-wood,
aromatic gum,[2] white and yellow sandalwood, flax, aloes,
ginger, incense, myrobolans of all kinds, very fine pearls and
pearls of a reddish color, which Marco Polo says are worth
more than the white ones,[3] and that may well be so in some
parts just as it is the case with the shells that are gathered
in Canaria and are sold for so great a price in the Mine of
Portugal. "There are infinite kinds of spices which have
been seen of which I do not care to speak for fear of prolixity."
All these are his words.

As to what he says of cinnamon, and aloes and ginger,
incense, myrobolans, sandal woods, I never saw them in this
island, at least I did not recognize them; what he says of
flax must mean *cabuya*[4] which are leaves like the *cavila* from
which thread is made and cloth or linen can be made from
it, but it is more like hemp cloth than linen. There are two
sorts of it, *cabuya* and *nequen;* *cabuya* is coarse and rough
and *nequen* is soft and delicate. Both are words of this
island Española. Storax gum I never smelled except in the
island of Cuba, but I did not see it, and this is certain that
in Cuba there must be trees of it, or of a gum that smells like
it, because we never smelled it except in the fires that the
Indians make of wood that they burn in their houses. It is
a most perfect perfume, certainly. I never knew of incense
being found in these islands.

Returning to the journey, Friday, August 17, he went 37
leagues, the sea being smooth, "to God our Lord," he says,
"may infinite thanks be given." He says that not finding
islands now, assures him that that land from whence he came
is a vast mainland, or where the Earthly Paradise is, "be-

---

[1] An arroba was twenty-five pounds.
[2] *Estoraque*, officinal storax, a gum used for incense.
[3] *Cf.* Marco Polo, bk. iii., ch. ii.
[4] Pita, the fibre of the American agave.

cause all say that it is at the end of the east, and this is the Earthly Paradise," [1] says he.

Saturday, between day and night, he went 39 leagues.

Sunday, August 19, he went in the day and the night 33 leagues, and reached land; and this was a very small island which he called Madama Beata, and which is now commonly so called. This is a small island of a matter of a league and a half close by this island of Española, and distant from this port of Sancto Domingo about 50 leagues and distant 15 leagues from the port of Yaquino, which is more to the west. There is next to it another smaller one which has a small but somewhat high mountain, which from a distance looks like a sail, and he named it Alto Velo.[2] He believed that the Beata was a small island which he called Sancta Catherina when he came by this southern coast, from the discovery of the island of Cuba, and distant from this port of Sancto Domingo 25 leagues, and is next to this island. It weighed upon him to have fallen off in his course so much, and he says it should not be counted strange, since during the nights he was from caution beating about to windward, for fear of running against some islands or shoals; there was therefore reason for this error, and thus in not following a straight course, the currents, which are very strong here, and which flow down towards the mainland and the west, must have carried the ships, without realizing it, so low. They run so violently there toward La Beata that it has happened that a ship has been eight months in those waters without being able to reach this port and that much of delay in coming from there here, has happened many times.

Therefore he anchored now between the Beata and this island, between which there are two leagues of sea, Monday, August 20. He then sent the boats to land to call Indians,

---

[1] *Cf.* the letter on the Third Voyage, Major, *Select Letters of Columbus,* p. 140, for Columbus's reasoning and beliefs about the Earthly Paradise or Garden of Eden; for Las Casas's discussion of the question, see *Historia de las Indias,* II. 275–306.

[2] High sail.

as there were villages there, in order to write of his arrival
to the Adelantado; having come at midday, he despatched
them. Twice there came to the ship six Indians, and one of
them carried a crossbow with its cord, and nut and rack,[1]
which caused him no small surprise, and he said, "May it
please God that no one is dead." And because from Sancto
Domingo the three ships must have been seen to pass down-
ward, and concluding that it certainly was the Admiral as he
was expecting him each day, the Adelantado started then in
a caravel and overtook the Admiral here. They both were
very much pleased to see each other. The Admiral having
asked him about the condition of the country, the Adelantado
recounted to him how Francisco Roldan had arisen with 80
men, with all the rest of the occurrences which had passed
in this island, since he left it. What he felt on hearing such
news, there is small need to recite.

He left there, Wednesday, August 22, and finally with some
difficulty because of the many currents and the north-east
breezes which are continuous and contrary there he arrived
at this port of Sancto Domingo, Friday, the last day of August
of the said year 1498, having set out from Isabela for Castile,
Thursday the tenth day of March, 1496, so that he delayed
in returning to this island two years and a half less nine days.

[1] The rack was used to bend the crossbow.

LETTER OF COLUMBUS TO THE NURSE OF PRINCE JOHN

INTRODUCTION

THIS letter was addressed by Columbus to Doña Juana de Torres, who had been a nurse of the lately deceased royal prince John, the son of Ferdinand and Isabella, and who was the sister of Antonio de Torres, who had accompanied Columbus on his second voyage and was subsequently a commander in other voyages to the New World. It was probably written on shipboard when Columbus was sent back to Spain in irons in the autumn of the year 1500. It is at once a cry of distress and an impassioned self-defence, and is one of the most important of the Admiral's writings for the student of his career and character.

In the letter to Santangel the discoverer announces his success in his long projected undertaking; in the letter to the nurse he is at the lowest point in the startling reverse of fortune that befell him because of the troubles in Santo Domingo, and in the letter on the fourth voyage he appears as one struggling against the most adverse circumstances to vindicate his career, and to demonstrate the value of what he had previously accomplished, and to crown those achievements by actually attaining the coast of Asia. Columbus regarded his defence as set forth in this letter as of such importance that he included it in the four codices or collections of documents and papers prepared in duplicate before his last voyage to authenticate his titles and honors and to secure their inheritance by his son. The text of the letter from which the present translation was made is that of the Paris Codex of the *Book of Privileges*, as it is called. This is regarded by Harrisse as the best. The translation is by George F. Barwick of the British Museum, and was originally published in *Christopher Columbus, Facsimile of his Own Book of Privileges*, 1502, edited by B. F. Stevens (London, 1903). The letter remained unpublished until it was printed in Spotorno's *Codice Diplomatico* in 1822. In 1825 it appeared again in Navarrete's *Viages*, in a slightly varying text. It was first published in English in the translation of the *Codice Diplomatico* issued in London in 1823 under the title of *Memorials of Columbus*, etc.

E. G. B.

TRANSCRIPT OF A LETTER WHICH THE ADMIRAL OF THE INDIES SENT TO THE NURSE OF PRINCE DON JOHN OF CASTILE

IN THE YEAR 1500 WHEN HE WAS RETURNING FROM THE INDIES AS A PRISONER

Most virtuous Lady: —

THOUGH my complaint of the world is new, its habit of ill-using is very ancient. I have had a thousand struggles with it, and have thus far withstood them all, but now neither arms nor counsels avail me, and it cruelly keeps me under water. Hope in the Creator of all men sustains me; His help was always very ready; on another occasion, and not long ago, when I was still more overwhelmed, he raised me with his right arm, saying, O man of little faith, arise, it is I; be not afraid.[1]

I came with so much cordial affection to serve these Princes, and have served them with such service, as has never been heard of or seen.

Of the new heaven and earth which our Lord made, when Saint John was writing the Apocalypse,[2] after what was spoken by the mouth of Isaiah,[3] he made me the messenger, and showed me where it lay. In all men there was disbelief, but to the Queen my Lady He gave the spirit of understanding,

---

[1] An echo of the words of Jesus to Peter when he began to sink, "O thou of little faith, wherefore didst thou doubt?" *Matthew*, XIV. 31.

[2] *Revelation*, XXI. 1. "And I saw a new heaven and a new earth; for the first heaven and the first earth were passed away."

[3] "For, behold, I create new heavens and a new earth." *Isaiah*, LXV. 17.

and great courage, and made her heiress of all, as a dear and much loved daughter. I went to take possession of all this in her royal name. They sought to make amends to her for the ignorance they had all shown by passing over their little knowledge, and talking of obstacles and expenses. Her Highness, on the other hand, approved of it, and supported it as far as she was able.

Seven years passed in discussion, and nine in execution.[1] During this time very remarkable and noteworthy things occurred whereof no idea at all had been formed. I have arrived at, and am in such a condition that there is no person so vile but thinks he may insult me; he shall be reckoned in the world as valor itself who is courageous enough not to consent to it.

If I were to steal the Indies or the land which lies towards them,[2] of which I am now speaking, from the altar of Saint Peter, and give them to the Moors, they could not show greater enmity towards me in Spain. Who would believe such a thing where there was always so much magnanimity?

I should have much desired to free myself from this affair had it been honorable towards my Queen to do so. The support of Our Lord and of Her Highness made me persevere; and to alleviate in some measure the sorrows which death had caused her,[3] I undertook a fresh voyage to the new heaven and earth which up to that time had remained hidden; and if it is not held there in esteem like the other voyages to the Indies, that is no wonder because it came to be looked upon as my work.

The Holy Spirit inflamed Saint Peter and twelve others with him, and they all fought here below, and their toils and hardships were many, but last of all they gained the victory.

[1] 1485–1491 inc. and 1492–1500 inc.

[2] *Sy yo robara las Yndias o tierra que jaz fase ellas*, etc. In the translation *jaz fase* is taken to stand for *yace hacia*. This supposition makes sense and is probably correct. The reading of the other text is " *que san face ellas.*" Navarrete says that neither one is intelligible.

[3] The death of Prince John, October 4, 1497.

This voyage to Paria [1] I thought would somewhat appease them on account of the pearls, and of the discovery of gold in Española. I ordered the pearls to be collected and fished for by people with whom an arrangement was made that I should return for them, and, as I understood, they were to be measured by the bushel.[2] If I did not write about this to their Highnesses, it was because I wished to have first of all done the same thing with the gold. The result to me in this has been the same as in many other things; I should not have lost them nor my honor, if I had sought my own advantage, and had allowed Española to be ruined, or if my privileges and contracts had been observed. And I say just the same about the gold which I had then collected, and [for] which with such great afflictions and toils I have, by divine power, almost perfected [the arrangements].

When I went from Paria I found almost half the people of Española in revolt,[3] and they have waged war against me until now, as against a Moor; and the Indians on the other side grievously [harassed me]. At this time Hojeda arrived [4] and tried to put the finishing stroke: he said that their Highnesses had sent him with promises of gifts, franchises and pay; he gathered together a great band, for in the whole of Española there are very few save vagabonds, and not one with wife and children. This Hojeda gave me great trouble; he was obliged to depart, and left word that he would soon return with more ships and people, and that he had left the royal person of the Queen our Lady at the point of death. Then Vincent Yañez [5] arrived with four caravels; there was dis-

---

[1] The name given to that part of the mainland of South America which Columbus discovered on his third voyage.

[2] *I.e.*, so great was their abundance.

[3] On this revolt, see Bourne, *Spain in America*, p. 49 *et seqq.*, and in greater detail, Irving, *Columbus*, ed. 1868, II. 109 *et seqq.*

[4] Hojeda sailed in May, 1499. Las Casas's account of his voyage is translated by Markham in his *Letters of Amerigo Vespucci*, Hakluyt Society (London, 1894), p. 78 *et seqq.* See also Irving, *Columbus*, III. 23–42 He was accompanied on this voyage by Amerigo Vespucci.

[5] Vicente Yañez Pinzon set sail from Palos, November 18, 1499. For his voyage, see Irving, *Columbus*, III. 49–58.

turbance and mistrust, but no mischief; the Indians talked of many others at the Canibales [Caribbee Islands] and in Paria; and afterwards spread the news of six other caravels, which were brought by a brother of the Alcalde,[1] but it was with malicious intent. This occurred at the very last, when the hope that their Highnesses would ever send any ships to the Indies was almost abandoned, nor did we expect them; and it was commonly reported that her Highness was dead.

A certain Adrian about this time endeavored to rise in rebellion again, as he had done previously, but Our Lord did not permit his evil purpose to succeed. I had purposed in myself never to touch a hair of anybody's head, but I lament to say that with this man, owing to his ingratitude, it was not possible to keep that resolve as I had intended; I should not have done less to my brother, if he had sought to kill me, and steal the dominion which my King and Queen had given me in trust.[2] This Adrian, as it appears, had sent Don Ferdinand[3] to Xaragua to collect some of his followers, and there a dispute arose with the Alcalde from which a deadly contest ensued, but he [Adrian] did not effect his purpose. The Alcalde seized him and a part of his band, and the fact was that he would have executed them if I had not prevented it; they were kept prisoners awaiting a caravel in which they might depart. The news of Hojeda which I told them, made them lose the hope that he would now come again.

For six months I had been prepared to return to their Highnesses with the good news of the gold, and to escape from governing a dissolute people, who fear neither God, nor their King and Queen, being full of vices and wickedness. I could have paid the people in full with six hundred thousand,[4] and for this purpose I had four millions of tenths and somewhat

[1] The Alcalde was Roldán, the leader of the revolt. He was alcalde mayor of the city of Isabela and of the whole island, *i.e.*, the chief justice. Las Casas, *Historia de las Indias*, II. 124.

[2] On the career in Española of Adrian de Muxica and his execution, see Irving, *Columbus*, II. 283 *et seqq.*

[3] Ferdinand de Guevara. See Irving, *Columbus*, II. 283 *et seqq.*

[4] *I.e.*, maravedis, equivalent to about $4000.

more, besides the third of the gold. Before my departure I many times begged their Highnesses to send there, at my expense, some one to take charge of the administration of justice; and after finding the Alcalde in arms I renewed my supplications to have either some troops or at least some servant of theirs with letters patent; for my reputation is such that even if I build churches and hospitals, they will always be called dens of thieves. They did indeed make provision at last, but it was the very contrary of what the matter demanded: may it be successful, since it was according to their good pleasure.

I was there for two years without being able to gain a decree of favor for myself or for those who went there, yet this man [1] brought a coffer full; whether they will all redound to their [Highnesses'] service, God knows. Indeed, to begin with, there are exemptions for twenty years, which is a man's lifetime; and gold is collected to such an extent that there was one person who became worth five marks [2] in four hours; whereof I will speak more fully later on.

If it would please their Highnesses to remove the grounds of a common saying of those who know my labors, that the calumny of the people has done me more harm than much service and the maintenance of their [Highnesses'] property and dominion has done me good, it would be a charity, and I should be re-established in my honor, and it would be talked about all over the world; for the undertaking is of such a nature that it must daily become more famous and in higher esteem.

When the commander Bobadilla came to Santo Domingo,[3] I was at La Vega, and the Adelantado [4] at Xaragua, where that Adrian had made a stand, but then all was quiet, and

---

[1] Bobadilla, the successor of Columbus as governor, who sent him back in chains.

[2] A mark was eight ounces or two-thirds of a Troy pound. Here it is probably the silver mark as a measure of value, which was about $3.25. If the word is used as a measure of weight of gold, it would be about $150.

[3] Bobadilla arrived at Santo Domingo August 23, 1500.

[4] Bartholomew Columbus.

the land rich and all men at peace. On the second day after his arrival he created himself Governor, and appointed officers and made executions, and proclaimed immunities of gold and tenths and in general of everything else for twenty years, which is a man's lifetime, and that he came to pay everybody in full up to that day, even though they had not rendered service; and he publicly notified that, as for me, he had charge to send me in irons, and my brothers likewise, as he has done, and that I should nevermore return thither, nor any other of my family; alleging a thousand disgraceful and discourteous things about me. All this took place on the second day after his arrival, as I have said, and while I was absent at a distance, without my knowing either of him or of his arrival.

Some letters of their Highnesses signed in blank, of which he brought a number, he filled up and sent to the Alcalde and to his company, with favors and commendations; to me he never sent either letter or messenger, nor has he done so to this day. Imagine what any one holding my office would think when one who endeavored to rob their Highnesses, and who has done so much evil and mischief, is honored and favored, while he who maintained it at such risks is degraded.

When I heard this, I thought that this affair would be like that of Hojeda or one of the others, but I restrained myself when I learnt for certain from the friars that their Highnesses had sent him. I wrote to him that his arrival was welcome, and that I was prepared to go to the Court and had sold all I possessed by auction; and that with respect to the immunities he should not be hasty, for both that matter and the government I would hand over to him immediately as smooth as my palm. And I wrote to the same effect to the friars, but neither he nor they gave me any answer. On the contrary, he put himself in a warlike attitude, and compelled all who went there to take an oath to him as Governor; and they told me that it was for twenty years.

Directly I knew of those immunities, I thought that I would repair such a great error and that he would be pleased, for he gave them without the need or occasion necessary in so vast a matter; and he gave to vagabond people what would have been excessive for a man who had brought wife and children. So I announced by word and letters that he could not use his patents because mine were those in force; and I showed them the immunities which Juan Aguado [1] brought. All this was done by me in order to gain time, so that their Highnesses might be informed of the condition of the country, and that they might have an opportunity of issuing fresh commands as to what would best promote their service in that respect.

It is useless to publish such immunities in the Indies; to the settlers who have taken up residence it is a pure gain, for the best lands are given to them, and at a low valuation they will be worth two hundred thousand at the end of the four years when the period of residence is ended, without their digging a spadeful in them. I would not speak thus if the settlers were married, but there are not six among them all who are not on the lookout to gather what they can and depart speedily. It would be a good thing if people should go from Castile, and also if it were known who and what they are, and if the country could be settled with honest people.

I had agreed with those settlers that they should pay the third of the gold, and the tenths, and this at their own request; and they received it as a great favor from their Highnesses. I reproved them when I heard that they ceased to do this, and hoped that the Commander would do likewise, but he did the contrary. He incensed them against me by saying that I wanted to deprive them of what their Highnesses had given them; and he endeavored to set them at variance with me, and did so; and he induced them to write to their Highnesses that they should never again send me back to the government, and I likewise make the same supplication to them for myself and for my whole family, as long as there are not different inhabitants. And he together with them ordered inquisitions concerning me for wickednesses the like whereof

---

[1] Juan Aguado arrived from Spain in October, 1495. Las Casas, *Historia de las Indias*, II. 109 *et seqq.*, gives a full account of his mission. See also Irving, *Columbus.* ed. 1868, II. 77 *et seqq.*

were never known in hell. Our Lord, who rescued Daniel and the three children,[1] is present with the same wisdom and power as he had then, and with the same means, if it should please him and be in accordance with his will.

I should know how to remedy all this, and the rest of what has been said and has taken place since I have been in the Indies, if my disposition would allow me to seek my own advantage, and if it seemed honorable to me to do so, but the maintenance of justice and the extension of the dominion of Her Highness has hitherto kept me down. Now that so much gold is found, a dispute arises as to which brings more profit, whether to go about robbing or to go to the mines. A hundred castellanos[2] are as easily obtained for a woman as for a farm, and it is very general, and there are plenty of dealers who go about looking for girls; those from nine to ten are now in demand, and for all ages a good price must be paid.

I assert that the violence of the calumny of turbulent persons has injured me more than my services have profited me; which is a bad example for the present and for the future. I take my oath that a number of men have gone to the Indies who did not deserve water in the sight of God and of the world; and now they are returning thither, and leave is granted them.[3]

I assert that when I declared that the Commander[4] could not grant immunities, I did what he desired, although I told him that it was to cause delay until their Highnesses should receive information from the country, and should command anew what might be for their service. He excited their enmity against me, and he seems, from what took place and from his behavior, to have come as my enemy and as a very vehement one; or else the report is true that he has spent much to ob-

---

[1] Cf. *Daniel*, chs. III. and VI.

[2] The castellano was one-sixth of an ounce, or in value about $3.

[3] See Bourne, *Spain in America*, p. 50, for Columbus's bitter characterization of the Spaniards in Española in 1498, and p. 46 for the royal authorization in June, 1497, to transport criminals to the island. The terrible consequences of this policy led the Spanish government later to adopt the strictest regulations controlling emigration to the New World. *Cf. Spain in America*, ch. XVI.

[4] Bobadilla was a knight commander of the military order of Calatrava.

tain this employment. I do not know more about it than what I hear. I never heard of an inquisitor gathering rebels together and accepting them, and others devoid of credit and unworthy of it, as witnesses against their governor.

If their Highnesses were to make a general inquisition there, I assure you that they would look upon it as a great wonder that the island does not founder.

I think your Ladyship will remember that when, after losing my sails, I was driven into Lisbon by a tempest, I was falsely accused of having gone there to the King in order to give him the Indies. Their Highnesses afterwards learned the contrary, and that it was entirely malicious. Although I may know but little, I do not think anyone considers me so stupid as not to know that even if the Indies were mine I could not uphold myself without the help of some prince. If this be so, where could I find better support and security than in the King and Queen our Lords, who have raised me from nothing to such great honor, and are the most exalted princes of the world on sea and on land, and who consider that I have rendered them service, and preserve to me my privileges and rewards; and if anyone infringes them, their Highnesses increase them still more, as was seen in the case of Juan Aguado; and they order great honor to be conferred upon me, and, as I have already said, their Highnesses have received service from me, and keep my sons in their household;[1] all which could by no means happen with another prince, for where there is no affection, everything else fails.

I have now spoken thus in reply to a malicious slander, but against my will, as it is a thing which should not recur to memory even in dreams; for the Commander Bobadilla maliciously seeks in this way to set his own conduct and actions in a brighter light; but I shall easily show him that his small knowledge and great cowardice, together with his inordinate cupidity, have caused him to fail therein.

---

[1] Diego Columbus had been appointed a page to Prince John in 1492. Navarrete, *Viages*, II. 17. At this time, 1500, both Diego and Ferdinand were pages in the Queen's household. *Historie*, ed. 1867, p. 276.

I have already said that I wrote to him and to the friars, and immediately set out, as I told him, almost alone, because all the people were with the Adelantado, and likewise in order to prevent suspicion on his part. When he heard this, he seized Don Diego [1] and sent him on board a caravel loaded with irons, and did the same to me upon my arrival, and afterwards to the Adelantado when he came; nor did I speak to him any more, nor to this day has he allowed anyone to speak to me; and I take my oath that I cannot understand why I am made a prisoner. He made it his first business to seize the gold, which he did without measuring or weighing it, and in my absence; he said that he wanted it to pay the people, and according to what I hear he assigned the chief part to himself and sent fresh exchangers for the exchanges. Of this gold I had put aside certain specimens, very big lumps, like the eggs of geese, hens, and pullets, and of many other shapes, which some persons had collected in a short space of time, in order that their Highnesses might be gladdened, and might comprehend the business upon seeing a quantity of large stones full of gold. This collection was the first to be given away, with malicious intent, so that their Highnesses should not hold the matter in any account until he has feathered his nest, which he is in great haste to do. Gold which is for melting diminishes at the fire; some chains which would weigh about twenty marks have never been seen again. I have been more distressed about this matter of the gold than even about the pearls, because I have not brought it to Her Highness.

The Commander at once set to work upon anything which he thought would injure me. I have already said that with six hundred thousand I could pay everyone without defrauding anybody, and that I had more than four millions of tenths and constabulary [dues], without touching the gold. He made some free gifts which are ridiculous, though I believe that he began by assigning the chief part to himself. Their Highnesses will find it out when they order an account to be obtained from him, especially if I should be present thereat. He does

[1] The younger brother of the Admiral.

nothing but reiterate that a large sum is owing, and it is what I have said, and even less. I have been much distressed that there should be sent concerning me an inquisitor who is aware that if the inquisition which he returns is very grave he will remain in possession of the government.

Would that it had pleased our Lord that their Highnesses had sent him or some one else two years ago, for I know that I should now be free from scandal and infamy, and that my honor would not be taken from me, nor should I lose it. God is just, and will make known the why and the wherefore.

They judge me over there as they would a governor who had gone to Sicily, or to a city or town placed under regular government, and where the laws can be observed in their entirety without fear of ruining everything; and I am greatly injured thereby. I ought to be judged as a captain who went from Spain to the Indies to conquer a numerous and warlike people, whose customs and religion are very contrary to ours; who live in rocks and mountains, without fixed settlements, and not like ourselves; and where, by the divine will, I have placed under the dominion of the King and Queen, our sovereigns, another world,[1] through which Spain, which was reckoned a poor country, has become the richest. I ought to be judged as a captain who for such a long time up to this day has borne arms without laying them aside for an hour, and by gentlemen adventurers and by customs and not by letters,[2] unless they were Greeks or Romans, or others of modern times of whom there are so many and such noble examples in Spain;[3] or otherwise I receive great injury, because in the Indies there is neither town nor settlement.

[1] *Un otro mundo.* See note, p. 352 above.

[2] *Caballeros de conquistas y del uso, y no de letras.* This should be: "Knights of Conquests and by profession and not of letters." *I.e.*, by nobles that have actually been conquerors and had conquered territory awarded to them and who are knights by practice or profession and not gentlemen of letters.

[3] What this means is not altogether clear. Apparently Columbus means that men of letters or lawyers in Greece and Rome, great conquering nations, would know what standards to apply in his case, and that there were some such men of breadth in Spain.

The gate to the gold and pearls is now open, and plenty of everything — precious stones, spices, and a thousand other things — may be surely expected, and never could a worse misfortune befall me; for by the name of our Lord the first voyage would yield them just as much as would the traffic of Arabia Felix as far as Mecca, as I wrote to their Highnesses by Antonio de Torres in my reply respecting the repartition of the sea and land with the Portuguese; and afterwards it would equal that of Calicut, as I told them and put in writing at the monastery of Mejorada.

The news of the gold that I said I would give is, that on the day of the Nativity, while I was much tormented, being harassed by wicked Christians and by Indians, and when I was on the point of giving up everything and, if possible, escaping from life, our Lord miraculously comforted me and said, "Fear not violence, I will provide for all things; the seven years of the term of the gold have not elapsed, and in that and in everything else I will afford thee a remedy." On that day I learned that there were eighty leagues of land with mines at every point thereof. The opinion now is that it is all one. Some have collected a hundred and twenty castellanos in one day, and others ninety, and even the number of two hundred and fifty has been reached. From fifty to seventy, and in many more cases from fifteen to fifty, is considered a good day's work, and many carry it on. The usual quantity is from six to twelve, and any one obtaining less than this is not satisfied. It seems too that these mines are like others, and do not yield equally every day. The mines are new, and so are the workers: it is the opinion of everybody that even if all Castile were to go there, every individual, however inexpert he might be, would not obtain less than one or two castellanos daily, and now it is only commencing. It is true that they keep Indians, but the business is in the hands of the Christians. Behold what discernment Bobadilla had, when he gave up everything for nothing, and four millions of tenths, without any reason or even being requested, and without first notifying it to their Highnesses. And this is not the only loss.

I know that my errors have not been committed with the intention of doing evil, and I believe that their Highnesses regard the matter just as I state it; and I know and see that they deal mercifully even with those who maliciously act to their disservice. I believe and consider it very certain that their clemency will be both greater and more abundant towards me, for I fell therein through ignorance and the force of circumstances, as they will know fully hereafter; and I indeed am their creature, and they will look upon my services, and will acknowledge day by day that they are much profited. They will place everything in the balance, even as Holy Scripture tells us good and evil will be at the day of judgment. If, however, they command that another person do judge me, which I cannot believe, and that it be by inquisition in the Indies, I very humbly beseech them to send thither two conscientious and honorable persons at my expense, who I believe will easily, now that gold is discovered, find five marks in four hours. In either case it is needful for them to provide for this matter.

The Commander on his arrival at Santo Domingo took up his abode in my house, and just as he found it so he appropriated everything to himself. Well and good; perhaps he was in want of it. A pirate never acted thus towards a merchant. About my papers I have a greater grievance, for he has so completely deprived me of them that I have never been able to obtain a single one from him; and those that would have been most useful in my exculpation are precisely those which he has kept most concealed. Behold the just and honest inquisitor! Whatever he may have done, they tell me that there has been an end to justice, except in an arbitrary form. God our Lord is present with his strength and wisdom, as of old, and always punishes in the end, especially ingratitude and injuries.

LETTER OF COLUMBUS ON THE FOURTH VOYAGE

INTRODUCTION

THE letter on Columbus's last voyage when he explored the coast of Central America and of the Isthmus of Panama was written when he was shipwrecked on the island of Jamaica, 1503. It is his last important writing and one of great significance in understanding his geographical conceptions.

The Spanish text of this letter is not older than the sixteenth century and perhaps not older than the seventeenth. The Spanish text was first published by Navarrete in his *Coleccion de los Viages y Descubrimientos*, 1825. An Italian translation, however, was published in 1505 and is commonly known as the *Lettera Rarissima*. Mr. John Boyd Thacher has reproduced this early Italian translation in facsimile in his *Christopher Columbus*, accompanied by a translation into English. Cesare de Lollis prepared a critical edition of the Spanish text for the *Raccolta Colombiana*, which was carefully collated with and in some instances corrected by this contemporary translation. Most of his changes in punctuation and textual emendations have been adopted in the present edition, and attention is called to them in the notes.

The translation is that of R. H. Major as published in the revised edition of his *Select Letters of Columbus*. It has been carefully revised by the present editor, and some important changes have been made. As hitherto published in English a good many passages in this letter have been so confused and obscure and some so absolutely unintelligible, that the late Justin Winsor characterized this last of the important writings of Columbus as "a sorrowful index of his wandering reason." [1]   Almost every one of these passages has yielded up the secret of its meaning either through a more exact translation or in the light of the textual emendations suggested by de Lollis or proposed by the present editor. Among such revisions and textual emendations attention may be called to those discussed on pp. 392, 396, 397.   As here published this letter of Columbus is as coherent and intelligible as his other writings.

The editor wishes here to acknowledge his obligations to Professor Henry R. Lang of Yale University, whom he has consulted in regard to perplexing passages or possible emendations, and from whom he has received valuable assistance.

The other important accounts of this voyage, or of the part of it covered by this letter, are the brief report by Diego de Porras, of which a translation is given in Thacher's *Columbus*, and those by Ferdinand Columbus in the *Historie* and Peter Martyr in his *De Rebus Oceanicis*.   On this voyage Las Casas's source was the account of Ferdinand Columbus.   Lollis presents some striking evidence to show that the accounts of Ferdinand Columbus and Peter Martyr were based upon the same original, a lost narrative of the Admiral.   It will be remembered, however, that Ferdinand accompanied his father on this voyage, and although only a boy of thirteen his narrative contains several passages of vivid personal recollection.   The editor has carefully compared Ferdinand's narrative with the account in this letter and noted the important differences.

E. G. B.

[1] *Christopher Columbus*, p 459; *cf.* also the passages quoted on p. 460.

THE FOURTH VOYAGE OF COLUMBUS

A Letter written by Don Christóbal Colon, Viceroy and Admiral of the Indies, to the most Christian and mighty King and Queen of Spain, our Sovereigns, in which are described the events of his voyage, and the countries, provinces, cities, rivers and other marvellous matters therein discovered, as well as the places where gold and other substances of great richness and value are to be found

Most Serene, and very high and mighty Princes, the King and Queen our Sovereigns: —

MY passage from Cadiz to the Canary occupied four days, and thence to the Indies sixteen days. From which I wrote, that my intention was to expedite my voyage as much as possible while I had good vessels, good crews and stores, and that Jamaica was the place to which I was bound. I wrote this in Dominica:[1] —

Up to the period of my reaching these shores I experienced most excellent weather, but the night of my arrival came on with a dreadful tempest, and the same bad weather has continued ever since. On reaching the island of Española[2] I despatched a packet of letters, by which I begged as a favor that a ship should be supplied me at my own cost in lieu of one of those that I had brought with me, which had become unseaworthy, and could no longer carry sail. The letters were taken, and your Highnesses will know if a reply has been given to them. For my part I was forbidden to go on

[1] The punctuation of this first paragraph has been changed in the light of the contemporary Italian translation known as the *Lettera Rarissima*, which is given in facsimile and English translation in Thacher's *Christopher Columbus*, II. 671 *et seqq.*

[2] June 29. Las Casas, III. 29.

shore;[1] the hearts of my people failed them lest I should take them further, and they said that if any danger were to befall them, they should receive no succor, but, on the contrary, in all probability have some great affront offered them. Moreover every man had it in his power to tell me that the new Governor would have the superintendence of the countries that I might acquire.[2]

The tempest was terrible throughout the night, all the ships were separated, and each one driven to the last extremity, without hope of anything but death; each of them also looked upon the loss of the rest as a matter of certainty. What man was ever born, not even excepting Job, who would not have been ready to die of despair at finding himself as I then was, in anxious fear for my own safety, and that of my son, my brother[3] and my friends, and yet refused permission either to land or to put into harbor on the shores which by God's mercy I had gained for Spain sweating blood?

But to return to the ships: although the tempest had so completely separated them from me as to leave me single, yet the Lord restored them to me in His own good time. The ship which we had the greatest fear for, had put out to sea to escape [being blown] toward the island. The *Gallega*[4] lost her boat and a great part of her provisions, which latter loss indeed all the ships suffered. The vessel in which I was, though dreadfully buffeted, was saved by our Lord's mercy from any injury whatever; my brother went in the ship that was unsound, and he under God was the cause of its being saved.

[1] By the letter of the King and Queen, March 14, 1502, Columbus had been forbidden to call at Española on the outward voyage. Las Casas, *Historia de las Indias*, III. 26.

[2] The new governor, Ovando, who had been sent out to supersede Bobadilla, had reached Santo Domingo in April of this year, 1502.

[3] Columbus was accompanied by his younger son Ferdinand and his elder brother Bartholomew. Las Casas, III. 25.

[4] The translation here follows Lollis's emendation of the text which changed the printed text, " *habia, echado á la mar, por escapar, fasta la isola la Gallega; perdio la barca,*" etc., to " *habia echado á la mar, por escapar fasta la isla; la Gallega perdio la barca.*" One of the ships was named *La Gallega*, and there is no island of that name in that region.

With this tempest I struggled on till I reached Jamaica, and there the sea became calm, but there was a strong current which carried me as far as the Queen's Garden [1] without seeing land. Hence as opportunity afforded I pushed on for the mainland, in spite of the wind and a fearful contrary current, against which I contended for sixty days, and after all only made seventy leagues. All this time I was unable to get into harbor, nor was there any cessation of the tempest, which was one continuation of rain, thunder and lightning; indeed it seemed as if it were the end of the world. I at length reached the Cape of Gracias á Dios, and after that the Lord granted me fair wind and tide; this was on the twelfth of September. [2]

[1] Columbus set forth from the harbor of Santo Domingo in the storm, Friday, July 1. The ships found refuge in the harbor of Azua on the following Sunday, July 3. (Ferdinand Columbus in the *Historie*, ed. 1867, pp. 286–287.) Azua is about 50 miles west of Santo Domingo in a straight line, but much farther by water. After a rest and repairs the Admiral sailed to Yaquimo, the present Jacmel in the territory of Hayti, into which port he went to escape another storm. He left Yaquimo, July 14. (Las Casas, III. 108 ; Ferdinand Columbus, *Historie*, p. 289.) He then passed south of Jamaica, and was carried by the currents northwest till he reached the Queen's Garden, a group of many small islands south of Cuba and east of the Isle of Pines, so named by him in 1494 on his exploration of the coast of Cuba.

[2] From the Queen's Garden he sailed south July 27 (the Porras narrative of this voyage, Navarrete, II. 283; in English in Thacher, *Columbus*, II. 640 *et seqq.*), and after a passage of ninety leagues sighted an island Saturday, July 30. (Porras in Thacher, II. 643.) This was the island of Guanaja about twelve leagues north of Trujillo, Honduras. (Las Casas, III. 109.) Here a landing was made and a canoe was encountered which was covered with an awning and contained Indians well clothed and a load of merchandise. Notwithstanding these indications of a more advanced culture than had hitherto been found, the Admiral decided not to explore the country of these Indians, which would have led him into Yucatan and possibly Mexico, but to search for the strait which he supposed separated Asia from the continental mass he had discovered on his third voyage (Paria, South America). He struck the mainland near Trujillo, naming the point Caxinas. At or near this place they landed Sunday, August 14, to say mass. (Las Casas, III. 112; Ferdinand Columbus, *Historie*, p. 295.) From this point he coasted very slowly, sailing in sight of land by day and anchoring at night, distressed by storms and headwinds, some days losing as much ground as could be gained in two, till September 12, when he reached Cape Gracias á Dios. (Las Casas, III. 113; *Historie*, p. 297; Porras narrative in Thacher, *Columbus*, II. 644.) It will be seen from this collation of the sources that the statements in our text are far from exact, that they are in fact a very

Eighty-eight days did this fearful tempest continue, during
which I was at sea, and saw neither sun nor stars; my ships
lay exposed, with sails torn, and anchors, rigging, cables,
boats and a great quantity of provisions lost; my people
were very weak and humbled in spirit, many of them promising to lead a religious life, and all making vows and promising to perform pilgrimages, while some of them would frequently go to their messmates to make confession.[1]   Other
tempests have been experienced, but never of so long a duration or so fearful as this: many whom we looked upon as brave
men, on several occasions showed considerable trepidation;
but the distress of my son who was with me grieved me to the
soul, and the more when I considered his tender age, for he
was but thirteen years old, and he enduring so much toil for
so long a time.   Our Lord, however, gave him strength even
to enable him to encourage the rest, and he worked as if he
had been eighty years at sea, and all this was a consolation to
me.   I myself had fallen sick, and was many times at the
point of death, but from a little cabin that I had caused to be

general and greatly exaggerated recollection of a most trying experience.
It will be remembered that Ferdinand was on this voyage, but his narrative
says nothing of any storm between July 14 when he left the Queen's Gardens
and the arrival at Guanaja, a passage which Porras says took three days.
This passage, however, Las Casas describes apparently on the basis of this
letter as having taken sixty days (*Historia*, III. 108).   Next the text of
the *Historie* presents a difficulty, for it places the tedious stormy voyage of
sixty leagues and *seventy* days between Caxinas (Trujillo) and Cape Gracias
á Dios (*Historie*, p. 296), although in another place it gives the beginning of
this coasting as after August 14 and the date of arrival at the Cape as September 12.   This last chronological difficulty may perhaps be accounted for
in this way: The original manuscript of the *Historie* may have had "XXX
dias," which a copyist or the Italian translator may have taken for "LXX
dias."

[1] A review of the chronology of the voyage in the preceding note will
show that no such storm of eighty-eight days' duration could have occurred
in the first part of this voyage.   Columbus was only seventy-four days in
going from Santo Domingo to Cabo Gracias á Dios. Either the text is wrong
or his memory was at fault.   The most probable conclusion is that in copying
either LXXXVIII got substituted for XXVIII or *Ochenta y ocho* for *Veinte
y ocho*.   In that case we should have almost exactly the time spent in going
from Trujillo to Cape Gracias á Dios, August 14 to September 12, and exact
agreement between our text, the *Historie*, and the Porras narrative.

constructed on deck, I directed our course. My brother was in the ship that was in the worst condition and the most exposed to danger; and my grief on this account was the greater that I brought him with me against his will.

Such is my fate, that the twenty years of service [1] through which I have passed with so much toil and danger, have profited me nothing, and at this very day I do not possess a roof in Spain that I can call my own; if I wish to eat or sleep, I have nowhere to go but to the inn or tavern, and most times lack wherewith to pay the bill. Another anxiety wrung my very heartstrings, which was the thought of my son Diego, whom I had left an orphan in Spain, and dispossessed of my honor and property, although I had looked upon it as a certainty, that your Majesties, as just and grateful Princes, would restore it to him in all respects with increase. [2]

I reached the land of Cariay,[3] where I stopped to repair my vessels and take in provisions, as well as to afford relaxation to the men, who had become very weak. I myself (who, as I said before, had been several times at the point of death) gained information respecting the gold mines of which I was in search, in the province of Ciamba;[4] and two Indians conducted me to Carambaru,[5] where the people (who go naked)

---

[1] Twenty years, speaking approximately. This letter was written in 1503, and Columbus entered the service of Spain in 1485.

[2] Diego was the heir of his father's titles. He was appointed governor of the Indies in 1508, but a prolonged lawsuit was necessary to establish his claims to inherit his father's rights.

[3] Their course was down the Mosquito coast. Cariay was near the mouth of the San Juan River of Nicaragua. Las Casas gives the date of the arrival at Cariarí, as he gives the name, as September 17 (III. 114). The *Historie* gives the date as September 5 and the name as Cariai (p. 297).

[4] Peter Martyr, *De Rebus Oceanicis* (ed. 1574), p. 239, says that Columbus called Ciamba the region which the inhabitants called Quiriquetana, a name which it would seem still survives in Chiriqui Lagoon just east of Almirante Bay. The name "Ciamba" appears on Martin Behaim's globe, 1492, as a province corresponding to Cochin-China. It is described in Marco Polo under the name "Chamba"; see Yule's *Marco Polo*, II. 248-252 (bk. III., ch. v.).

[5] Carambaru is the present Almirante Bay, about on the border between Costa Rica and Panama. Las Casas describes the bay as six leagues long and over three broad with many islands and coves. He gives the name

wear golden mirrors round their necks, which they will neither
sell, give, nor part with for any consideration. They named
to me many places on the sea-coast where there were both
gold and mines. The last that they mentioned was Veragua,[1]
which was five-and-twenty leagues distant from the place
where we then were. I started with the intention of visiting
all of them, but when I had reached the middle of my journey
I learned that there were other mines at so short a distance
that they might be reached in two days. I determined on
sending to see them. It was on the eve of St. Simon and St.
Jude,[2] which was the day fixed for our departure; but that
night there arose so violent a storm, that we were forced to
go wherever it drove us, and the Indian who was to conduct
us to the mines was with us all the time. As I had found every
thing true that had been told me in the different places which
I had visited, I felt satisfied it would be the same with respect
to Ciguare,[3] which according to their account, is nine days

as Caravaró (III. 118). Ferdinand Columbus's account is practically
identical.

[1] Veragua in this letter includes practically all of the present republic of
Panama. The western quarter of it was granted to Luis Colon, the Admiral's
grandson, in 1537, as a dukedom in partial compensation for his renouncing
his hereditary rights. Hence the title Dukes of Veragua borne by the Admiral's descendants. The name still survives in geography in that of the
little island Escudo de Veragua, which lies off the northern coast.

[2] The eve or vigil of St. Simon and St. Jude is October 27. According to
the narrative in the *Historie*, on October 7, they went ashore at the channel
of Cerabora (Carambaru). A few days later they went on to Aburema.
October 17 they left Aburema and went twelve leagues to Guaigo, where they
landed. Thence they went to Cateva (Catiba, Las Casas) and cast anchor in
a large river (the Chagres). Thence easterly to Cobrava; thence to five
towns, among which was Beragua (Veragua); the next day to Cubiga. The
distance from Cerabora to Cubiga was fifty leagues. Without landing, the
Admiral went on to Belporto (Puerto Bello), which he so named. ("Puerto
Bello, which was a matter of six leagues from what we now call El Nombre
de Dios." Las Casas, III. 121.) He arrived at Puerto Bello November 2,
and remained there seven days on account of the rains and bad weather.
(*Historie*, pp. 302–306.) Apparently Columbus put this period of bad weather
a few days too early in his recollection of it.

[3] Ciguare. An outlying province of the Mayas lying on the Pacific side
of southern Costa Rica. Peter Martyr, *De Rebus Oceanicis*, p. 240, says,
"In this great tract (*i.e.*, where the Admiral was) are two districts, the near
one called Taia, and the further one Maia."

journey across the country westward: they tell me there is a
great quantity of gold there, and that the inhabitants wear
coral ornaments on their heads, and very large coral bracelets
and anklets, with which article also they adorn and inlay
their seats, boxes, and tables. They also said that the women
there wore necklaces hanging down to their shoulders. All
the people agree in the report I now repeat, and their account
is so favorable that I should be content with the tithe of the
advantages that their description holds out. They are all
likewise acquainted with the pepper-plant;[1] according to the
account of these people, the inhabitants of Ciguare are accustomed to hold fairs and markets for carrying on their commerce,
and they showed me also the mode and form in which they
transact their various exchanges; others assert that their ships
carry cannon, and that the men go clothed and use bows
and arrows, swords and cuirasses, and that on shore they have
horses which they use in battle, and that they wear rich
clothes and have good things.[2]   They also say that the sea sur-
rounds Ciguare, and that at ten days' journey from thence is
the river Ganges; these lands appear to hold the same relation
to Veragua, as Tortosa to Fontarabia, or Pisa to Venice.[3]
When I left Carambaru and reached the places in its neighborhood, which I have mentioned above as being spoken of
by the Indians, I found the customs of the people correspond
with the accounts that had been given of them, except as regarded the golden mirrors: any man who had one of them
would willingly part with it for three hawks'-bells,[4] although
they were equivalent in weight to ten or fifteen ducats. These
people resemble the natives of Española in all their habits.

[1] See p. 311, note 5.

[2] Probably *casas*, houses, should be the reading here. In the corresponding passage of the contemporary Italian version the word is "houses." This
information, mixed as it is with Columbus's misinterpretations of the Indian
signs and distorted by his preconceptions, was first made public in the
Italian translation of this letter in 1505 and then gave Europe its first inti-
mations of the culture of the Mayas.

[3] *I.e.*, in being on either side of a peninsula, Tortosa and Fontarabia
being on opposite sides of the narrowest part of the Spanish peninsula.

[4] See p. 300, note 1.

They have various modes of collecting the gold, none of which will bear comparison with the plans adopted by the Christians.

All that I have here stated is from hearsay. This, however, I know, that in the year ninety-four I sailed twenty-four degrees to the westward in nine hours,[1] and there can be no mistake upon the subject, because there was an eclipse; the sun was in Libra and the moon in Aries.[2] What I had learned by the mouth of these people I already knew in detail from books. Ptolemy thought that he had satisfactorily corrected[3] Marinus, and yet this latter appears to have come very near to the truth. Ptolemy placed Catigara[4] at a distance of twelve lines to the west of his meridian, which he fixes at two degrees and a third beyond Cape St. Vincent, in Portugal. Marinus comprised the earth and its limits in fifteen lines.[5]

[1] The Spanish reads, "Lo que yo sé es que el año de noventa y cuatro en veinte y cuatros grados al Poniente en termino de nueve horas." The translation in the text and that in Thacher (II. 687) of the Italian makes nonsense. The translation should be "what I know is that in the year '94 (1494) I sailed westward on the 24th parallel (lit. on 24 degrees) a total of nine hours (lit. to a limit of nine hours)." That is, he reckoned that he had gone $\frac{9}{24}$ round the world on the 24th parallel, and he knew it because there was an eclipse by which he found out the difference in time between Europe and where he was. The "termino" of nine hours refers to the western limit of his exploration of the southern coast of Cuba when he concluded it was a projection of the mainland of Asia. After reaching the conclusion that this is the correct interpretation of this passage, I discovered that it had been given by Humboldt in his *Kritische Untersuchungen über die historische Entwickelung der geographischen Kenntnisse von der Neuen Welt*, I. 553, and by Peschel in his *Zeitalter der Entdeckungen*, p. 97, note 2. It may be objected to this explanation that in reality Columbus had only gone about 75 degrees west of Cape St. Vincent in Portugal. The accurate calculation of longitude at that time, however, was impossible, and as will be seen in the following note Columbus's calculation was biassed by powerful preconceptions.

[2] In his *Libro de Profecias* Columbus recorded the data of this eclipse which took place February 29, 1494, from which he drew the conclusion, "The difference between the middle of the island Jamaica in the Indies and the island of Cadiz in Spain is seven hours and fifteen minutes." Navarrete, *Viages*, II. 272.

[3] Reading *remendiado* or *remendado* instead of *remedado*.

[4] Catigara was in China on the east side of the Gulf of Tonquin.

[5] Marinus of Tyre divided the earth into 24 meridians, 15 degrees or one hour apart. His first meridian passed the Fortunate Isles, which he supposed to be $2\frac{1}{4}$ degrees west of Cape St. Vincent, and his fifteenth through

Marinus on Ethiopia gives a description covering more than twenty-four degrees beyond the equinoctial line, and now that the Portuguese have sailed there they find it correct.[1] Ptolemy says also that the most southern land is the first boundary, and that it does not go lower down than fifteen degrees and a third.[2] The world is but small; out of seven divisions of it

Catigara, southeastern China. The inhabited world embraced fifteen of these lines, 225 degrees, and the unknown portion east of India and west of Spain, nine lines, or hours, or 135 degrees. *Cf.* Vignaud, *Toscanelli and Columbus*, p. 74; Bunbury, *History of Ancient Geography*, II. 519 *et seqq.* Columbus, therefore, according to his calculations, had in 1494 completely covered this unknown section and reached India (or China), and so had demonstrated the correctness of Marinus's views. In reality his strong preconceptions as to where he was distorted his calculations of the longitude. Ptolemy corrected Marinus's estimate of 225 degrees from Cape St. Vincent to Sera in China, and, as noted in Columbus's letter, placed Catigara in China (on the east side of the Gulf of Tonquin) at twelve lines or 180 degrees west of his meridian (2½ degrees west of Cape St. Vincent). If Ptolemy was right, Columbus had not reached India (or more exactly China) or come, on his own calculation, within 45 degrees or 2700 geographical miles of it measured on the equator. The outline reproduction of the map of Bartholomew Columbus made after his return from this voyage given in Channing's *Student's History of the United States*, p. 27 (photographic reproduction in Bourne, *Spain in America*, p. 96) illustrates the Admiral's ideas and conclusions. This region (*i.e.*, Costa Rica and Panama) is a southern extension of Cochin-China and Cambodia and is connected with *Mondo Novo, i.e.*, South America.

[1] The translation here adopts the emended text of Lollis, substituting "ali[e]nde" for "al Indo" in the sentence "Marino en Ethiopía escribe al Indo la línea equinoçial." *Raccolta Colombiana*, parte I., tomo II., p. 184. The translation of the unamended text as printed by Major was "the same author describes the Indus in Ethiopia as being more than four and twenty degrees from the equinoctial line." Apparently the 24 should be 44. With these changes the statements in the text agree with Columbus's marginalia to the *Imago Mundi*, where he notes that the Cape of Good Hope is Agesinba and that Bartholomew Diaz found it to be 45 degrees south of the equator. "This," he goes on, "agrees with the dictum of Marinus, whom Ptolemy corrects, in regard to the expedition to the Garamantes, who said it traversed 27,500 stadia beyond the equinoctial." *Raccolta Colombiana*, parte II., tomo II., p. 377. On Marinus's exaggerated estimate of the distance covered by the Romans in tropical Africa, see Bunbury, *History of Ancient Geography*, II. 524.

[2] This is unintelligible. The Spanish is, "Tolomeo diz que la tierra mas austral es el plazo primero." The meaning of *plazo* is not "boundary" but "term" (allotted time). The reading should be: "la tierra mas austral es el praso promontorio," and the translation should be, "Ptolemy says that the most southern land is the promontory of Prasum," etc. Prasum promon-

the dry part occupies six, and the seventh is entirely covered by water.[1] Experience has shown it, and I have written it with quotations from the Holy Scripture, in other letters, where I have treated of the situation of the terrestrial paradise, as approved by the Holy Church;[2] and I say that the world is not so large as vulgar opinion makes it, and that one degree of the equinoctial line measures fifty-six miles and two-thirds; and this may be proved to a nicety.[3]

But I leave this subject, which it is not my intention now to treat upon, but simply to give a narrative of my laborious and painful voyage, although of all my voyages it is the most honorable and advantageous. I have said that on the eve of St. Simon and St. Jude I ran before the wind wherever it took me, without power to resist it; at length I found shelter for ten days from the roughness of the sea and the tempest overhead, and resolved not to attempt to go back to the mines, which I regarded as already in our possession.[4] When I started in pursuance of my voyage it was under a heavy rain, and reaching the harbor of Bastimentos I put in, though

torium was Ptolemy's southern limit of the world. He placed it at about 16 degrees south latitude. See Bunbury, *History of Ancient Geography*, II. 572, and Smith's *Dictionary of Greek and Roman Geography*, art. "Prasum Promontorium"; also Ptolemy's *Geography*, bk. IV., ch. IX., the descriptive matter relating to Map 4 on Africa.

[1] *II. Esdras*, VI. 42, see p. 358, note 1.

[2] See the Letter of Columbus on his Third Voyage. Major, *Select Letters of Columbus*, p. 141.

[3] Ptolemy reckoned the length of the degree on the equator at 62½ miles. The shorter measurement of 56⅔ was the estimate adopted by the Arab astronomer Alfragan in the ninth century and known to Columbus through Cardinal d'Ailly's *Imago Mundi*, the source of much if not most of his information on the geographical knowledge and opinions of former times. Cardinal d'Ailly's source of information about Alfragan was Roger Bacon's *Opus Majus*. Columbus was deeply impressed with Alfragan's estimate of the length of the degree and annotated the passages in the *Imago Mundi*. *Cf. Raccolta Colombiana*, Parte I., tomo II., pp. 378, 407, and frequently. See this whole question in Vignaud, *Toscanelli and Columbus*, p. 79 *et seqq.*

[4] In Puerto Bello. See p. 394, note 2. Porto Bello, to use the Anglicized form, became the great shipping port on the north side of the isthmus for the trade with Peru. *Cf.* Bourne, *Spain in America*, p. 292.

much against my will.[1] The storm and a rapid current kept
me in for fourteen days, when I again set sail, but not with
favorable weather. After I had made fifteen leagues with great
exertions, the wind and the current drove me back [2] again
with great fury, but in again making for the port which I had
quitted, I found on the way another port, which I named
Retrete, where I put in for shelter with as much risk as regret,
the ships being in sad condition, and my crews and myself
exceedingly fatigued.[3] I remained there fifteen days, kept in
by stress of weather, and when I fancied my troubles were at
an end, I found them only begun. It was then that I changed
my resolution with respect to proceeding to the mines, and
proposed doing something in the interim, until the weather
should prove more favorable for my voyage.[4] I had already
made four leagues when the storm recommenced, and wearied
me to such a degree that I absolutely knew not what to do;
my wound reopened, and for nine days my life was despaired
of; never was the sea seen so high, so terrific, and so covered
with foam; not only did the wind oppose our proceeding onward, but it also rendered it highly dangerous to run in for
any headland, and kept me in that sea which seemed to me
as a sea of blood, seething like a cauldron on a mighty fire.
Never did the sky look more fearful; during one day and one
night it burned like a furnace, and every instant I looked to
see if my masts and my sails were not destroyed; these

[1] Columbus left Porto Bello November 9 and went eight leagues, but the
next day he turned back four and took refuge at what is now Nombre de
Dios. From the abundance of maize fields he named it Port of Provisions
(Puerto de Bastimentos). *Historie*, p. 306.

[2] *Me reposó atrás il viento*, etc. For *reposó* the text apparently should
be either *repuso*, " put back," or *rempujó*, " drove back," and the translation is based on this supposition.

[3] They remained at Bastimentos till November 23, when they went on to
Guiga, but did not tarry but pushed on to a little harbor (November 26),
which the Admiral called Retrete (Closet) because it was so small that it
could hold only five or six vessels and the entrance was only fifteen or twenty
paces wide. *Historie*, p. 306.

[4] That is, Columbus turns back to explore the mines on account of the
violence of the east and northeast winds. This was December 5. *Historie*,
p. 309.

flashes came with such alarming fury that we all thought the
ships must have been consumed. All this time the waters
from heaven never ceased, not to say that it rained, for it was
like a repetition of the deluge. The men were at this time so
crushed in spirit that they longed for death as a deliverance
from so many martyrdoms. Twice already had the ships
suffered loss in boats, anchors, and rigging, and were now lying
bare without sails.

When it pleased our Lord, I returned to Puerto Gordo,[1]
where I recruited my condition as well as I could. I then
once more turned towards Veragua; for my voyage, although
I was [ready] for it, the wind and current were still contrary.[2]
I arrived at nearly the same spot as before, and there again
the wind and currents still opposed my progress; and once
again I was compelled to put into port, not daring to await the
opposition of Saturn[3] with Mars so tossed on an exposed
coast; for it almost always brings on a tempest or severe
weather. This was on Christmas-day, about the hour of
mass.

Thus, after all these fatigues, I had once more to return to
the spot from whence I started; and when the new year had
set in, I returned again to my task: but although I had fine
weather for my voyage, the ships were no longer in a sailing
condition, and my people were either dying or very sick. On
the day of the Epiphany,[4] I reached Veragua in a state of ex-

[1] Not mentioned in the *Historie* by name. It was the place where they
stayed from December 26 to January 3 to repair the ship *Gallega* as appears in
the *Probanzas del Almirante*. Navarrete, *Viages*, III. 600. It was between
Rio de los Lagartos and Puerto Bello. Lollis, *Raccolta Colombiana*, Parte I.,
tomo II., p. 187.

[2] Adopting de Lollis's text and punctuation.

[3] *La oposicion de Saturno con Marte tan desvaratado en costa brava*, adopting de Lollis's text following the suggestion of the contemporary Italian
translation. According to the doctrines of astrology the influence of Saturn
was malign. "When Saturn is in the first degree of Aries, and any other
Planet in the first degree of Libra, they being now an hundred and eighty
degrees each from other, are said to be in Opposition: A bad Aspect."
William Lilly, *Christian Astrology* (London, 1647), p. 27.

[4] Epiphany, January 6. It will be remembered that Columbus had
passed Veragua the previous October when working eastward. See p. 394,

haustion; there, by our Lord's goodness, I found a river and a safe harbor, although at the entrance there were only ten spans of water. I succeeded in making an entry, but with great difficulty; and on the following day the storm recommenced, and had I been still on the outside at that time, I should have been unable to enter on account of the reef. It rained without ceasing until the fourteenth of February, so that I could find no opportunity of penetrating into the interior, nor of recruiting my condition in any respect whatever; and on the twenty-fourth of January, when I considered myself in perfect safety, the river suddenly rose with great violence to a considerable height, breaking my cables and the breastfasts,[1] and nearly carrying away my ships altogether, which certainly appeared to me to be in greater danger than ever. Our Lord, however, brought a remedy as He has always done. I do not know if any one else ever suffered greater trials.

On the sixth of February, while it was still raining, I sent seventy men on shore to go into the interior, and at five leagues' distance they found several mines. The Indians who went with them conducted them to a very lofty mountain, and thence showing them the country all around, as far as the eye could reach, told them there was gold in every part, and that, towards the west, the mines extended twenty days' journey; they also recounted the names of the towns and villages where there was more or less of it. I afterwards learned that

note 2. He now found he could enter the river of Veragua, but found another near by called by the Indians Yebra, but which Columbus named Belem in memory of the coming of the three kings (the wise men of the East) to Bethlehem. (Las Casas, III. 128; Porras in Thacher, II. 645.) The name is still preserved attached to the river.

[1] *Proeses.* In nautical Spanish *prois* or *proiza* is a breastfast or headfast, that is a large cable for fastening a ship to a wharf or another ship. In Portuguese *proiz* is a stone or tree on shore to which the hawsers are fastened. Major interpreted it in this sense, translating the words *las amarras y proeses,* "the cables and the supports to which they were fastened." The interpretation given first seems to me the correct one, especially as Ferdinand says that the flood came so suddenly that they could not get the cables on land. *Historie,* p. 315.

2 D

the Quibian,[1] who had lent these Indians, had ordered them to show the distant mines, and which belonged to an enemy of his; but that in his own territory one man might, if he would, collect in ten days as much as a child could carry.[2] I bring with me some Indians, his servants, who are witnesses of this fact. The boats went up to the spot where the dwellings of these people are situated; and, after four hours, my brother returned with the guides, all of them bringing back gold which they had collected at that place. The gold must be abundant, and of good quality, for none of these men had ever seen mines before; very many of them had never seen pure gold, and most of them were seamen and lads. Having building materials in abundance, I established a settlement, and made many presents to the Quibian, which is the name they gave to the lord of the country. I plainly saw that harmony would not last long, for the natives are of a very rough disposition, and the Spaniards very encroaching; and, moreover, I had taken possession of land belonging to the Quibian. When he saw what we did, and found the traffic increasing, he resolved upon burning the houses, and putting us all to death; but his project did not succeed, for we took him prisoner, together with his wives, his children, and his servants. His captivity, it is true, lasted but a short time, for he eluded the custody of a trustworthy man, into whose charge he had been given, with a guard of men; and his sons escaped from a ship, in which they had been placed under the special charge of the master.

[1] *Quibian* is a title, as indicated a few lines further on, and not a proper name as Major, Irving, Markham, and others following Las Casas have taken it to be. The Spanish is uniformly "El Quibian." Peter Martyr says: "They call a kinglet (*regulus*) Cacicus, as we have said elsewhere, in other places Quebi, in some places also Tiba. A chief, in some places Sacchus, in others Jurá." *De Rebus Oceanicis*, p. 241.

[2] "*Una mozada de oro.*" *Mozada* is not given in any of the Spanish dictionaries I have consulted. The Academy dictionary gives *mojada* as a square measure, deriving it from the low Latin *modiata* from *modius*. Perhaps one should read *mojada* instead of *mozada* and give it a meaning similar to that of *modius* or about a peck. Major's translation follows the explanation of De Verneuil, who says: "*Mozada signifie la mesure que peut porter un jeune garçon.*"

In the month of January the mouth of the river was entirely closed up,[1] and in April the vessels were so eaten by the shipworm,[2] that they could scarcely be kept above water. At this time the river forced a channel for itself, by which I managed, with great difficulty, to extricate three of them after I had unloaded them. The boats were then sent back into the river for water and salt, but the sea became so high and furious, that it afforded them no chance of exit; upon which the Indians collected themselves together in great numbers, and made an attack upon the boats, and at length massacred the men.[3] My brother, and all the rest of our people, were in a ship which remained inside; I was alone, outside, upon that dangerous coast, suffering from a severe fever and worn with fatigue. All hope of escape was gone. I toiled up to the highest part of the ship, and, with a voice of fear crying, and very urgently, I called upon your Highnesses' war-captains in every direction for help, but there was no reply. At length, groaning with exhaustion, I fell asleep, and heard a compassionate voice address me thus: "O fool, and slow to believe and to serve thy God, the God of all! what did He do more for Moses, or for David his servant, than He has done for thee? From thine infancy He has kept thee under His constant and watchful care. When He saw thee arrived at an age which suited His designs respecting thee, He brought wonderful renown to thy name throughout

---

[1] The mouth of the river was closed by sand thrown up by the violent storms outside. *Historie*, p. 321.

[2] The teredo.

[3] During the weeks that he was shut in the River Belem Columbus had his brother explore the country. The prospects for a successful colony led him to build a small settlement and to plan to return to Spain for re-enforcements and supplies. The story is told in detail in the *Historie* and by Irving, *Columbus*, II. 425–450, and more briefly by Markham, *Columbus*, pp. 259–267. This was the first settlement projected on the American Continent. The hostility of the Indians culminating in this attack rendered the execution of the project impracticable. In the manuscript copy of Las Casas's *Historia de las Indias* Las Casas noted on the margin of the passage containing the account of this incident, "This was the first settlement that the Spaniards made on the mainland, although in a short time it came to naught." See Thacher, *Columbus*, II. 608.

all the land. He gave thee for thine own the Indies, which form so rich a portion of the world, and thou hast divided them as it pleased thee, for He gave thee power to do so. He gave thee also the keys of those barriers of the ocean sea which were closed with such mighty chains; [1] and thou wast obeyed through many lands, and gained an honorable fame throughout Christendom. What did he more for the people of Israel, when he brought them out of Egypt? [2] or for David, whom from a shepherd He made to be king in Judea? Turn to Him, and acknowledge thine error — His mercy is infinite. Thine old age shall not prevent thee from accomplishing any great undertaking. He holds under His sway many very great possessions. Abraham had exceeded a hundred years of age when he begat Isaac; nor was Sarah young. Thou criest out for uncertain help: answer, who has afflicted thee so much and so often, God or the world? The privileges promised by God, He never fails in bestowing; nor does He ever declare, after a service has been rendered Him, that such was not agreeable with His intention, or that He had regarded the matter in another light; nor does he inflict suffering, in order to give effect to the manifestation of His power. His word goes according to the letter; and He performs all his promises with interest. This is [his] custom. Thus I have told thee what thy Creator has done for thee, and what He does for all men. Just now He gave me a specimen of the reward of so many toils and dangers incurred by thee in the service of others." [2]

I heard all this, as it were, in a trance; but I had no answer to give in definite words, and could but weep for my errors.

---

[1] De Lollis points out that these striking words are a paraphrase of the famous lines in Seneca's *Medea*, Chorus, Act II.: —

> Venient annis saecula seris
> Quibus Oceanus vincula rerum
> Laxet, et ingens pateat tellus,
> Tethysque novos detegat orbes
> Nec sit terris ultima Thule.

Columbus copied these verses into his *Libro de las Profecias* and translated them. Navarrete, *Viages*, II. 272.

[2] Accepting de Lollis's emended text.

He who spoke to me, whoever it was, concluded by saying, —
"Fear not, but trust; all these tribulations are recorded on
marble, and not without cause." I arose as soon as I could;
and at the end of nine days there came fine weather, but not
sufficiently so to allow of drawing the vessels out of the river.
I collected the men who were on land, and, in fact, all of them
that I could, because there were not enough to admit of one
party remaining on shore while another stayed on board to
work the vessels. I myself should have remained with my men
to defend the settlement, had your Highnesses known of it;
but the fear that ships might never reach the spot where we
were, as well as the thought, that when provision is to be
made for bringing help, everything will be provided,[1] made
me decide upon leaving. I departed, in the name of the
Holy Trinity, on Easter night,[2] with the ships rotten, worm-
eaten and full of holes. One of them I left at Belen, with
a supply of necessaries; I did the same at Belpuerto. I then
had only two left, and they in the same state as the others.
I was without boats or provisions, and in this condition I
had to cross seven thousand miles of sea; or, as an alterna-
tive, to die on the passage with my son, my brother, and so
many of my people. Let those who are accustomed to finding fault and censuring ask, while they sit in security at
home, "Why did you not do so and so under such circumstances?" I wish they now had this voyage to make.
I verily believe that another journey of another kind awaits
them, or our faith is nothing.

On the thirteenth of May I reached the province of Mago
[Mango],[3] which borders on Cathay, and thence I started

---

[1] "Quando se aia de proveer de socorro, se proveera de todo."

[2] April 16, 1503.

[3] Cuba. According to Ferdinand Columbus the course was as follows:
The Admiral followed the coast of the isthmus eastward beyond El Retrete
to a place he named Marmoro (near Punto de Mosquitos) somewhat west of
the entrance to the Gulf of Darien; then May 1 in response to the urgency of
the pilots he turned north. May 10 they sighted two little islands, Caymanos
Chicos, and the 12th they reached the Queen's Garden just south of Cuba
(see p. 391, note 1). The next day they landed in Cuba and secured
supplies. It is significant of the tenacity of Columbus's conviction that

for the island of Española. I sailed two days with a good
wind, after which it became contrary. The route that I followed called forth all my care to avoid the numerous islands,
that I might not be stranded on the shoals that lie in their
neighborhood. The sea was very tempestuous, and I was
driven backward under bare poles. I anchored at an island,
where I lost, at one stroke, three anchors; and, at midnight,
when the weather was such that the world appeared to be
coming to an end, the cables of the other ship broke, and it
came down upon my vessel with such force that it was a
wonder we were not dashed to pieces; the single anchor that
remained to me was, next to the Lord, our only preservation.
After six days, when the weather became calm, I resumed my
journey, having already lost all my tackle; my ships were
pierced by borers more than a honey-comb and the crew entirely paralyzed with fear and in despair. I reached the
island a little beyond the point at which I first arrived at it,
and there I turned in to recover myself after the storm;[1] but
I afterwards put into a much safer port in the same island.
After eight days I put to sea again, and reached Jamaica by
the end of June;[2] but always beating against contrary winds,
and with the ships in the worst possible condition.   With
three pumps, and the use of pots and kettles, we could scarcely
clear the water that came into the ship, there being no remedy
but this for the mischief done by the ship-worm.   I steered in

Cuba was a part of the mainland of Asia that he here calls it Mago (*i.e.*,
Mango).   June 12, 1494, when he had explored the southern coast of Cuba,
he reached this conviction and compelled his officers and crew to take oath
that "it (*i.e.*, Cuba) is mainland and in particular the province of Mango."
Navarrete, *Viages*, II. 144. (The affidavits are translated in Thacher, *Columbus*,
II. 327.)   Mangi (southern China) is described by Marco Polo at great length.
In the second Toscanelli letter Quinsay is said to be "in the province of
Mangi, *i.e.*, near the province of Cathay." It is noted several times in
Columbus's marginalia to Marco Polo.

[1] *Allí me torné á reposar atrás la fortuna.* De Lollis, following the Italian
translation, reads: *Allí me tornó á reposar atrás la fortuna*, etc.   "There the
storm returned to drive me back; I stopped in the same island in a safer
port." As this gives an unknown meaning to *reposar*, he suggests that Columbus may have written *repujar*, "to drive."

[2] June 23. *Historie*, p. 334.

such a manner as to come as near as possible to Española, from which we were twenty-eight leagues distant, but I afterwards wished I had not done so, for the other ship which was half under water was obliged to run in for a port. I determined on keeping the sea in spite of the weather, and my vessel was on the very point of sinking when our Lord miraculously brought us upon land. Who will believe what I now write? I assert that in this letter I have not related one hundredth part of the wonderful events that occurred in this voyage; those who were with the Admiral can bear witness to it. If your Highnesses would be graciously pleased to send to my help a ship of above sixty-four tons, with two hundred quintals of biscuits and other provisions, there would then be sufficient to carry me and my crew from Española to Spain. I have already said that there are not twenty-eight leagues between Jamaica and Española; and I should not have gone there, even if the ships had been in a fit condition for so doing, because your Highnesses ordered me not to land there. God knows if this command has proved of any service. I send this letter by means of and by the hands of Indians; it will be a miracle if it reaches its destination.

This is the account I have to give of my voyage. The men who accompanied me were a hundred and fifty in number, among whom were many calculated for pilots and good sailors, but none of them can explain whither I went nor whence I came;[1] the reason is very simple: I started from a point above the port of Brazil[2] in Española. The storm prevented me from following my intended route, for I was obliged to go wherever the wind drove me; at the same time I fell very sick, and there was no one who had navigated in these parts

[1] On the contrary the narrative of Diego de Porras, which he prepared after his return to Spain in November, 1504, is a much clearer account of the voyage in most respects than this letter of Columbus's. For it, see Thacher, *Columbus*, II. 640–646. Porras relates that during this voyage the Admiral took all the charts away that the seamen had had. Thacher, *Columbus*, II. 646.

[2] "*El puerto de Jaquimo* [Jacmel], which he called the port of Brasil." Las Casas, *Historia*, III. 108.

before.   However, after some days, the wind and sea became tranquil, and the storm was succeeded by a calm, but accompanied with rapid currents.   I put into harbor at an island called Isla de las Pozas, and then steered for mainland;[1] but it is impossible to give a correct account of all our movements, because I was carried away by the current so many days without seeing land.   I ascertained, however, by the compass and by observation, that I moved parallel with the coast of the mainland.   No one could tell under what part of the heavens we were, and when I set out from there to come to the island of Española, the pilots thought we had come to the island of St. John, whereas it was the land of Mango, four hundred leagues to the westward of where they said.[2]   Let them answer and say if they know where Veragua is situated.   I assert that they can give no other account than that they went to lands, where there was an abundance of gold, and this they can certify surely enough; but they do not know the way to return thither for such a purpose; they would be obliged to go on a voyage of discovery as much as if they had never been there before.

There is a mode of reckoning derived from astronomy which is sure and safe, and a sufficient guide to any one who understands it.   This resembles a prophetic vision.[3]   The Indies ships[4] do not sail except with the wind abaft, but this is not because they are badly built or clumsy, but because the strong currents in those parts, together with the wind, render it impossible to sail with the bowline,[5] for in one day they would lose as much way as they might have made in seven; for the same reason I could make no use of caravels, even though they

[1] Cuba.

[2] The pilots thought that they were east of Española when Columbus turned north, and consequently thought that Cuba (Mango) was Porto Rico (San Juan).   Cf. Historie, p. 333.

[3] I.e., in that it is clear to one who understands it, and blind to one who does not.

[4] Las naos de las Indias, i.e., the large ships for the Indies, i.e., Española.

[5] Bow-lines are ropes employed to keep the windward edges of the principal sails steady, and are only used when the wind is so unfavorable that the sails must be all braced sideways, or close hauled to the wind.   (Major.)

were Portuguese lateens.[1] This is the cause that they do not sail unless with a regular breeze, and they will sometimes stay in harbor waiting for this seven or eight months at a time; nor is this anything wonderful, for the same very often occurs in Spain.

The nation of which Pope Pius II. describes the situation and characteristics has now been found,[2] excepting the horses with the saddles and poitrels and bridles of gold; but this is not to be wondered at, for the lands on the sea-coast are only inhabited by fishermen, and moreover I made no stay there, because I was in haste to proceed on my voyage. In Cariay[3] and the neighboring country there are great enchanters of a very fearful character. They would have given the world to prevent my remaining there an hour. When I arrived they sent me immediately two girls very showily dressed; the eldest could not be more than eleven years of age and the other seven, and both exhibited so much immodesty, that more could not be expected from public women; they carried concealed about them a magic powder; when they came I gave them some articles to dress themselves out with, and directly sent them back to the shore.[4] I saw here, built

[1] *I.e.*, rigged with lateen sails in the Portuguese fashion.

[2] Columbus, in his marginal notes to his copy of the *Historia Rerum ubique Gestarum* of Pope Pius II. (Aeneas Sylvius Piccolomini; Venice, 1477), summarized the description of the Massagetae in ch. XII. in part as follows: they "use golden girths and golden bridles and silver breast-pieces and have no iron but plenty of copper and gold." *Raccolta Colombiana*, parte I., tomo II., p. 300. This description of the Massagetae goes back to Herodotus. While some habits ascribed to the Massagetae were like what Columbus observed in Veragua, their home was nowhere near eastern China.

[3] See p. 393, note 3.

[4] The account in the *Historie* is radically at variance with this. The girls were brought on board and "showed themselves very brave since although the Christians in looks, acts, and race were very strange, they gave no signs of distress or sadness, but maintained a cheerful and modest (*honesto*) bearing, wherefore they were very well treated by the Admiral who gave them clothes and something to eat and then sent them back." *Historie*, p. 299. Ferdinand gives the ages as eight and fourteen and says nothing of witchcraft except that the Indians were frightened and thought they were being bewitched when Bartholomew the next day ordered the ships' clerks to write down the replies he got to his questions; *ibid.*

on a mountain, a sepulchre as large as a house, and elaborately sculptured; the body lay uncovered and embalmed in it. They also spoke to me of other very excellent works of art.[1] There are many species of animals both small and large, and very different from those of our country. I had a present of two pigs, and an Irish dog was afraid to face them. A crossbowman had wounded an animal like a monkey,[2] except that it was larger, and had a face like a man's; the arrow had pierced it from the neck to the tail, and since it was fierce he was obliged to cut off an arm and a leg; the pig bristled up on seeing it and tried to get away. I, when I saw this, ordered the *begare*[3] as it is called to be thrown to the pig where he was, and though the animal was nearly dead, and the arrow had passed quite through his body, yet he threw his tail round the snout of the boar, and then holding him firmly, seized him by the nape of the neck with his remaining hand, as if he were engaged with an enemy. This action was so novel and so extraordinary, that I have thought it worth while to describe it here. There is a great variety of animals here, but they all die of *barra*.[4] I saw some very large fowls (the feathers of which resemble wool),[5] lions, stags, fallow-deer and birds.

When we were so harassed with our troubles at sea, some of our men imagined that we were under the influence of

[1] A specimen of the Maya sculptures, of which such imposing remains are found in Yucatan. The translation follows Lollis's emendation, which substitutes *mirrado* for *mirando*.

[2] *Gato paulo.* On this name, see p. 341, note 3. Ferdinand, in the *Historie*, relates this incident in more detail, from which it is clear that the pigs were peccaries which had been captured by the men. On the other hand, Ulloa, the Italian translator of the *Historie*, mistranslated *gato paulo* by "gatto," "cat."

[3] *Begare.* Columbus in recollecting this incident transferred to the monkey the Indian name of the wild pigs. The *begare* is the "peccary," a native of America. Oviedo, lib. xii., cap. xx, gives *baquira* as the name of wild pigs in Nicaragua, and *baquira* and *begare* are obviously identical.

[4] For the word *barra* no explanation can be offered except what is derived from the context. As the Italian has *diverse malattie*, "divers diseases," de Lollis suggests that *barra* should be *varias* and that *maladias* was somehow dropped from the text.

[5] *Leones.* The American lion or puma.

sorcery, and even to this day entertain the same notion. Some of the people whom I discovered eat men, as was evidenced by the brutality of their countenances. They say that there are great mines of copper in the country, of which they make hatchets [1] and other elaborate articles both cast and soldered; they also make of it forges, with all the apparatus of the goldsmith, and crucibles. The inhabitants go clothed; and in that province I saw some large sheets of cotton very elaborately and cleverly worked, and others very delicately painted in colors.[2] They tell me that more inland towards Cathay they have them interwoven with gold. For want of an interpreter we were able to learn but very little respecting these countries, or what they contain. Although the country is very thickly peopled, yet each nation has a very different language; indeed so much so, that they can no more understand each other than we understand the Arabs. I think, however, that this applies to the barbarians on the sea-coast, and not to the people who live more inland. When I discovered the Indies, I said that they composed the richest lordship in the world; I spoke of gold and pearls and precious stones, of spices and the traffic that might be carried on in them; and because all these things were not forthcoming at once I was abused. This punishment causes me to refrain from relating anything but what the natives tell me. One thing I can venture upon stating, because there are so many witnesses of it, viz., that in this land of Veragua I saw more signs of gold in the first two days than I saw in Española during fours years, and that there is not a more fertile or better cultivated country in all the world, nor one whose inhabitants are more timid; added to which there is a good harbor, a beautiful river, and the whole place is capable of being easily put into a state of defence. All this tends to the security of the Christians and the permanency of their sover-

[1] A misunderstanding. The Mayas made no metal tools. Brinton, *The American Race*, p. 156.

[2] Possibly Columbus may have seen some Maya codices, of which such remarkable specimens have been preserved.

eignty, while it affords the hope of great increase and honor to the Christian religion; moreover the road hither will be as short as that to Española, because there is a certainty of a fair wind for the passage. Your Highnesses are as much lords of this country as of Xerez or Toledo; your ships if they should go there, go to your own house. From there they will take gold; in other lands to have what there is in them, they will have to take it by force or retire empty-handed, and on the land they will have to trust their persons in the hands of a savage.[1]

Of the other [matter] that I refrain from saying, I have already said why I kept silent. I do not speak so, neither [do I say] that I make a threefold affirmation in all that I have ever said or written nor that I am at the source.[2] The Genoese, Venetians and all other nations that possess pearls, precious stones, and other articles of value, take them to the ends of the world to exchange them for gold. Gold is most excellent; gold is treasure, and he who possesses it does all he wishes to in this world, and succeeds in helping souls into paradise. They say that when one of the lords of the country of Veragua dies, they bury all the gold he possessed with his body. There were brought to Solomon at one journey[3] six hundred and sixty-six quintals of gold, besides what the merchants and sailors brought, and that which was paid in Arabia. Of this gold he made two hundred lances[4] and three hundred shields, and the flooring[5] which was to be above them

---

[1] Considering Columbus's experience at Veragua this account exhibits boundless optimism. Still it is not to be forgotten that through the conquest of Mexico to the north this prediction was rather strikingly fulfilled.

[2] It is not clear to what Columbus refers in this sentence.

[3] *De un camino.* The texts to which Columbus refers just below show that this should read *de un año*, in one year.

[4] In the Latin version of Josephus used by Columbus the Greek θυρεός, a target, was rendered *lancea.* See *Raccolta Colombiana*, parte I., tomo II., p. 367.

[5] *Tablado.* In the Italian translation *tavolato*, a "partition wall," "wainscoting," also "floor." *Tablado* also means "scaffold" and "stage" or "staging." We have here a curious series of mistakes. The Greek text of Josephus has ἐκπώματα, "cups." The old Latin translator, perhaps having a defective text, took ἐκπώματα apparently to be equivalent

was also of gold, and ornamented with precious stones; many
other things he made likewise of gold, and a great number of
vessels of great size, which he enriched with precious stones.
This is related by Josephus in his Chronicle *De Antiquita-
tibus;* mention is also made of it in the Chronicles and in
the Book of Kings.[1] Josephus thinks that this gold was found
in the Aurea;[2] if it were so, I contend that these mines of
the Aurea are identical with those of Veragua, which, as I
have said before, extends westward twenty days' journey, and
they are at an equal distance from the Pole and the Line.[3]
Solomon bought all of it, — gold, precious stones, and silver,
— but your Majesties need only send to seek them to have them
at your pleasure.   David, in his will, left three thousand quintals of Indian gold to Solomon, to assist in building the Temple;
and, according to Josephus, it came from these lands.[4]   Jerusalem and Mount Sion are to be rebuilt by the hands of Christians, who it is to be God told by the mouth of His prophet in
the fourteenth Psalm.[5]   The Abbot Joaquim said that he who

to πώματα, which has as its secondary meaning, "lids," and translated it
by the uncommon word *coopercula,* "lids" (*cf.* Georges, *Lateinischdeutsches
Handwörterbuch, sub voce cooperculum*).   The meaning of this word Columbus
guessed at, not having the text before him to see the connection, and from
its derivation from *cooperio,* "to cover," took it to be a "covering" in the
sense of flooring, or perhaps ceiling, above where the shields were hung "in
the house of the forest of Lebanon," and rendered it *tablado.*   The whole
passage from the old Latin version (published in 1470 and frequently
later), Columbus copied into a fly-leaf of his copy of the *Historia Rerum
ubique Gestarum* of Pope Pius II.   See *Raccolta Colombiana,* parte I., tomo
II., pp. 366–367.
   [1] Josephus, *Antiquities of the Jews,* bk. VIII., ch. VII., sect. 4; *I. Kings,*
x. 14, 15; *II. Chronicles,* IX. 13, 14.
   [2] The Chersonesus Aurea of Ptolemy, or the Malay Peninsula.
   [3] That is, Veragua and the Golden Chersonese are in the same
latitude.
   [4] Josephus wrote that the gold came from the "Land of Gold," "*a terra
que vocatur aurea,*" as the passage in the Latin version reads.   The Greek
is, ἀπὸ τῆς χρυσῆς καλουμένης γῆς.   Josephus gives no further identification
of the location.
   [5] I have not been able to verify this reference.   There is nothing in the
fourteenth Psalm relating to this matter, nor is the fourteenth Psalm mentioned among the many citations from the Psalms in the *Libro de las
Profecias.*

should do this was to come from Spain;[1] Saint Jerome showed
the holy woman the way to accomplish it;[2] and the emperor
of Cathay, a long time ago, sent for wise men to instruct him
in the faith of Christ.[3] Who will offer himself for this work?[4]
Should any one do so, I pledge myself, in the name of God,
to convey him safely thither, provided the Lord permits me
to return to Spain.

The people who have sailed with me have passed through
incredible toil and danger, and I beseech your Highnesses,
since they are poor, to pay them promptly, and to be gracious
to each of them according to their respective merits; for I
can safely assert, that to my belief they are the bearers of the
best news that ever was carried to Spain. With respect to
the gold which belongs to the Quibian of Veragua, and other
chiefs in the neighboring country, although it appears by the
accounts we have received of it to be very abundant, I do not
think it would be well or desirable, on the part of your Highnesses, to take possession of it in the way of plunder; by fair
dealing, scandal and disrepute will be avoided, and all the gold
will thus reach your Highnesses' treasury without the loss of
a grain.

[1] In his *Libro de las Profecias* Columbus wrote, "El abad Johachín,
calabrés, diso que habia de salir de España quien havía de redificar la Casa
del Monte Sion." "The abbot Joachim, the Calabrian, said that he who
was destined to rebuild the House of Mount Sion was to come from Spain."
Lollis remarks that Columbus interpreted in his own way the "Oraculum
Turcicum," which concludes the thirty prophecies of Joachim of Flora in
regard to the popes. In the edition (Venice, 1589) which Lollis had seen,
this prophecy was interpreted to mean Charles VIII. of France. *Raccolta
Colombiana*, parte II., tomo II., p. 83.

[2] The reference to St. Jerome I have not found in Columbus's marginalia.

[3] The father and uncle of Marco Polo had been given this mission by
Cublay Kaan. See Marco Polo, bk. I., ch. VII. Opposite the passage in
his copy of the Latin Marco Polo which he had, Columbus wrote, "magnus kam
misit legatos ad pontificem." *Raccolta Colombiana*, parte II., tomo II., p. 446.

[4] The recovery of the Holy Sepulchre had been long a cherished object
with Columbus. See the Journal of the First Voyage, December 26; the
letter to Pope Alexander VI., February, 1502 (Navarrete, *Viages*, II. 280),
and his *Libro de Profecias*, a collection of Scripture texts compiled under his
supervision relating to the restoration of Zion, etc. *Raccolta Colombiana*,
parte I., tomo II., pp. 77–160.

With one month of fair weather I shall complete my voyage. As I was deficient in ships, I did not persist in delaying my course; but in everything that concerns your Highnesses' service, I trust in Him who made me, and I hope also that my health will be re-established. I think your Highnesses will remember that I had intended to build some ships in a new manner, but the shortness of the time did not permit it. I had certainly foreseen how things would be. I think more of this opening for commerce, and of the lordship over such extensive mines, than of all that has been done in the Indies.[1] This is not a child to be left to the care of a stepmother.

I never think of Española, and Paria, and the other countries, without shedding tears. I thought that what had occurred there would have been an example for others; on the contrary, these settlements are now in a languid state, although not dead, and the malady is incurable, or at least very extensive. Let him who brought the evil come now and cure it, if he knows the remedy, or how to apply it; but when a disturbance is on foot, every one is ready to take the lead. It used to be the custom to give thanks and promotion to him who placed his person in jeopardy; but there is no justice in allowing the man who opposed this undertaking, to enjoy the fruits of it with his children. Those who left the Indies, avoiding the toils consequent upon the enterprise, and speaking evil of it and me, have since returned with official appointments, — such is the case now in Veragua: it is an evil example, and profitless both as regards the business in which we are embarked, and as respects the general maintenance of justice. The fear of this, with other sufficient considerations, which I clearly foresaw, caused me to beg your Highnesses, previously to my coming to discover these islands and mainland, to grant me permission to govern in your royal name. Your Highnesses granted my request; and it was a privilege and treaty granted under the royal seal and oath, by which I

---

[1] An opinion abundantly justified through the conquest of Mexico and the establishment of the kingdom of New Spain.

was nominated viceroy, and admiral, and governor-general of all: and your Highnesses limited the extent of my government to a hundred leagues beyond the Azores and Cape Verde islands, by a line passing from one pole to the other, and gave me ample power over all that I might discover beyond this line; all which is more fully described in the official document.[1]

But the most important affair of all, and that which cries most loudly for redress, remains inexplicable to this moment. For seven years was I at your royal court, where every one to whom the enterprise was mentioned treated it as ridiculous; but now there is not a man, down to the very tailors, who does not beg to be allowed to become a discoverer. There is reason to believe, that they make the voyage only for plunder, and that they are permitted to do so, to the great disparagement of my honor, and the detriment of the undertaking itself.[2] It is right to give God His own, — and to Caesar[3] that which belongs to him.[4] This is a just sentiment, and proceeds from just feelings. The lands in this part of the world, which are now under your Highnesses' sway, are richer and more extensive than those of any other Christian power, and yet, after that I had, by the Divine will, placed them under your high and royal sovereignty, and was on the point of bringing your majesties into the receipt of a very great and unexpected revenue; and while I was waiting for ships, to convey me in safety, and with a heart full of joy, to your royal presence, victoriously to announce the news of the gold that I had discovered, I was arrested and thrown, with my two brothers,

[1] See the Capitulation, pp. 77, 78 above. The limit mentioned was fixed by the Papal Demarcation line; the limit agreed upon by Spain and Portugal was 370 leagues west of the Cape Verde Islands.

[2] A reference to such voyages as those of Vicente Yañez Pinzon, Hojeda, Diego de Lepe, and Rodrigo de Bastidas which occurred in 1499–1502. *Cf.* Bourne, *Spain in America*, pp. 67–71, and for details Irving, *Columbus*, III. 15–62.

[3] Accepting de Lollis's emendation *á César* instead of the MS. reading *açetar* which Navarrete printed *aceptar.* The Italian has *a Cesaro.*

[4] "Render therefore unto Caesar the things which are Caesar's; and unto God, the things which are God's." *Matthew*, XXII. 21.

loaded with irons, into a ship, stripped, and very ill-treated, without being allowed any appeal to justice.[1]

Who could believe, that a poor foreigner would have risen against your Highnesses, in such a place, without any motive or argument on his side; without even the assistance of any other prince upon which to rely; but on the contrary, amongst your own vassals and natural subjects, and with my sons staying at your royal court? I was twenty-eight years old when I came into your Highnesses' service,[2] and now I have not a hair upon me that is not gray; my body is infirm, and all that was left to me, as well as to my brothers, has been taken away and sold, even to the frock that I wore, to my great dishonor. I cannot but believe that this was done without your royal permission. The restitution of my honor, the reparation of my losses, and the punishment of those who have inflicted them, will redound to the honor of your royal character; a similar punishment also is due to those who plundered me of my pearls, and who have brought a disparagement upon the privileges of my admiralty. Great and unexampled will be the glory and fame of your Highnesses, if you do this; and the memory of your Highnesses, as just and grateful sovereigns, will survive as a bright example to Spain in future ages. The honest devotedness I have always shown to your Majesties' service, and the so unmerited outrage with which it has been repaid, will not allow my soul to keep silence, however much I may wish it: I implore your Highnesses to forgive my complaints. I am indeed in as ruined a condition as I have related; hitherto I have wept over others; — may Heaven now

[1] At Española in 1500 by Bobadilla. *Cf.* the letter to the nurse above, p. 380.

[2] This is one of the most important passages bearing upon the age of Columbus. As he came to Spain at the end of 1484 according to Ferdinand Columbus, *Historie*, ch. xii., Peschel fixed his birth in 1456, *Zeitalter der Entdeckungen*, p. 76. The majority of modern critics, however, have agreed upon the basis of notarial documents in Genoa that 1446 was the date of his birth and propose therefore to emend the text here by substituting "treinta y ocho" for "veinte y ocho." On the various dates set for his birth see Vignaud, *The Real Birth-date of Christopher Columbus*. Vignaud fixes upon 1451.

2 E

have mercy upon me, and may the earth weep for me. With regard to temporal things, I have not even a blanca,[1] for an offering; and in spiritual things, I have ceased here in the Indies from observing the prescribed forms of religion. Solitary in my trouble, sick, and in daily expectation of death, surrounded by a million of hostile savages full of cruelty, and thus separated from the blessed sacraments of our holy Church, how will my soul be forgotten if it be separated from the body in this foreign land? Weep for me, whoever has charity, truth, and justice! I did not come out on this voyage to gain to myself honor or wealth; this is a certain fact, for at that time all hope of such a thing was dead. I do not lie when I say, that I went to your Highnesses with honest purpose of heart, and sincere zeal in your cause. I humbly beseech your Highnesses, that if it please God to rescue me from this place, you will graciously sanction my pilgrimage to Rome and other holy places. May the Holy Trinity protect your Highnesses' lives, and add to the prosperity of your exalted position.

Done in the Indies, in the island of Jamaica, on the seventh of July, in the year one thousand five hundred and three.

[1] *Blanca,* a copper coin worth about one-third of a cent.

ORIGINAL NARRATIVES OF THE
VOYAGES OF JOHN CABOT

INTRODUCTION

JOHN CABOT, the Venetian sailor who took the first English ship across the Atlantic, was not a writer like Columbus, and consequently our knowledge of his projects and his achievements is limited to what is derived from the reports of other men who knew him or his son and from certain official documents. In general our material may be classified into: (*a*) English official documents, (*b*) reports derived from John Cabot himself, and (*c*) reports or records derived more or less directly from Sebastian Cabot. The materials in *a* and *b* are harmonious; those in classes *b* and *c*, on the other hand, are practically irreconcilable. The result of this conflict of testimony has been to discredit Sebastian Cabot and to lead many scholars to believe that he tried to ascribe to himself what his father did. Other critics reluctant to bring so serious a charge against a man who held honorable positions in Spain and later in England believe that the material in class *c* relates to the second voyage — that of 1498, and that by a mistake it was in the minds of the narrators confused with the voyage of 1497. For a presentation of all the original material the reader may be referred to H. Harrisse, *John Cabot the Discoverer of North America, and Sebastian his Son* (London, 1896), and to G. E. Weare, *Cabot's Discovery of North America* (London, 1897). G. P. Winship, *Cabot Bibliography* (London, 1900), gives a complete guide to the Cabot literature. For a brief account of the voyages and of the Cabot question see E. G. Bourne, *Spain in America* (New York, 1904), pp. 54–63. The most important recent monograph is H. P. Biggar, *The Voy-*

ages of the Cabots and of the Corte-Reals, in *Revue Hispanique,* tome X. (Paris, 1903).

The material presented here consists of the private letters of two Italians sojourning in London in 1497–1498, and the official despatch of the junior Spanish ambassador at the English court.

E. G. B.

THE VOYAGES OF JOHN CABOT

LETTER OF LORENZO PASQUALIGO TO HIS BROTHERS ALVISE AND FRANCESCO, MERCHANTS IN VENICE [1]

THE Venetian, our countryman, who went with a ship from Bristol to find new islands, has returned, and says that 700 leagues hence he discovered mainland, the territory of the Grand Cham (*Gram Cam*).[2] He coasted for 300 leagues and landed; he did not see any person, but he has brought hither to the King certain snares which had been set to catch game, and a needle for making nets; he also found some cut trees, wherefore he supposed there were inhabitants. Being in doubt he returned to his ship.

He was three months on the voyage, and this is certain, and on his return he saw two islands [3] but would not land,

[1] This letter was received in Venice on September 23, 1497, and a copy of it was incorporated by Marino Sanuto in his diary. It was first brought to light by Rawdon Brown in his *Ragguagli sulla Vita e sulle Opere di Marin Sanuto*, etc. (Venezia, 1837). It was published in English in a generally accessible form in 1864 in the *Calendar of State Papers, Venetian Series*, I. 262, edited by Rawdon Brown. The translation here given is a revision of Brown's version. Another translation is printed in Markham, *The Journal of Columbus* (London, 1893).

[2] This reference to the Grand Cham probably indicates familiarity with Columbus's views of what he had discovered as expressed in his letters to Santangel and to Sanchez; see above, p. 268.

The landfall of John Cabot has been the subject of prolonged discussion. Labrador, Newfoundland, and Cape Breton are the principal places advocated. Of late years, owing to the vigorous and learned arguments of Dr. S. E. Dawson there has been an increasing disposition to accept Cape Breton on Cape Breton Island as the most probable location. See Winship, *Cabot Bibliography*, for the literature.

[3] The words "to starboard" have been inserted at this point in all English translations. Biggar has pointed out that the words *al dreto* so translated are Venetian dialect for *addietro*, which is an alternate form for the more

423

so as not to lose time, as he was short of provisions. The King is much pleased with this. He says that the tides are slack and do not flow as they do here.

The King has promised that in the spring our country-man shall have ten ships, armed to his order, and at his re-quest has conceded him all the prisoners, except traitors, to go with him as he has requested. The King has also given him money wherewith to amuse himself till then,[1] and he is now at Bristol with his wife, who is also Venetian, and with his sons; his name is Zuam Talbot,[2] and he is styled the great admiral. Vast honor is paid him; he dresses in silk, and these English run after him like mad people, so that he can enlist as many of them as he pleases, and a number of our own rogues besides.

The discoverer of these things planted on his new-found land a large cross, with one flag of England and another of St. Mark, by reason of his being a Venetian, so that our ban-ner has floated very far afield.

London, 23 August 1497.

FIRST LETTER OF RAIMONDO DE SONCINO, AGENT OF THE DUKE OF MILAN, TO THE DUKE[3]

. . . Also some months ago his Majesty sent out a Vene-tian, who is a very good mariner, and has good skill in dis-covering new islands, and he has returned safe, and has found two very large and fertile new islands; having likewise dis-

common *indietro*, back. The earlier translators thought *al dreto* equivalent to *al dritto*, on the right. *Al tornar al dreto* means simply "in going back."

[1] "August 10, 1497 : To hym that founde the New Isle, 10£." British Museum, Add. MSS. No. 7099, 12 Henry VII., fol. 41. From Weare, *Cabot's Discovery of North America*, 124.

[2] So in Sanuto's text. This form indicates perhaps that Pasqualigo had only heard the name and not seen it written.

[3] This letter was found in the archives of the Sforza family in Milan. The manuscript is apparently no longer extant. There are two somewhat diver-gent texts. The one translated here is the one sent by Rawdon Brown to the Public Record Office in London. Both are printed in Weare, *Cabot's Discovery*, pp. 142–143. The translation given here is by Rawdon Brown as printed in the *Calendar of State Papers, Venetian Series*, I. 259–260.

covered the Seven Cities,[1] 400 leagues from England, on the
western passage. This next spring his Majesty means to
send him with fifteen or twenty ships.

SECOND LETTER OF RAIMONDO DE SONCINO TO THE DUKE OF MILAN [2]

Most Illustrious and Excellent My Lord:—

Perhaps among your Excellency's many occupations, it
may not displease you to learn how his Majesty here has won
a part of Asia without a stroke of the sword. There is in
this kingdom a Venetian fellow, Master John Caboto by name,
of fine mind, greatly skilled in navigation, who seeing that
those most serene kings, first he of Portugal, and then the one
of Spain, have occupied unknown islands, determined to make
a like acquisition for his Majesty aforesaid.[3] And having obtained royal grants that he should have the usufruct of all
that he should discover, provided that the ownership of the
same is reserved to the crown, with a small ship and eighteen
persons he committed himself to fortune; and having set out
from Bristol, a western port of this kingdom, and passed the
western limits of Ireland, and then standing to the northward he began to sail toward the Oriental regions, leaving
(after a few days) the North Star on his right hand; and,

[1] The Seven Cities was a legendary island in the Atlantic. They are all
placed and named on the legendary island of Antilia on the map of Grazioso
Benincasa in 1482. See E. G. Bourne, *Spain in America*, pp. 6 and 7, and
Kretschmer, *Die Entdeckung Amerikas*, Atlas, plate 4. Columbus reported
in Portugal that he had discovered Antilia (see p. 225, note 1) ; hence the deduction either of John Cabot or of Raimondo that the region explored by Cabot,
being far to the west in the ocean, was the same as that visited by Columbus.
Cf. also art. " Brazil, Island of," *Encyclopaedia Britannica*.

[2] This letter is preserved in the Archivio di Stato in Milan. It was first
published in the *Annuario Scientifico del* 1865 (Milan, 1866). It was first
printed in English in Winsor, *Narrative and Critical History of America*, III.
54–55 (Boston, 1884), in the chapter by Charles Deane, entitled "The Voyages of the Cabots." This translation was revised by Professor B. H. Nash
of Harvard University and is given here with only one or two slight changes.

[3] In this passage Cabot's immediate impulse is attributed to the voyages
of Columbus and their results.

having wandered about considerably, at last he struck mainland, where, having planted the royal banner and taken possession on behalf of this King, and taken certain tokens, he
has returned thence.   The said Master John, as being foreign-
born and poor, would not be believed if his comrades, who are
almost all Englishmen and from Bristol, did not testify that
what he says is true.   This Master John has the description
of the world in a chart, and also in a solid globe which he has
made, and he shows where he landed, and that going toward
the east he passed considerably beyond the country of the
Tanais.[1]   And they say that it is a very good and temperate
country, and they think that Brazil-wood[2] and silk grow
there; and they affirm that that sea is covered with fishes,

---

[1] No satisfactory explanation of this can be given.   Bellemo, in the *Raccolta Colombiana*, pt. III., vol. I., p. 197, interprets this sentence to mean that
Cabot showed on the globe the place he had reached on the voyage and then
to that statement the remark is added, referring to earlier journeys, "and going
toward the east he has passed considerably beyond the land of the Tanais."
Tanais is the Latin name for the Don, and at the mouth of the Don was the important Venetian trading station of La Tana.   *Cf.* Biggar, *Voyages of the
Cabots and Corte-Reals*, pp. 33–34, note.   Biggar dissents from this interpretation.   I would offer the conjecture that "the land of the Tanais" stands for the
land of Tana.   In Marco Polo the kingdom of Tana, on the western side of
India, is described as powerful and having an extensive commerce.   See
Marco Polo, pt. III., ch. xxx.   Raimondo, if unfamiliar with Marco
Polo, would understand La Tana by Tana and then naturally assume that
"the country of Tana" was a slip for "country of the Tanais."   Cabot on
the other hand might have heard of Tana when in Mecca without getting
any very definite idea of its location except that it was far to the East in
India.   The phrase "toward the East," like the one earlier in the letter
"toward the Oriental regions," is used of the ultimate destination, not the
direction, and of the destination as a known spot always thought of in
Europe as "the East."

[2] *El brasilio* for *el legno brasilio*.   Brazil wood was an East Indian red
wood imported into Europe.   It is the *Caesalpina sappan*.   Its bright color
led to its being compared to glowing coals, *brazia, brascia*, etc., Eng. brazier,
and then to its being called, as it were, "glowing coals wood," *lignum brasile,
lignum brasilium*, etc., and in Italian most commonly *brasile* and *verzino*, a
popular corruption.   Heyd, *Histoire du Commerce du Levant au Moyen-Age*,
II. 587.   On the transference of the name of this wood to a mythical island
in the Atlantic and then, after the discoveries, to the present country of
Brazil which produced dye-woods similar to *Brasilio*, see Yule's art. "Brazil,
Island of," *Encyclopaedia Britannica*, and Winsor, *Narrative and Critical History*, I. 49–51.

which are caught not only with the net but with baskets, a
stone being tied to them in order that the baskets may sink
in the water. And this I heard the said Master John relate.

And the aforesaid Englishmen, his comrades, say that they
will bring so many fishes that this kingdom will no longer
have need of Iceland, from which country there comes a very
great store of fish which are called stock-fish.[1] But Master
John has set his mind on something greater; for he expects
to go farther on toward the East [2] from that place already occupied, constantly hugging the shore, until he shall be over
against an island, by him called Cipango, situated in the
equinoctial region, where he thinks all the spices of the world,
and also the precious stones, originate;[3] and he says that in
former times he was at Mecca, whither spices are brought by
caravans from distant countries,[4] and that those who brought
them, on being asked where the said spices grow, answered
that they do not know, but that other caravans come to their
homes with this merchandise from distant countries, and these
[caravans] again say that they are brought to them from other

---

[1] *Stochfissi*. The English word "stockfish" Italianized. Of the English
fish trade with Iceland, Biggar gives a full account, *Voyages of the Cabots*,
pp. 53–62, making frequent citations from G. W. Dasent, *Icelandic Annals*,
IV. 427–437. He quotes also a passage from the *Libell of English Policy*,
1436, beginning:

> "Of Yseland to wryte is lytille nede
> Save of stokfische;" etc.

[2] *El Levante*, here again as a known place, oriented from Europe. His
destination, not the direction of his route.

[3] In Cabot's mind the Cipango of Marco Polo is confused with the Spice
Islands. Marco Polo says nothing of the production of spices in his account
of Cipango. The confusion is probably to be traced to Columbus's reports
that he had discovered Cipango and that the islands he had discovered
produced spices.

[4] From 1425 Jiddah on the east shore of the Red Sea rapidly displaced
Aden as an emporium of the spice trade where the cargoes were transshipped
from Indian to Egyptian vessels. Jiddah is the port of entry for Mecca,
distant about forty-five miles, and Mecca became a great spice market. See
Heyd, *Histoire du Commerce du Levant au Moyen-Age*, II. 445 *et seqq.*, and
Biggar, *Voyages of the Cabots and Corte-Reals*, pp. 31–36. Biggar quotes
interesting passages on the Mecca trade from *The Travels of Ludovico di
Varthema*, Hakluyt Society (London, 1863).

remote regions. And he argues thus, — that if the Orientals affirmed to the Southerners that these things come from a distance from them, and so from hand to hand, presupposing the rotundity of the earth, it must be that the last ones get them at the North toward the West;[1] and he said it in such a way, that, having nothing to gain or lose by it, I too believe it: and what is more, the King here, who is wise and not lavish, likewise puts some faith in him; for (ever) since his return he has made good provision for him, as the same Master John tells me. And it is said that, in the spring, his Majesty afore-named will fit out some ships, and will besides give him all the convicts, and they will go to that country to make a colony, by means of which they hope to establish in London a greater emporium of spices than there is in Alexandria; and the chief men of the enterprise are of Bristol, great sailors, who, now that they know where to go, say that it is not a voyage of more than fifteen days, nor do they ever have storms after they get away from Hibernia. I have also talked with a Bur-gundian, a comrade of Master John's, who confirms every-thing, and wishes to return thither because the Admiral (for so Master John already entitles himself)[2] has given him an island; and he has given another one to a barber of his from Castiglione-of-Genoa, and both of them regard themselves as Counts, nor does my Lord the Admiral esteem himself any-thing less than a Prince. I think that with this expedition there will go several poor Italian monks, who have all been promised bishoprics. And, as I have become a friend of the Admiral's, if I wished to go thither I should get an archbish-opric. But I have thought that the benefices which your

---

[1] *I.e.*, a place far enough east from Arabia to be thought of as west from Europe. After making all due allowances one may be excused for feeling some misgiving whether John Cabot actually ever was in Mecca. While some of the spices and eastern commodities were brought overland by caravan from Ormuz or Bassora, the greater part came by water to Jiddah. At Jiddah he could hardly have failed to get fairly accurate information as to where the spices came from. That one who had seen that great commerce should have remained so much in the dark as to conclude that spices came from northeastern Asia is strange enough.

[2] In imitation of Columbus.

Excellency has in store for me are a surer thing; and therefore I beg that if these should fall vacant in my absence, you
will cause possession to be given to me, taking measures to
do this rather where it is needed, in order that they be not
taken from me by others, who because they are present can
be more diligent than I, who in this country have been brought
to the pass of eating ten or twelve dishes at every meal, and
sitting at table three hours at a time twice a day,[1] for the sake
of your Excellency, to whom I humbly commend myself.

Your Excellency's

Very humble servant,
RAIMONDO.

London, Dec. 18, 1497.

DESPATCH TO FERDINAND AND ISABELLA FROM PEDRO DE AYALA JUNIOR AMBASSADOR AT THE COURT OF ENGLAND, JULY 25, 1498 [2]

I THINK your Majesties have already heard that the King
of England has equipped a fleet in order to discover certain
islands and mainland which he was informed some people from

---

[1] English social joys in the fifteenth century did not appeal to the more
refined Italians. An interesting parallel to this comment of Raimondo de
Soncino is to be found in Vespasiano's life of Poggio. "Pope Martin sent
him with letters to England. He strongly condemned their life, consuming
the time in eating and drinking. He was used to say in pleasantry that
oftentimes being invited by those prelates or English gentlemen to dinner or
to supper and staying four hours at the table he must needs rise from the table
many times to wash his eyes with cold water so as not to fall asleep." Vespasiano da Bisticci, *Vite di Uomini Illustri del Secolo XV*. (Florence, 1859),
p. 420.

[2] The original is in the archives at Simancas partly in cipher. It was discovered and deciphered by Bergenroth and published in the *Calendar of
State Papers, Spanish Series*, I., pp. 176–177. The Spanish text was published
by Harrisse, *Jean et Sébastien Cabot*, pp. 329–330, and in Weare, *Cabot's
Discovery*, pp. 160–161. Bergenroth's translation is given here, carefully
revised. The contents of this letter were briefly summarized in a despatch
to the Catholic sovereigns by Dr. Puebla, their senior ambassador, which was
transmitted at or about the same time with that of Ayala. The Puebla
despatch, which contains nothing not in the Ayala despatch, can be seen in
Weare, p. 159.

Bristol, who manned a few ships [1] for the same purpose last year, had found. I have seen the map which the discoverer has made, who is another Genoese, like Colon [and?] [2] who has been in Seville and in Lisbon, asking assistance for this discovery. The people of Bristol have, for the last seven years, sent out every year two, three, or four light ships (*caravelas*), in search of the island of Brazil and the seven cities,[3] according to the fancy of this Genoese. The King determined to send out [ships], because, the year before, they brought certain news that they had found land. The fleet consisted of five vessels, which carried provisions for one year. It is said that one of them, in which another Fai [Friar?] Buil [4] went, has returned to Ireland in great distress, the ship being much damaged. The Genoese continued his voyage. I, having seen the route which they took, and the distance they sailed, find that what they have found, or what they are in search of, is what your Highnesses already possess since it is, in fine, what fell to your Highnesses by the treaty with Portugal.[5] It is expected that they will be back in the month of September. I inform your Highnesses in regard to it. The king of England has often spoken to me on this subject. He hoped to derive great advantage from it. I think it is not further distant than four hundred leagues. I told him that, in my opinion, the land was already in the possession of your Majesties; but, though I gave him my reasons, he did not like it. Because I believe that your Highnesses will presently receive information in regard to all this matter, and the chart or map which this man has made, I do not now send it; it is here and it, according to my opinion, is false, in order to make it appear that they are not the said islands.

[1] In this Ayala would seem to have been misinformed. *Cf.* pp. 423, 425.

[2] The "and" is not in the original, but is supplied by all the editors. It is not absolutely certain that it belongs there. If it does, the passage implies that Cabot had recently been in Seville and Lisbon to enlist interest in his second voyage.

[3] This information is not elsewhere confirmed. On Brazil and the Seven Cities, see p. 426, note 2, and p. 425, note 1.

[4] One Friar Buil went with Columbus on his second voyage.

[5] The treaty of Tordesillas, June 7, 1494; see p. 323, note 3.

INDEX

2 F